DOUBLE PARADOX

DISCARD

DOUBLE PARADOX

Rapid Growth and Rising
Corruption in China

Andrew Wedeman

CORNELL UNIVERSITY PRESS   ITHACA AND LONDON

Copyright © 2012 by Cornell University

First published 2012 by Cornell University Press
First printing, Cornell Paperbacks, 2012
Printed in the United States of America

Library of Congress Cataloging-in-Publication Data

Wedeman, Andrew Hall, 1958–
    Double paradox : rapid growth and rising corruption in China / Andrew Wedeman.
      p. cm.
    Includes bibliographical references and index.
    ISBN 978-0-8014-5046-4 (cloth : alk. paper)
    ISBN 978-0-8014-7776-8 (pbk. : alk. paper)
    1. Corruption—China.   2. Political corruption—China.   3. Economic development—China.   4. China—Economic conditions—1949–   I. Title.
    JQ1509.5.C6W39   2012
    364.1'3230951—dc23   2011037091

Cornell University Press strives to use environmentally responsible suppliers and materials to the fullest extent possible in the publishing of its books. Such materials include vegetable-based, low-VOC inks and acid-free papers that are recycled, totally chlorine-free, or partly composed of nonwood fibers. For further information, visit our website at www.cornellpress.cornell.edu.

Cloth printing   10 9 8 7 6 5 4 3 2 1
Paperback printing   10 9 8 7 6 5 4 3 2 1

To my daughter, Maggie Wedeman, and wife, Kelly Eaton, who have lived with this book for the past decade and a half.

Contents

Preface and Acknowledgments

I began thinking about this book in the mid-1990s after reading Paolo Mauro's article "Corruption and Growth" wherein he demonstrated that the statistical correlation between corruption and growth was negative. At the time, Transparency International had just begun publishing its Corruption Perception Index. In light of Mauro's work, I was struck by the fact that in 1996 China was ranked as the sixth most corrupt country in the world, and yet that year its growth rate was ten percent, which was *down* slightly from the past several years. At the time, moreover, evidence was coming out that, far from being paragons of honest government, both Japan and South Korea had deep histories of corruption that involved not only low-level politicians but the leaders of their ruling parties. In 1996 I wrote an article comparing the political economy of corruption in Zaire, the Philippines, and South Korea. While looting by the Mobutu regime certainly destroyed the Zairian economy and systematic rent scraping by Marcos hollowed out the Philippine economy, I argued, in South Korea it appeared that corruption provided a way for the ruling party to cash in on rapid growth and so provided an incentive to promote economic development. Thereafter, I discovered data on the number of party members punished by the various provincial wings of the Discipline Inspection Commission of the Chinese Communist Party (CCP), which prompted more questions. It appeared that provinces with the highest growth rates and reputations for being "one step ahead" in the adoption of economic reforms also were the provinces with the highest incidence of disciplinary actions. In that 1996 article, "Rotting from the Head Down," I endeavored to show that rather than being negatively correlated with corruption, growth rates were positively correlated with the incidence of corruption. The paper was roundly—and appropriately—rejected by the reviewers at *Comparative Politics,* who pointed out how little I then understood about the complexity of trying to analyze the political economy of corruption and how to handle data on corruption in China. They did, however, suggest that there was perhaps something to the argument. It was a good question: whether rising corruption had affected growth rates in China in the manner suggest by Mauro, who had become part of a growing cadre of economists at institutions such as the World Bank, the International Monetary Fund, and the United States Agency for International Development calling for a systematic attack on corruption as a way to promote growth in the developing world.

I had also become intrigued by corruption in China during the spring and early summer of 1995, when I began to receive promotional materials for the Seventh International Anticorruption Conference, to be held in Beijing in October. I was interested in attending but was perplexed that I kept receiving new brochures. It was only after reading reports on the suicide of Beijing Vice Mayor Wang Baosen and the arrest of Beijing First Secretary Chen Xitong on corruption charges that I had my answer. Wang had been among the co-chairs of the conference, and the reason for the new brochures was that his picture had been deleted to paper over the fact that one of the co-chairs of a major international anticorruption conference had killed himself after being found to have been deeply involved in an elaborate corruption scheme wherein Wang and Chen had collected tens of millions of dollars in "commissions" from real estate developers seeking leases for prime blocks of real estate in downtown Beijing. (In a touch of added irony, the conference was to be headquartered at the Century Hotel where Chen Xitong's son, who was convicted on bribery charges related to his father's activities, was general manager.) I subsequently wrote an analysis of the Chen Xitong case for the *China Review* and was fascinated by the complexity of the scandal and the politics of the investigation.

In the summer of 1997, I was asked to give a talk on corruption in China at the Universities Service Centre at the Chinese University of Hong Kong. Much to my surprise, since I was at the time a junior scholar, a reporter from the *South China Morning Post* attended the talk and interviewed me afterward. The following day, Ivan Tang published a story on the talk in which he declared that I had argued that "corruption has helped boost economic growth on the mainland."[1] I quickly checked with my mentor Rick Baum, who had attended the talk, and was assured that I had not in fact said that. I had, instead, suggested that the argument that corruption negatively affects growth was problematic because several of the most successful cases of economic development (Japan and South Korea) had experienced deep-seated corruption during their economic takeoffs; China appeared to be one of these outliers. But having been publicly associated with the link between rapid growth in China and worsening corruption, I felt compelled to formulate a much better explanation for their co-existence than I had given Tang, which was that corruption was not slowing growth because a lot of the dirty money was being invested in China.

At the time, I was spending part of each summer at the Universities Services Centre poring through the Chinese press in search of stories on corruption, a laborious task in the days before searchable digital media and the absence of a reliable index for most of the Chinese print media. As I scanned the papers each day, I was amazed at the amount of information in papers such as *Jiancha Ribao* (Procurator's Daily) and *Fazhi Ribao* (Legal Daily) and returned to my home university each fall with stacks of Xerox copies. As my colleagues and acquaintances became aware of my work on corruption in China, they frequently asked me, first, if it was dangerous to research corruption in China and, second, if I was able to get any information. As my file cabinets and bookshelves filled up, it was clear to me that the problem was not getting data on corruption. Rather, the problem was figuring out what to do with an overwhelming amount of data that did not seem to make sense. I could explain how corruption and growth worked together in Japan and South Korea, but none of the arguments worked for China. In Japan and South Korea, "political corruption" in the form of monies paid to the ruling party by big business had provided the financial glue that bound the otherwise fractious right wing together, kept the ruling party from splitting into rival factions, and gave it a financial-political stake in ensuring the growth and profitability of business allies. The Chinese Communist Party, on the other hand, was not dependent for its political strength on monies extracted from business. Nor did it need a "profit" motive to promote rapid growth. On the contrary, it seems clear that the party saw rapid growth as a political necessity because of the twin legacies of the Great Leap Forward and the Cultural Revolution, and subsequently Tiananmen. Moreover, it was pretty clear that whereas corruption in Japan and South Korea was "structural" and institutionalized, in China it was anarchic and predatory. Corrupt officials were not, it seemed to me, scraping off a share of the gains companies earned from the government's pro-growth economic policies; in most cases they were simply preying on companies, stealing a share of their profits in return for not doing them harm or, in many other cases, stealing from the state itself. Corruption in China more closely resembled corruption in Zaire than it did corruption in Japan. I thus came up with the notion of the "double paradox": the core issue was not whether one could have corruption and growth, which we could explain by examining the political economy of the developmental states in Japan and South Korea, but how it was possible to sustain rapid growth given high levels of predatory corruption in which officials seem to be engaged in looting the economy.

Work on what had become a book project progressed slowly as I struggled to understand China's anticorruption apparatus and slowly learned how to interpret the data. Studying corruption is extraordinarily difficult because whatever data are available describe at best the tip of an iceberg that cannot be seen or measured. In fact, all that we can see are those instances in which individuals are caught and, in the case of China, which the government decides to publicize. Interviewing is frustrating because those who have real insight are also those who are patently unwilling to talk, and those who are willing to talk often have only indirect knowledge. Moreover, in the case of China the sheer number of cases—tens of thousands each year—is simply overwhelming and at best detailed information is available on only a fraction of the total. One thus faces a lot of trees without being able to see the true extent of the forest. And yet the key to understanding the impact of corruption lies in the ability of the analyst to figure out the shape of the forest by looking at a lot of trees.

In this book I present my best understanding of the shape and tenor of corruption in post-Mao China and seek to explain why the Chinese economy has continued to grow rapidly even after corruption intensified in the 1990s. The resulting argument is my best attempt to reconcile the double paradox of rapid growth and intensifying corruption. I will not claim the argument is without flaws. I do, however, think it addresses a critically important question. Ever since we became aware that corruption worsened in China after the advent of reform, people have been predicting that corruption will prove fatal to China's economy and the survival of the communist party. China is, in fact, often portrayed as a deeply corrupt polity in which political power and public authority have become nothing more than means for self enrichment. To many both inside and outside China, the regime is riddled to its core by corruption. It is essentially a kleptocracy in which honest officials are vastly outnumbered by corrupt officials and even the inner core of the party leadership is directly or indirectly involved in plunder. Many are also convinced that although the CCP claims to be engaged in a "war on corruption," the fight is a form of Beijing Opera—what Monty Python called "Bad Red Guard Theater"—in which actors frantically run about the stage amidst a great din and occasionally drag out a "villain" for a public pillorying. But for all the sound and fury, it is just a show, and the only corrupt officials who get caught are the small fry, the unlucky, the clueless, and those without political allies. If a senior official is punished, they argue, it is because he lost out in the game of factional politics or has been selected as a sacrificial "tiger." Whatever data the regime decides to release, they claim, are "lies" designed to deceive the public into thinking the regime is dedicated to the fight, when in reality the party understands that even though corruption may well prove fatal to its grip on power and is undermining the economy, earnestly fighting corruption would certainly kill the party even quicker. They conclude that the senior leadership talks boldly about the war on corruption as a battle to the death, but in reality it turns a blind eye to the corruption of their wives, children, relatives, friends, and subordinates.

On a certain level, I do not disagree with many of these views. China's quarter-century fight against corruption is no doubt in part an exercise in public relations and has not succeeded in curbing corruption. It is certainly true that for every corrupt official who gets caught there are more who evade capture either because they are lucky or because they are politically protected. Nor is there any question that all the data we have are incomplete and cannot tell us the true extent of corruption. I agree that corruption is a very serious problem in China, and

I reject suggestions that perhaps "corruption with Chinese characteristics" has somehow promoted growth or works differently from corruption in other parts of the world. Nevertheless, we have to recognize that despite predictions that corruption will spiral out of control, the Chinese economy has continued to grow at a remarkable pace. Since the conventional wisdom in economics argues—and the empirical results seem to prove—that corruption and growth are negatively correlated, we cannot, therefore, avoid asking why worsening corruption did not wreak much greater damage on the Chinese economy. Why has high-speed growth in China survived the worsening of corruption?

In writing this book I have accumulated many debts. I owe much to those who contributed directly or indirectly, knowingly or unknowingly, to my efforts. First and foremost, I owe a deep debt to my wife, Kelly Eaton, and daughter, Maggie Wedeman, both of whom have endured my long nights and weekends in the office as well as, I hope, enjoyed the many trips to Hong Kong, Taiwan, and China while I conducted my fieldwork. I wish to thank Jean Hong, former assistant director of the Universities Service Centre, who for so many years provided me with a place to conduct my work and encouraged my efforts. Many others have contributed to my efforts to understand corruption in China, including Melanie Manion, Ting Gong, Yan Sun, Clayton Dube, Dali Yang, Li Lianjiang, Ma Jun, Ethan Michelson, Ren Jianming, Flora Sapio, Shawn Shieh, Yuan Baixun, Richard Xiao, and Richard Baum, to name but a few. I owe a particularly important intellectual debt to Guo Yong at Qinghua University whose pioneering work on the use of case data proved central to my efforts to resolve the paradoxes of growth and corruption in China.

Over the years, the Department of Political Science and the Research Council of the University of Nebraska-Lincoln have provided financial support for my fieldwork. I also thank the Fulbright Foundation, which granted me a year-long research appointment at Taiwan National University, during which I conducted the fieldwork on which the section on machine politics in Taiwan is based, and the Hopkins Nanjing Center, where I spent two fruitful years plowing through mountains of case data and building databases. I am also grateful to Roger Haydon at Cornell University Press who encouraged me year after year to stick with this project and who has now shepherded the book into print, as well as the two readers who provided insightful suggestions on how to improve the original manuscript. I also am in debt to Candace Akins, Martha Walsh, and Eric Giuscffi who labored to clean up my often sloppy editing. I would be particularly remiss if I did not, finally, recognize the work of all the Chinese and Western journalists whose reports form the core of my data and the many anonymous individuals who told me the tales and provided the anecdotes that helped me make sense of the things I read and the data I gathered.

A DOUBLE PARADOX

The political economy of post-Mao China is a tale of two Chinas. The first China in this tale experienced an economic miracle.[1] Between 1979 and 2010, China's economy grew at an average rate of 8.75 percent, three full percentage points more than the South Korean economy (5.64 percent) and five times the average of the U.S. economy (1.64 percent).[2] China's gross domestic product (GDP) per capita increased thirteenfold according to the International Monetary Fund's World Economic Outlook.[3] By comparison, the South Korean economy managed a net gain of less than half that of China. The U.S. and Japanese economies grew by about a tenth of China's growth rate. China did not lead the world in average growth or total net gain in GDP—that honor went to Equatorial Guinea, which embraced what might be called the "Beverly Hillbillies" model of development. After being dirt poor and mired in an endless cycle of despotic rule and economic decline, Equatorial Guinea suddenly struck oil and became, overtly, rich over night. But China's economic success was, in gross terms, impressive enough to put it among the ranks of the "economic miracles."

The second China in this tale faces rapidly worsening corruption.[4] Corruption, defined here as the improper use of public authority for private gain or advantage, was not unknown during the Maoist period. With the advent of reform, corruption became increasingly common and, more important, more intense. The number of economic crime cases "filed" by the procuratorate (i.e., cases in which a criminal indictment was handed down) increased dramatically, rising from 9,000 in 1980, the first year that China's first Criminal Code was in force, to 28,000 in 1985, and nearly doubling the following year when the Communist

Party launched its second post-Mao, anticorruption campaign.[5] The 1989 anticorruption campaign pushed the number of filings to more than 77,000. After the 1989 campaign, the total number of cases filed progressively diminished, but even though the regime may have been charging fewer officials each year, the "intensity" of corruption increased. The number of senior officials shot up over fivefold, from 190 in 1988 to 1,118 in 1990, then doubled to 2,285 in 1995. By 2000, the regime was indicting over 2,500 senior officials a year. Bribe size, albeit crudely measured, grew at an explosive pace, jumping from ¥4,000 in 1984 to ¥54,000 ten years later, then almost tripling to ¥140,000 in 1998, and doubling again to ¥273,000 in 2005.[6] As tangible evidence of worsening corruption appeared, analysts at Political Risk Services shifted upward their subjective estimates of the economic risk from corruption, and by the mid-1990s they and other indexers deemed China among the top quarter of corrupt countries in the world.[7]

If we juxtapose the two Chinas in this tale, we confront a paradox. According to economists, there is a robust negative correlation between corruption and growth. Using econometric analyses and cross-national indices of corruption based on experts' subjective estimates of the level of corruption, first Paolo Mauro and later other economists found that higher levels of corruption correlated with lower growth rates, with a one point increase in corruption (on a one to ten scale) resulting in a one percent decrease in growth.[8] Although a one percent drop in growth might not seem large, given average growth rates of 1.73 percent between 1980 and 2006 and the fact that a mere 2.46 percent separated the top quartile of economic performers from the bottom quartile, a one percent shift in growth would be highly significant.[9] Moreover, in the Corruption Perceptions Index (CPI) compiled by Transparency International (TI), average scores for the most corrupt quartile of cases between 1995 and 2006 were also separated from the average scores for the least corrupt quartile by roughly 2.52 points.[10] For a country with a CPI score equal to the 1992–2006 CPI average (5.96) and an average 1980–2006 GDP per capita growth rate (1.73 percent), a one-point shift in its corruption score would have moved it close to the top quartile (7.50) in terms of corruption and into the lower second quartile in terms of growth. A two-point increase should cause a "typical" country with an average CPI score to become among the most corrupt countries, push its economy from a modest positive growth rate (1.73 percent) to a negative growth rate, and put it among the bottom quartile of economic performers.

Because China's CPI score increased by two points between 1992 and 1996, the new orthodoxy on corruption suggests that growth rates should have fallen and economic development slowed.[11] Yet in the case of China, we see rising corruption, high growth rates, *and* high-speed economic development (see Figure 1.1). Growth rates reached double-digit levels during the mid-1990s, even though the

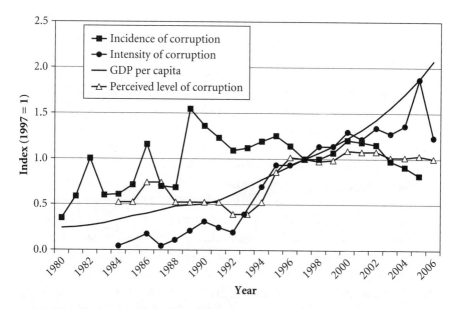

FIGURE 1.1. Corruption and development in China, 1980–2006
Sources: Incidence and severity calculated using data in *Zhongguo Jiancha Nianjian* [Procuratorial Yearbook of China] (Beijing: Zhongguo Jiancha Chubanshe, various years), and *Zhongguo Tongji Nianjian* [Statistical Yearbook of China] (Beijing: Zhongguo Tongji Chubanshe, various years). Perceived level of corruption index is a composite index calculated using data from Political Risk Services, *International Country Risk Guide;* Transparency International, "Corruption Perceptions Index," available at http://www.transparency.org/policy_research/surveys_indices/cpi, accessed September 12, 2008; and World Bank, "Worldwide Governance Indicators, 1996–2008," available at http://worldbank.org/governance/wgi/index.asp, accessed October 8, 2008. Data provided to author by PRS Group in 2005. Per capita GDP index calculated based on data in International Monetary Fund, *World Economic Outlook* Database, April 2008, available at http://imf.org/external/pubs/ft/weo/2008/01/weodata/index.aspx, accessed October 8, 2008.
Note: The 1997 revision of China's Criminal Code resulted in a significant decrease in the number of cases filed. Much of the drop can, however, be attributed to the decriminalization of a range of low-level offenses, most of which result in administrative punishments rather than criminal convictions. It is my contention, therefore, that if we control for the changes in the law, there was not a dramatic change in the procuratorial caseload. I have, therefore, "normalized" the data for 1997 and 1998 by creating an index in which 1997 and 1998 equal zero. For purposes of comparison, I then calculate the total number of cases using the total filed in 1997. The actual number of cases filed after 1997 is thus considerably less than appears here. The data are, therefore, meant for illustrative purposes only and do not reflect the actual number of cases filed after 1997.

perceived level of corruption doubled between the mid-1980s and the mid-1990s. We can, in fact, identify three distinct contradictions between the new orthodoxy on corruption and the Chinese case. First, the incidence of corruption, as imperfectly measured by number of arrests per 10,000 public employees indicted on corruption charges (or what I call the "revealed rate of corruption") clearly increased before the economy roared into high gear in the early 1990s. Second, the period of most rapid growth (the mid-1990s) coincided with the intensification of corruption, as measured by the number of senior officials charged with corruption and a crude measure of bribe size (derived by calculating the average amount of funds recovered from prosecutions per case). Third, rapid growth continued, even though the perceived level of corruption, the subjective estimate by experts of the actual level of corruption, more than doubled. The Chinese economy has, it would seem, flourished even as corruption worsened.

My primary purpose in this book is to resolve the apparent contradiction between worsening corruption and continuing rapid growth in China. It is not just that we face a simple contradiction between the new orthodoxy that increasing corruption lowers growth rates and, hence, should retard development and the evidence of a concurrent worsening of corruption and continued rapid growth in China. Rather, we face a double paradox of corruption and growth. It might seem logical that the primary paradox (worsening corruption and rapid growth) somehow derives from flaws in the logic of the new orthodoxy and the use of spurious correlations to "prove" its core hypothesis. I begin, however, not by rejecting the argument that *ceteris paribus* higher levels of corruption have negative effects on economic performance—on the contrary, I accept that proposition as generally true. Even a casual survey of corruption and economic performance in the less-developed world yields too many examples of economy-crippling corruption to doubt the basic conclusions of the new orthodoxy.

We can, however, point to instances in which countries that enjoyed considerable economic success did so despite being dogged by high levels of corruption—corruption that was often deeply embedded within their political systems, and in some cases corruption that was arguably central to the smooth operation of their political systems. Japan, South Korea, and Taiwan, for example, all had political systems that were highly corrupt, yet all were able to achieve rapid economic development. As I argue in the case studies of South Korea and Taiwan presented in chapter 2, corruption in these cases was essentially institutionalized in ways that forged and sustained a symbiotic relationship between conservative, pro-development political parties and business interests. In broad terms, corruption in those cases provided a mechanism through which a portion of the gains earned by business was funneled back to politicians who favored a set of broadly pro-growth macroeconomic policies. The recipients of corrupt political contributions then used dirty money to purchase political support and thereby managed to build stable, pro-growth, generally right-wing political coalitions. Corruption was a necessary precondition for rapid growth, not because corruption fueled rapid growth, but rather because absent such corruption (or more specifically what Chalmers Johnson has termed "structural corruption") political instability threatened to slow or even harm economic growth.[12] Thereafter, structural corruption created both an ongoing political rationale for the right to continue to enact policies that facilitated profitability for its business allies and an ongoing political dependency on business for the dirty money needed to maintain unity on the right. I recognize, however, that these examples of "developmental corruption" are exceptions to the general rule that corruption harms economic growth. Hence, we can resolve the first paradox of corruption and rapid growth by recognizing that, in some minority of cases, corruption resolved core political contradictions and lowered political barriers to rapid economic growth.

China, however, simply does not fit the developmental corruption model. Qualitative analysis reveals that corruption in China bears a stronger resemblance to the more common form, what I describe as "predatory corruption" in chapter 3. Corruption was never integral to the construction or maintenance of China's ruling communist party, and the party was never dependent on a symbiotic relationship with business either to maintain its grip on power or to provide incentives to enact and support pro-growth policies. On the contrary, corruption served as a means for individual officials or groups of officials to siphon off a share of the gains from growth. Corruption in China was similar to that in many of the worst examples of endemic and economically destructive corruption elsewhere in the developing world. The second paradox we confront in China is the paradox of concurrent predatory corruption and rapid growth. China stands out, not simply because it is an example of coincident high levels of corruption and rapid growth but because it is a perhaps singular contemporary example of coincidental high levels of predatory corruption and rapid growth.

The argument I advance derives in part from recognition of qualitative differences in corruption and builds on the work of Sun Yan and Ting Gong, as well as that of Guo Yong. In particular, I draw on two sets of arguments. First, I follow them in arguing that deepening reform fueled worsening corruption and also that corruption evolved and morphed as the economy restructured. According to Ting Gong, corruption underwent a major evolution in the 1990s as the deepening of reform loosened the state's grip on the economy and created a range of new opportunities for corruption.[13] Whereas most corruption in the 1980s involved officials arbitraging between the state's centrally planned economy and the emerging market economy, liberalization and marketization in the

1990s afforded them new chances to rack in illegal money in areas such as real estate, finance, and business while also creating new opportunities for tax evasion, financial fraud, stock manipulation, and smuggling.[14] Gong thus suggests that the economic reforms fueling China's rapid economic growth also spawned the post-Mao surge in corruption. As the economy grew, moreover, corruption shifted from a largely individualized form of power abuse into what Gong terms "collective corruption," which allowed corrupt officials and their confederates outside the party state to pursue greater illegal gains and to reduce the risk of exposure by forming protective networks—known colloquially as "protective umbrellas" (baosan).[15] Thus corruption was a dynamic consequence of reform, not some sort of cultural artifact or entrenched institutional pathology.[16] This is not to suggest that culture and institutions did not matter. Clearly, cultural factors such as guanxi (particularistic relations) and a culture that emphasizes gift giving and banqueting create an environment in which the line between acceptable social interactions and corruption is blurred and easily crossed.[17] Similarly, the organizational involution of the Chinese Communist Party—its failure to evolve into a professionalized Weberian bureaucracy—and hence the existence of a political system in which laws and regulations remain imperfect and political loyalties dominate were also conducive to corruption.[18]

In the second set of arguments, I follow Sun and others in seeing corruption not as a single form of political pathology but rather as a complex set of different behaviors whereby officials seek personal profits from the misuse of their official powers. Like Sun, I assume that different types of corruption have different economic consequences and that some forms will be more economically destructive than others. She proposes that corruption in post-Mao China involved a mixture of "transactive" and "nontransactive" corruption and that the latter, which involves various forms of what amounts to plunder and theft, generally has more negative effects than the former, which primarily involves bribes paid to either obtain some good or avoid suffering some bad at the hands of corrupt officials.[19] Building on earlier work examining why the post-Soviet economy suffered so badly when corruption exploded in the early 1990s whereas China seemed to escape the presumed ill effects of rampant corruption, Sun proposes that certain forms of transactive corruption serve to break down institutional rigidities and can help push marketization forward.[20] She does not, however, argue for the existence of growth-inducing "corruption with Chinese characteristics." Instead, she correctly recognizes that corruption in China involved positive and negative transactive corruption, as well as a considerable amount of highly predatory nontransactive corruption, particularly in poor, rural, and undeveloped localities. She thus ends with a model in which high aggregate rates of growth were the product of corruption in relatively developed and wealthy areas that linked corrupt cadres and the emerging entrepreneurial class together into pro-growth coalitions, even as corruption wreaked its normal destruction elsewhere. Jane Duckett, Chengze Simon Fan, Herschel I. Grossman, Jean Oi, and Andrew Walder reach similar conclusions, arguing that in some localities corruption and the opportunity for personal profit served as an incentive for cadres to support economic reform and development.[21]

Although these various authors see the worsening of corruption as a byprod-uct of China's incremental and evolving economic reforms and recognize that some forms of corruption may result in profit-seeking collusion between officials and entrepreneurs, ultimately all remain wedded to the belief that while intensi-fying corruption and rapid growth may coexist in the short term, they are inher-ently contradictory. The negative effects of corruption will manifest themselves, presumably in economic crisis or even collapse. Sun, for example, addresses why the Chinese economy accelerated in the 1990s even as corruption intensified. She argues that although corruption had contributed to the marketization of the economy in the 1980s by tearing apart many of the Maoist-era impediments to economic activity, in the 1990s corruption acted to distort the economy, creat-ing an appearance of rapid growth but a reality of worsening misdistribution of wealth. Corruption undermined the institutional integrity of the state, leav-ing it vulnerable to crisis.[22] Gong is less explicit in addressing the issue, choos-ing instead to posit that the key to sustaining current economic success lies in effective anticorruption work that will prevent corruption from precipitating a debilitating political and/or economic crisis.[23] Minxin Pei sees worsening cor-ruption as leading to rapid but poor-quality growth that could stagnate or even collapse with an external shock.[24] Hilton Root concludes that systematic corrup-tion threatens to transform China into an "outlaw economy" in which "private mafias" earn "great fortunes."[25]

In many respects, my argument about why China has sustained a long period of concurrent rapid growth and intensifying corruption parallels that of Sun, Gong, and others. In common with the current conventional wisdom, I reject the notion that corruption encourages growth or that somehow corruption with Chinese characteristics is different from corruption elsewhere. Instead, I posit that reform progressively created new opportunities for corruption and that the deepening of reform spawned intensifying corruption, particularly in the 1990s. In some instances, corruption allowed officials to cash in on gains from rapid economic growth, and the possibility of illicit gain gave them incentives to promote profit making by business interests while recognizing that in many cases corruption involved the sort of predatory plunder that necessarily harms economic activity. But whereas most analysts assume that corruption feeds on the economy and that as it worsens it begins to bite into the muscle and even the bones of the economy, I contend that in the Chinese case corruption has fed off growth and has tended to concentrate on areas where reform created "windfall profits" by transferring valuable assets from the state to the market. In most cases, corruption was not limited to a one-time diversion of a share of the gains realized from transfers, and in many areas a dense, contradictory, and often arbitrary regulatory system allowed officials not directly party to transfers to extract a share of profits from the market. And yet, even in many of these cases, corrupt officials are ultimately cashing in on new value created by reform rather than feeding off the existing stock of value.

Three specific elements constitute my overall argument about why China's rapid economic growth has survived not only an intensification of corruption broadly defined but very significant levels of overtly predatory corruption. First, corruption intensified after the first rounds of reform unleashed the pent-up potential of the Chinese economy. The sequencing of reform and corruption, therefore, played a critical role in determining how corruption affected growth. Second, corruption was linked to the commodification of previously undervalued resources and their transfer from the state to the market. Third, as corruption intensified, the party and state fought back with an anticorruption program that, while perhaps highly imperfect and at best only partially effective, nevertheless prevented corruption from reaching even higher levels or spinning out of control.

Most analysts of corruption in postreform China assume that corruption began to spread rapidly in the 1980s. To the extent that we can measure corruption, it is true that the total number of reported cases increased dramatically between 1980 and 1989–90. Focusing on the total number of reported cases, however, cloaks a slightly more complicated pattern in which the number of low-level cases exploded in the 1980s but high-level, high-stakes corruption did not increase until later. As noted, and as I argue in chapter 4, corruption intensified in the 1990s at a point when growth rates had shot up into double digits. This implies that the intensification of corruption was a likely consequence of rapid growth and that, rather than create a priori barriers to accelerated growth, high-level, high-stakes corruption fed off an already dynamic and growing economy.

In my view, the intensification of corruption was a direct response to the economic boom and the deepening reform that followed Deng Xiaoping's 1992 "Southern Tour" and subsequent adoption of a more aggressive reform policy. Although previous rounds of reform had created a wide array of opportunities for corruption, most early corruption involved arbitraging between low in-plan prices and higher market prices, leveraging access to scarce commodities or resources, and protecting unauthorized business activity. Corrupt officials were able to rake off relatively small bribes and kickbacks. The further loosening of economic regulations that began in 1993 created new opportunities in the corporate, real estate, and financial sectors involving the de facto transfer of vast amounts of value from the state to either the managers of state-owned enterprises or a new class of private-sector entrepreneurs. In these circumstances, corrupt officials could amass illegal fortunes by brokering transfers and skimming off a percentage of the windfall profits created by the gulf between the nominal value of assets and their emerging market value.

The intensification of corruption in the 1990s was, therefore, an endogenous function of the deepening reform and the transition to a market-based economy, because it was partially driven by the commodification of state-owned resources and the transfer of value from the state to nonstate business actors, including the emerging state-managerial class.[26] This is not to suggest that the intensification of corruption in the 1990s was not harmful to the economy. There seems little question that it did result in substantial economic costs.[27] But the cost of corruption was less than the gains from growth, with the result that corruption was feeding off the margin rather than consuming the lion's share of gains from growth.

In my argument, commodification is linked to the intensification of corruption and central to the very nature of corruption. In broad terms, economic reform in China has entailed the transformation of productive assets into commodities. Under the old planned economy, assets were administered and controlled by the state or collective units. Value, in the form of price, was largely fixed by administrative fiat. Economic reforms have progressively transferred assets from the command sector to the market, where their value is fixed by supply and demand, albeit with some continuing regulation by the state. In most cases, significant gaps existed between the state-set value and the market price; when assets were transferred from the command economy to the market, these gaps created rents. In theory, the state should have captured these rents by raising the state-set value to approximate the market price. In practice, rents have generally been split between officials and those taking control of marketized assets, with the latter kicking back a share of their windfall profits to the former as bribes or "commissions." In other cases, officials have simply arrogated valuable state assets or allowed their relatives or friends to commandeer them. Officials have also become silent partners in various "private" ventures based on former state assets. Shortages were a secondary source of corruption, particularly in the first decade of reform. Officials with access to scarce resources were able to leverage "considerations" from those seeking to obtain scarce goods or to divert commodities designated for in-plan use and priced below market levels for the black market and thus to profit directly.

The tremendous expansion of the infrastructure needed to support rapid economic growth has also driven increases in corruption. According to official budgetary statistics, between 1978 and 2006, central and local governments allocated

¥3.74 trillion (US$489 billion) for the regular budget and an additional ¥15.2 trillion (US$1.99 trillion) from the "extra budget" for capital construction.[28] Since then, the government has launched a massive campaign to expand infrastructure that includes building almost 19,000 kilometers of high-speed rail lines at an estimated cost of ¥4 trillion (US$597 billion), a US$228 (¥1.5 trillion) expansion of the country's air networks, further expansion of the highway system, and the construction of new urban infrastructure, including subway and light-rail systems.[29] Public infrastructure projects are notorious for corruption, not only in China but also in virtually all countries (e.g., Boston's Big Dig project). It is hardly surprising that the boom in infrastructural investment, which coincidentally really began in the mid-1990s, has helped fuel a rise in corruption and that the huge sums of money being spent have contributed to the intensification of corruption.

Not all corruption can be traced to the process of commodification, shortages, or public works. To a considerable extent, sustained high levels of corruption can be attributed to the same factors that drive corruption elsewhere, including, among others: excessive red tape; poorly defined and imperfectly enforced rules and procedures; regulatory slack and excess; bureaucratism; lack of transparency; and, above all, inadequate accountability. Nevertheless, if the structural transformation and commodification of the Chinese economy has driven worsening corruption and has played a significant role in the intensification of corruption, we might expect that pressure and incentives for corruption will decrease. This will occur as the economy moves closer to full marketization, as the rents created by gaps between the administratively set and market prices of assets controlled by the state are eliminated by the transfer of these assets to the market, and as price decontrol eliminates other rents and distortions. Similarly, we would anticipate that, so long as public spending on infrastructure remains high, so will corruption linked to capital construction. We can thus identify two major factors driving the worsening of corruption: the transformation of the Chinese economy and the development of new infrastructure. In these areas, rising corruption is clearly an endogenous part of the growth process rather than an a priori barrier to growth. In a sense, therefore, we might consider both the overall increase in the level of corruption, which began in the early 1980s, and the intensification of corruption, which occurred in the mid-1990s, as transitional/transformational costs. In sum, corruption has been the price China has had to pay for the transformation from a command to a market economy and for the construction of the physical infrastructure required to support that transition and the expansion of the economy.

Another reason I believe that corruption did not stifle rapid growth in China was that after a somewhat half-hearted start in the early 1980s, the regime steadily fought corruption. Although sometimes dismissed as ineffectual or even derided as farcical, China's war on corruption began in the early 1980s and has continued for three decades. Between 1980 and 2006, the People's Procuratorate, the judicial institution responsible for investigating and prosecuting criminal activity, has filed criminal charges in more than 1.1 million cases involving "economic crime" and indicted approximately 30,000 senior officials, including roughly 60 officials holding the rank of deputy minister or above.[30] Between 1980 and 2005, the People's Court system accepted roughly the same number of cases.[31] Although data are currently missing for the early years, between 1985 and 2005 the courts sentenced more than 650,000 individuals to prison terms, including 227,000 who were sentenced to five or more years. Obviously incomplete data published by Amnesty International and press reports indicate that at least 1,000 individuals received suspended death sentences or were executed for economic crimes between 1980 and 2006.[32] The number of party members disciplined for economic crimes by the Discipline Inspection Commission (DIC), which is a nonjudicial political institution, is less certain because only the total number of disciplinary cases is regularly reported and at present data are available only for the period 1992–2006. Based on these data and data on the breakdown of cases by provincial party disciplinary organs, it appears that upward of 875,000 individuals were cited for disciplinary infractions involving economic offensives. A small percentage of these (around 6 percent) were handed over to judicial authorities for criminal investigation. Many more, at least 150,000 were, however, expelled from the party. It is also highly likely that a significant percentage of those convicted on economic crime charges were in fact party members and/or state officials.[33]

China's ongoing war on corruption may not have greatly reduced the actual level of corruption, but it has had a positive effect. At a very basic level, it appears to have prevented corruption from spiraling out of control. Rising corruption can create a vicious cycle.[34] Assuming that a regime's anticorruption resources are finite, as more officials become corrupt, the odds they will be caught decrease. As the risk of capture decreases, the expected value of engaging in corruption will increase and hence the likelihood that previously "honest" officials will "go bad" will also increase. As more officials become corrupt, the strain on the regime's anticorruption resources will increase further. At some point, the strain will become so great that corruption can overwhelm the regime's anticorruption abilities and corruption will spiral out of control.

Because it entered the reform period with a rudimentary anticorruption capability, China might well have seen corruption spiral out of control.[35] At first, the party did not seem to take the threat of corruption very seriously, and it was not until after corruption helped trigger massive antigovernment demonstrations in the spring of 1989 that the "war on corruption" began in earnest. Since then, the regime has steadily fought corruption. The efficacy of China's war on corruption is subject to debate, with many deeming it a failure. As I argue in chapter 6, a more nuanced assessment seems to indicate that while the regime has made little progress in reducing corruption, it has succeeded in controlling corruption in the minimal sense that it has prevented corruption from spiraling upward.[36] China's approach to anticorruption work is, however, structured in ways that work best at detecting and deterring low-level corruption and create incentives for corrupt officials to increase the level of bribes demanded and graft undertaken.[37]

Because the regime's anticorruption drive were concurrent with structural changes driven by the evolving reform program, efforts to attack corruption must be placed in this larger context. First, as noted, during the early years of reform, chronic shortages and rationing created numerous opportunities for street-level bureaucrats and grassroots cadres to leverage "considerations" from consumers. A person who wanted to buy a bicycle in the early 1980s often had to obtain a ration coupon from his unit, and in such a situation it often made sense to hand the individual responsible for issuing coupons a carton of Double Happiness cigarettes and a couple bottles of *erguotou baijiu* (white liquor). Workers seeking job transfers and students seeking permission to take the college entrance examination also had incentives to use gifts, including red envelopes containing bribes, to get in through the "back door" (*zou houmen*). By the mid-1990s, shortages of basic consumer goods had ceased, eliminating the need for citizens to pay bribes to obtain them. People continued to seek entry through the back door but increasingly could get in through the front door. Similarly, businesses continued to have to wine and dine officials. As regulations became more clearly defined and low-level officials' latitude in interpreting them decreased, however, banqueting tended to become more a way of building social networks based on insider connections (*guanxi*) than a necessary business activity. Because the regime's war on corruption tended to fall most heavily on the "small fry" rather than the "big tigers," it arguably combined with structural change to reduce the overall level of corruption.

Second, pervasive shortages during the early reform period also fueled corruption in the form of arbitrage between in-plan prices and market prices. Throughout the 1980s, commodities were priced according to whether the buyer was designated as operating within the state economic plan or operated outside the plan; in-plan prices generally were much lower than market prices. Officials and cadres with access to supplies of in-plan commodities could make fast and illegal profits by selling on the market. Official profiteering (*guandao*) and speculation were common. The basis for illegal official arbitrage was largely eliminated by the early 1990s by the gradual phasing out of planned prices as a result of both official price reform and an informal process in which rent seeking and black marketeering pushed officially set prices toward market-clearing levels and by the marketization of the Chinese economy. This reduced one of the major forms of high-level corruption of the early reform period. The massive 1989 anticorruption campaign, which specifically targeted *guandao*, thus began at a time when differences between in-plan and market prices had begun to narrow.

Third, the ongoing anticorruption drive and structural changes helped push the locus of high-level corruption upward, causing a reduction in the anarchic nature of corruption and facilitating the growth of what Andrei Schleifer and Robert Vishny have called the "industrial organization" of corruption.[38] As corruption becomes the purview of more senior officials, new incentives to limit predatory extractions emerge and restructure corrupt transactions in ways that are beneficial for both corrupt officials and business interests. Schleifer and Vishny's model implies that corrupt officials are more likely to strike a balance between the amount of illegal money extracted and the potential profits accruing from illegal transactions. Corruption becomes increasingly "organized" and in some instances "monopolized." As corruption becomes more organized, it becomes predictable and reliable in the sense that businesses are increasingly able to engage in "one stop" bribery rather than having to run a gauntlet of corrupt mid- and low-level officials.

Thus, even though the absolute size of illegal transactions increased dramatically during the 1990s, it appears that corruption was less likely to "kill the goose that laid the golden eggs" by subjecting it to a multiplicity of demands for illegal payoffs that ultimately "plucked the goose bare" and sapped its health. Officials were, I contend, more likely to understand that feeding and caring for the goose would give them a steady stream of golden eggs, rather than killing the goose to plunder its golden innards. This was not simply a change in heart on the part of corrupt officials. The success of reform and the expectation that the economy would continue to grow, in my view, helped convince corrupt cadres and officials that it was better to look to a long-term income stream than to seek to maximize short-term extractions. Ironically, a new interest in long-term income streams rather than maximizing short-term plunder would also give senior officials incentives to reduce corruption among their subordinates because competition for bribes and free-lance corruption might create excessive pressure on businesses.

To conclude, I assert that concurrent high levels of predatory corruption and rapid growth in China were possible because of the dynamic interaction between economic reform and corruption. When Deng Xiaoping and his allies launched the first tentative reforms in 1978–79, corruption was not a serious problem and existed mostly in the form of privilege seeking and petty bribery. As the economy began to respond to the loosening of controls, growth rates edged upward and corruption began to worsen as officials took advantage of the rents created by shortages and the dual-track price system. By the mid-1990s, shortages had largely disappeared and prices had been forced upward to market-clearing levels. After a second round of reforms in 1993 moved the economy much closer to the market, the economy roared into high gear. Senior officials now found themselves in positions to extract large "considerations" for their role in brokering the transfer of state-controlled assets to the emerging private sector or from the corporatization of state-owned enterprises. As a result, corruption intensified in the mid-1990s. The regime's steady, if less than perfect, anticorruption effort, however, kept corruption from spiraling out of control. The economy thus continued to grow rapidly, even as corruption intensified.

As I argued at the beginning of this chapter, what is most perplexing about the concurrent intensification of corruption and continued rapid growth is not that it contradicts the current economic orthodoxy that corruption and growth are negatively correlated but that we confront a double paradox. Not only did China experience rising corruption and rising growth rates, but corruption in China has conformed more closely to the predatory forms of corruption directly associated with economic decline or stagnation, not the rare form of developmental corruption found in Japan, South Korea, and Taiwan. In seeking to resolve the double paradox of corruption and rapid growth in China, therefore, this book begins with a comparative analysis of corruption and growth elsewhere. In chapter 2, I examine developmental corruption in South Korea and Taiwan, focusing on the role of corruption in the formation and consolidation of pro-growth "developmental alliances" that linked the ruling party's political interests to the economic interests of big business. In chapter 3, I draw on a variety of cases including post-1968 Equatorial Guinea, Zaire during the Mobutu era (1965–97), Haiti under the Duvaliers (1957–86), the Dominican Republic during the Trujillo years (1930–61), and the Central African Republic during the Bokassa period (1966–79) to illustrate how endemic corruption leads to economic crisis. Then, I shift the focus to China. In chapter 4, I detail the sequencing of corruption and growth and outline its different forms and manifestations. In chapter 5, I explore the dynamic consequences of the commodification of China's economy. I assess the impact of the Chinese Communist Party's ongoing war on corruption in chapter 6. In the conclusion, I endeavor to pull the complex strands of my analysis together, in part by reference to the United States in the nineteenth and early twentieth centuries. Like China's today, the economy of the United States developed and matured during an era when corruption—mostly in an anarchic form of localized machine politics—was widespread. Parallels between the two cases, in fact, suggest that while China is unique in the contemporary world in the sense that it alone seems to have weathered the intensification of corruption without seeing growth rates fall, in a larger historical perspective there may be precedent for the coexistence of high levels of corruption and rapid systemic change and economic growth.

DEVELOPMENTAL CORRUPTION

Although economists have found a robust and negative correlation between corruption and growth, there are seeming exceptions to the rule, including most prominently Japan, South Korea, and Taiwan where we have evidence of extensive and deep-seated corruption existing alongside rapid economic growth. In fact, the heyday of each country's "economic miracle" occurred during a period of high levels of political corruption.

During the 1980s, proponents of the "developmental state" model tended to downplay the importance of corruption in East Asia. Chalmers Johnson, for example, admitted the existence of extensive "structural corruption" (*kozo oshoku*) in Japan but brushed it aside, arguing that corrupt politicians merely reigned while honest technocrats ruled.[1] Similarly, Ezra Vogel wrote, "It is understood that politicians receive funds from people seeking favors and that they have some obligations to respond to these requests." Yet, he concluded that while Japanese politicians received considerable gifts and favors, "The distortion of public policy to favor certain vested interests on the basis of political contributions is probably not great," although "there have been several well-known incidents of such manipulations."[2] Even in a history of "political bribery" that documents repeated political scandals in Japan, Richard Mitchell notes that while corruption existed among parliamentarians, both the bureaucracy and judiciary were "remarkably free of corruption."[3] In Taiwan, Robert Wade asserts, corruption was "much diminished" by the 1970s after Chiang Ch'ing-kuo launched a crackdown of such severity that government officials were afraid not only to accept bribes but even to be seen in "bars, dance halls, and expensive restaurants." To the extent that corruption existed, it was small scale, predictable, and limited to minor overcharging on public works projects. As a result, he concluded, corruption existed mostly at the subnational level "where nothing major for the national development effort is at stake."[4] In a careful econometric analysis, Beatrice Weder found no evidence to support the claim that corruption in East Asia did not have the same negative effect as elsewhere.[5] In a 1997 Asian Development Bank report, Jeffery Sachs and Steve Radelet went even further, arguing that one of the reasons for East Asia's superior economic performance was that corruption was "less extensive" than in other regions.[6]

Despite claims that corruption in East Asia was less severe than in other regions or that what Westerners deemed "corrupt" was in fact nothing more than the "Asian way" of doing business, in my view, "political corruption," or what has been called "structural corruption," mostly in the form of under-the-table, illicit "contributions" from big business to the ruling party, was an integral part of politics.[7] In all three cases, "dirty money" bound together and sustained the conservative, pro-business political coalitions found at the core of the so-called developmental state. Moreover, I contend that in these cases, structural corruption was a necessary precondition for rapid growth. Prior to initiating the macroeconomic policy regimes associated with rapid growth, would-be conservative leaders in two of the three cases (Japan and South Korea) had to contend with potentially paralyzing internecine political battles within the right wing. In Taiwan, the ruling Kuomintang (KMT), which had been forced to flee to the island after suffering a crushing defeat on the Chinese mainland by the Chinese Communist Party, faced a potentially serious threat from its sullen and alienated "native" majority, many of whom viewed it as an alien, colonial regime. In all three cases, the right turned to machine politics to create stable ruling coalitions.

As defined by Johnson in his 1982 analysis of the Japanese Ministry of International Trade and Industry (MITI), the developmental state was a mutated form of capitalism in which highly skilled technocrats, working in intimate concert with business, skillfully navigated the product and business cycles and manipulated state economic policy in ways that ensured maximum economic growth.[8] In Johnson's formulation, the development state appeared to be a quasi-authoritarian form of technocracy in which politicians reigned but bureaucrats ruled. Within the bureaucracy, economic policy was guided by a small circle of core offices staffed by the best and brightest graduates of Japan's top universities who worked in a meritocracy where only the very best rose to the top ranks. Electoral and parliamentary politics were essentially a political theater in which parliamentary debate created an appearance of democracy. In reality, politicians only served to buffer the technocrats from society, and elections provided a means of gauging the public mood without necessarily allowing the public to directly influence the legislative or policy agendas. Similarly, Peter Evans described the development state as simultaneously "embedded" and "autonomous" by which he meant that it was sensitive to the demands of society and key interests but had power to dominate the policy process.[9] Ideologically, the development state was motivated by "GNP-ism," an ideology in which the role of government was to raise incomes and constantly increase national economic power.

Although the developmental state was initially presented as a "new" and perhaps higher political form, in fact, as Johnson later recognized, the technocracies that putatively led the Japanese, Korean, and Taiwanese "miracles" rested on a foundation of old-fashioned machine politics.[10] The core of the developmental state was formed by a collusive relationship between business and political power.[11] Business provided the political resources (mostly money) that allowed conservative, pro-business political leaders to build stable political coalitions by binding together what would otherwise have been a series of rival and often hostile factions, each more interested in power than policy per se. Using funds obtained from the business sector, the "big bosses" provided factional leaders with a monetary buy-in. The factional bosses, in turn, doled out funds to rank-and-file politicians who used the money to fund local "constituent organizations," pay community organizers to mobilize voters, and ultimately, if necessary, to buy the votes needed to win elections and thereby ensure conservative control of government.

Control of government enabled the ruling coalition to harness state policies to the goal of consolidating its grip on power and repaying its business supporters with a combination of "public goods" in the form of broadly pro-business macroeconomic policies; "private goods" in the form of government subsidies, tax breaks, government contracts, and rents; and pork-barrel spending aimed toward its supporters at large. The new result was a pro-business system of redistributive politics that drew its sustenance from both business profits and government revenues. However, the costly nature of sustaining a machine in which base money, not some higher ideology, ultimately bound the ruling coalition together demanded that the ruling party not simply repay its business allies but embrace a set of developmentalist policies so that the economy would grow and thereby generate the increased profits needed to meet the ever-increasing financial demands of machine politics.

This is not to suggest that political leaders in Japan, South Korea, and Taiwan only embraced "GNP-ism" for instrumental political reasons. On the contrary, other factors, including security concerns emanating from serious external threats, were critical, particularly in the South Korean and Taiwanese cases. The close relationship of these regimes with the United States and pressure from Washington to embrace market economics also helped ensure that they embraced pro-business economic strategies. Nor do I wish to imply that machine politics per se was a powerful engine of growth. Machine politics is by its nature corrupt because it is designed to profit the few, economically and politically, and to do so by manipulating policies in ways that generate rents, create inefficiencies, and ultimately allow politicians and business to obtain illicit income. Machine politics is, however, a way of coping with a potentially unstable political environment—one splintered by factionalism, plagued by political infighting, and suffering from deep polarization—where ideological factors and shared identities are insufficient to bind together stable ruling coalitions. In such an environment, the mercenary nature of machine politics, with its emphasis on direct material reward, and the machine's ability to provide tangible payoffs to those factions and politicians that join the coalition (and, conversely to punish those who do not) can provide a way to create a modicum of political stability.

The cash nexus linking business and politics, finally, serves to structure the political interests of the machine in ways that push it toward pro-business, pro-growth macroeconomic policies. In this construct, the machine's "developmental" interests are motivated not by the desire of political leaders or technocrats to advance the "national interest," though these may play a role, but rather by the ruling coalition's fundamental political interest in power. As David Kang suggests, the political fortunes of the ruling party and the profit-making interests of business are bound together in ways that make them "mutual hostages" to sustained economic growth.[12] According to Barbara Geddes, the result is a "Janus faced" system that depends on a combination of graft and growth.[13]

In the sections that follow, I examine the role of political corruption in South Korea and Taiwan. In the interest of brevity, I do not include an in-depth case study of Japan because it has already been well documented and discussed. In each case, I assert that to lay a foundation for rapid growth, it was first necessary to overcome political divisions that threatened to fragment the conservative, pro-market, pro-business right wing into warring fractions and thus open the way for the rise of the left. In the case of South Korea, by the late 1950s and early 1960s, the right was badly fragmented. Bitter infighting followed the fall of President Syngman Rhee and the overnight collapse of the ruling Liberal Party. Political loyalties were localized and personalized, thus ensuring that most politicians saw themselves as independent operators. After seizing power in a military coup in 1961, Park Chung-hee, who immediately found himself under intense pressure from the United States to restore civilian rule, had to somehow forge a new coalition in a political environment where instrumental politics prevailed. He did so by ruthlessly centralizing control over the collection of political money and establishing a new political machine. Politicians who bought into the system were rewarded while those who choose to remain independent faced a dearth of political money. On Taiwan, President Chiang Kai-shek also found it expedient to turn to machine politics. In addition to needing to purge the ruling KMT party of the corrupt, ineffectual, and demoralized following the 1949 retreat from the mainland, Chiang needed to forge ties with the local political leaders of a population that was hardly favorable to the transplanted regime. Like Park, Chiang created a vast political machine that doled out a variety of incentives to those who joined its ranks while starving those who opposed it.

Although these two developmental coalitions were constructed differently, in both South Korea and Taiwan the relationship between money and power was symbiotic, though often tinged with a strong element of coercion. In South Korea, Park provided cheap capital and other policy-induced incentives to companies willing to fulfill his periodic demands for political cash. On Taiwan, Chiang relied much more heavily on publicly owned industries and the state to provide a web of patronage and opportunities (such as access to local franchises, rural credit institutions, and less rigorous enforcement of rules and regulations) that could be used to co-opt local politicians. Regardless of differences in the structures of these two machines, the contrast between what I term "developmental corruption" in these cases and the more common form of "degenerative corruption" known in the popular literature as "kleptocracy" was stark.[14] Whereas corruption in a kleptocracy channels wealth and resources out of the state and economy and into the pockets of the thieves in power, political corruption in the developmental states drew money out of the business sector and pumped it into political organizations where it was used to give the ruling party an "unfair" advantage over the opposition. Political corruption thus allowed the right to "cheat" the political system.[15]

Moreover, in both South Korea and Taiwan, political corruption was not "black" in the sense that money politics involved criminal activity of varying shades of grayness. That is, money was more often than not paid not as "bribes" to "purchase" a specific policy or favor or to bend a particular rule. Business generally handed money over, often using legal or at least quasi-legal mechanisms, with the expectation that the payments would help maintain the right's grip on power and that right-wing governments would skew policy in favor of business, particularly big business. This does not mean that individual corruption did not occur or that right-wing politicians did not siphon some of the money their machines collected from the business sector into their own pockets. They did. Rather, I suggest that the balance between the "gray" political corruption associated with irregular campaign finances and blacker forms of corruption involving private plunder tilted toward the gray area of political corruption more than in other regions.

South Korea

In contrast to Japan, where the developmental state rested on a relatively stable foundation of money politics and a collusive relationship between conservative politicians and big business, the developmental state in South Korea was better characterized as based on a coerced alliance between the ruling party and big business. In key respects, the functional relationship was the same. In return for financial support from big business, the ruling party put in place a macroeconomic policy regime that heavily favored the growth of big business.

In the South Korean version of the developmental state, the ruling party's approach to big business was much more heavy-handed, with the ruling party often engaging in what amounted to "political extortion" to extract money from big business. Even so, the South Korean right faced chronic problems in forging the stable coalition needed to perpetuate its grip on power and, as in Japan, relied on a system of political redistribution to bind its fractious parts together, using money extracted from big business as the essential "glue." The conservative-business alliance was not one of equals, and the impetus for the formation of the developmental alliance came from the political side, which first extorted the money needed to forge a new right-wing political coalition and then established a system of patron-client relations wherein the ruling party provided its business clients with cheap capital, repressed labor costs, and doled out oligopolistic privileges in return for a cut of the resulting profits. Given the coercive nature of the politics-business nexus in South Korea, as major firms, known in Korean as *chaebol*, grew from economic weaklings into powerful, diversified business empires, the balance of power shifted in their favor. In the process, the relationship between the South Korean right and big business soured and ultimately the original alliance collapsed, but not until after the South Korean economy had made dramatic gains and achieved a self-sustaining pattern of growth.

The abrupt end of Japanese colonial rule in August 1948 ushered in a period of prolonged political chaos and instability as a myriad of political groups formed, dissolved, and reformed in a dizzy scramble to fill the political vacuum created by the collapse of the old colonial administration.[16] Out of the chaos, the U.S. Occupation selected Syngman Rhee, a Princeton-trained PhD, who had campaigned tirelessly and without success for Korean independence during the interwar years. An old-fashioned autocrat, Rhee managed to entrench himself in power and in August 1948 became the head of the newly formed Republic of

Korea. The formation of the new Rhee government did not, however, bring order to the South Korean political scene. On the contrary, the newly elected National Assembly suffered from chronic fractionalism and political fragmentation. In August 1945, fifty-four political parties formed. By June 1946, the number of parties had increased to 107 and then 344. Of these, forty-nine contested the first National Assembly elections in 1948.[17] Two years later, thirty-eight parties fielded candidates in the second election, and in 1956 twenty-eight parties vied for National Assembly seats. Large numbers of independents also contested elections during the early years of the republic, with the number ranging from 417 in the 1948 election to 1,513 in the 1950 election, 797 in the 1954 election, 357 in the 1958 election, and 1,010 in the 1960 election. As a result, independents occupied a significant share of the seats in the assembly (45 percent) in 1948 and constituted a majority (62 percent) in 1950. It was not until 1954 that Rhee's governing party controlled a majority of assembly seats; even then, independent legislators accounted for 31 percent of the seats.[18]

During this time, party loyalties were fluid due in part to the lack of a strong ideological foundation and in part to the low salience of party identification at the local level.[19] Politicians were putatively motivated by egoist greed, not ideology. According to Quee-young Kim, during the Rhee era, "in the simplest terms, party politics…can be pictured as a struggle between men who expended their wealth to increase it and men who used political office to augment it."[20] As a result, the National Assembly was riven by a "myriad of schisms" carried over from the chaotic days of 1945.[21] From the beginning of his time in office, Rhee was locked in a bitter power struggle with the Democratic Party, the party that had essentially put him power.[22] Even after Rhee cobbled the right-wing parties together to form the Liberal Party in 1951, factionalism continued.[23] In part, the failure of the Liberal Party to coalesce into a strong party was the result of the underlying fragmentation of Korean politics. Rhee, however, greatly contributed to the instability. Seeing himself as a paternalist leader, he did not want party politics to infringe on his authority.[24] Instead, he sought to forge a personalized politics based on absolute personal loyalty. He refused, therefore, to share power with the party and instead appointed his cronies and henchmen to key positions of power.[25]

In 1952, when the National Assembly balked at amending the constitution so he could stand for a third term as president, Rhee resorted to violence and intimidation aimed not only at the opposition parties but also at "disloyal" members of his own party.[26] In the years that followed, he kept the party in disequilibrium by constantly reshuffling the cabinet and playing one group off against another in order to prevent his own party from becoming a threat to his personal power.[27] Appointments were made on the basis of loyalty to Rhee and his key lieutenant

Yi Ki-bung, the speaker of the National Assembly.[28] The bureaucracy, meanwhile, was wracked by "backbiting, conspiracy, and factional struggles" as well as "petty jealousies, rivalry for favor of the superior, sycophancy, and deliberate obstruction."[29] As the Liberal Party degenerated into a fragile collection of self-serving politicians grouped into two rival factions and lost whatever support it had immediately after the Korean War, Rhee came to rely increasingly on the national police and vote fraud to ensure that he and the party "won" elections.[30]

In addition to being politically unstable and institutionally weak, the Rhee regime suffered from what some have characterized as a combination of endemic low-level corruption and high-level corruption. High-level corruption involved the sale of former Japanese-owned industries and state property at bargain-basement prices to Rhee's allies, the granting of loans to favored businessmen at interest rates well below the rate of inflation, the illegal auctioning off of import licenses and foreign exchange quotas to those willing to contribute to the ruling Liberal Party, and the letting of sweetheart contracts to political supporters.[31] Military supply contracts were a particularly lucrative source of illicit income, and Rhee was known not only to demand that the military contribute a portion of the kickbacks it got from suppliers to the party but even to siphon funds out of the military budget to support his political activities.[32] Rhee also allegedly raised political funds by selling war materiel (petrol, automobiles, spare parts, etc.) and military food supplies on the black market and by diverting money from funds earmarked for the purchase of food for the army.[33]

Endemic low-level bureaucratic corruption was also a significant problem. Bureaucrats demanded bribes to perform routine duties, embezzled public funds, and extorted "voluntary contributions" from citizens. Businessmen evaded taxes by bribing assessors and collectors. Customs inspectors allowed illegal imports in return for a cut of the black-market profits.[34]

The resulting combination of high- and low-level corruption led to the formation of a new class of political capitalists who profited directly from their connections with Rhee and the rents he sold them. In return, the political capitalists bankrolled his regime and the ruling Liberal Party.[35] In the 1960 election, for example, the business sector allegedly provided 94 percent of the roughly ₩5.4 billion (US$6.5 million) the ruling party raised. (Liberal Party candidates contributed the remaining ₩300 million). Of the total ₩5.1 billion in business contributions, ₩2.9 billion (53 percent) came in the form of "donations" while the remaining ₩2.2 billion (41 percent) came from kickbacks from some 30 businessmen who were given cut-rate government loans totaling ₩7.79 billion just before the election.[36]

In the spring of 1960, the Rhee regime imploded after student demonstrators took to the streets to protest the rigging of the 1960 presidential election and what they saw as a police-led wave of terror aimed at the opposition.[37] In a matter of weeks, the demonstrations swelled into a nationwide revolt against the Rhee government. During the political turmoil of the next several months, the national police disintegrated and the military, which was under heavy U.S. pressure not to act, balked at the prospect of having to suppress the demonstrations with bloody force.[38] After Rhee resigned and left the country for exile in the United States, his regime quickly failed and an interim government was formed by Chang Myon (also known as John Chang), a leading member of the opposition and former vice president (1956–60).[39] Both Chang's interim government and the government he formed after the establishment of the Second Republic in July 1960 were crippled by factional conflict. The Democratic Party quickly split into rival wings, and in November 1960 the "Old Faction" bolted and became the main opposition to Chang's rump Democratic Party, which itself was, according to Kim Se-jin, a "conglomeration of disgruntled opposition forces" consumed by a fight for the spoils of power.[40] Even the student "revolutionaries" who had led the charge against the corrupt Rhee regime succumbed to the corrupting effects of power.[41]

Corruption continued at endemic levels after the collapse of the Rhee regime. Bribes had to be paid to members of the National Assembly to ensure passage of legislation. Businesses continued to pay off tax authorities in order to evade taxes.[42] Members of the ruling Democratic Party continued to accept payoffs from businessmen in return for being allowed to make windfall profits.[43] Chang's party, however, lost what had been the most lucrative source of illegal political money during the Rhee period when the United States forced an end to the practice of requiring businesses receiving U.S. aid dollars to kick back the difference between the official and black-market exchange rates. To offset this loss, Chang lifted the outright ban on "luxury" imports from Japan and began extracting "contributions," in Japanese yen, from firms seeking highly profitable import licenses.[44]

Despite his need for political money, Chang nevertheless turned against the political capitalists who had financed Rhee's regime, threatening them with criminal prosecution.[45] Although popular in the charged political environment of 1960–61, Chang's attack on the political capitalists exacerbated the political instability and economic chaos that followed the overthrow of Rhee's First Republic, and hostility between Chang and big business contributed to Chang's failure to forge a stable governing majority in the National Assembly. Chang's position was further undermined when he pressured the army high command to hand over ₩1.7 billion (US$2.5 million) to his political war chest, a move that prompted the chief of staff to resign and helped set the stage for a military coup in May 1961.[46]

The new junta, formally known as the Military Revolutionary Council, immediately dissolved all political parties and social organizations, blaming "corrupt, faction-ridden politicians" for Korea's endless political upheavals.[47] Soon thereafter, it banned 5,000 politicians whose egotism, it said, had brought the nation to the brink of ruin.[48] Henceforth, coup leader General Park Chung-hee declared, Korea would purse an "administrated" form of democracy without political parties and would rely instead on a mass political movement, the People's Movement for National Reconstruction, as a means for political participation. The junta, which was quickly re-formed as the Supreme Council for National Reconstruction, was, however, wracked by bitter infighting, and it was not until early 1963 that Park finally muscled most of his rivals out of the way.[49]

Once his rivals were gone, Park faced a series of new political challenges. From the time of the coup onward he was under intense U.S. pressure to restore civilian rule as quickly as possible, and in August 1961 he announced that it would be restored in two years.[50] Transitioning to civilian rule confronted Park with a series of major challenges. It demanded that he, or any other would-be officer-turned-civilian-politician, set up a political party to contest presidential and National Assembly elections. Park was also under considerable pressure to bring corruption under control and to crack down on the rampant political profiteering that had become the norm under Rhee and Chang. Moreover, if he was to consolidate power, Park had to revive South Korea's faltering economy.

Park moved quickly to attack corruption and profiteering, calling for a "surgical operation" to "excise" the nation of "a malignant social, political, and economic tumor."[51] Less than two weeks after the coup, the government announced the formation of a committee to investigate and punish those guilty of "illicit accumulation of wealth" and arrested the heads of many of South Korea's leading companies.[52] Soon thereafter, the regime cracked down on hooliganism, prostitution, smuggling, black marketeering, and loan sharking (and arrested some 2,000 alleged communists).[53] The newly formed Korean Central Intelligence Agency (KCIA), meanwhile, moved against corruption within the state bureaucracy. Shortly after its establishment in June 1961, it initiated a screening of 41,000 government employees and ultimately charged 1,863 with either corruption or "antirevolutionary" (i.e., antiregime) activity.[54]

The first crackdown was unsuccessful, and corruption at all levels remained a problem.[55] High-level corruption, in fact, reached such proportions in the late 1960s that critics damned the regime as being controlled by "five thieves"—generals, senior bureaucrats, industrialists, cabinet politicians, and members of the National Assembly—and described the wealthy residential quarter of Seoul as the "thieves' village."[56] Faced with mounting criticism, Park launched a renewed crackdown in 1971, during which 4,000 government officials were punished for corruption.[57]

Park's second anticorruption campaign also failed, and by the mid-1970s visible high-level corruption had once again become a source of public cynicism.[58] The imposition of the quasi-authoritarian Yushin Constitution in 1972, however, meant that public discussion of corruption abated during the later Park years. At the same time, under the "cult of austerity" of the Yushin (revitalizing) regime, visible displays of wealth were frowned on, and Park ordered occasional "show trials" of senior officials caught violating restrictions on the sale and importation of luxury goods.[59] Fear of the KCIA, which was widely believed to have such a vast network of informants that nothing escaped its attention, reinforced the disincentives for rank-and-file bureaucrats to engage in corruption.[60] Nevertheless, corrupt exchanges continued, as evidenced by the 1978 scandal involving the Hyundai Corporation and its sale of luxury apartments to senior bureaucrats at below-market prices; many of the bureaucrats made fast profits by immediately reselling the apartments at their true market value.[61] Ultimately, Park only partially curbed bureaucratic corruption, driving it deeper underground without really killing it.

Under the leadership of Kim Jong-pil, Park's nephew-in-law and a key confederate in the May 1961 coup, the KCIA set about addressing the second major challenge facing Park in the run-up to democratic elections: forming a new ruling party.[62] Kim created a highly centralized organization, which he named the Democratic Republican Party (DRP), designed to knit together the fractious Korean right. As noted above, Korean political parties have traditionally been characterized by extreme factionalism. In part, chronic factionalism reflected the highly personalized and nonideological nature of conservative politics, particularly in the Korean countryside. Deep-seated regionalism further fragmented the South Korea polity. Kim thus had to engineer a system that would pull together a "herd of cats," a mass of politicians with strong local ties who could mobilize the voters needed to win seats using particularistic appeals and personal connections. Kim's system would then need to impose sufficient discipline to ensure that the right-wing leadership could control the National Assembly. In part, the new regime addressed the problem of chronic political fragmentation by stipulating that only party-affiliated candidates could stand for election to the National Assembly and that members of the National Assembly who bolted their party would lose their seats.[63] Kim also relied on the KCIA to pressure politicians to join the new party. Kim's strategy emphasized "funds instead of guns" to attract political activists into the ranks of the DRP.[64] Not surprisingly, the DRP attracted political opportunists and the "free-floating elements" that had populated the fringes of the political establishment during the Rhee period.[65]

Building a party, particularly one populated by substantial numbers of political mercenaries required money. At first, Kim Jung-pil relied on a Rube

Goldberg–like system wherein he funded the right through a combination of KCIA funds and illegal imports of Datsun sedans and pinball machines.[66] Kim started construction on a complex of bars, bathhouses, and dancehalls (known as the Walker Hill Resort) designed to soak up U.S. GIs' "entertainment" dollars after Park shut down Seoul's red-light district.[67] Like Rhee and Chang, Kim took money from speculators and allegedly manipulated the stock market.[68] Foreign companies, including Japanese firms and investors seeking to skirt restrictions on Japanese involvement in the South Korean economy and hide the source of their investments, were another supplier of under-the-table money.[69] The Japanese government, finally, allegedly gave Park a ₩2.6 billion (US$20 million) secret contribution after Park lowered South Korea's demands for war reparation and agreed to move forward with diplomatic normalization.[70]

Park, however, saw a need for a more stable system of financial funding, for which he turned to big business: the *chaebol*. He arrested many of Rhee's business cronies on charges of corruption and profiteering and then made them an offer. If they would fund his new regime, he would drop (or suspend) all the charges against them.[71] Further, in return for political "donations," Park offered them access to cheap capital. In the immediate aftermath of the coup, the military government had nationalized the banks, restricted access to foreign capital, and centralized the allocation of capital.[72] Because loans and credits required the approval of the Blue House (i.e., the president), Park was positioned to determine which firms had access to investment capital and at what political price.[73]

Park thus made the DRP's system of political fund raising more systematic and, in the process, he shifted control of illegal fund raising away from Kim Jungpil, who he correctly saw as a potential rival, into his own hands and those of his inner staff. A new system of political corruption quickly emerged. Whereas Rhee, and to a lesser extent Chang, had sold rents and favors in a haphazard, piecemeal manner, Park institutionalized a system of surreptitious "contributions." Although he continued to sell rents, in the main Park was in the business of selling cheap capital. He was able to control the price of capital because he controlled the banks and hence could set interest rates for select borrowers at or just below the rate of inflation.[74] To obtain this cheap capital, the *chaebol* had to agree to four things. First, they had to pay Park a commission up front to obtain discounted loans.[75] Second, they had to agree to invest the capital in accordance with state investment priorities, which stressed export-oriented industrialization in the 1960s and later the development of heavy and chemical industries. Third, they had to kick back a percentage of their profits to Park. Fourth, they were to make "charitable donations" to the New Community Movement (Saemaul), a government-led program to improve conditions in the villages.[76] Park also was willing to provide additional state support for the *chaebol*, including support in the suppression of wages and unionization, direct export subsidies, and indirect subsidies in the form of an overvalued exchange rate. And he was willing to actively support individual *chaebol* by controlling entry into key sectors and allowing them to engage in a variety of monopolistic and oligopolistic practices. But, once again, to get Park's support the *chaebol* had to provide him with the secret funds (*bi chagum*) needed to maintain his grip on power and to preserve the political foundations of his developmental state, including the cost of maintaining a majority in the National Assembly.[77]

Establishment of a centralized system of illicit fund raising capable of generating large sums of money gave Park the tools necessary to tackle the twin problems of political instability and endemic factionalism.[78] From the beginning, Park's attempts to forge unity on the right were hampered by factionalism. The junta (officially known as the Supreme Council for National Reconstruction [SCNR]) was itself split into warring factions, and Kim Jong-pil's attempt to form the DRP was seen as an internal power grab. Park himself clearly saw the existence of a strong party organization as a potential political threat to executive power. Park, therefore, played to Kim's factional rivals in the early days, ultimately forcing Kim into exile, only to quickly shift his support to Kim's faction when the "nonmainstream" faction grew in power.[79] Park, in other words, faced the double task of forging unity among politicians with strong local bases and weak political loyalties, while concurrently preventing the party from emerging as a threat. He thus turned to a strategy of that we might call "divide and subordinate" based on a system of centralized financial dependency wherein individual politicians were rendered heavily dependent on the Blue House for their political sustenance.

Paradoxically, the nature of Korean politics facilitated this strategy. Like their Japanese counterparts, conservative Korean politicians relied on local political machines to knit together networks of local political brokers and generate votes. DRP politicians maintained two parallel sets of local organizations. On the one hand, they controlled the official district party organization (*kong chojik*). Although nominally under the organizational authority of the party, the *kong chojik* were in reality personalistic machines bound together by personal ties, kinship, and opportunism. In the same manner as a political boss in the United States, Korean politicians bought constituents' loyalty by dispensing "tangible benefits and favors."[80] The *kong chojik* is itself organized in a hierarchical manner reaching down from the district to the precinct, polling station, block, and finally to the neighborhood, with local notables (*yuji*) acting as political brokers responsible for turning out the vote come election day.[81] The party subsidies helped cover staff, office, and other costs associated with operating the *kong chojik*.[82] Additional funds were raised via candidates' supporters' associations (*huwonhoe*).[83] Politicians also relied on a variety of parallel informal vote-gathering machines (*sa chojik*) to mobilize support. Unlike the *kong chojik* which operated on a district-wide basis, *sa chojik* tended to be more narrowly focused and were often organized along functional lines. Like the *kong chojik*, the *sa chojik* were based on particularistic ties.[84]

As was also true in Japan during the heyday of dominance by the Liberal Democratic Party (LDP), political resources flowed from politicians to their constituents, not the other way around. Politicians were, of course, expected to intercede on behalf of their supporters with the police and the bureaucracy. Expectations, however, went much further. First, politicians were to bring home the bacon by steering government resources into their districts. Second, they were expected to work their districts: hosting banquets, sponsoring clubs, handing out envelopes with cash at weddings, providing condolence money to the bereaved at funerals, helping the poor out with school fees, relieving farmers' thirst with *mak-kolii* (rice alcohol) at harvest time, and helping arrange government jobs for locals.[85] Third, candidates were expected to distribute vote-buying money.[86] Failure to redistribute tangible benefits could prove politically fatal, even for members of the ruling party, because supporters were notoriously willing to shift their loyalties to whomever better provided for their "needs."[87] For an ambitious politician, therefore, membership in the ruling party and hence access to governmental resources and officials had considerable, if perhaps mercenary, benefits.[88]

Strict election laws that set spending levels at a tiny fraction of the totals needed to sustain a politician's local machine and electoral efforts created a final hedge against fragmentation on the right. According to the election laws implemented in 1963, candidates could only raise funds directly from fellow party members. Contributions from others had to be funneled through the *huwonhoe*. Under these rules, conservative candidates either had to self-finance or had to depend on back-channel subsidies from the party center.[89] If candidates raised money illegally on their own, they made themselves vulnerable to politically motivated legal punishment if they fell afoul of Park. This is not to imply that conservative politicians did not raise money legally. Presumably, most did, but they also had to raise money illegally out of political necessity because party subsidies and legally raised funds were rarely sufficient to cover a politician's costs. Illegal fund raising and campaigning, therefore, rendered the "mercenary" conservative politicians (as well as opposition politicians who were also forced to engage in the same sorts of illegal activities) hostage to their party. The KCIA and police, finally, continued to play an active role in elections during the 1960s and 1970s. "Mavericks" who bucked the party thus not only risked prosecution for illegal fund raising but also faced the possibility of harassment, intimidation, and vote rigging.[90]

Funds and KCIA muscle enabled Park to cobble together a party of rightists and opportunists, but he was never able to achieve the stable political dominance enjoyed by the Japanese LDP. On the contrary, Park and the DRP faced serious challenges from what should have been a weak opposition.[91] In the 1963 National Assembly elections, the opposition split into four major parties with the result that the DRP managed to win an 88-seat majority even though its candidates only received a third of the total vote. Park himself squeaked by with a less than 2 percent margin over the opposition candidate Yun Po-sun. Four years later, Park defeated Yun by ten points and the DRP increased its share of the vote in the National Assembly election to 50.6 percent, taking 102 out of 175 seats. In 1971, the DRP saw its share of the vote fall to 47.7 percent but nevertheless hung on to its National Assembly majority, while Park beat opposition candidate Kim Dae-jung by eight points.[92] Despite his repeated electoral victories, Park was increasingly worried by the opposition's strong showings, and in 1972 he revoked the Third Republic Constitution and replaced it with a new system that ensured that the ruling party would control the National Assembly, even if the opposition were to win a majority of its elected seats.[93]

This rigging of the electoral game notwithstanding, Park and the DRP could not escape the need for constant flows of political money to funds its local operations and buy the loyalty of its stalwarts. Because that money came primarily from the business sector and the *chaebol*, Park had strong political incentives to promote their growth. The relationship forged between the Blue House and the *chaebol* addressed Park's challenge to build a viable ruling coalition and put in place mechanisms for addressing his third challenge: breaking the cycle of low growth rates and underdevelopment that had dogged both the Rhee and Chang regimes. By the late 1960s Park had forged a developmental alliance that in key respects mirrored the developmental alliance between the LDP and big business in Japan. Money extracted from big business was used for building a political machine that bound together the otherwise fractious South Korean right, thereby creating the political stability needed to sustain rapid economic growth. In recompense for their support, Park provided the *chaebol* with cheap capital but with the caveat that they must use it to invest in growth producing ventures, including support for the emerging export industrial sector. The alliance was successful both politically and economically. The economy began to grow more rapidly after Park consolidated power.

Developmental corruption in South Korea diverged from the pattern that emerged in Japan. First, whereas the Japanese developmental alliance rested to a considerable extent on shared values linking the LDP to big business, from its inception the South Korean developmental alliance was held together by a combination of mutual reciprocity and coercion. Like Rhee, Park continued to rely on the secret police to suppress opposition, not only from the formal opposition parties but also within his own party. It was also understood that businesses ignored Park at considerable peril. As a result, when Park strong-armed the Korean Federation of Industry (KFI) for money, the money had to be delivered.[94] Those that failed to deliver could expect to see their access to capital cut off and faced swift regulatory retaliation.[95] Second, and directly related to the pervious point, from the beginning the relationship between political power and economic power was far more conflict ridden, with the result that the South Korean developmental alliance began to break down after Park was assassinated by Kim Jae-kyu, the head of the KCIA, in October 1979.

Park's assassination ushered in a chaotic return to democracy that ended in December 1979 when General Chun Doo-hwan staged a coup d'état. Although he may have fancied himself the political reincarnation of Park, Chun was a very different, and considerably less honest, man. Like Park, Chun extorted money from the *chaebol*, often relying on the same coercive tactics. But whereas Park was able to cast his extractions in paternalistic terms, Chun lacked the pseudo-charismatic aura that enabled Park to portray himself as the source of the *chaebol* fortune. Moreover, whereas Park cultivated an image of personal integrity, Chun was seen as blatantly venal because he not only forced the *chaebol* to contribute to his new Democratic Justice Party (DJP), he also pocketed a considerable share of what he collected from the *chaebol*, something Park apparently never did. Chun forced the *chaebol* to donate money to a variety of organizations controlled by members of his family, who skimmed off a good share of these funds.[96]

Increasing tension between Chun and the *chaebol* was indicative of more fundamental changes in the structure of the state-business relationship. By the late 1970s, the power of the *chaebol* had begun to rival that of the state as the *chaebol* came to dominate the economy and as the increasing concentration of economic power in the hands of the largest *chaebol* gave them oligopolistic economic power. Convinced that the mounting power of the *chaebol* was a threat to his shaky regime, Chun initiated a series of "reforms" that would have weakened the most powerful *chaebol* and reduced state support. These initiatives included banking deregulation, a new antimonopoly law, and regulations aimed at de-concentrating corporate ownership.[97]

The impact of Chun's reforms on the regime-*chaebol* relationship was complex. On the one hand, banking deregulation and the growth of nonbank financial institutions appeared to increase the financial autonomy of the *chaebol* by reducing their dependence on the state for capital.[98] At the same time, however, tighter enforcement of antimonopoly laws and the de-concentration policy threatened to break up the "octopus-legged" *chaebol*.[99] Ironically, the privatization of the banks proved to be the key source of increasing tensions and ultimately caused a shift from a cooperative state-corporate relationship to a contradictory relationship.

Privatization of the banks was a two-edged sword from the perspective of both the state and the *chaebol*. On the one hand, privatization afforded the *chaebol* new opportunities to extend their influence and obtain greater control over capital. Conversely, privatization decreased the power of the state. At the same time, privatization implied an increasing role for the state as the provider of cheap capital, a reliable source of new funds for the heavily leveraged *chaebol*, and the ultimate guarantor against bankruptcy. Most *chaebol* were technically bankrupt, having borrowed heavily during the days when Park had kept interest rates on policy loans below the rate of inflation and had ordered the banks to lend liberally to the *chaebol*, particularly those involved in the development of the heavy and chemical industries. The *chaebol* had, therefore, built up excessive amounts of debt. When the economy began to decelerate in the early 1980s, the banks found themselves holding large amounts of nonperforming loans. In the past, bad corporate debt had not been a serious problem because the state effectively guaranteed repayment of most loans given to the *chaebol*. With privatization, however, the banks would either have to write off these loans or declare them in default. As a result, a significant number of firms, including subsidiaries of major *chaebol*, faced the prospect of bankruptcy as a result of privatization. Even those who did not go bankrupt would have to pay much higher interest rates, and poor performers were apt to find them selves unable to obtain new financing.

Privatization, therefore, created new conflicts between the banks, credit-worthy borrowers seeking new loans for investment purposes, and debtors seeking discounted bailout loans. Because both the banks and debtors had to look to the central Bank of Korea for the discounted capital that could be rediscounted and lent out as bailout loans or as new cut-rate policy loans, the state found itself at the center of the emerging conflict at the same time that regime efforts to de-concentrate corporate ownership and to curb the monopolistic or oligopolistic power of the *chaebol* created conflicts between business and the state. The position of the Chun regime was further complicated by its own lack of political legitimacy and the increasing strength of the opposition.[100] Combined with competition among the *chaebol* for control over the emerging private banking and nonbank financial sectors, tight credit and slow growth during the early 1980s increased conflicts between Chun and the *chaebol* and ultimately fragmented the old developmental alliance.[101]

In this environment, the inherently rival interests of the *chaebol* led them to reject the old system wherein they had contributed to the ruling party with the expectation that it would provide a generally favorable business environment and suppress the price of capital. They favored one in which political contributions became a means to buy particularistic benefits, often in the form of discounted policy loans and government contracts, and to protect themselves from the danger of aggressive government enforcement of the deconcentration and antimonopoly policies. The old cooperative system was further undermined by the eruption of open conflict between Chun and the KFI in 1983–84, which had hitherto served as the business community's peak association and primary conduit for negotiating relations with the state. Conflict between the KFI and the Chun government specifically robbed the business community of a means of centralizing and coordinating political donations, thus forcing individual *chaebol* to deal directly with the regime at the same time that rivalry among the *chaebol* was increasing and contradictions between the regime and the business community were intensifying. Ultimately, in the later 1980s these contradictions and tension led to what amounted to a *chaebol* revolt wherein several *chaebol* found themselves in open and direct conflict with either Chun or his successor Roh Tae-woo. In 1985, for example, the chairman of the Kukje Corporations, a relatively small *chaebol*, spurned Chun's demands for "contributions" to charitable trusts known to act as conduits for embezzlement, after which Chun ordered the company disbanded. Seven years later during the 1992 presidential election, relations between the Hyundai Corporation and the ruling party had become so strained that Hyundai founder Chung Yu-young ran against the ruling party candidate Kim Young-sam.[102]

Although the developmental alliance in South Korea was clearly breaking apart by the mid-1980s, and the Chun and Roh regimes were become increasing corrupt, the fact remains that Park's efforts at machine building based on money extorted from the *chaebol* in the 1960s set the stage for sustained development during the 1970s and into the 1990s. Park faced the same essential problem that the Japanese right and big business faced in the early 1950s: chronic political fragmentation, bitter faction infighting, and the danger of political instability. Following the 1961 coup, Park "solved" these problems by forcing the *chaebol* to give him the financial wherewithal to buy up the loyalty of a motley collection of self-interested, often mercenary local politicians. He supplemented the lure of money with strong-arm tactics and classic pork-barrel politics to concurrently dissuade free-lancing and encourage politicians to look to the government for the "goods" voters expected them to "deliver." As such, Park was much more akin to Boss Tweed than the "Unique Miracle" Francisco Macias of Equatorial Guinea (see chapter 3) in that he used dirty money, the corrupt inclinations of individual politicians, and the profit-making interests of big business to forge an alliance whose political interests were more intimately linked to rapid economic development and the political income generated thereby rather than plunder. Park failed, however, to create an institutionalized machine like the Japanese LDP, and the Chun regime that seized power after his assassination clearly degenerated into something more closely resembling a racketeering state. Nevertheless, by the time that occurred, the South Korean economy had broken out of the trap of chronic underdevelopment.

Taiwan

In attempting to consolidate its grip on power and set the stage for sustained rapid growth, the Kuomintang faced an even more daunting challenge than conservatives in either Japan or South Korea. Whereas conservatives in Japan and South Korea had to knit together fractious right wings, the leaders of the Kuomintang had to create a stable political foundation for growth in a political environment characterized by high levels of suspicion and even hostility between the party and a large segment of the population. In key respects, the KMT was a colonial regime imported from the mainland after the Japanese surrender in August 1945, and in the immediate aftermath of retrocession the regime appeared more intent on plundering than liberating or governing. Officials and troops looted wartime stocks, dismantled Japanese-built industries and shipped their machinery to the scrap metal yards of Shanghai, seized Japanese-owned property, took over Japanese-owned companies, and engaged in widespread petty thievery.[103] Corrupt officials demanded bribes for cutting through the dense forest of red tape they themselves created.[104] Mainlanders appointed to manage public enterprises taken over from the Japanese milked them dry.[105] Moreover, Kuomintang officials acted as if the Taiwanese were "Japanese collaborators" and "traitors to the motherland" who had somehow failed to prevent the Japanese takeover in 1895. Tensions thus began to build almost from the day the first Chinese troops disembarked in Keelung and Kaohsiung. On February 28, 1947, a minor brawl involving a woman selling black-market cigarettes and police triggered a short-lived rebellion known on Taiwan as the "2–28 Incident" because of the day it erupted. The revolt was quickly suppressed, and in a wave of "white terror" the Nationalist government arrested, imprisoned, and executed tens of thousands of "native" Taiwanese.[106] Conditions worsened in 1949 when the Nationalist collapse on the mainland led to an influx of upward of two million refugees, including half a million soldiers.[107]

After evacuating to Taiwan, the rump KMT leadership not only faced the immediate problem of warding off an attack by the People's Liberation Army, it confronted a triple political task if the party was to survive over the long term. First, it had to stabilize and cleanse a party that was in shambles as a result of the defeat on the mainland and had been ravaged by years of corruption, factionalism, and demoralization.[108] Second, it had to find a means to reduce its reliance on the iron fist to control the island's "Taiwanese" population.[109] Third, it had to build an economy capable of supporting the island's now swollen population and generating the sustained rapid economic growth that would give the population a reason to accept KMT rule.

To address the problems of intraparty decay, Chiang Kai-shek initiated a two-year reorganization that returned the KMT to its earlier Leninist structure.[110] Party members were grouped into cells and their behavior closely monitored. A system of party committees was established to facilitated oversight and control over the government, social organizations, and businesses. A major recruitment drive expanded party membership dramatically, increasing the number of party members from an estimated 50,000 in 1950 to 282,000 in 1952, then doubled the number to over 600,000 in 1961, with the result that by the early 1960s party members constituted about one in ten adults on the island.[111] Finally, the party penetrated local society by establishing a system of offices extending down to the township level whose full-time staff was tasked with providing a variety of free services and acting as intermediaries between citizens and the state bureaucracy, courts, and police.[112] At the local level, the KMT party chairman was a key political actor. Responsible for ensuring the election of party candidates, or at least independents allied with the party, he also oversaw the allocation of patronage, mediated political and community problems, and worked closely with provincial and national party organizations. Normally an outsider, the local KMT chairman essentially acted as the party's "ambassador plenipotentiary."[113]

The reorganization drive culled the party ranks of those guilty of flagrant corruption, indiscipline, and dereliction of duty. The number of party members expelled for corruption was low because many of those who had grown rich from graft during the civil war chose not to make the trip to Taiwan but instead fled to Hong Kong, the United States, or elsewhere. Bureaucratic corruption was thus curtailed, not eliminated.[114] Corruption remained widespread particularly at the subnational and local levels throughout the 1950s and 1960s.[115] According to Allan Cole, poorly paid officials felt they deserved a slice of profits earned by businessmen, and businessmen were willing to pay bribes as long as the "squeeze" was not excessive.[116] During the 1950s, serious overvaluation of the New Taiwan Dollar also fueled a combination of rent seeking by private profiteers and corruption among officials involved in the allocation of foreign currency and import licenses.[117]

Evidence of serious high-level corruption surfaced in 1969 with the exposure of the Banana Scandal in which senior officials, including the governor of the Central Bank of Taiwan and the former chief of personnel administration, were found to have skimmed off millions of dollars by falsifying export receipts and accepting kickbacks from the Kaohsiung Fruit Cooperative.[118] In 1972, Chiang Kai-shek's son and designated heir Chiang Ch'ing-kuo launched a new anticorruption campaign aimed at breaking the "unholy alliances" between civil servants and businessmen. Officials were ordered to report any social contract with businessmen and were warned not to put on lavish banquets, elaborate weddings, or large funerals.[119] They were banned from patronizing "hostess" bars, and the police began raiding nightclubs and bars, demanding identification, and recording the names of civil servants they caught. Officials caught three times were subject to dismissal.[120] Chiang went so far as to prosecute senior members of the powerful Taiwan Garrison Command for their involvement in smuggling and sent Wang Chang-yi, Chiang Kai-shek's former secretary, to prison for his role in the Banana Scandal.[121] In the short term, the 1972 campaign had a chilling effect of closing off many of the more common ways for civil servants and businessmen to "socialize." Bureaucrats suspected of corruption were often shunted off to positions with little power, a technique that tended to obscure the level of bureaucratic corruption but also had the effect of keeping the ranks of those with real authority relatively clean. Even so, Robert Wade reports that contractors expected to kick back 8 to 10 percent of the value of public contracts; customs officials skimmed off around 10 percent of the value of meat and liquor imports and would prevent goods from clearing customs if they were not paid off; and businessmen understood that if a bureaucrat complained about his low salary and the high cost of living, that this was a signal that a "gift" of cash should be given.[122] It appears, therefore, that corruption continued at both the local and national levels but was "controlled" and "tolerable."[123]

Although the severity of bureaucratic corruption during the post-1949 period is somewhat unclear, it is nevertheless clear that it was not a central factor in shaping or deforming state economic policy. The bureaucracies charged with making and supervising macroeconomic policy were staffed with well-paid technocrats.[124] Hence, even though low-level corruption might have been common, the state was, in Geddes's terms, split into a largely corruption-free technocracy and a more corrupt administration.[125]

Even so, the developmental alliance in Taiwan rested on a much broader foundation of money and power that bound the KMT to the economy and rendered the business sector heavily, if not utterly, dependent on the party and the party-controlled state. The party "solved" its macro political and economic problems by creating a vast machine that operated not only on a political level, but also on an economic level that in many ways surpassed the scale and scope of the Japanese and South Korean developmental machines.

Construction of the economic foundation of what would become the Taiwanese version of the development machine began immediately after the island's retrocession in 1945 and included the creation of an economic structure in which KMT and the state controlled the "commanding heights." They placed both mainland industrialists, who dominated the large-enterprise sector and later the Taiwanese entrepreneurs who populated the small and medium enterprise sector, in dependent relationships. The party then increased its economic leverage by building a sprawling network of party-owned companies. Control over public resources and the profits generated by party-owned enterprises allowed the regime to construct a political machine linking the mainlander-dominated KMT to the Taiwanese-dominated "local factions" (*difang paixi*) that structured local politics and placed them in a similarly dependent relationship.

Construction of the Taiwanese development machine began with the adoption of a land reform program that broke the political back of the landlord class and with the formation of an extensive state-owned industrial sector. Begun in 1949, the land reform program first reduced rents; then sold off public lands, including land formerly owned by Japanese, to small farmers; and in 1953 transferred the ownership of most rented land to the tiller.[126] Transfer of ownership was accomplished by having the state purchase land from landlords, with 70 percent of the purchase price being paid in the form of land bonds and the remaining 30 percent in stocks in four state-owned enterprises. Tenant farmers then purchased the land from the state and paid for the land in installments over a ten-year period. Income from these payments was used to pay interest on the land bonds issued to landlords. Both stock and land bonds could be resold, and many former landlord families, fearing that the stocks and bonds would prove valueless in the long term, quickly sold them and either lived off the proceeds or invested in small businesses. A few ex-landlords and other entrepreneurs opted to speculate in stocks and land bonds and were thereby able to accumulate the capital needed to become industrialists and investors. In rather short order and with minimal resistance, the KMT regime managed to eliminate the landlord class and hence one source of resistance to its rule.

Concurrent with the land reform, the state built up the system of farmers, fishermen, and water conservancy associations, many of which dated to the Japanese colonial era.[127] The purpose of these associations was twofold. First, they acted as the agent for the state rice, fertilizer, and fruit-export monopolies; marketed other crops; operated rice mills; and provided agricultural extension services to farmers.[128] Second, their credit departments became the primary source of credit in rural areas. In addition to acting as a savings and loan bank for their members, the associations served "as agents for the Land Bank, the Cooperative Bank, the Farmers Bank of China and different government agencies in the supply of agricultural credit."[129] By arbitraging between bank interest rates and the interest rate on loans to farmers, the associations provided a rich source of semi-licit income.[130] Control over the associations, and hence the flow of credit, thus because a key source of power in the countryside.[131] The associations were, as one author put it, "succulent meat" (*fei rou*), and control over them was much prized.[132]

Control over local government was a second source of local political power. Although local governments had little legislative autonomy, they nevertheless controlled key sources of patronage, the allocation of public works contracts, the assignment of public franchises and monopolies (e.g., public transportation), and preferential access to bank loans.[133] In addition, control over local government in urban areas allowed local factions to name the members of urban planning committees and hence manipulate the distribution of land-use rights, control zoning regulations, and enabled their allies to profit from land speculation and real estate development.[134] Finally, local officials were positioned to grant tacit operating rights for illegal casinos, dance halls, nightclubs, and massage parlors.[135]

Local elections thus became the focus of intense conflict between contending "local factions" (*difang paixi*). Based initially on long-standing family and clan relationships, local factions were relatively permanent but informal coalitions organized to contend for political power at the county, township, and association levels.[136] In general, local factions were nonideological and formed around prominent local figures and local officials. Local factions rarely extend across counties.[137] Even so, local factions played critical roles at the provincial level. Up until the mid-1980s, in fact, over half the KMT members of the Taiwan Provincial Assembly were associated with specific local factions.[138] Factional politics was, finally, congruent with the ROC's Single Non-transferable Vote with Multimember Districts (SNTVMMD) electoral system wherein the ruling party had to successfully run multiple candidates in legislative elections but could win seats on the basis of small, compact groups.[139]

Like U.S. political machines, local factions in Taiwan entered politics to obtain the spoils of power and channel patronage and public spending to their supporters. Unlike their U.S. counterparts, however, local factions in Taiwan lacked political autonomy. Although local governments and the farmers' associations were a rich source of political resources, the money behind them came from the central and provincial governments. Chronically short of locally generated revenues, local governments depended heavily on budgetary subsidies from the Taiwan provincial and central governments. During the years of KMT hegemony, subsidies were directed to localities controlled by local factions loyal to the party.[140] If a locality came under the sustained control of the opposition, it faced the very real prospect of fiscal starvation.[141]

Most local factions were dominated by KMT members or allied themselves with the party. In either case, local politicians' commitment to the party was generally instrumental.[142] By the same token, the KMT's commitment to local factions was equally mercenary. Although the party saw local factions as useful allies, it understood they could be dangerous "independent kingdoms" if they became too deeply entrenched in power. The party, therefore, played games of divide and conquer: alternating its support between rival local factions, building up weak factions in areas where a particular local faction was strong, and even backing nonfaction candidates to prevent the local factions from consolidating their grip on local power.[143] The local factions, in turn, played games designed to undermine the KMT's ability to operate independently and might boycott party nominees if they were not affiliated with the faction, endorse the party's nominee but then remain passive during the election, or shift their support to opposition candidates.[144]

The factions were, therefore, rival political machines that relied on a combination of familial and personalistic connections, promises of patronage and access to pubic resources, mediation with the state bureaucracy, and vote buying to build the electoral bases that would allow them to contend for control of various local offices.[145] And even though the factions derived their power from their allegiance to the KMT, the KMT was beholden to them because faction leaders and members, most of whom were ethnic Taiwanese rather than mainlanders, were able to mobilize voters and ensure the party's electoral power even in areas where the party per se was seen as a "foreign" occupier.[146]

At the grassroots level, the key actors were the local fixers or ward heelers, known in the Minnan dialect spoken by "native" Taiwanese as the *tiau-a-ka*.[147] The *tiau-a-ka* were generally locally prominent men involved in business or employed as local officials with the sort of strong community ties that would allow them to cobble together blocks of voters. Would-be *tiau-a-ka* generally entered politics by first establishing social connections with a group of local voters, often by assisting them in dealing with the government, helping them find jobs, and perhaps providing small loans and grants to help defray wedding and funeral expenses, pay school fees, or to start up a small business. More broadly, an aspiring *tiau-a-ka* needed to build "connections" not only within the local community but also with government officials and other powerful figures outside the community, which he could draw on to "help" his neighbors and associates.[148] Having achieved a role as a community or neighborhood leader, a would-be *tiau-a-ka* began building ties with one of the local factions, often by helping out in local elections and other political activities. Once identified as a local political activist, the *tiau-a-ku* would be incorporated into the faction's electoral machine come election time. In the run up to an election, the local party leaders would begin building their "vote-buying machine" by establishing an informal coordinating board and selecting a core group of political brokers. Afterward, these brokers selected the large number of street-level *tiau-a-ka*, responsible for identifying voters who were already inclined to support the party and those who might be induced to vote for it if they were "correctly approached." After calculating how many votes the faction would need to buy to win the election, the faction's leadership would give its *tiau-a-ka* funds for various political activities, including banquets, outings, etc. On the eve of the election, the *tiau-a-ka* would offer would-be supporters and wavering voters small sums of money or other "gifts."[149]

The money to fund a faction's operations, including vote buying, generally came not from the KMT but from the candidates themselves. Would-be candidates generally had to first "buy" the party's nomination by contributing large sums to the party's coffers and then fund their own campaigns.[150] Candidates also faced the possibility of having to pay rivals to drop out of the race for the party's nomination.[151] Despite these up-front, out-of-pocket costs, successful candidates could expect to reap a net profit from their "investment" in the form of "payments" and "contributions" from their core supporters, who, in turn, assumed their "investments" would be repaid in the forms of patronage, government contracts, franchises, and other favors that "their" man could provide once in office.[152] KMT funds were, however, more likely to be made available to candidates running for county-level offices, particularly those in areas where the opposition threatened party control.

In addition to funding elections, local politicians spent considerable sums maintaining their standing among voters. They were expected to be major contributors to community projects, including school construction and road-paving projects; hand out cash to the bereaved at funerals and to members of wedding parties; extend small loans to needy constituents; pay medical bills; and give subsidies to students attending high schools and universities.[153] Local politicians were also expected to generously support local temples and charities.[154]

Politics was, in short, an expensive profession. But it could also be very profitable. The profits from politics appear to have come primarily from the connections politicians built up during their years in office rather than from milking the public treasury. Local government budgets were simply too small to permit large-scale looting. As a result, politicians generally cashed in after leaving office by going into (or, in most cases, back into) business, either as managers of state- or party-owned companies or as "liaison officers" working for private companies but specializing in dealing with and massaging their former political colleagues and government officials.[155]

The KMT's political machine incorporated the local factions and penetrated the labor force through the state-owned industrial sector and its unions. The large state sector was a rich source of employment for party members and loyalists.

According to Fred Riggs, in the early post-1949 years, employees of state-owned companies constituted 46 percent of total industrial employment and numbered upward of 68,000.[156] In 1966, state-owned industries accounted for a much smaller percentage of the total industrial workforce (11.41 percent).[157] Even so, the total number of workers employed by state-owned companies had increased to perhaps as many as 72,000.[158] In most state-owned enterprises, managerial and staff positions were held by mainlanders, who frequently secured their positions through nepotism and party connections. Taiwanese workers, on the other hand, were bound to the party first by the existence of a hierarchy of intracompany party organizations staffed by KMT cadres (who were paid by the company) tasked with political indoctrination and policing.[159] Workers were thus under pressure to demonstrate their political reliability and loyalty both as a means of ensuring continued employment and as a prerequisite for promotion.[160] Second, Taiwanese workers were bound to the party via the company union, which was also controlled by the party.[161] Union activism offered Taiwanese workers opportunities to move off the shop floor and the possibility of promotion to staff positions. Moreover, union posts also brought with them access to union funds and opportunities for illicit self-enrichment.[162]

Whereas Park developed the DRP into a political machine first in anticipation of democratic elections and then in the face of strong electoral opposition, prior to the 1980s KMT control over the national political apparatus was not at risk. On the contrary, at the national level, the declaration of martial law in 1947 and the enactment of the Temporary Provisions Effective during the Period of the Communist Rebellion in 1948 suspended national elections and gave the party a de facto political monopoly. At the subnational level, where popular elections were introduced as early as 1946 and extended to the provincial level in 1951, control over the state gave the KMT access to a wide array of political resources (patronage, loans, public works contracts, public franchises, etc.) that it distributed to those who helped maintain its grip on elected offices. Despite the draconian measures backstopping KMT power, the party's power was never absolute, and over the years it faced increasingly serious challenges from both independents and the coalition of anti-KMT politicians known as the *dangwai* (literally, those outside the party), who began to contest elections for the "supplemental seats" added to the Legislative Yuan during the 1970s and 1980s.[163] In this context of "creeping democratization," redistributive politics helped linked the mainlander-dominated KMT to Taiwanese society and mitigate the potentially negative effects of the cleavages created in the immediate postretrocession period. More critically, ties between the party and local factions created a *modus vivendi* that allowed the party to cooperate with local political actors in the pursuit and maintenance of political stability. The KMT's political machine was, of course, backstopped by a massive security apparatus that reportedly employed 30,000 secret police and used martial law to ruthlessly crush overt opposition to KMT rule, as well as the Taiwan Garrison Command which administered the martial law.[164]

Over time, increasing competition drove the cost of local elections up dramatically. In theory, campaign spending was strictly limited and the amount that candidates could spend was relatively small.[165] In reality, candidates often spent many times more than the law allowed. According to Chao, by the 1980s a viable campaign for a basic executive post, the hamlet chief, cost an average of NT (New Taiwan Dollars) $500,000 to NT$1 million (US$ 14,000–28,000), village or town council NT$1–2 million (US$28,000–56,000), village or township head NT$10–20 million (US$280,000–560,000), county council member NT$30–80 million (US$843,000–2.2 million), and county magistrate NT$100–500 million (US$2.8–14 million).[166]

As costs increased, the party began to look to wealthy businessmen, popularly known as "golden cows" *(jin niu)* who could independently afford the expense of campaigning.[167] The party also built ties with the Taiwanese underworld. Prior to the 1980s, organized crime played a secondary role in local elections: buying votes, intimidating voters, and strong-arming opposition candidates in return for protection from police interference and awards of public works construction contracts.[168] By the 1990s, gangsters had moved from the back rows to the political forefront as gang members began standing for election.[169] The rise of mafia politics *(heidao zhengzhi)* and the increasing role of organized crime's "black gold" *(heijin)* in politics not only corrupted the Taiwanese electoral system and drew the KMT into a series of "unholy alliances," it ultimately weakened the party's political machine and its ability to maintain local political hegemony, leading to the rise of independent candidates and mavericks, politicians who claimed the party label but ran without having secured its formal nomination.[170] In the long run, the instrumental loyalties that tied local factions to the KMT also proved to be a source of weakness because they helped cast KMT candidates as political mercenaries, drawn to politics by a desire for power and personal gain rather than a sense of public duty.[171] Nevertheless, the fact remains that during the critical take-off phase of Taiwan's economic development the KMT's machine-style approach to politics knit together a complex united front that connected the party, local Taiwanese politicians, businessmen, and organized crime by giving them a common instrumental interest in maintaining KMT control over Taiwan's governmental hierarchy.

Although machine-style politics helped enmesh the KMT into the ethnic Taiwanese polity, a combination of state-owned industries, large-scale private industries, and a sector of party-owned companies also embedded the party into the economy, tied key economic interests to the party, and linked the party's long-term political interest in maintaining its grip on power to the rapid growth of the Taiwanese economy. Just as the party created a political machine to consolidate its grip on the Taiwanese policy, it constructed a parallel machine to control and dominate the economy.

The state sector was built on a foundation of confiscated Japanese enterprises. During the early years of KMT rule, Governor Chen Yi adopted a statist development strategy based on the socialization of the means of production and government monopolization.[172] Between October 1945 and early 1946, in addition to assuming control of land, property, and material belonging to the Japanese military administration and the colonial government, the ROC confiscated a total of 775 Japanese-owned industrial firms, 85 Taiwanese-owned firms, and assets worth OT (Old Taiwan Dollars) $9.5 billion.[173] Of these, 399 were nationalized and transferred to the control of the central government, the Taiwan provincial government, or local governments. The remaining firms were either sold or shut down. The newly formed state sector included all of the major banks and financial institutions; state monopolies in aluminum, iron and steel, and petroleum; a state tobacco and alcohol monopoly; provincial companies controlling the production of sugar, electricity, paper, cement, shipbuilding, and machine machining; public firms involved in mining, agriculture, forestry, shipping, insurance, and construction; and state-controlled administrations for railways, roads, ports, and telecommunications.[174] As a result, the state sector accounted for upward of 90 percent of the island's economy in the immediate post-retrocession period.[175] After Chen Yi was recalled, the island's new governor Wei Tao-ming backed away from Chen's socialist policies and allowed the growth of the private sector.[176] The state sector, however, remained quite large, accounting for over half of total capital formation and industrial production in 1959. Until 1967, state-owned companies accounted for more than a third of total manufacturing enterprises.[177]

Even after extensive growth of the private sectors during the 1960s and the concurrent privatization of a limited number of state-owned enterprises, the state sector continued to account for over a fifth of industrial production until the 1990s.[178] Many state owned enterprises were granted monopolies or dominated particular sectors (e.g., energy, electrical power, munitions and other defense-related materials, copper, oil, aluminum, steel, petrochemicals, shipbuilding, heavy machinery, and chemical fertilizers).[179] In the wake of the 1973 global oil crisis, the state sector expanded with the establishment of the China Petroleum Corporation, China Petrochemical Development Corporation, and China Shipbuilding Corporation.[180] As of 1989, the state sector included a total of 122 enterprises, of which 29 were controlled by the national government, 40 by the provincial government, ten by the municipal governments in Taipei and Kaohsiung, eight by county governments, and 35 by the Vocational Assistance Commission for Retired Servicemen (VAR).[181] Even though the "state" (i.e., the central government, provincial governments, and local governments) owned these state-owned enterprises (SOEs), they were de facto controlled by the KMT because, as Karl Fields points out, "virtually all top-level management positions" were held by KMT party members.[182]

Politically, the size of the state sector was important for two reasons. First, the state sector included all of Taiwan's major banks and financial institutions. So long as it controlled the state, the KMT controlled the allocation of capital and rendered the business sector dependent on the party. During the 1950s, all the banks were state owned. Between 1959 and 1961, three privately owned banks were allowed to form. Nevertheless, as of 1964, banks controlled by the central and provincial governments accounted for 81 percent of total bank assets. Of the remainder, half of the assets belonged to the China Development Corporation, 20 percent of whose shares belonged to the state.[183] In 1991, according to Karl Fields, the state still controlled twenty-one of Taiwan's twenty-four banks and these state-controlled banks accounted for 98 percent of total deposits, with the seven largest state-controlled banks accounting for 90 percent of total deposits.[184]

Second, control over the state sector positioned the party to dominate the private sector. The private sector during the early post-1949 period initially included ethnic Taiwanese businessmen who had built networks of merchant enterprises during the Japanese colonial period or had acquired Japanese businesses and assets during the chaotic period following the August 1945 surrender. A number of these were then able to parlay their initial capital into much larger sums by engaging in underground money lending.[185] A number of large landowners, including the "five big families," were also able to acquire significant ownership shares in the four public corporations that were "privatized" during the land reform by using their stock to compensate landlords for the land transferred to tenant farmers.[186] In 1948–49, an influx of capitalists fleeing the communist takeover of the mainland created a new class of "émigré industrialists" concentrated in the textile sector. Most of these émigré textile industrialists were already closely tied to the state-controlled banks and were often known political allies of the regime.[187] Regardless of their origins, private-sector capitalists were dependent on the party-state which controlled the banks, access to sectors where restricted competition created rents, the issuing of business licenses, the levying of taxes, delivery of supplies of electricity, and the allocation of key materials. Loyalty to the party, in short, was a prerequisite for doing business.[188] The adoption of a neomercantilist Import Substitution Industrialization (ISI) regime in the early 1950s reinforced the émigré industrialists' dependency on the state.

Under the terms of the policy, the state-controlled imports of raw cotton and rationed supplies to individual firms, selling the raw cotton to them at a third of the black market price, thus ensuring that favored firms reaped high profits from the sale of finished cloth.[189] Over time, many of these companies coalesced into enterprise groups (*guanxi qiye*), networks of companies linked together through family ties, cross-ownership, and personalistic relations (*guanxi*), which came to dominate the large-enterprise sector of the Taiwanese economy. Although nominally privately owned, many of these enterprise groups were linked to the party, which often cemented their informal ties by granting them "oligopolistic rent-seeking opportunities and political access."[190]

Like most sectors of the economy, the KMT penetrated the emerging private sector through a variety of corporatist-like structures.[191] The party, for example, controlled the National Federation of Industries (NFI), the National Federation of Commerce (NFC), and the National Association for the Promotion of Industry and Commerce (NAPIC).[192] Sectoral trade associations were, in turn, the state's "handmaidens" with responsibility to pass government instructions down to their members rather than lobby on their behalf.[193] The KMT Social Affairs Department was, in fact, responsible for supervising the election of association officials, and the leaders of the peak associations were hand picked by the party chairman. In addition, large private enterprises were informally required to place retired military officers in key management positions, thus positioning the state security apparatus and the party to keep a close eye on corporate affairs. Companies also frequently hired mainlanders with political connections to serve as liaisons to the state and party.[194] In return for their loyalty, executives were given access to the party chairman's inner circle and senior government officials.[195]

When the limits of import-substitution industrialization were reached in the late 1950s, the KMT instituted a series of economic reforms that spawned a new sector populated by small and medium-size enterprises (SMEs) engaged in export-oriented production, often acting as subcontractors for Japanese manufacturers. In theory, these largely Taiwanese-owned SMEs should have been more independent of the KMT machine than the state-owned sector and mainlander-controlled large enterprises. In reality, they too were indirectly dependent on the party. Not only did they need access to foreign exchange and credit, which the state had a heavy hand in controlling, they were also vulnerable to regulatory pressures and often required inputs produced by upstream firms controlled by the state, the party, or enterprise groups allied with the state.[196] The SME section thus also existed in a state of semidependence and vulnerability.

The final pillar of the KMT political machine was a network of party-owned corporations, known informally as KMT Inc. The KMT had established party-owned enterprises before the 1949 retreat. Early on, the KMT concentrated its business activities in areas such as publishing and media, areas obviously important to its political operations. After the retreat to Taiwan, the party incrementally built a sprawling business empire that reached into the heart of the Taiwanese economy. During the 1950s, the party set up manufacturing companies (textiles, plastics, and machinery), an import-export company, and a construction company.[197] The following decade, it established the Taiwan Stock Exchange Corporation, became involved in insurance, expanded its manufacturing interests (adding pharmaceuticals and cement), launched a deep-sea fishing venture, built the island's first (and for many years only) television broadcasting company, opened a movie studio, and went into the business of supplying natural gas. In 1959, the party participated in the founding of the China Development Corporation (CDC) with some of Taiwan's largest industrialists. Overtly, the purpose of the CDC was to establish an alternative to U.S. aid, which the government concluded would be phased out in the early 1960s, by facilitating foreign borrowing and long-term lending to Taiwan-based companies.[198] In practice, of course, the party's stake in the CDC gave it control over the allocation of credit raised overseas.

Until the 1970s, the party-owned sector remained relatively small and the KMT relied mainly on the state sector, which it controlled, for patronage and finances.[199] During the 1970s and 1980s, the party significantly expanded its business holdings, particularly in the financial sector.[200] At one time, the party held a stake in more than two hundred companies both on Taiwan and overseas, including some fifty companies in which it controlled a majority stake.[201] In addition, the party controlled substantial amounts of real estate, including tracts purchased from the state at very favorable prices during the 1980s and early 1990s.[202]

Although the party owned some enterprises outright, the real political power of KMT Inc. derived from the web of its investments in private companies. Seven holding companies formed the core of KMT Inc.; the first of which, Central Investment Holdings, was established in 1971. By far the largest of the KMT holding companies, as of 1993, Central Investment held stocks in companies in a multitude of sectors, including finance, petrochemicals, construction, cement, and manufacturing with an estimated value of NT$72.87 billion (US$2.7 billion) in 1994. Four years later the party set up Hua Hsia Investment Holdings, which had estimated holdings in 1996 of NT$6.50 billion (US$240 million).[203] A much smaller company, Hua Hsia owned shares in a variety of newspapers, television broadcasters, and other media companies. In 1979, the party formed Kuang Hwa Investment Holdings, which invested in a wide array of companies in a variety of sectors including gas and high technology and had an estimated value of NT$22.87 billion (US$860 million) in the mid-1990s. Nine years later, the party established four more holding companies, Chi Sheng Industrial Holdings (valued in 1996 at NT$1.91 billion [US$71 million]), which held stocks in companies concentrated in the construction and real estate development sectors; Jen Hwa Investment Holdings (NT$3.44 billion [US$127 million]), which owned stocks in mostly high-tech companies; Kingdom Investment Holdings, which was invested in companies in the insurance business; and Asia Pacific Holding Company (NT$1.55 billion [US$57 million]), which specialized in foreign investment.[204] In 1993, the party reorganized its corporate holdings, transferred all its shares to its seven holding companies, and then placed them under the control of the newly established Business Management Committee (BMC), thus separating its business interests from the KMT's Central Finance Committee (CFC) and consolidating the party's now sprawling corporate empire. By then, KMT Inc. was worth something on the order of US$4 billion. Other estimates put the total value of KMT Inc. as high as US$36 billion in 1993.[205]

The reach of KMT Inc. was only partly a function of its corporate empire and its stock portfolio.[206] By investing in a wide range of firms, the party built a network of business partners that included many of Taiwan's leading industrialists, capitalists, and traders, many of them party members. Even businessmen who were not partners with KMT Inc. had reasons to cultivate the party since its considerable capital assets made it a potential investor. Finally, KMT Inc. was invested in the state sector and held a stake in at least forty-two SOEs.[207]

In his novel *The Octopus: A Story of California*, Frank Norris described the Southern Pacific Railroad as a powerful beast whose tentacles reached down into the very bowels of the California economy and threatened to squeeze the life out of it.[208] The reach of the KMT far exceeded Norris's vision of the Southern Pacific. The party completely penetrated Taiwanese society. It controlled the state, military, and secret police. State-owned enterprises provided it with a large stock of patronage. Through the state, the KMT controlled the banks and hence the allocation of capital. Its stalwarts controlled the farmers' associations, fishermen's associations, irrigation cooperatives, and a host of functional and civic associations. Control over company unions gave the party both a means to stifle worker activism and feather-bedding opportunities for those ready, willing, and able to support the party. Party-owned enterprises earned the party profits to finance its central operations, created patronage for its loyalists, and forged partnerships that bound a wide array of capitalists and industrialists to the perpetuation of party control. In short, the party not only controlled the commanding heights of the Taiwanese economy, it penetrated deep into the valleys and hollows of Taiwanese society, with the result that even the largely Taiwanese-controlled

SMEs and the export sector were caught within its many tentacles. The KMT machine was truly an octopus, one far bigger than Norris's fictional Southern Pacific octopus.

And yet, the KMT octopus was neither a parasite nor a leech that sucked Taiwan dry. It certainly drew its sustenance and vigor out of the economy and often manipulated the economy in ways that bestowed rents and other advantages on the state, party, and social structures it controlled. But the health and viability of the party political-cum-economic machine depended on the overall health of the Taiwanese economy. At a fundamental level, the party needed strong economic growth to legitimate its claim to power and provide the economic foundation for resisting the CCP-controlled mainland, a need that was considerably reinforced by uncertainty about the U.S. commitment to the KMT and the survival of the Republic of China. Jobs and growth were, therefore, a political necessity. The party needed a strong economy for much less grandiose reasons. To begin with, a strong economy created profit-making opportunities for party-owned enterprises (POEs) and their business partners. Strong profits, in turn, ensured that the party's coffers would be full and it could outspend its rivals many times over. Profits also made the party attractive to business interests. Over time, profits depended increasingly on export earnings and hence on the SME sector, which the party did not control in the same manner that it controlled the state and KMT Inc. The party had strong incentives, therefore, to encourage and facilitate the rapid growth of these largely Taiwanese-owned companies.

As Peter Evans argues, because it was deeply embedded in the economy, the KMT had strong incentives to pursue rapid growth.[209] The party was, ultimately, a political-cum-economic body which sought not only political power but also the economic profits it needed to survive in a somewhat hostile and ever more competitive political environment. In a sense, the party was autonomous because it controlled an authoritarian state that for three and a half decades enabled it to stymie challenges to its grip on power. And yet the party was not hegemonic. From the beginning, democratic elections at the local level and the imperative to overcome the hostility created during the plunder and terror of the first post-retrocession years forced the party to cultivate the Taiwanese population. Over time, the party's deepening involvement in the economy rendered it increasingly dependent on its business "partners" and the overall health of the Taiwanese economy. Moreover, because the party's political and economic interests depended on the health of the Taiwanese-dominated export sector, the party was, in Kang's terms, a "hostage," but a hostage who, in turn, held its captor captive because Taiwanese SMEs could not long survive if they were to wage open political war against the party.[210] In a sense, therefore, the party machine effectively internalized the developmental alliance that formed the political and economic foundation for rapid economic growth.

Prior to the 1997 Asian Economic Crisis, it was common to hear that the "dragons" and "tigers" of East Asia had created a new form of capitalism. The so-called developmental state was said to be a new and smarter political animal, one that understood the economics of development and had embraced a new ideology called "GNP-ism." There is no question that during the 1960s, 1970s, and 1980s, the growth rates in the economies of Japan, South Korea, and Taiwan allowed them to rapidly move from the ranks of the underdeveloped world into the developing world and then into the ranks of the developed world. These "economic miracles" were based on a form of politics most often associated with the corrupt excesses of the post–Civil War period in the United States, or what is often called the "Gilded Age": the political machine. That being the case, one might wonder if perhaps Boss Tweed and Tammany Hall had more to do with the Asian Economic Miracle than did Adam Smith and the University of Chicago's neoclassical brand of free-market economics.

The answer is no. Boss Tweed was not the cause of rapid economic growth in South Korea and Taiwan. Rapid growth in these cases was the result of export-promoting economic policies, integration into the international market economy, and regimes that sought rapid economic growth as a hedge against external threats and a source of domestic legitimacy. Machine politics was, however, a necessary precondition. Before these economies could begin to grow rapidly, a stable political foundation had to be laid. In South Korea, Syngman Rhee's attempt to impose stability from above through increasing authoritarianism led to the collapse of the conservative Liberal Party and ushered in a period of chronic political instability under Chang Myon. General Park Chung-hee ended the turmoil by staging a military coup in 1961 but was forced by the United States to allow a return to democracy in 1963. To have any hope of retaining power in free elections, Park had to somehow forge a winning coalition out of the fractious Korean right. In the case of Taiwan, the Leninist KMT found itself forced to operate in a political environment soured by the 2–28 uprising and the white terror that followed its suppression and compelled to grapple with the legacy of defeat in the civil war. The party had to reach out to local Taiwanese political actors and get them to support the mainlander-dominated regime. The same problem also confronted Japan, where internecine infighting between the rival Liberal and Democratic parties combined with the impending reunification of the warring wings of the antibusiness Japanese Socialist Party and rising labor militancy threatened to create an unstable political environment at a time when the Japanese economy was struggling to complete postwar reconstruction and cope with the end of the Korean War boom.

In all these instances, the conservative political leadership built alliances with powerful economic actors and set up political machines based on redistributive politics. In Korea, Park and Kim Jong-pil first strong-armed (literally) the business sector into providing the money necessary to form the Democratic Republican Party (DRP) and then Park continued to squeeze business for the money needed to buy the loyalty of local politicians. In return, Park channeled cheap capital to his supporters and helped build the powerful *chaebol* that would come to dominate the South Korean economy.

The Taiwanese case was more complicated. On the one hand, Chiang Kai-shek relied much more heavily on an iron fist to control the island. But he too forged alliances with local Taiwanese factions and offered access to patronage, profit-making opportunities, and credit in return for their support while also building an alliance with the island's industrialists and capitalists. Unlike Park, the KMT moved into the economy, building the network of corporate holdings that would eventually become known as KMT Inc. In both cases, short, rapid economic development was built on a foundation of pork, graft, and machine politics.[211]

Because they were allied with and dependent on the business sector for the political resources needed to sustain them, the South Korean and Taiwanese political machines became developmental machines. Politics was expensive and the mercenary nature of the machines' stalwarts meant that holding the machine together and retaining the ruling parties' grip on power required constant injections of political money.[212] Only a profitable business sector was capable of satisfying the ruling parties' need for money. The base political interest in retaining power, therefore, virtually mandated that these ruling parties enact economic policy regimes that favored high-speed growth. The scale of the parties' monetary requirements was also such that they had to enact relatively broad-based policies that benefited a range of businesses, not a select few. Businesses, in turn, had good reason to pay the political bills of these ruling parties. So long as the ruling parties facilitated their profit making and the economies expanded, illegal contributions yielded positive returns. Oftentimes, not contributing could have had direct negative consequences (denial of access to capital, regulatory harassment, etc.). Most major business players had to pay to play, and only those who paid profited. In short, rapid growth justified paying the cost of keeping the ruling party in power.

Not everybody, of course, profited. Labor and consumers in particular bore a considerable share of the cost of the promotion of high-speed growth. In addition, over time, systems based on "honest" political graft tended to become increasingly mired in classically dishonest and dysfunctional graft. Chun and

Roh clearly redirected money that had flowed through the president's office and into the coffers of the DRP during the Park era into their pockets, those of their families, and to their inner set of cronies. By the mid-1980s, the South Korean developmental machine was clearly degenerating into an instrument for presidential plunder. Taiwan, meanwhile, saw a rise in gangster politics in the 1990s and an influx of "black gold." In the formative stages of rapid growth in these economies, however, it was graft that created the conservative parties that put together pro-growth economic regimes and sustained them in power as each economy took off.

In conclusion, in South Korea and Taiwan developmental corruption was a necessary precondition because it forged and sustained developmental coalitions and because it was structured in ways that created powerful political incentives for ruling parties to promote growth and hence to grow the profits from which they drew their financial sustenance. It was not the sole factor, of course, but it was an important factor.

If corruption can create political machines and give them powerful political incentives to promote rapid growth and private profit making, then the first paradox of high levels of corruption and rapid growth is explained by the utility of machine politics in the formation of developmental alliances in otherwise unstable political environments. Like the more common form of corruption, or what we might call degenerative corruption, developmental corruption siphons money out of the economy. But whereas the bulk of money plundered by politicians in other systems ends up in their pocket and is either stashed away in foreign safe havens or squandered on wine, women, and the like, a considerable share of the money siphoned out of the business sector in instances of developmental corruption is funneled into turning weak and factious political parties into political machines, which then promote the profit-making interests of the business sectors that support them financially. As a broad approximation, therefore, we can resolve the first paradox of concurrent extensive corruption and rapid growth. Even though the political machine may be a venal, mercenary, and inefficient institution, in certain circumstances the fact that it is a form of political institution whose purpose is to sustain its grip on power means it is likely to act like what Mancur Olson calls a "stationary bandit": it looks more to long-term income than does a de-institutionalized regime of "roving bandits" whose lack of a long time horizon leads them to loot and plunder.[213]

Solving the first paradox of corruption and development, unfortunately, does not help explain the concurrence of intensifying corruption and rapid growth in China. Whereas it was necessary to strengthen political parties and imbue them with political incentives to promote rapid growth in South Korea and Taiwan, China already had a powerful political machine, the Chinese Communist

Party (CCP). In the late 1970s Deng Xiaoping and his allies saw rapid growth as critical to the restoring the party's battered legitimacy. After a decade of reform, the party's incentives for a headlong pursuit of rapid growth were renewed by antigovernment protests in 1989 (protests triggered to a considerable extent by popular outrage over mounting official corruption), which convinced Deng that new reforms were needed to accelerate growth and to dramatically increase household incomes. Nor did the party need the financial support of business to sustain its grip on power because its financial needs were well taken care of. From an institutional perspective, therefore, developmental corruption was a necessary precondition for rapid growth. Moreover, whereas developmental corruption tends to be structural in the sense that it is a semiregularized and organized part of the political system, degenerative corruption tends to be much more anarchic, with individual officials, including the political leadership, using their authority to grab whatever they can. In the case of post-Mao China, Ting Gong, Shawn Shieh, Lu Xiaobo, Thomas Bickford, James Mulvenon, and others have argued for the existence of organizational, institutional, and collective corruption, and there is certainly evidence of public institutions using their organizational power to engage in corrupt activity and of webs or rings of officials colluding with private interests for corrupt purposes. However, there is no evidence that corruption in China is centrally organized as was the case in South Korea and Taiwan.[214] On the contrary, the evidence suggests that corruption in contemporary China is essentially anarchy and hence bears a much stronger resemblance to the forms of corruption associated with degenerative corruption and economic decline than it does to the forms of corruption associated with developmental corruption and economic progress. The ultimate challenge in explaining the concurrence of worsening corruption and rapid growth in post-1978 China is thus explaining why such rapid growth was possible even as the "wrong" kind of corruption spread and, perhaps more specifically, why rapid growth continued despite the intensification of corruption as high-level, high-stakes corruption worsened.

DEGENERATIVE CORRUPTION

Because China does not fit the pattern I describe as "developmental corruption," it would appear that examining the workings of the ruling political machines in South Korea and Taiwan provides little analytical leverage to help solve the second paradox of concurrent high-speed growth and serious predatory corruption; that is, corruption that plunders the economy and is hence a more direct threat to growth. In fact, by more precisely examining why machine politics might be compatible with rapid growth in the abstract, and contrasting the incentives embedded in machine politics with those embedded in other more predatory forms of corruption, we can begin to see why a combination of rapid growth and intense corruption was possible in post-Mao China.

Machine politics is defined by two core mechanisms: transactive corruption and redistributive politics. Transactive corruption refers to the exchanges and deals between the machine and private interests, including business interests, whereby power is manipulated for money. Redistributive politics refers to the deployment and reallocation of money for political purposes, including coalition building and the purchase of political loyalty. As argued below, political machines often support economic growth because growth increases the amount of resources from which they can draw the political money needed to fund their redistributive activities. Moreover, those who control the machine are apt to find that private interests are more willing to make "contributions" if they believe such payments will yield profits or other gains.[1] Thus, what made developmental corruption work in South Korea and Taiwan was that both parties to the corrupt and collusive transactions saw these exchanges as beneficial, with politicians gaining power on the one hand and business interests earning profits on the other. And, though each may have entered a Faustian bargain with the devil of corruption, and their illicit relations may have imposed costs on the public at large, the net result of the deal was rapid economic growth made possible by the construction of a stable though perhaps mercenary ruling coalition.

The cost of these Faustian bargains was much less than the alternative: degenerative corruption. In the abstract, developmental corruption can be thought of as a form of organized crime wherein the political mafioso extort a percentage of the profits of legitimate—and illegitimate—businesses in exchange for enacting pro-business macroeconomic policy regimes. Degenerative corruption, by contrast, more closely resembles a mugging or liquor store stickup because it involves much higher levels of what has been termed, awkwardly perhaps, "auto-corruption" and a one way flow of "plunder."[2] Developmental corruption is thus parasitical in that the political machine sucks its sustenance from an economy but does not necessarily intend to kill its economic host. Degenerative corruption, by contrast, is predatory in that it feeds directly on an economy and its vitals. Both may do considerable harm, but degenerative corruption is much more likely to prove fatal and manifest its worse effects more quickly.

It is critically important to understand that in calling the machine-style corruption in South Korea and Taiwan "developmental" while characterizing other systems of corruption as "degenerative" I do not wish to imply that developmental corruption is "good corruption" or that corruption somehow accelerated growth in these two cases.[3] In South Korea and Taiwan, corruption contributed to growth by helping to resolve underlying political problems and by reinforcing the regimes' incentives to promote growth. But the key to successful development was a combination of the exogenously derived determination of these regimes to pursue growth and the success of the business sector. To the extent that developmental corruption contributed to growth, it did so only as a means to other ends and to the extent that it contained the negative effects of political fragmentation.

With due recognition that there is no such thing as good corruption or growth-enhancing corruption, in the pages that follow I develop an alternative argument. Although there is no good corruption, there is clearly bad and worse corruption: the corruption that has negative effects, and the corruption that can have potentially catastrophic effects. Building on my analysis of the role of transactive corruption in South Korea and Taiwan, I contrast that pattern with the degenerative corruption I associate with official plunder and what others have described as kleptocracy.

To illustrate the differences between degenerative and more benign forms of corruption, I begin this chapter with a theoretical discussion of corruption as a process. Great effort has been expended in the past on defining corruption, and yet after decades of controversy most definitions boil down to J. S. Nye's classic formulation:

> Corruption is behavior which deviates from the formal duties of a public role because of private-regarding...pecuniary or status gains; or violates rules against the exercise of certain types of private-regarding influence.[4]

I do not seek to add to this debate but rather focus on corruption as process and the implications of differing forms of corruption for economic growth. In the main, my goal is to specify the differential effects of what others have termed auto-corruption and transactive corruption.[5] In very simple terms, auto-corruption involves public officials looting state assets or plundering the private sector and hence creates an essentially one-way flow of benefits. Transactive corruption involves illicit exchanges between state and nonstate actors in which public officials "sell" their authority to private actors seeking some sort of improper positive benefit or hoping to avoid some unwanted negative consequence. I then map the distinction between plunder and transactive corruption to the distinction between degenerative and developmental corruption by associating plunder with the most degenerative forms of corruption and transactive corruption with its less destructive forms.

The first part of this chapter delves into the theoretical differences between degenerative and developmental corruption. The second part focuses on the dynamics of degenerative corruption in a number of extreme cases of kleptocracy. A final section analyzes the case of Equatorial Guinea, the one country in which GDP has grown faster than China and yet which has a history of crippling corruption.

Corruption and Growth

At a very broad and abstract level, the difference between degenerative corruption and developmental corruption resides in the difference between auto-corruption and transactive corruption. Auto-corruption, in simple terms, is corruption involving a single party, while transactive corruption involves multiple parties. In the former, corrupt officials prey on the state, the economy, and society, expropriating public and private resources and assets to their private use and control. In the latter, corrupt officials engage in illicit exchanges with private parties, selling their authority to those willing to pay a price to obtain certain outcomes. Although the basic distinction between these two forms of corruption may be simple, the implications of their differences are sufficiently profound that auto-corruption tends to yield degenerative corruption while transactive corruption has the potential, and I must stress only the potential, to yield positive economic outcomes in the form of developmental corruption. Degenerative corruption and developmental corruption are, of course, stylized ideal types, and the pattern of corruption we observe in practice is generally a mix of auto-corruption and transactive corruption that shades off toward degenerative corruption on the one hand and toward developmental corruption on the other hand. Nevertheless, we can think about auto-corruption in its purest form as kleptocracy, a system of unchecked, predatory plunder, while transactive corruption shades off into a form of centrally organized and orchestrated exchanges between politicians and powerful private parties that has been described as "structural corruption."[6]

Auto-corruption is really nothing more than a fancy, academic term for theft. Just as a robber uses a gun to rob a liquor store or a bank, an official engaged in auto-corruption uses his authority to expropriate assets. In some cases, the process may be simple: the president empties the treasury, diverts royalties from the sale of raw materials, skims off money from foreign loans, and ships off his loot to secret bank accounts in Switzerland, the Cayman Islands, or the Jersey Islands; the minister diverts his department's budget, squeezes the salaries of his subordinates, and uses the money to buy expensive real estate on the Riviera and purchase luxury yachts; mid-level officials embezzle public money so they can buy Mercedes Benz sedans and live the high life; while low-ranking bureaucrats put their hands into the till and make off with the petty cash fund. More often than not, auto-corruption involves much less flagrant and obvious means, and much more complicated machinations and processes. Thus, for example, a corrupt president might set up a series of special budgetary accounts which he alone controls. Corrupt ministers and military officers might create phantom bureaucrats and soldiers so they can pocket their pay and allowances. Bureaucrats might purchase goods and services from shell companies they own. Auto-corruption can also involve looting the private sector. Corrupt officials, for example, might seize plantations from their owners and convert them into their personal property or commandeer private automobiles and houses. Street-level bureaucrats, police officers, and soldiers might force citizens to provide them food and drink without charge, pilfer shops, or simply rob them at gunpoint. Ultimately, regardless of the form it takes, auto-corruption is a process whereby corrupt officials plunder, stealing public and private resources and appropriating them to their own use. The flow of resources and benefits is, therefore, one way and as such auto-corruption is associated with embezzlement, plunder, pillage, and looting.

Auto-corruption can take place not only on an individual level but also on a regime level, in which case it is generally associated with what is known as kleptocracy. In dictionary terms, this is a "government of thieves"; in Sinnathamby

Rajaratnam's terms, it is a government "of the corrupt, for the corrupt, and by the corrupt."[7] In a stereotypical kleptocracy, corruption permeates the entire political system, infecting not only ordinary officials and functionaries but even the political leadership.[8] Unbridled and flagrant corruption is, in fact, often one of the hallmarks of a true kleptocracy. The state and public authority become means of corrupt expropriation and are, in a fundamental sense, transformed into an instrument for corruption. The state, in other words, becomes a "predatory autocracy."[9]

Although corruption may be ubiquitous in a true kleptocracy, it is not necessarily anarchic. On the contrary, not only might the kleptocrat in chief use the state to enrich himself, but pervasive corruption often serves to secure his hold on power. By franchising out opportunities for corruption, the kleptocratic ruler creates a mafia-style network of power that binds his subordinates together in a common enterprise based on plunder. Odd though it might seem, most kleptocrats are not smash-and-grab looters—or what Mancur Olson described as "roving bandits"—but instead tend to seek to consolidate their grip on power and fight tenaciously to hold onto power, in many cases even after their depredations have destroyed many of the most valuable sources of plunder.[10] Kleptocracy can, in fact, become highly institutionalized and morph into what H. E. Chehabi and Juan Linz describe as the "sultanistic state," whose primary function is the material benefit of the ruler, his family, court, and cronies.[11] Less well-entrenched kleptocracies, including those whose rulers lack access to either the external aid or income from resource exploitation are apt to degenerate into "mafia" or "criminal" states in which political fragmentation fuels the rise of predatory warlords whose income and survival depends not on looting the empty coffers of the state but on the systematic and brutal looting of the societies over which they hold sway.[12] In theory, private parties can also capture the state and use it to appropriate public and private resources to their control, but we have few if any examples of a state being fully colonized by nonstate actors, hell-bent on plunder.[13]

Despite the tenacity with which kleptocrats and sultans cling to power, there is little question that rampant auto-corruption ultimately proves economically destructive, particularly when it reaches high levels. Unchecked plunder not only denudes society and the economy of valuable resources, it also destroys property rights. Further, it either drives out legitimate economic activity in which any visible source of wealth is apt to become a target of official looters, pushes it underground into more easily concealed black marketing, or triggers capital flight to foreign safe havens. Moreover, unrestrained plunder—or even the threat or fear of plunder—can destroy incentives for long-term investments that might yield sustained economic growth. Why, after all, make an investment that might not yield profits for years if unchecked corruption will wipe out those profits or if corrupt officials will expropriate the investment as soon as it begins to make a profit? Insecurity and fear can wreak havoc not only on society but on the ranks of corrupt officialdom as well. Faced with the possibility of a sudden fall from grace, corrupt officials have incentives to either consume their ill-gotten loot or to stash it away in foreign safe havens with the hope that if the regime collapses or they fall out with the thief in chief, they can escape into a gilded exile. Moreover, if the future is clouded with doubt and danger, it makes sense for corrupt officials to grab as much as they can and as fast as they can: it might not be there tomorrow—or they might not be.

In sum, because auto-corruption entails a one-way transfer of public and private resources to the pockets of corrupt officials, and plunder wreaks havoc on property rights and generates high levels of insecurity, the consequences of auto-corruption tend to be direct and relatively immediate, once it reaches significant levels. Left unchecked, auto-corruption is apt to trigger a vicious downward economic cycle. For these reasons, I describe auto-corruption as "degenerative corruption." In crude terms, at very high levels auto-corruption acts like a vampire, sucking the lifeblood out of an economy and destroying the property rights and institutions that hold it together.[14]

Whereas auto-corruption involves a one-way transfer of resources from the state and economy into the hands of corrupt officials, transactive corruption is a two-way exchange of resources between corrupt officials and private parties. In the case of bribery, which is arguably the primary form of transactive corruption, an official accepts cash or some other benefit from a private party and in return performs some sort of service or hands over some good. Corrupt transactions can be quid pro quo in nature such that illicit payments to the official are directly or immediately tied to how the official exercises her authority (e.g., a twenty-dollar bill slipped out the window to a police officer in return for a "warning" instead of a speeding ticket). Corruption can also involve much more complex and indirect exchanges based on diffuse reciprocity wherein a private party gives an official a series of gifts or loans without asking for any sort of favor but with the understanding that the official will help the private party in the future. Similarly, a company may employ a law firm in which a politician is a partner to perform legitimate legal work on its behalf but with the expectation that the politician will give the company access when it wants to lobby for certain policies or use his influence to help it get on the inside track in bidding for public contracts. The political boss of a city might never take a bribe but might allow businesses to believe if they use his sister-in-law's firm to print advertisements, they are more likely to win contracts from the city. An entrepreneur might secretly sell shares in his company to an official's wife at a favorable price with the expectation that the official will steer business opportunities and confidential information his way because the official stands to profit if the company profits. Or a bureaucrat might steer jobs toward a particular heating contractor because his wife's brother is a secret partner.

Thus, whereas quid pro quo bribery links the actions of the participating parties directly, corrupt transactions based on diffuse reciprocity involve indirect, long-term exchange relationships whereby both parties seeks illicit mutual gain. As these relationships become more indirect and reciprocity more diffuse, it often becomes hard to link illicit payments and considerations paid to favors and contracts delivered.[15] In some cases, in fact, corruption may become virtually invisible or appear as little more than a set of cozy ties between political leaders and the courthouse clique of insiders.[16]

Corrupt transactions may involve either symmetric (equal) or asymmetric exchanges. The value of bribes paid is often, in fact, much smaller than the value of what officials hand over to their partners in crime, a phenomenon known in economics as Tullock's Paradox.[17] Even if the allocation of benefits is unequal, both parties may nevertheless consider themselves better off if the gain for a corrupt transaction is greater than the opportunity cost of honesty.[18] Corrupt transactions may also involve negative favors—that is, favors that shield the private party from some sort of sanction or penalty. Thus, for example, a health inspector might demand bribes from a restaurant that has violated health standards. In such a case, the victim might benefit from paying the bribe if it enables her to avoid being shut down and forced to pay the cost of remedial clean up, in which case the victim would profit at the cost of her customers' stomachs and gastrointestinal tracks. Similarly, a factory manager might profit by buying off environmental inspectors to avoid paying the cost of installing pollution-abatement filters and wastewater treatment facilities (or operating those already installed). In other words, bribes may not only allow private parties to obtain illicit gains, they may also allow them to avoid legitimate costs. By the same token, criminals and gangsters may pay bribes to the police, officials, and politicians in return for protection of their illegal activities and the profits they derive there from.[19] The well-documented problem of the Hong Kong police force with syndicated corruption provides a fitting example of how seemingly predatory extortion by police may facilitate illicit profit seeking by members of the criminal underworld.[20]

This is not, however, to imply that bribes are not sometimes extorted. Obviously, in many instances corrupt officials shake down private parties using threat of investigation or throw up thickets of red tape that can only be cut if "speed money" is paid. The terms of trade can, in fact, become so far tilted against the private party that the flow of resources becomes essentially one way. When bribery shades off into official extortion and blackmail, it ceases to be an exchange and becomes plunder. Short of that, so long as both parties obtain some gain, whether it is a positive in the form of net profit or a negative in the form of cost avoidance, transactive corruption presumably leaves both the corrupt official and his briber better off. This does not mean transactive corruption is costless. On the contrary, corrupt transactions are likely to benefit the parties to the exchanges while imposing costs on others (e.g., competitors and the public). It is unlikely therefore that transactive corruption per se has direct growth-enhancing potential. Moreover, auto- and transactive corruption are hardly mutually exclusive. Most often, corruption involves elements of both. What we might call "mixed corruption," corruption that combines elements of plunder and bribery, is, in fact, apt to characterize most situations. Because assumption leads us to expect that the costs of auto-corruption (plunder) are a priori greater than those of transactive corruption (bribery), it follows that the aggregate impact of corruption will be a function of the mix, with those cases where auto-corruption predominates suffering greater and, perhaps more critically, obvious economic problems than those where transactive corruption predominates.

To summarize, although we can construct a set of conditions in which certain forms of corruption can have positive—or, perhaps more accurately, nonnegative—consequences, such conditions are, I would posit, rare. For developmental corruption to work as argued in chapter 2, those who construct political machines must have economic growth and development as one of their long-term political goals. If this is case, then the use of structural corruption to facilitate the construction of stable, pro-growth political coalitions becomes a means to that end. If, however, the political leadership is less interested in promoting real growth and development but is instead more interested in self-enrichment or more concerned with the immediate political security, then attempts to use corruption to construct developmental alliances are apt to fail and give way to predatory corruption. Left unchecked, they can culminate in kleptocracy. As we see in the case of South Korea, developmental corruption can easily turn into predatory corruption if the supreme leadership becomes more venal and self serving over time or begins to lose control over lieutenants and operatives. Corruption and strong economic performance, in short, can coexist but only under very restrictive and likely transitory conditions. It is, therefore, perhaps not surprising that examples of rapid growth and successful growth combined with relatively high levels of corruption, even when corruption takes the form I describe as developmental corruption, are rare and that the more common pattern of high levels of corruption and poor economic performance, or even economic decline, predominates.

Having deduced why the aggregate correlation between corruption and growth ought to be negative even given outliers such as Japan, South Korea, and Taiwan, we still confront the problem of China. As argued in chapter 2, China simply does not fit the developmental corruption model. All of the economic functions I ascribe to the developmental machine—its utility in countering factionalism and providing for greater political stability, its role in linking those with political power to those holding economic power, and its ability to merge political and business interests together in ways that give the regime incentives to promote growth—were largely provided by the institution of the CCP and its political imperatives. But if China does not fit the developmental model, does it fit the model of degenerative corruption? In some circles, China is, in fact, portrayed as a kleptocracy where corrupt officials run wild. Although there may be some examples of unbridled political plunder, a more focused examination suggests the states beset by wholesale pillage are apt to be states that have already suffered near-complete institutional implosions and whose most basic governmental structures have failed. Those cases in which corruption has reached massive levels, by contrast, tend to be ones in which the state institution has not failed per se but rather has been converted into institutions for predatory corruption. In the pages that follow, I examine a number of the more well known of these examples of kleptocracy with an eye to determining if corruption in China conforms more closely to this pattern than that of developmental corruption.

As I hope to demonstrate, systematic degenerative corruption is often not a form of plunder whereby the kleptocrat in charge simply grabs whatever riches are to be found but is rather the conversion of core political and business institutions into mechanisms for the kleptocrat in charge to progressively monopolize profit-yielding activities. Systematic and relatively organized plunder by those at the very top is then complimented by much more anarchic plunder by their underlings. As those at the top steal from the state, other state officials are apt to find their salaries go missing and benefits unpaid. Vested with various increments of public authority, mid-level bureaucrats create mechanisms that allow them to extract bribes and kickbacks from the public, while street-level bureaucrats, police, and soldiers do what they can to get by. The result is a more complex mix of corruption than suggested by the "roving bandit" and his thirst for loot but one in which a band of stationary bandits settle into a pattern of systematic plunder that over the long term drains the local economy of its vitality.

In the remaining pages of this chapter, I detail the degenerative and even catastrophic effects of kleptocracy by first describing a series of relatively well-known cases (Zaire, Haiti, and the Dominican Republic) and some lesser-studied examples (Nicaragua, Central African Empire). I then provide a more detailed case study of what one critic has called "true pillage" in Equatorial Guinea, the one economy that outgrew the post-Mao economy—at least on paper.[21]

Kleptocracy

As defined in the previous section, kleptocracy denotes a state ruled by thieves in which corrupt officials transform the state into an instrument of private plunder. Despite the obvious association with looting, kleptocrats rarely move in, grab what they can, and quickly flee abroad to gorge on their ill-gotten loot. Instead, kleptocracy tends to be a system wherein "power tends to corrupt and absolute power corrupts absolutely," to use Lord Acton's famous dictum. Not satisfied with enjoying the trappings of power, kleptocracy begins to emerge when the ruler, not just his minions and henchmen, turns to corruption as a means of personal enrichment and uses his authority to divert resources away from the state and into his own pockets. Kleptocracy is, however, seldom simply the result of "presidential corruption."[22] Rather, kleptocracy comes from a much wider and deeper usurpation of public authority because corruption not only afflicts the ruler and other state officials but subverts public policy to the private interests of those in power. Systematic plunder thus becomes an integral part of the political system.[23] Kleptocracies are, almost by definition, "weak states" in which rulers find themselves confronting strongmen who must be eliminated, contained, or placated.[24] In many cases, corruption becomes a means of buying off these threats. In return for pledges of loyalty, the rulers of such weak states grant strongmen the right to plunder segments of the state and the economy, with the result that systematic plunder expands beyond the presidential palace and deep into the ranks and bowels of the state and society, transforming the state into one of thieves.

Zaire is perhaps the most frequently cited example of unbridled corruption and brazen kleptocracy. During his years in power, Mobutu routinely and systematically diverted money from the state treasury, the central bank, the state-owned mineral monopoly, and a host of other sources. Mobutu exported much of what he stole, allegedly transferring upward of US$100 million a year to banks in Switzerland and elsewhere in Europe. Not content to live off public revenues alone, Mobutu acquired extensive business interests, including plantations and shares in major businesses, and reaped additional profits by engaging in smuggling, sometimes using military aircraft.[25] Mobutu's immediate subordinates also stole what they could get their hands on, while street-level bureaucrats, police, and soldiers, all of whom frequently went unpaid as a result of embezzlement by their superiors, engaged in extortion, sometimes at gunpoint.[26] The net result was a bare treasury that left the state unable to function, a massive outflow of hard currency that stripped the Zairian economy of investable capital, and a wholesale assault on property rights that drove economic activity underground.[27] Kleptocracy and the anarchy that accompanies it can, therefore, be linked fairly directly to the collapse of the Zairian economy during the late 1980s and early 1990s.

To a considerable extent, Sierra Leone replicates the Zairian example. Following independence, President Albert Margai first bankrupted the national agricultural marketing board through his efforts to buy off his rivals, thereby causing the almost complete collapse of the agricultural export sector. Margai then formed an intimate relationship with Lebanese merchants involved in the sprawling black market for illegal diamonds. By forcing the national diamond monopsony to keep its purchase price well below the world price, Margai and his Lebanese confederates were able to skim off huge profits from smuggled diamonds, part of which Margai plowed into payoffs to his political allies, but at a crippling cost to the state treasury. After toppling Margai in a coup, President Siaka Stevens organized a new national diamond monopsony in which key political allies were given the right to siphon off a substantial share of the income while using the state authority to clamp down on illegal production and smuggling. Having thus deprived the state treasury of a key source of public revenues, Stevens spent what little remained in the treasury on a series of grandiose construction projects, each involving a sizable corruption coefficient for the officials involved, while also racking up huge foreign debts. Stevens retired in 1985 and was succeeded by former commander of the army Joseph Momoh. President Momoh launched a massive anticorruption campaign, the primary result of which was not substantial reduction in corruption but destruction of what remained of the formal economy and the entrenchment of a new cadre of corrupt officials. When Momoh was overthrown by a group of junior officers in 1992, an investigation into corruption showed that Momoh, Vice President Abduai Conteh, the commander of the Sierra Leone army, the inspector of the police, and numerous other senior officials had diverted massive amounts of public money to their own use. Momoh alone had reportedly accumulated at least US$3 million in cash and close to US$15 million in property, admittedly small change compared to the takings of other kleptocrats. Nevertheless, the damage to the economy was so severe and the breakdown of control so complete, that rebels backed by Liberian strongman Charles Taylor were able to wrest control over the diamond and gold fields and use the money earned by exporting blood diamonds to fund a war that pushed the country into anarchy and a brutal civil war.[28]

Overt plunder represents only one form of unchecked corruption. Examination of other infamous instances of kleptocracy reveals that systematic plunder often takes much more complex forms that involve not only outright looting but a pervasive effort to transform the state and economy into personal prebends for the ruler, his family, and his inner circle of cronies.[29] The absence of an open assault on the state treasury and private property does not mean, however, that endemic corruption in these other examples did not result in massive economic destruction in places such as Haiti, the Dominican Republic, Nicaragua, and what was once known as the Central African Empire.

After he was legitimately elected in 1957, Haiti's Francois "Papa Doc" Duvalier built a system of state predation that would have put Mobutu to shame.[30] After he ruthlessly crushed all centers of possible opposition, including the army which had played kingmaker in the preceding decades, in a series of purges, and hence secured himself from all possible threats, Duvalier systematically plundered the state, economy, and society. He began by moving large blocks of public money, including all income from the state tobacco monopoly (which also controlled the sale of flour, sugar, automobiles, alcohol, and electronics) and a new mandatory state-run old-age pension system off budget. Purchases of state lottery tickets were made mandatory and the income diverted. Businesses and even schoolchildren were required to make voluntary contributions to funds to build a new capital, Duvalierville, and for economic development. The president colluded with foreign companies, signing contracts with them and then splitting the money allocated to pay for projects with them. In 1957, he secured a US$4 million loan from a Cuban bank and then split it three to one with members of the regime of Fulgencio Batista in Havana. Papa Doc even engaged in outright extortion, holding businessmen hostage in the presidential palace until they agreed to buy worthless government securities or cut the president into their businesses.[31] Contributions extracted for national defense after aborted invasion attempts by members of the opposition, allegedly with the backing of Castro, went straight into Papa Doc's pockets. Petty corruption and extortion reached endemic levels as the regime's largely unpaid thugs, known as the Tonton Macoutes (a term based on the Creole for "bogeyman"), shook down businesses and citizens, stole from businesses, and arbitrarily collected tolls and license fees from the public. Even people seeking to flee the terror or who had fallen afoul of Papa Doc reportedly had to buy their exit permits from senior members of the Tonton Macoutes. According to Michel-Rolph Trouillot, corruption quickly grew from being an undesirable administrative pathology to the regime's raison d'être; in Yolaine Armand's terms, the goal of politics was "to obtain and guarantee one's enjoyment of unrestricted power and material advantages."[32] Mats Lundahl describes Duvalier's creation of an unprecedented system of graft based on "pure gangsterism and extortion."[33]

The anarchy and terror of the early Duvalier years made normal business and commerce impossible. Fearing for their lives, the mulatto bourgeoisie, which had formed the heart of Haiti's business community prior to 1957, fled. Foreign businessmen packed up and left. Tourists stayed away in droves. During the mid-1960s, conditions deteriorated steadily as Duvalier, having secured himself politically, began to siphon of an estimated US$10 million a year into his own pockets.[34] As a result, between 1960 and 1970 the Haitian economy contracted at an annual rate in excess of 2 percent.[35]

The Haitian economy, however, never collapsed. Instead, once the mulatto bourgeoisie had been broken politically and his grip on power consolidated, Duvalier eased off the reign of terror and entered a new alliance with foreign capital seeking a source of cheap labor. The new alliance with U.S. investors reopened the doors to foreign aid, most of which had been curtailed during early 1960s. Tourism also revived, thus increasing the inflow of hard currency. As a result, the Haitian economy experienced a period of surprisingly rapid growth, albeit one that was concentrated almost entirely in the export processing and tourism sectors. As investment and tourist dollars flowed in, Jean-Claude "Baby Doc" Duvalier, who succeeded his father upon Papa Doc's death in 1971, and the members of the new technocracy that replaced the Tonton Macoutes, continued to skim off the top. By 1984, Baby Doc had reportedly amassed a fortune of over US$450 million, while his mother had one of over US$1.5 billion.[36] Baby Doc Duvalier thus rode the wave of growth, extracting payments and commissions from foreign investors. The Haitian state, however, did not because the export-processing sector was exempt from taxation. The state's coffers remained bare despite export-oriented industrialization. Corruption and contractor fraud, meanwhile, skimmed off most of the aid dollars long before they reached Haiti's poor. As a result, economic conditions deteriorated because the growth of the 1970s and 1980s witnessed increasing concentration of wealth in the hands of the Duvaliers and their cronies.[37] By the time Baby Doc Duvalier eventually agreed to go into exile in 1986 (after losing the support of the remnants of the old Tonton Macoutes and, much more critically, the administration of Ronald Reagan), corruption had effectively hollowed out the economy and left Haiti one of the poorest countries in the world.[38]

Whereas looting was the modal form of corruption in Zaire and Haiti, the Dominican Republic during the Rafael Trujillo years (1930–61) and Nicaragua during the era of the Somoza family dynasty (1937–79) provide examples of a markedly different form of rapacious corruption.[39] Like Mobutu and the Duvaliers, Trujillo and the Somozas used political power to pursue private wealth. But instead of looting the economy, they sought to take it over by building up extensive, octopus-like business empires that enabled them to tap directly into existing sources of wealth and to scrap off rents created by the manipulation of public policy.

Trujillo began by using his power, first as army chief of staff and then president, to set up a series of monopolies controlled by firms in which he held an interest. He started with a monopoly on the distribution of milk and then gained control over the sale of meat through the creation of a slaughterhouse monopoly.

Shortly thereafter, he created a system of export licensing for cocoa that enabled him to gain control over that sector. By the mid-1930s, his monopoly interests extended into the production of salt, tobacco products, army boots, edible oils, matches, lumber, and furniture, as well as the export of coffee and rice. His wife, meanwhile, set up a scheme whereby government employees had to insure their paychecks by signing them over to a firm she controlled, which advanced them their pay minus a 2 percent service charge. Trujillo himself collected an additional 10 percent of public employees' pay in the form of a mandatory deduction for dues to the ruling Partido Dominicano, of which he was the head. A further percentage of workers' paychecks was siphoned off through a worker's compensation scheme run by a Trujillo-controlled firm.

Trujillo used his income from these schemes to buy shares in existing firms. As his power grew, he increasingly used coercion to force the owners of profitable business to sell their shares to him at well below their market value. By the late 1930s, Trujillo had amassed a fortune reportedly worth US$1.5 million and controlled an estimated 40 percent of the nation's wealth.[40] In 1941, he acquired de facto control of the dominant National City Bank, which then became the Banco de Reservas, and of the Corporacion Dominicana de Electricidad after both were nationalized. Trujillo was thus positioned to control the allocation of capital and electric power and ensure that his firms received easy and cheap access to these resources.

During the economic boom triggered by rapid increases in the demand for Dominican products during World War II, Trujillo extended his business interests to include a stake in firms engaged in the manufacture of cement, chocolate, industrial alcohol, beverages, liquor, paper, cardboard, flour, nails, bottles and glass, marble, medicine, paint, sacks, cord and knitted goods, textiles, and clothing. By the late 1940s, therefore, Trujillo had used his political power to penetrate into virtually all corners of the Dominican economy, creating that Stanislav Andreski has characterized as a form of "patrimonial statism" in which virtually everything of value belonged to Trujillo, the "Benefactor of the Fatherland."[41] His political power, moreover, allowed Trujillo-owned firms to pay no taxes, receive free electricity from the nationalized electric power industry, and draw on unpaid convict, military, and public employee labor, thus inflating their profitability considerably. Moreover, if Trujillo-owned firms began to lose money, he sold them to the state at their nominal value, only to buy them back when their profits revived.[42] The Dominican state, in short, had become a means to advance Trujillo's private interests.

Flush with earnings from these ventures, Trujillo next moved into the sugar industry. Long a bastion of foreign capital, the sugar industry quickly fell under Trujillo's control as the owners of one sugar mill after another decided to sell out to firms controlled by the president rather than face the threat of labor unrest and government harassment. By 1956, Trujillo controlled twelve of the Dominican Republic's sixteen sugar mills, with just one remaining in foreign hands.[43] By the time of his assassination in 1961, Trujillo controlled upward of 80 percent of Dominican industry and employed 45 percent of the nation's labor force. Given his control over the state, which employed 15 percent of the labor force, this meant that over half of the Dominican population depended on the generalissimo for their income.[44]

Although Trujillo used state power to further his private increases and to ultimately transform the Dominican economy into a "private business,"[45] the economy grew rapidly during his rule and underwent extensive industrialization and urbanization. Moreover, in contrast to the anarchy and brazen plunder characteristic of the Mobutu regime and the early Duvalier years, the Dominican Republic remained relatively stable throughout his tenure. Growth, however, took place in a way that almost exclusively benefited Trujillo and his inner circle by concentrating wealth in their hands. The wages and living standards of ordinary Dominicans did not, therefore, keep pace with the overall growth of the economy. More important, growth was accompanied by monopolization and the transformation of the state into a servant of Trujillo's private interests, with the result that the economy became increasingly distorted as it grew. In the process, property rights were undermined by his frequent use of state power to gain control over key sectors and firms, and the state treasury became a means to subsidize Trujillo's business interests. Trujillo's corruption was not limited to the use of state power to help expand his business holdings. For example, during the 1959 invasion crisis, Trujillo and various confederates embezzled US$44 million from the US$50 million allocated for arms purchases.[46] Thus, even though Trujillo did not crudely loot the Dominican economy, his corruption of state power to his private interests largely crippled the market-based economy and left the Dominican Republic with an economic system that more closely resembled the private estate of a feudal baron than a modern industrial economy.

To a considerable extent, the case of Nicaragua under the Somozas parallels that of the Dominican Republic. After assuming power, Anastasio Somoza García, the commander of the Nicaraguan National Guard, farmed out segments of the state to his political loyalists, granting them concessions, contracts, jobs, and tax exemptions, while also tolerating widespread diversion of budgetary funds into officials' pockets through ruses such as padded payrolls.[47] Somoza tapped into a variety of sources of illegal income, including accepting contributions and commissions for granting gold, rubber, and timber concessions; collecting protection money from illegal prostitution, gambling, smuggling, and bootlegging racketeers; selling smuggled goods; and illegally exporting cattle to Costa Rica.[48]

During World War II, he bought properties confiscated from German nationals at a fraction of their real value and took over properties seized from supporters of the Sandino rebels. Somoza also used blackmail to acquire profitable enterprises. By the mid-1940s, Somoza had become the largest landowner in Nicaragua and had diversified from cattle ranching and coffee plantations into sugar production, light manufacturing, cement production, insurance, electric power generation, and real estate. By 1945, Anastasio Somoza Garcia reportedly had a personal fortune of US$10–60 million. During the 1950s, Somoza acquired new business interests, including a monopoly on the production of pasteurized milk, new textile concerns, the directorship of the Pacific Railway Corporation, and ownership of shipping and airline companies. To finance new acquisitions and support his growing concerns, Somoza drew on state development funds and credit, put his employees on the public payroll, and diverted state assets to the use of his private business interests.

After Anastasio Somoza Garcia's assassination in 1956, his sons continued to build the family's business empire, moving into the manufacture of shoes, construction, food processing, automotive sales, tobacco processing, and meat packing, using state-subsidized credit and treasury money to fund their expanding business interests. The Somozas also extorted bribes from firms seeking licenses, concessions, and public contracts and skimmed off foreign aid money. The family reaped windfall profits after the 1972 Managua earthquake by embezzling aid funds and speculating in real estate. By 1974, Anastasio Somoza Debayle had built his own fortune to an estimated US$400 million.

As was true in the Dominican Republic, the Nicaraguan economy grew even as the Somozas relentlessly expanded their business holdings and transformed the state into a tool of their private financial interests. Between 1928 and 1944, the economy grew 145 percent. After a recession brought on by falling commodity prices in 1956, the economy continued to expand, growing two and a half times between 1960 and 1975.[49] But unlike Trujillo, the Somozas never gained true economic hegemony, and even at the height of their power Nicaragua continued to be dominated by an oligarchy of powerful economic interests. The overall pattern of corruption was, nevertheless, the same as that found in the Dominican Republic in that the Somozas used their political power to construct a vast business empire rather than simply looting the treasury and plundering the private economy. To the extent that they did loot and plunder, it was to secure resources to expand their business holdings and to create rents that enhanced the profitability of their business concerns.[50]

The case of Colonel, later Marshal and then Emperor, Jean-Bedel Bokassa in the Central African Republic/Empire replicates this general pattern. On the one hand, he siphoned off a share of the annual subsidy the French government paid to keep his bankrupt regime afloat.[51] He took in additional money by skimming off part of the profits of the diamond export monopoly run by a consortium of U.S., French, Dutch, and Israeli firms which by the late 1960s was generating US$7.3 million in revenues for the state. It was widely understood that anybody dealing in diamonds had to donate money to Bokassa and that it was *de rigueur* that Bokassa be appointed to the board of firms engaging in diamond mining and export. When several members of the diamond export consortium refused to pay him hundreds of millions of Central African Francs (CFA) in renewal fees in 1969, Bokassa abolished this system and granted a new monopoly to a firm, Centradiam, owned by a Greek tycoon and of which Bokassa owned a major share. Unlike its predecessor, Centradiam paid no royalties or taxes to the government and so Bokassa's income increased considerably. Several years later, a group of Middle Eastern businessmen and international arms dealers, including Adnan Khashoggi, paid Bokassa handsomely to allow a new firm, SADECA, to move into the diamond export market. Bokassa also received a third of the profits from ivory exports and was widely assumed to receive a part of the profits earned by French firms engaged in hardwood exports and beer production. In addition to these sources of income, Bokassa owned a variety of enterprises engaged in light manufacturing, coffee and cocoa processing, textiles, and real estate, and he controlled a construction firm that received lucrative public works contracts. Much like Trujillo, Bokassa used his authority to support his firms, forcing the government to buy their products at inflated prices while subsidizing them with free inputs from the state such as gasoline. Bokassa-controlled firms, of course, paid no taxes. Much of Bokassa's income was quickly exported to France, where he bought a variety of expensive real estate, and Switzerland, where it was stashed in Swiss banks for safekeeping. In all, according to prosecutors at his 1986 trial, Bokassa pocketed US$54 million between 1966 and 1979, not a huge sum by comparative standards but princely compared to per capita income in his country.

When we look into the details of how some of the world's most corrupt leaders extract money from the state and the economy, it becomes clear that pure plunder (e.g., rampant theft of public resources, extortion, and looting) constitutes only one facet of endemic corruption and kleptocracy. Politicians such as the Duvaliers, Trujillo, the Somozas, and Bokassa systematically plundered state resources and undoubtedly stashed a considerable share of what they stole overseas. But in almost every case, they also invested part of their income at home. The pattern is, in fact, one wherein political power is used to construct sprawling business empires that not only occupy the commanding heights of the domestic economy but which reach into even the most mundane corners. Thus, Trujillo not only sought to dominate the highly profitable sugar export sector, he also built monopolies on slaughter of cattle and distribution of milk. The Somozas not only acquired extensive coffee and ranching interests but were also involved in the manufacture of matches and shoes. Their business empires were so extensive that it appears that Trujillo and the Somozas wanted to squeeze every last penny out of their economies. Elsewhere, Ferdinand Marcos in the Philippines and Suharto in Indonesia followed much the same pattern, siphoning off government funds while constructing webs of business interests and alliances with private businessmen that enabled them amass personal fortunes.

More often than not, endemic plunder did not result in immediate economic crisis. In some cases, severe political instability induced both by rampant corruption and reigns of terror did result in periods of sharp economic decline as foreign capital fled to safer shores and domestic capital moved underground. For the most part, however, once the reign of terror ended and a modicum of political stability returned, the economy rebounded and in a number of cases entered a period of robust growth, even though corruption tended to increase as these regimes became consolidated. This was very much the case in Haiti, the Dominican Republic, and Nicaragua. In all three cases, endemic corruption accompanied rapid industrialization. In the cases of the Dominican Republic and Nicaragua, in fact, the leading role played by corrupt leaders in the development of new industrial sectors and to a considerable extent growth was a function of the expanding business activities of firms and sectors controlled by Trujillo and the Somozas.

A closer examination of the pattern of growth and industrialization, however, reveals that endemic corruption produced short-term growth without leading to sustainable long-term development. The business empires of corrupt leaders depended on the state for a considerable share of their profits. In many cases, they received monopoly rights from the state that created rent-inflated profits but cost consumers and stunted the economy at large. In other cases, they received heavily subsidized capital or even free capital from the state as well as other subsidized inputs such as convict labor and free electricity. In many cases, a share, sometimes a considerable share, of the profits, and even the working capital, of these subsidized business empires was exported abroad. To maintain themselves and to continue to expand, therefore, these empires were highly dependent on constant injections of plundered public resources. The resulting combination of monopolization, subsidization, concentration, profit exports, and plunder was such that in most cases growth led to the progressive hollowing out of the economy. The fact that the growth of leaders' corrupt business empires often came at the expense of other domestic firms and capitalists who were either forced to sell out or driven out of business exacerbated the problem of hollowing out. In the long run, therefore, endemic corruption and corrupt leaders' relentless pursuit of new sources of licit and illicit private income led to the emergence of regimes that were not only dependent on corruption for growth but which could not survive without constant injections of money looted from the public treasury and ultimately from the economy itself. This created a vicious cycle of corruption, economic decline, and an ever-mounting burden from corruption.

True Pillage

The extent of kleptocracy in the cases discussed thus far pales in comparison to the unbridled pillage that the rulers of Equatorial Guinea have subjected their county to since it became independent of Spain in 1968. Whereas Duvalier, Trujillo, the Somozas, and even Bukasso squeezed a tremendous amount of wealth out their economies and wrought considerable damage on their countries in the process, Equatorial Guinea's two presidents stripped that nation's economy bare.

On the surface, Equatorial Guinea might appear to be prospering today. As noted in chapter 1, Equatorial Guinea alone out performed China in terms of net increase in GDP per capita since 1978. At a basic level, this is hardly surprising. Desperately poor and with a tiny population,[52] Equatorial Guinea struck it rich in the mid-1990s following the discovery of large offshore reserves of oil and natural gas.[53] As oil production rose from 5,000 barrels a day in 1995 to roughly 400,000 barrels per day in 2007, and natural gas production rose from essentially nothing to 45 billion cubic feet annually in 2006, oil revenues shot up from US$3 million in 1993 to US$3.3 billion in 2006.[54] Three years later, rising oil prices had reportedly pushed annual revenues to over US$7 billion.[55] As a result, according to the International Monetary Fund, per capita GDP rocketed from US$294 in 1990 to US$10,435 in 2007, a rise which has prompted some to predict that Equatorial Guinea will become an African Kuwait.[56]

At the same time that its economy has grown, Equatorial Guinea has suffered from some of the world's worst corruption. When Transparency International added it to its Corruption Perceptions Index in 2005, Equatorial Guinea was ranked the seventh most-corrupt government out of 158, with a score of 8.1 out of a maximum of 10. In 2008, Transparency International ranked it the ninth most-corrupt country out of 179.[57] Equatorial Guinea's World Bank governance score has also shown a marked worsening of corruption. This measure rose from 3.55 (out of a possible 5) in 1996, at which point it was deemed the twentieth most-corrupt government, to 4.12 in 2004, making it the fourth most-corrupt government in the world.[58] Corruption is so severe in Equatorial Guinea that it has been described as "a concentrated distillate of all the woes of post-colonial Africa": beset by "corruption," "nepotism," "tribalism," "brutality," and "megalomania."[59] Others have branded it "one of the most criminalized states in the world," describing it as "an oil kleptocracy" in which the president considers the state his personal property and the ruling elites are engaged in "true pillaging."[60] Since 1993, President Theodoro Obiang Ngeuma has allegedly stashed upward of US$2–3 billion in secret offshore accounts.[61] According to Hazel McFerson, the ruling elite has stolen "virtually" everything.[62]

At a very simple level, the concurrence of rapid growth and endemic corruption in Equatorial Guinea is easy to explain. Foreign oil companies, whose exports account for over 90 percent of the country's export earnings, pump crude out of the ground and pour money into the hands of the governing elite. On paper, therefore, the economy grows at a dizzying rate, but in reality almost none of the money enters the economy. Instead, it is constantly siphoned off, exported to offshore bank accounts, and sunk into expensive real estate in Europe, the United States, and elsewhere. Much of that money and the fraction that actually enters the country are then squandered by Equatorial Guinea's tiny jet-setting elite. Oil money has not left the country visually unchanged: a building boom has transformed the downtown of the capital, Malabo, from a decrepit wreck lacking sewage and electricity into an overtly modern city of glass and concrete office blocs. Behind this façade, however, most of city's residents still have no access to running water or electricity.[63]

The country remains desperately poor. According to the United Nations' 2007–8 *The Human Development Index*, the country ranked 127 out of 177, even though its per capita GNP made Equatorial Guinea the seventy-third least-poor economy. Corruption has thus kept most of Equatorial Guinea poor largely because the elites have looted most of the income from oil.

Equatorial Guinea's problems with corruption did not, however, begin with the oil boom. On the contrary, corruption has been a crippling problem since the country received its independence. For most of the pre–oil boom period, corruption weighed so heavily on the Equatorial Guinean economy that it had essentially collapsed by the mid-1970s. At best, estimates of per capita GDP from the Penn World Tables and the International Monetary Fund (IMF) show the economy as essentially flat-lining until the oil boom. Estimates by other observers imply that per capita income fell by over half from US$170 at the time of independence to US$75 by the mid-1970s.[64]

The demise of the Equatorial Guinean economy following independence can be directly and easily ascribed to the combined effects of endemic predatory corruption and a prolonged reign of terror. Prior to independence, the economy had developed at a reasonably healthy rate as Spanish planters built a thriving export economy based on plantation agriculture on the island of Fernando Po (now known as Bioko) using labor imported first from Liberia and then later Nigeria, and timber exports from the mainland enclave of Rio Muni.[65] The profitability of the colony's economy was, however, more than partly due to its status of as a Spanish colony. Exports from the colony not only enjoyed preferential tariff rates in Spain but were sold in Spain at prices above those prevailing on the world market.[66] By and large, the rents generated by the concessions granted to the island by the Franco government accrued to Spanish-controlled syndicates. Fernando Po was, nevertheless, prosperous by regional standards.[67]

Faced with the decolonization of most of its European possessions in West Africa during the late 1950s and early 1960s, Spain initially sought to permanently incorporate its West African possessions by making Fernando Po and Rio Muni provinces, only to later succumb to mounting international pressure to grant them independence. The prospect of independence, however, revealed deep divisions between the Bubi population of Fernando Po and the much larger Fang population of Rio Muni. More prosperous but badly outnumbered, many on the island favored either continued association with Spain or separation from the mainland.[68] The emerging Fang leadership, on the other hand, favored independence and union of the two halves of what was then known as Spanish Guinea. In the end, the Fangs' power in numbers prevailed, and the first presidential election in 1968 brought Francisco Macias Nguema, a Fang, to power. Born a member of the powerful Esangui clan, Macias began his career as a low-level colonial official. Said to be not terribly intelligent and lacking more than a rudimentary education, Macias worked his way up through the ranks largely by cultivating relationships with Spanish officials, often by impressing them with his willingness to treat other Guineans with contempt.[69] Believing him to be a malleable protégé, Spanish officials came to see Macias as willing to protect and preserve Spain's vested interests after independence and so they lent their tacit support to his campaign for president.

Macias, however, had acquired a deep antipathy toward the Spanish during his years of service to them and had become, moreover, a protégé of Garcia Trevijano, a Spanish lawyer turned entrepreneur with ambitions to wrest control of the island's economy from the established Spanish syndicates. Once in power, Macias quickly turned on entrenched Spanish interests. In February 1969, a wave of harassment of whites by members of Macias's newly established youth militia precipitated a mass exodus of whites, including the planters, managers, and technicians who supervised Fernando Po's export economy. As the Europeans left, Macias seized their property, converting plantations into state-run farms and shutting down almost the entire retail sector by ordering the establishment of a system of state-run stores. In the process, 15,000 local retail workers were thrown out of work.[70] Subsequently, plantation workers imported from Nigeria under contract came under attack. After nearly one hundred Nigerians were killed in 1970–71, 20,000 deserted Fernando Po, complaining that they had been held in virtual slavery by Macias's plantation managers.[71] In 1975, amid renewed evidence of slave-like conditions and constant attacks on workers by regime thugs, the Nigerian government evacuated the last 25,000 of its nationals. Macias replaced the Nigerians with an estimated 45,000 forced laborers shipped over from Rio Muni.[72] Managed by inexperienced state officials and staffed with unwilling—and often unfed—corvee laborers, the output of Equatorial Guinea's once-profitable cocoa and coffee plantations declined rapidly, depriving the country of the bulk of its export earnings. As those earnings fell, Macias exacerbated conditions by granting his pal Trevijano a monopoly on international trade. Prices for imports soon skyrocketed and stocks of imported food dwindled. Imports of machinery and spare parts ceased, with the result that machinery needed to support the plantation economy could not be maintained. Within a few years, the country's electrical system collapsed and the rudimentary road system crumbled.

In March 1969, hard on the heels of his attack on Spanish economic interests, Macias claimed that members of the political opposition had organized a coup attempt and used the alleged plot as an excuse to unleash a new reign of terror.[73] The terror, which continued throughout the next decade, helped further destroy the economy. Faced with the risk of sudden confiscation of property, arrest, and summary execution, a third of the population fled abroad. To stem the exodus, Macias imposed a system of internal travel restrictions and checkpoints that made movement—and hence domestic trade—virtually impossible. He also ordered all ships, boats, and canoes impounded, which immediately ruined the local fishing industry and deprived the population of its major source of protein. (Macias sold fishing rights to the Soviets, who exported the bulk of the fish from trawlers pulled from the Bight of Bonny without landing anything.) The terror soon degenerated into near anarchy as the unpaid and undisciplined army and militia turned to pillaging shops, looting farms, and robbing civilians in broad daylight. By the mid-1970s, markets had been stripped bare. Unable to find food, people were forced back into subsistence agriculture and scavenging. Most cities and towns were largely deserted as the population moved back into the bush. Even the state bureaucracy collapsed. Without budgets or funds to meet payrolls, most offices simply ceased to function as officials disappeared. Government employees frequently had to leave the cities to search for food.

Ultimately, corruption and terror proved to be Macias's undoing. After declaring himself the "Unique Miracle" and claiming that it was God's will that he should lead the nation, his fears of plots against him led Macias to abandon the capital (Santa Isabel, later renamed Malibo) on Fernando Po. He withdrew to his home village of Nsegayong deep in the jungles of western Rio Muni, where he lived in a bunker-like palace guarded by Cubans and North Koreans.[74] Government revenues, including royalties from French logging companies and the

Soviet fishing operations, were remitted to the personal control of the president, and the country's cash reserves were allegedly stuffed into suitcases stored in the president's office.[75]

By the late 1970s, there was nothing left to extort or plunder.[76] Unpaid and unable to find sufficient plunder to keep their troops fed, a delegation of officers, including the younger brother of Teodoro Obiang Nguema (Macias's nephew who held the posts of military governor of Fernando Po and commandant of the Black Beach Prison where regime opponents were tortured and brutally executed) went to Nsegayong to beg Macias for money. Macias promptly put them in front of a firing squad and ordered the arrest of other officers of the National Guard. The executions apparently signaled to Obiang and other members of the ruling clan that even blood relatives were no longer safe from the terror. Faced with the choice between death and drastic action, Obiang launched a coup in August 1979, seizing control of Fernando Po and Bata, the de facto capital of Rio Muni. Macias ordered a counterattack by loyal units led by Cuban and North Korean officers, but it failed and Obiang's forces quickly advanced on Nsegayong. After putting up stiff but short-lived resistance, Macias's forces collapsed and he was captured after several weeks on the run.

The fall of Macias (who was executed after a speedy trial that carefully avoided the large body of evidence implicating Obiang and other coup leaders in the terror and corruption) brought an end to the terror and a reopening of the country to the outside world. The coup did not, however, end the plunder. If anything, the plundering worsened. As international aid started to flow in and efforts to rehabilitate the export sector began, Obiang and his inner circle (most of whom were either members of his immediate family or fellow clansmen) grabbed whatever they could. Companies seeking government contracts and concessions were informed that they had to pay bribes and kickbacks to senior officials. The amounts demanded were often so high that many would-be investors quit the country soon after arriving. Obiang privatized Macias's state farms but then either took them over himself or gave them to his henchmen. Petty corruption among street-level bureaucrats continued unabated.[77] The one-time thugs and killers of the Macias era thus morphed into a new regime of "tropical gangsters" under which the Equatorial Guinean economy remained a ruin.[78] According to one visitor, "The economy is dead and corruption is the game."[79] By early 1993, things had become so bad that the IMF announced it was suspending all aid and would leave the country to its own crumbling devices.[80]

The discovery of large offshore oil deposits in the early 1990s radically changed the economic picture but not Equatorial Guinea's political economy of corruption.[81] The influx of petro-dollars created a new and unprecedented source of corrupt money. The primary problem facing Obiang and his cronies was how to get their hands on the oil money. The 1977 Foreign Corrupt Practices Act made it illegal for U.S. oil companies, which held the bulk of the exploration and exploitation concessions, to make direct payments to foreign officials and required them to make royalty payments to official government accounts. Obiang, however, sidestepped that restriction. He first ordered the oil companies to deposit royalties into a series of offshore accounts controlled by the president and his inner circle and then declared all information on oil revenues a state secret.[82] Funds were either used to pay "expenses" incurred by the president and his family, redeposited into his personal accounts or the personal accounts of government officials, or transferred to other offshore banks, from whence they disappeared into a maze of shell companies.[83] In return for at best tacitly conniving with Obiang in his diversion of oil royalties, the major oil companies (ExxonMobil, Hess, and Marathon) received concessionary terms whereby Equatorial Guinea earned about half of what other governments in the Gulf of Guinea are paid for their oil.[84]

Kickbacks by the oil companies put oil money into the pockets of government officials through a labyrinth of channels. For instance, they purchased or leased properties owned by officials, paying prices far above the local market price.[85] They entered into local partnership with shell companies owned by members of the ruling elite, with the local partner obtaining a significant stake and hence the rights to a substantial slice of the profits while putting up only a fraction of the nominal value of their shares.[86] ExxonMobil, for example, sold the Abayak Corporation a 15 percent share in Mobil Oil Guinea Equatorial, its local oil distribution company, for a mere US$2,300. Marathon Oil, meanwhile, partnered with GEOGAM, a nominally state-owned company, to build two major oil refineries. In reality, Abayak held a 75 percent interest in GEOGAM and was itself controlled by President Obiang and his chief advisor, Hassan Hachem. Despite its apparent size, Abayak's headquarters consisted of six unoccupied offices, and investigators were unable to determine exactly how much capital GEOGAM had put into the refinery ventures.

Service contracts provided a second avenue for kickbacks. ExxonMobil and Hess, for example, contracted with Sonavi, a firm controlled by Obiang's brother, Armengol Ondo Nguema, for security services. Marathon Oil hired its local workers through a human resources firm controlled by a former minister.[87] Oil companies routinely awarded construction contracts to the Bomden Corporation, which was controlled by Julian Ndong Nkuma, the head of the presidential security detail, to companies owned by Agustin Ndong Ona, the military governor of Rio Muni, or to firms controlled by former Premier Angel Serefin Seriche Dougon and former State Secretary for Hydrocarbon Industries Miguel Abia Biteo. President Obiang reportedly owned both of the major supermarkets in Malabo that catered to expatriatess. Several oil companies paid school fees and living expenses for the children of high government officials, including the president's son and heir apparent Teodorin, who for a number of years tried to establish himself as a rap music promoter in Los Angeles.

In addition to skimming off oil revenues, members of the ruling elite obtained lucrative timber concessions. Teodorin Obiang, for example, owned at least four different lumber companies and held a large stake in Geasa, the major domestic airline. According to rumors, senior government officials are involved in illegal arms trafficking. Nearly two dozen Equatorial Guinean diplomats have been implicated in drug smuggling using the diplomatic pouch to move supplies of drugs, and it is alleged that the county has become a major way station for heroin destined for western Europe.[88] Elite control over the economy was so complete that it was said that members of the elite collected tolls as the gatekeepers for every significant sector.

Corruption was by no means limited to the ruling elite. Government ministries have been found to have phony payrolls that include thousands of phantom officials and to have used funds skimmed off from the budget to finance illegal loan sharking.[89] Customs officials routinely demanded tips from travelers arriving in Malabo. Soldiers continued to shake people down in broad daylight for beer money.[90]

Given all the evidence of his direct involvement in grand corruption, it is truly ironic that Obiang has repeatedly sacked the entire cabinet, charging that his ministers were corrupt, and has had low-ranking officials periodically arrested on charges of corruption.[91] Even more audacious, in the spring of 2006 Equatorial Guinea hosted an international ethics workshop organized by TRACE International, a U.S.-based nonprofit that provides antibribery compliance services to multinational corporations.[92]

Superficially, Equatorial Guinea resembles China as an example of rapid growth in a context of extreme corruption. It is obvious, however, that the two cases diverge in the most critical aspects. Rampant predatory corruption, combined with a reign of political terror, clearly crippled the Equatorial Guinean economy for almost two and a half decades, and there is little reason to assume that it would not have remained an economic failure if oil had not been discovered in the early 1990s. Thereafter, oil revenues created a façade of rapid economic growth even as corrupt officials diverted most if not all of the profits from oil production into their private offshore bank accounts. Assuming the allegations of arms trafficking and drug smuggling are true, what is perhaps most noteworthy about the case of Equatorial Guinea is not the extent of corruption so much as the sheer greed of the ruling elite. Not content to simply grab the bulk of the county's oil revenues, the ruling elite set up a system that allows it to profit from virtually the entire range of economic activities directly and indirectly associated with the oil boom and to engage in criminal activity while hiding behind the authority of the state.

An examination of some of the worst examples of corrupt regimes reveals a number of critical factors. First, and perhaps foremost, roving bandits are rare. All of the kleptocrats examined in this chapter were truly stationary bandits. None of them sought to quickly fill his pockets and abscond. All of them clung tenaciously to power and spent considerable effort on entrenching their regimes. At the same time, however, all engaged in wholesale plunder in the sense that they seemed determined to wring as much illicit wealth out of the economy as possible. All are thus cases where corruption was not a simply a matter of degree. On the contrary, all of the cases discussed in this chapter are examples of fundamentally corrupt regimes or what McFerson has termed "hyper-corruption," — states in which the function of political power was the illicit extraction of wealth.[93]

Second, the means by which these kleptocrats plundered their economies were complex and indirect. It is, in fact, almost startling the extent to which they sought to colonize their economies by creating webs of illicit extraction. Rather than brazenly loot the treasury directly or simply steal tax revenues, most of them went into business, setting up corporate interests that allowed them to tap into the economy and scrape off profits. In a twisted sense, therefore, the interests of the political leadership came to be tied to those of the economy but in a way that led the political leadership to stress private profit making by their corporate interests. In the process, they tended to so severely distort the economy that the growth of their corporate empires came at the expense of overall economic performance. Their business interests were, in other words, parasitic in the sense that they ended up sapping the strength of the economy and contributed to its debilitation.

Third, with the exception of Equatorial Guinea, most of these economies experienced an initial period of growth even as kleptocracy was being established. Over time, however, corruption so severely damaged property rights that the economy first stagnated and in the long term economic decline set in. Equatorial Guinea, in contrast, experienced a prolonged period of economic failure that can be directly attributed first to Macias's reign of terror and then to Obiang's systematic plundering of the economy. In the mid-1990s, the discovery of oil and the resulting oil boom overtly led to rapid economic growth. But oil money only created a façade of growth in the sense that it rebuilt downtown Malabo, transforming it from a decrepit and decaying wreck to a new city with high-rise office buildings, but left the rest of the country no better than it was under Macias. The benefits of the oil boom were thus confined to Obiang's family and his inner circle of political cronies.

It is important to recognize, however, that corruption was not the only source of economic destruction. In the cases examined in this chapter, it was clearly a combination of endemic corruption and either systematic political terror or the collapse of order that assaulted the economic fundamentals. Faced with threats of confiscation or extortion and chronic physical danger, engaging in business as usual, let alone sustained investment, must have seemed like pure folly.[94] Under such conditions, it would have been surprising if capital had not fled abroad or into the informal economy and if the private sector did not collapse. As such, the net result of kleptocracy was politically induced underdevelopment and economic catastrophe.

In addition to the examples of developmental corruption discussed in chapter 2 and the kleptocracy discussed in this chapter are many examples of economies where high levels of corruption have been associated with faltering economic performance or the emergence of "bubble economies." The Philippines, Indonesia, and Thailand have been called examples of crony capitalism where a small clique of businessmen profit from cozy relationships with the president, his family, and other members of the political inner circles. India, on the other hand, is said to suffer from a plague of bureaucratic and political corruption in which abundant red tape can only be parted by bribery. Following the demise of the Soviet Union, Russia and most of the other former Soviet bloc countries experienced a surge in corruption which many associate with the collapse of their economies and, particularly in the case of Russia, the emergence of a criminalized economic oligarchy and widespread organized crime. There are, in short, numerous examples of economically destructive corruption.

These examples reinforce the peculiarity of the Chinese case. Despite its reputation for rampant corruption, it would be hard to equate corruption in contemporary China with that I describe in Equatorial Guinea, Zaire, or Sierra Leone where elites engaged in wholesale plunder. Nor would it seem reasonable to say that corruption in China resembled that found in Haiti, the Dominican Republic, Nicaragua, or the Central African Empire. Instead, perhaps the best macro-description of corruption in China is that it is widespread but anarchic and involves significant individual officials and rings of officials taking advantage of their public authority to leverage private benefits. As such, corruption is not structural and hierarchical as was the case in the developmental states of South Korea and Taiwan. Nor is corruption in China characterized by systematic plunder like the hyper-corrupt kleptocracies found in Equatorial Guinea and Zaire. Herein we once again confront the core dilemma: how could the Chinese economy grow at almost 10 percent annually for almost a quarter-century even as corruption worsened?

In the chapters that follow, I argue that sustained rapid growth in China was possible even as corruption intensified for three major reasons. First, rather than an a priori barrier to a surge in growth rates, corruption worsened after the advent of rapid growth. Second, the rapid transformation of the Chinese economy during the 1990s created a series of windfall profits as undervalued assets were transferred from state control to the market and much of the most intense corruption involved officials skimming off a share of these profits. Third, and perhaps most critical, unlike the states of the former Soviet Union, China entered this period of rapid growth and intensifying corruption with its core political and administrative institutions intact and at a time when the party was actively seeking to strengthen state institutions. Thus, when corruption surged, the party responded with a sustained anticorruption effort. While that may not have significantly reduced corruption to date, it has served as a check and hence has arguably prevented corruption from becoming even worse than it has been thus far.

SEQUENCING AND CORRUPTION

Reform did not produce corruption in contemporary China. Corruption existed before reform, albeit mostly in discreet and often petty forms. Reform did, however, lead to a surge in corruption by opening up new opportunities for officials to use their authority to enrich themselves. As reform unfolded, corruption also evolved. In the early years, corruption fed off a combination of rents created by price distortions left over from the prereform period and widespread shortages, which allowed officials to arbitrage between the in-plan prices and market prices. By the early 1990s, shortages had largely been replaced by glut conditions as production of goods increased and most rents had dissipated.[1] The deepening of market reforms that followed Deng Xiaoping's 1992 Southern Tour, however, brought new opportunities for corruption. More important, market reforms also brought high-level, high-stakes corruption as valuable assets, including land and property controlled by the state bureaucracy, began to be transferred to private or corporate control. Once again, rents fueled corruption as officials, including senior officials, grabbed and skimmed off part of the difference between the nominal value of state assets and their emerging market value. Reform thus begat increased corruption and then drove the intensification of corruption.

If corruption worsened as reform deepened, why did corruption not thwart the reformers' efforts to raise growth rates? And why did intensifying corruption not derail reform and bring growth rates down? The answer is twofold. First, because corruption was limited at the beginning of the reform period, reformers did not have to tackle entrenched corruption at the same time they adopted economic reforms designed to raise growth rates. In most cases, high levels of corruption are an a priori barrier to growth, which stifles efforts to stimulate rapid growth in their infancy. Because corruption was not a serious problem initially, when reform stimulated the Chinese economy it had a chance to enter dynamic growth *before* corruption reached significant levels.

Second, corruption fed off the economic contradictions created by China's ad hoc, incremental reform with new reforms creating new opportunities for corruption as the deepening of reform closed off or reduced opportunities and incentives for earlier forms. Different forms of corruption thus ebbed and flowed over the course of the 1980s and 1990s. Deng and his allies did not set off to fully marketize China's economy. On the contrary, they sought to breathe new life into the moribund Maoist economy by allowing the dismantling of collectivized agriculture and then giving industrial enterprises greater incentives to improve productivity. As much as possible, they sought to preserve the socialist nature of the economy. As a result, they rejected privatization of the state sector and, instead, sought to grow a parallel "collective sector" that would be organized on the basis of local social ownership and would operate outside the planned economy.[2] To preserve the planned sector, they rejected privatization and adopted a dual-track price system in which commodities were priced according to whether their buyers and sellers were in-plan or out-plan. Those operating within the plan would pay low, state-fixed prices. Those operating outside the plan would pay higher—but still regulated—market prices.

The dual-track price system created immediate incentives for arbitrage. Given gaps between in-plan and market prices, officials and enterprises that could buy at the in-plan price could make considerable profits by illegally diverting commodities to the market. Shortages of commodities reinforced the incentives for corruption by creating shadow black-market prices above the legal market prices set by the state. Diversion of commodities from the plan to the market fueled corruption (both in its classic sense and also in the form of institutional corruption and local protectionism [*difang baohu zhuyi*]) and drove a process of informal price reform whereby de facto prices were driven toward market-clearing levels.[3] As prices approached market-clearing levels, the incentives and opportunities for corruption decreased. Corruption thus became part of an informal, bottom-up process that undermined the dual-track price system and helped set the stage for price reforms in the 1990s that essentially "rectified the names," so to speak, by eliminating fixed in-plan prices.[4] Once administratively induced price distortions were largely eliminated, the incentives for official profiteering though arbitrage trading radically diminished and this form of corruption began to disappear.

Even as official profiteering was waning, the regime's decision to deepen reforms by "corporatizing" the state sector and allowing the emergence of a substantial private sector following Deng's 1992 Southern Tour opened new opportunities for high-level corruption. The regime's decision to begin leasing state-owned land to real estate developers created additional opportunities for new corruption.[5] Absent a functioning market to fix the value of state-controlled assets and property, officials responsible for overseeing asset transfers were in a position to cash in by fixing the price of these assets low, then leveraging kickbacks from their buyers. Managers of state-owned enterprises and of the state-owned banks were also positioned to improperly rake in considerable sums by manipulating the terms on which state-owned enterprises were transformed into corporations and land leased out to developers. The illicit windfall gains obtained from manipulating the transfer of assets from the state to the market were theoretically one-time profits derived from artificial rents.

Once transferred and valued at market levels, these rents should have dissipated. Because the Chinese Communist Party rejected a quick, wholesale privatization scheme in favor of more protracted incremental transitions in which the state retained control over parts of the industrial, commercial, and financial sectors, these transfers involved a series of deals—some of them partial and conditional—spread out over a long period. Nevertheless, in theory once a majority of state assets have been transferred and their market value established, opportunities for this form of high-level corruption should also diminish.

Similarly, the surge in infrastructural development and the expenditure of huge sums on public construction contributed to the spread of corruption. Public works projects are notorious worldwide for graft, skimming, and kickbacks.[6] Contractors often pay upfront bribes to the officials responsible for awarding contracts, then kick back a percentage of the value of each contract. Officials skim off funds by awarding contracts to shell companies they control. Inspectors leverage bribes and payoffs, either for overlooking shoddy or incorrectly done work or by threatening to find problems that would require costly remedial repair.[7] Banks and others involved in financing frequently expect commissions and consulting fees for helping to ensure that loans are made in a timely fashion and do not get caught up in red tape. Given that state spending on capital construction and investment in new fixed assets (IFA) increased steadily and significantly during the reform period, it is hardly surprising that corruption increased in the 1990s.[8] Barring a dramatic improvement in the efficacy of China's anticorruption efforts, we ought to anticipate that continued high levels of infrastructural spending and construction will sustain elevated levels of corruption.

During the 1980s and 1990s, high tariff barriers and restrictions on the import of various goods, including automobiles, helped trigger a surge in smuggling. In the most famous case, a ring of smugglers led by Lai Changxing colluded with a host of public officials, including a deputy minister of public security, to import illegally ¥53 billion (US$6.4 billion) in vegetable oil, automobiles, cigarettes, and

4.5 million tons of refined petroleum. In an earlier case, two hundred officials in Zhanjiang (Guangdong) were arrested for their involvement with a ¥10 billion (US$1.2 billion) smuggling operation.[9] China's entry into the World Trade Organization (WTO) in 2001, and the resulting substantial reduction in tariffs, cut down on the profits from smuggling and hence the resources on which smugglers could draw to pay off officials; but smuggling did not, of course, disappear overnight. Entry into the WTO and lower tariff barriers, over the long run, however, should reduce the incentives for smuggling and the corruption that it fuels.

Not all corruption emanated from the contradictions created by incremental reform and the surge in infrastructural spending. The general loosening of political pressures that accompanied economic reforms clearly created a new culture of corruption in which officials were much more likely to abuse their powers. In some instances, this culture manifested itself in privilege taking, including banqueting and travel at public expense, nepotism (such as jobs for relatives, children, mistresses, and lovers), and improper use of official residences and vehicles. Bribery spread. Doctors began to expect red envelopes stuffed with cash as a prerequisite for treatments. Teachers and professors also began to accept gifts from students, particularly around the time of final examinations. In the process, the old petty bribe of a carton of Double Happiness cigarettes and a couple of bottles of *baijiu* was soon replaced by Rolex watches, cases of imported French wine, and, of course, bottles of XO cognac and Johnny Walker Black Label, plus the occasional loan of an expensive imported car, use of a luxury apartment, or the payment of pricy overseas college tuition for an official's daughter or son. To an extent, the spread of these forms of corruption can be related to the general increase in wealth caused by economic reform and growth. In the old days, after all, the best many would-be bribers could muster would have been relatively modest sums. As incomes rose, so did the sums private citizens could afford. Moreover, as private citizens, including emerging entrepreneurs and businessmen, enjoyed higher incomes, many cadres and officials came to expect that they should benefit as well and saw gifts as an appropriate way for businessmen and entrepreneurs to share a bit of the bounty created by China's economic boom.

Measuring Corruption

The preceding arguments about why growth remained high even as corruption worsened and intensified rests in the first place on my claim that reform preceded the surge in high-level corruption. In order to demonstrate my claim, it is necessary to plot the level of corruption over time. This is not an easy task. Corruption is, as is oft said, notoriously hard to measure. Officials engaged in auto-corruption are naturally hard to detect. Their crimes generally take place in private, and those involved have strong incentives to keep the crimes well hidden. Their subordinates and superiors also have incentives to cover up these acts or to involve themselves as accomplices. Similarly, parties to corrupt transactions have strong incentives to keep their misdeeds out of sight. Like narcotics sales and trafficking, corruption is thus a hidden, though not a victimless, crime seen only by those involved; it remains invisible until authorities stumble upon evidence of criminal activity or otherwise ferret it out.

Hard measures of corruption such as data on indictments, arrests, trials, and convictions, therefore, can tell only part of the story because they reflect only the percentage of corrupt activities in which the deeds were detected and the parties involved were prosecuted. As such, these data measure what we might call the revealed rate of corruption (RRC), not the actual rate of corruption (ARC). Data derived from the RRC suffer from two serious deficiencies. First, changes in the data are driven in part by variations in the intensity of enforcement. Assuming that the ARC remains at some constant level, the RRC may go up if the authorities intensify their anticorruption efforts. Conversely, the RRC will go down if they slack off. Variability in the intensity of enforcement is a major issue in China where highly observable spikes in the RRC (1982, 1986, and 1989) were the direct result of the launching of anticorruption campaigns. We have to assume, therefore, that the gap between the ARC and the RRC has varied significantly over time. Because we know when the authorities launched anticorruption campaigns, some of the variation in the ARC-RRC gap is clearly knowable.[10] Even if we control for known fluctuations, we can never be sure that the RRC is a linear function of the ARC. So long as the RRC cannot be assumed to be a linear function of the ARC, it cannot be taken as a fully reliable proxy.

Second, if we wish to assess changes in the ARC over time, the RRC is problematic because it measures when officials stop being corrupt—because they are indicated or arrested—not when they start being corrupt. Assuming that enforcement is imperfect, there will be a lag between when an official commits a crime and when he or she is caught. An alternative measure that we might call the emerging rate of corruption (ERC) based on when officials first turn to corruption would thus provide a much better means of tracking when China's surge in corruption began. Unfortunately, there are no systematic published data directly measuring the ERC. In theory, it is possible to calculate the ERC by analyzing data on individual cases of corruption. The efficacy of this method is, however, limited by the availability of case data. Chinese sources, including the mass media, publish a considerable amount of case data. But the number of cases in which sufficiently detailed data are provided is invariably a tiny fraction of the total number of cases prosecuted each year. Further, the quality and quantity of case data for the early reform period are even more limited, making it more difficult to measure the ERC during the early 1980s—which is the most critical period for my argument. Moreover, cases reported in the media and other sources cannot be assumed to be a representative sample because not only is the regime likely to filter what the media report, the media are likely to focus on cases involving senior officials, large sums of money, and—increasingly given the commercialization of the Chinese domestic media—sex, drugs, gambling, or other moral scandal. Far from a representative sample, therefore, the case data yield a sample dominated by high-visibility cases. Ironically, the skewed nature of the case data makes them useful in tracking the ERC for high-level, high-stakes corruption, that is, the sort of corruption we assume will have the most economically significant impact.

Guo Yong, on the other hand, argues that the most critical measure of the level of corruption is neither the RRC nor the ERC but what we might term the cumulative level of corruption (CLC). Guo correctly points out that during any given period, some percentage of corrupt officials will evade detection, thus creating a pool of hidden corruption.[11] Once again using data culled from individual cases, it is possible to estimate the aggregate number of corrupt officials rather than measuring only those who get caught. Because it includes all corrupt officials, the CLC much more closely approximates the ARC than the either the ERC or the RRC—but not perfectly. Because both the ERC and CLC can only be derived using case data, both are driven by the RRC. Assuming that some officials never get caught, the CLC will represent only that share of corrupt officials who ultimately get caught. Finally, because the data needed to calculate the CLC become available only after a corrupt official is caught, there is an inevitable reporting lag that depresses the CLC in years closest to the present because of undercounting of officials who will get caught in the future.

Despite such limitations, the CLC provides important information that cannot be obtained from other measures. Although movement in the CLC is a function of the interaction between the ERC and RRC, it need not move in tandem or parallel with either of them. If roughly as many corrupt officials are caught each year (as reflected in the RRC) as heretofore honest officials turn bad (as reflected in the ERC), then the size of this hidden pool will remain relatively constant. If, however, the RRC is lower than the ERC, then the size of the hidden pool will swell. Conversely, if the RRC is higher than the ERC, then over time the hidden pool will shrink. In theory, therefore, we can infer something about the interaction between the observable RRC and the unknowable ARC, including at least an imperfect sense of whether the gap between them is widening or narrowing.

Given the shortcomings associated with using hard data, many of those who study corruption and its effects have turned to alternative measures, including indices derived from polls that ask experts and businessmen to provide their best guess about the level of corruption. In recent years, indices of the perceived level of corruption (PLC) have become relatively sophisticated, with most relying on multiple polls and some using advanced statistical techniques to account for factors that cannot be measured directly.[12] Although PLC-based indices presumably incorporate some degree of insider knowledge about the extent of corruption—knowledge derived from direct experience or from information obtained from sources that are more "in the know"—we have to assume that what drives the PLC is actually the RRC. Analysts and experts presumably base a significant part of their estimates of the PLC on the sorts of visible signals that emanate from changes in the RRC. This appears to be the case in China, where a composite index based on the most widely used PLC indices tracks closely with the RRC, albeit with a fairly significant gap during the late 1980s when the 1989 anticorruption campaign produced a surge in the RRC while the PLC remained relatively constant (see Figure 4.1). This gap can, however, be explained by two factors. First, for the 1980s the composite index is based solely on the PRS Group's International Country Risk Guide, which, according to its authors, measures risk associated with corruption, not the level of corruption. In this light, the sudden increase in corruption need not signal that risk has increased. For instance, analysts who might have initially thought the massive 1989 crackdown would drive down the ARC and lowered their estimates in 1990–91 presumably began revising their estimates upward in the early 1990s when the drumbeat of reports on corruption made it clear that dramatic gains had not been made, with the result that the gap between the indices closed in the mid-1990s.

A final problem in trying to examine the genesis of China's crisis of corruption is that we have very limited data on the years before reform. First, most of the institutions responsible for investigating and prosecuting corruption and official misconduct (the procuratorate in the case of the judicial system and the Discipline Inspection Commission in the case of the party) were either formally disbanded or ceased to function during the Cultural Revolution. Only the courts continued to function, albeit often acting as revolutionary tribunals rather than real courts of law. Some data on prosecutions are available for only a very limited number of provinces but, to the best of my knowledge, no national-level data are available.

Second, prior to 1979, China did not have a formal criminal code that defined corruption and differentiated it from other offenses. During the Cultural Revolution period, the definition of corruption was only ad hoc and tended to involve political criteria linked to the intense factional and class struggles of the times.[13] Differences in definitions, therefore, make comparison of data from the prereform and postreform periods imprecise.

Third, the war against corruption involves four major institutions: the procuratorate, which is part of the judicial system and is charged with investigating and, where warranted, criminally prosecuting corrupt officials; the courts, which are

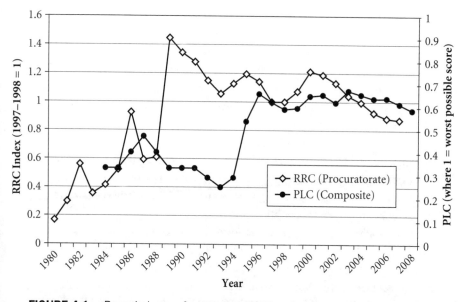

FIGURE 4.1. Revealed rate of corruption (RRC) and perceived level of corruption (PLC), 1980–2008

Sources: RRC index based on data in *Zhongguo Jiancha Nianjian* [Procuratorial Yearbook of China] (Beijing: Zhongguo Jiancha Chubanshe, various years). Composite PLC index based on data from Transparency International, "Corruption Perceptions Index," available at http://www.transparency.org/, accessed April 18, 2008; Political and Economic Risk Consultancy, "Corruption in Asia," available at http://www.asiarisk.com, accessed April 18, 2008; and World Bank, "Governance Index," available at http://www.worldbank.org/wbi/governance/, accessed April 18, 2008. *Notes:* Composite PLC represents the average of individual indices, with the original scores normalized as a percentage of the maximum possible score. Transparency International and World Bank indices are inverted so that the worst score (most corrupt) is the maximum score. In the case of the World Bank governance index, I have used a linear transformation to shift the scale from −2.5 to +2.5 to a 1 to 6 scale. The revealed rate of corruption has been normalized to control for changes in the legal definition of corruption resulting from the 1997 revision of the PRC Criminal Code. Scores for years prior to 1997 were thus normalized as a percentage of number of cases filed in 1997, and scores for years after 1998 were normalized as a percentage of number of cases filed in 1998. My assumption here is that, adjusting for the change in definitions, the revealed rate of corruption was roughly the same in 1997 and 1998.

responsible for trying criminal cases of corruption brought before them by the procuratorate; the discipline inspection commission (DIC), which is responsible for policing and disciplining members of the party but lacks judicial power; and the Ministry of Supervision, which is responsible for policing and disciplining state officials but has no judicial power.[14] In practice, because their jurisdictions overlap, the DIC and Ministry of Supervision function as unified institutions.[15] In theory, these institutions ought to work in an articulated manner, with the DIC-Supervision system conducting preliminary investigations, then imposing party or administrative sanctions on individuals found guilty of noncriminal offenses and passing individuals suspected of more serious offenses on to the procuratorate for criminal investigation and possible prosecution by the courts. In reality, differences in jurisdiction and in definitions of corruption make the gearing between the three systems less than perfect. The DIC's jurisdiction, for instance, includes a wide variety of offenses that do not involve corruption per se. It is responsible, for example, for punishing party members who violate the one-child policy and, of course, political offenses.

Even though we lack aggregate national-level data on the distribution of the caseload of the DIC, data from a number of provinces suggest that corruption cases account for about half the DIC's total caseload and that economic offenses as a percentage of the total caseload increased from perhaps a fifth in the mid-1980s to more than half in the early 2000s.[16] The DIC does not publish data on a regular basis or in any detail. On a national level, therefore, we have incomplete data on the total number of party disciplinary actions. National data are also available only beginning in 1992. Provincial gazetteers providing systematic data for some provinces are available for earlier years, and provincial yearbooks generally include a section on the activities of the provincial DIC, but the quality of the data is uneven and incomplete. Data on the supervisory system are also available in provincial yearbooks but are also of uneven quality. Moreover, reporting on the supervisory system is often incorporated into reports on the activities of the party disciplinary system, making it hard to differentiate their activities.

In general, the best data we have are on the procuratorate. Since 1987, it has published an annual yearbook, *Zhongguo Jiancha Nianjian* [Procuratorial Yearbook of China], which provides aggregate data on economic and disciplinary crimes and a breakdown of the data by type of offense. The yearbook also contains reports on individual provinces. Additional data are available from provincial yearbooks and gazetteers, which provide data on the prereform period. Because the procuratorate was defunct during the Cultural Revolution, there are no data for much of the 1960s and 1970s. The courts published national-level data in the *Zhongguo Falu Nianjian* [China Legal Yearbook] but only beginning in the later 1980s. Very limited amounts of earlier data are available and only on a provincial level. Reporting by the provincial courts on trials and convictions for economic crimes is spotty. The law yearbook, for example, does not include reports for all provinces, and the entries in provincial yearbooks are of considerably poorer quality than those reporting on the activities of the procuratorate. Moreover, the courts aggregate economic crime in a different manner from the procuratorate, with the result that data from the two systems are not entirely comparable.[17] The differences between these data are, nevertheless, close enough that they can be used in tandem.

In sum, the data we have are imperfect. There are significant gaps; the most systematic data we have primarily measure the RRC, which measures the intensity of enforcement and is an imperfect proxy for the ARC (which we cannot measure); and we can only calculate the ERC and CLC using case data that that are heavily biased toward high-profile cases. On the surface, it might appear that, given the limitations of the data, attempting to determine when corruption took off and whether it took off after policy reforms began to stimulate rapid economic growth would be futile. Nevertheless, I believe it is possible to demonstrate that reform preceded the worsening of corruption. In particular, I believe we have sufficient data to demonstrate conclusively that high-level corruption, the form that ought to have the most detrimental impact on economic performance, did not begin to increase and intensify until the early 1990s—a decade after the advent of reform and the acceleration of economic growth in China. Ultimately, of course, we are forced to triangulate, using the various measures as references to estimate changes in the unknowable ARC and changes in the nature of corruption. Since my argument that the sequencing of reform and corruption allowed China to experience rapid growth despite worsening and intensifying corruption, the key issue herein is when did the ARC begin to increase significantly and, more exactly, when did high-level corruption take off?

Genesis

Rampant corruption was among the first problems the CCP faced after its victory over the Guomindang.[18] The Nationalist-dominated Republic of China (ROC) government was widely seen as riddled by corruption, and many believe corruption contributed to its demise. Because the CCP inherited the administrative apparatus of the ROC, rooting out corruption and deeply entrenched bureaucratism (*guanliao zhuyi*) was seen as critically important. The party also found itself confronted with a wave of corruption and privilege seeking by its long-time stalwarts. Many cadres were ex-peasants who often had grown up in poverty and endured years of hardship and danger. Some were thus quick to use their new public authority to grab at the spoils of war and behave in the arrogant manner characteristic of past victorious peasant rebels. In Mao's words, they succumbed to the "sugar-coated bullets" of power.

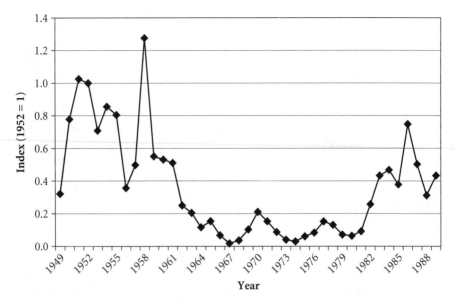

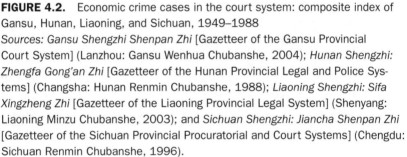

FIGURE 4.2. Economic crime cases in the court system: composite index of Gansu, Hunan, Liaoning, and Sichuan, 1949–1988
Sources: Gansu Shengzhi Shenpan Zhi [Gazetteer of the Gansu Provincial Court System] (Lanzhou: Gansu Wenhua Chubanshe, 2004); *Hunan Shengzhi: Zhengfa Gong'an Zhi* [Gazetteer of the Hunan Provincial Legal and Police Systems] (Changsha: Hunan Renmin Chubanshe, 1988); *Liaoning Shengzhi: Sifa Xingzheng Zhi* [Gazetteer of the Liaoning Provincial Legal System] (Shenyang: Liaoning Minzu Chubanshe, 2003); and *Sichuan Shengzhi: Jiancha Shenpan Zhi* [Gazetteer of the Sichuan Provincial Procuratorial and Court Systems] (Chengdu: Sichuan Renmin Chubanshe, 1996).

The party thus launched the Three Antis Campaign in August 1951, the Five Antis Campaign in January 1952, and the New Three Antis Campaign in January 1953. Each of these campaigns targeted corruption within the political and economic systems. The campaign against "hidden counterrevolutionaries" in July 1955 and the 1957 Party Rectification campaign also attacked abuse of official power and sought to root out politically suspect officials and cadres.[19] The impact of these early anticorruption campaigns is evident in the available data on court cases involving economic crime, which show major increases in campaign years (see Figure 4.2). The Great Leap Forward produced a second spike in 1958.

For the most part, those accused of corruption in the early days were apparently guilty of relatively minor offenses. According to Lu, of those charged with corruption during the 1951–52 Three Antis Campaign, only 2.8 percent were charged with embezzling more than ¥1,000, an admittedly princely sum, given that workers in state-owned industries earned an average annual wage of less than ¥500 in 1952.[20] Overall, three quarters of those charged were exempted from punishment, 21 percent received administrative penalties, and only 3.6 percent were charged with criminal offenses. In the end, just over 9,942 of the over 290,000 first accused of graft went to prison. Among those convicted, sixty-seven received life sentences, forty-two were given death sentences, and nine received suspended death sentences.[21]

Data on the extent of corruption in the early 1960s are very limited. Partial data, however, suggest that although the number of economic crime cases handled by the judicial system dropped significantly during the early 1960s, corruption remained a significant problem. In the first seven months of 1963, for example, twelve provinces including Hebei, Shanxi, Hunan, Guangdong, Liaoning, Heilongjiang, and Sichuan reported "ferreting out" 250,254 cases of speculation (*touji*), including 827 involving sums in excess of ¥10,000 and 26,105 involving sums between ¥1,000 and ¥10,000. These cases were uncovered in the course of implementing the Four Cleans Campaign against corrupt acts committed in rural areas during the Great Leap Forward (1958–59) and the three years of hardship that followed.[22] In the case of Hunan, at least, these cases were not handled by the procuratorate but were dealt with on an ad-hoc basis within the context of a series of mass campaigns, including the Socialist Education Movement.[23] In Jiangxi, the provincial procuratorate launched a new Three Antis Campaign in 1960 that uncovered 23,679 individuals who had committed various corrupt acts, including 2,853 involving sums between ¥200 and ¥1,000 and 308 involving sums over ¥1,000. Two years later, Jiangxi launched a second Five Antis Campaign, which was followed by another crackdown in 1965 after publication of the "Twenty Three Articles," a high-level document in which the Maoists called an attack on those within the party said to have taken the "capitalist road."[24]

By the late 1950s, the judicial system was under a political cloud, and at the local level the offices of the procuratorate, public security, and the courts were generally merged into a unified organization (*gongjianfa lianhe bangong*) in 1958 or 1959. After 1966, procuratorial work in many localities became paralyzed (*tanfei*) and was suspended (*zhongdian*) until 1967 or 1968, when the remnants of the judicial organs came under military control (*junguan*), only to be disbanded the following year.[25] In some localities, the procuratorial bureaus were reestablished in 1971, but not as independent organs. Instead, they were once again placed under military control. Elsewhere, it appears that local procuratorates simply ceased to function during the early part of the Cultural Revolution but were not formally disbanded until the early 1970s. Although there was undoubtedly considerable variation across localities, the overall pattern was one of institutional decline followed by paralysis and then collapse. At the central level, the Supreme

People's Procuratorate essentially ceased functioning in August 1966. In December 1966, Jiang Qing and the radicals called for the complete destruction of the public security, procuratorial, and legal systems, and in late 1968 the legal system was formally abolished. The party DIC also ceased functioning and was eliminated at the Ninth Party Congress in 1969.[26]

The judicial system was reconstituted by about 1978 and once again began to function. The courts had continued to function, but amidst the chaos and political infighting of the Cultural Revolution, regular judicial work seems to have slowed to a halt and the number of court cases involving economic crime remained very low until the advent of the reform period in 1978–79.

A low level of prosecution between 1966 and the late 1970s does not mean corruption had disappeared. On the contrary, there is evidence of corruption throughout this period. As Dennis Woodward points out, even though the left destroyed the formal institutions, eradicating corruption remained a theme throughout the Cultural Revolution and was prominently featured in a series of rural campaigns during 1969–72.[27] Shortly after the Ninth Party Congress, a new national attack on waste, graft, and speculation, known as the One Attack, Three Antis (*yida sanfan*) Campaign, was launched in 1970.[28] The campaign saw a significant jump in the number of trials for economic crime, at least in the provinces for which data are available, but quickly degenerated into a new factional fight as those in power used it to brand their political enemies as corrupt.[29]

Despite renewed attacks, a form of pseudo-corruption was spreading, primarily as a complex system based on a particularistic relationship, known in Chinese as *guanxi* whereby contacts are used to seek favors and to gain access to goods and services by going through the backdoor (*zou houmen*).[30] Reliance on inside connections had become increasingly common during the hard years of the early 1960s when food and other goods were in chronic short supply and the only way to get them was to cultivate the officials and cadres who controlled access.[31] In this environment, money was of little direct use, and with the elimination of the private sector there were no longer private interests willing to bribe officials, as had been the case in the early days. The key to the backdoor was, therefore, the cultivation of relationships and barter or brokering exchanges of goods and services. In part, *guanxi* derived from social connections, including extended kinship; shared local identity, school ties, work experience, or military service; and shared hardship. An individual could also spin networks (*guanxi wang*) by linking members of his or her immediate circles and their contacts with other *guanxi* networks. *Guanxi* could also be constructed through favors and gifts. In general, during the Cultural Revolution and on into the 1980s, the currency of gift giving was generally rather mundane—bottles of *baijiu*, meat, cigarettes, etc.—but valuable given pervasive shortages.[32] Small gifts and favors were more easily camouflaged and hidden, which was critical at a time when cadres were often under tight political scrutiny. According to Lu, *guanxi* connections were particularly important for obtaining the opportunity to join the People's Liberation Army, getting into college, and securing permission for those youths who had been sent to work in the country side or what was widely called "sent down to the countryside or up to the mountains" (*xiaxiang shangshan*) during the Cultural Revolution to return to the cities and to the positions they had held before being purged.[33] Privilege seeking, which Lu describes as a form of feudalistic "prebendalism," also spread during the Cultural Revolution, as cadres sought to append access to scarce goods and services to the perquisites of office.[34]

The overt decline in corruption associated with the Cultural Revolution was not, therefore, the result of a significant decrease in the extent of official corruption. It was more a function of institutional changes that subsumed corruption, transforming it from a legal and disciplinary matter involving the misuse of public authority into a political problem associated with revisionism, class struggle, and "taking the capitalist road." It gave rise to a culture of connections and gift giving whereby individuals sought to manipulate the formal structures of power to private advantage. By dismantling the judiciary, the Cultural Revolution also disguised the extent and severity of corruption, making it very difficult to measure and analyze due to the lack of data.

Following the reestablishment of the procuratorate in 1978, the number of economic crime cases in which formal charges were filed each year rose sharply. Between 1980 (the first year for which data are available) and 1989 (see Figure 4.3), the number of cases filed jumped eight and a half fold from 9,000 to more than 77,000. In three of those years (1982, 1986, and 1989), anticorruption campaigns produced distinct spikes in the number of cases filed. After 1989, the number of cases filed tended to decrease each year. In 1997, a new criminal code redefined corruption and decriminalized a range of low-level offenses. This produced a sharp drop in the number of cases filed. The drop is, however, misleading. Before the revision of the criminal code, the procuratorate filed formal charges in a wide range of minor cases which were then adjudicated within the procuratorate and ended up with the imposition of various administrative sanctions rather than criminal prosecution. Others went to court but resulted in either short prison sentences or nonprison punishments. After 1997, these cases were dealt with as administrative infractions by the accused official's home institution or were adjudicated by the Ministry of Supervision system. In practice, therefore, the revision of the criminal code created a significant discontinuity in the data by shifting minor offenses out of the judicial system. If we assume that the core rate of corruption was not affected by the decriminalization of low-level corruption and treat the drop in cases filed between 1997 and 1998 as

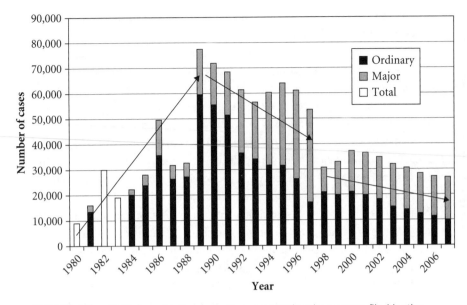

FIGURE 4.3. China's surge in corruption: economic crime cases filed by the procuratorate, 1980–2007

Source: Zhongguo Jiancha Nianjian [Procuratorial Yearbook of China] (Beijing: Zhongguo Jiancha Chubanshe, 1987–2008); Zuigao Renmin Jiancha Gongzuo Baogao [Work Report of the Supreme People's Procuratorate], 1980–87, available at http://www.spp.gov.cn/site2006/region/00018.html, accessed September 30, 2009.

Note: The term "ordinary" in this figure simply refers to those cases that were not classified as "major." I have superimposed a series of lines to indicate the overall trend in each of the three periods. Data on the number of major cases filed are not available for 1980 and 1982–83.

a disjuncture rather than as a decrease, then we see a third phase in the data in which the procuratorate's caseload has either leveled off or gradually diminished since 1998.

The overall trend in economic crime cases filed by the procuratorate appears to conform to the general assumption that the advent of reform triggered a surge in corruption. There are several problems with that assumption. First, we have to assume that low levels of corruption in the prereform period were at least partially a function of artificially low levels of enforcement. As noted previously, the procuratorial and party disciplinary systems had become paralyzed during the early stages of the Cultural Revolution and were still under institutional reconstruction when the first reforms were announced.[35] The regime's anticorruption capabilities were, therefore, presumably weak when economic reforms began to loosen controls. Enforcement was thus likely lax and the gap between the ARC and RRC larger than it would be later as the regime's anticorruption capabilities improved. Second, the data used to track corruption come from the RRC, which measures enforcement, not corruption per se. If we assume anticorruption efforts are reactive, then the upward trend in the data is presumably a joint function of rising corruption and increased anticorruption efforts triggered by perceived increases in corruption.

With those caveats in mind, the available data suggest that at the beginning of the reform era, corruption was relatively limited, though hardly nonexistent. Moreover, the data imply that low-level corruption predominated. In the early years, most of the cases filed by the procuratorate were ordinary cases (see Table 4.1). Until 1989, major cases (*da'an*—those involving more than ¥10,000) accounted for fewer than a fifth of the total filed, and relatively few senior officials were charged. Between 1983 and 1987, the procuratorate charged a total of 309 individuals holding positions at the level of county leader or higher (classified as "important cases" [*yao'an*] in Chinese legal parlance) with economic crimes, an average of sixty-two a year, less than two-tenths of one percentage of the total number of cases filed. In 1988–89, by contrast, 932 senior officials were arrested, including 742 during the 1989 anticorruption campaign.[36] To the limited extent we can tell based on the available case data, although some of the major cases filed in these early days involved corruption dating back to the Maoist era, in most instances officials turned to corruption after the advent of the reform.[37] If our small sample of high-profile cases provides some clue about the unfolding of corruption, the data suggest that the major surge took place in the mid-1980s, that is, after the adoption of rural reform and the first round of urban reforms.

In sum, data from the pre- and early postreform periods suggest that whereas the number of corruption cases investigated and prosecuted during the 1950s was high, the rate of prosecution began to drop off in the early 1960s, then fell to close to zero during the Cultural Revolution not because corruption disappeared but because the institutions responsible for anticorruption work were paralyzed and pulverized as a result of political turmoil. Following the end of the Cultural Revolution, the DIC and then the procuratorate were reformed and anticorruption work resumed. During the early 1980s, the number of indictments began to rise, and by 1989 the number of cases filed was nearly nine times what it had been in 1980. The post-1979 surge was, however, primarily in the form of ordinary corruption involving officials holding ranks below the leadership at the county and higher levels. More critically, to the extent we can infer patterns based on data from high-profile cases, the surge began after the advent of reform, which implies that the initial push to accelerate growth occurred when the extent of corruption was relatively low. Corruption, in short, worsened in the 1980s. But,

TABLE 4.1   Economic crime cases filed by the procuratorate, 1980–89

YEAR	ECONOMIC CRIME CASES FILED	MAJOR CASES FILED	ORDINARY CASES FILED	PERCENTAGE, MAJOR (%)	SENIOR CADRES CHARGED
1980	9,000	—	—	—	—
1981	16,000	2,512	13,488	15.70	—
1982	30,000	—	—	—	—
1983	19,000	—	—	—	
1984	22,200	2,100	20,100	9.46	
1985	28,000	4,208	23,792	15.03	
1986	49,557	13,888	35,669	28.02	
1987	31,737	5,392	26,345	16.99	
1988	32,626	5,450	27,176	16.70	190
1989	77,432	17,842	59,590	23.04	742

Source: Zhongguo Jiancha Nianjian [Procuratorial Yearbook of China] (Beijing: Zhongguo Jiancha Chubanshe, 1987–91).
Notes: Major cases defined as those involving over ¥10,000. Senior cadres defined as those holding leadership positions at the county level and above.

as I show in the following section, it was not until the early 1990s that high-level corruption began to intensify.

Intensification

In assessing the severity of corruption, we ought to distinguish between volume and intensity. Volume (the number of cases) essentially measures the broad extent of corruption. Aggregate RSS data, such as those reported in the previous section, measure volume. Intensity, on the other hand, measures the relative severity of cases. Not all cases are, after all, of the same magnitude, and some forms of corruption are likely to have greater economic impact. For instance, we might easily assume that a cop on the beat who shakes down a dozen speeders each week for bribes of $20 rather than issuing tickets will wreak much less harm to the political structures of law and order than will a high-level official who first accepts thousands of dollars from bankers in return for ignoring evidence they are engaging in reckless predatory lending and then accepts thousands more dollars for arranging a state-funded bailout after the bank's bad loans threaten to drive it into bankruptcy. It also seems logical to assume that although low-ranking street-level bureaucrats and officials may be able to manipulate the law to allow them to profit from their public authority, senior officials can do much greater damage if they systematically bend the rules and pervert public policy to secure illicit profits for themselves and their cronies. If we accept these assumptions, then it follows that although the surge in ordinary corruption documented in the previous section may well have had negative consequences for growth in post-Mao China, whatever damage that surge caused would have been compounded by a surge in high-level, high-stakes corruption. In terms of the overarching argument I raise in this chapter, it follows that if corruption was primarily at a low level with low stakes during the early reform period, it would have been a lesser threat to efforts to significantly stimulate the economy in the first place. The drag on the economy would presumably also be less if corruption did not begin to intensify until after the economy was already in high gear.

The available quantitative data allow us to measure the intensity of corruption three ways: (1) the percentage of cases filed that were classified as "major" by the judicial system, (2) the amount of funds recovered per case filed (or what we might call for convenience "average bribe size"), and (3) the number of senior officials charged as a percentage of all cases filed. Of these, the first two are problematic.

Between 1979 and 1997, graft and bribery cases were classified as major if they involved in excess of ¥10,000. Misappropriation cases were classified as major if they involved over ¥50,000. In 1997, the revised criminal code raised the thresholds upward to ¥50,000 and ¥150,000 respectively. Absent inflation and rising income, a fixed monetary definition might provide a reliable indicator of severity over time. China, however, has experienced both inflation and rapidly rising income since the advent of reform. According to official data, between 1979 and 1997, inflation drove consumer prices up 416 percent.[38] During that same period, the average annual industrial wage increased from ¥668 to ¥6,444, a nearly tenfold increase. As a result, the purchasing power of the major case threshold for bribery and graft fell from ¥10,000 to the equivalent of ¥2,400 and its value relative to the average annual industrial wage shrank from a ratio of 14:1 to 1.6:1. What had been a truly princely sum at the start of the reform had thus become much more modest by the time the criminal code was revised in 1997.[39] Assuming that corrupt cadres seek to maintain the value of their illicit income by raising their demands and pilferage to offset inflation and rising wages, the steady rise in the number of cases that surpassed the threshold for "major" status should not be surprising since to obtain the same purchasing power that a bribe of ¥10,000 brought in 1979, a corrupt cadre would have had to collect close to ¥40,000 in 1997, and to obtain the same value relative to her legal wages she would have had to demand close to ¥90,000.

Despite its decline in real value, the monetary threshold for major cases is not without salience. On the contrary, even though inflation and rising wages may have rendered ¥10,000 less valuable and princely, the penalties associated with major cases did not change between 1979 and 1997. As a result, corrupt officials were in effect running a significant risk for what had become a relatively paltry sum by the mid-1990s. Inflation and rising wages also had an impact on the lower threshold for a criminal indictment. According to the 1979 legal guidelines, an individual charged with graft or bribery involving less than ¥2,000 can be exempted from criminal prosecution.[40] Between 1979 and 1997, inflation cut the real value of this floor from ¥2,000 to under ¥500, with the result that by the mid-1990s individuals risked criminal prosecution for accepting bribes that were worth a quarter of what they had been in the early 1980s. Keeping thresholds fixed, therefore, meant that as incomes rose and inflation cut the real value of the renminbi (RMB), thus creating pressures to raise modal bribe sizes, more offenders were likely to cross the line separating major from ordinary corruption.

My estimation of average bribe size is also imperfect. The procuratorate publishes figures for how much money it recovers from the prosecution of economic cases each year. Exactly how it derives these figures is not clear, and it is not known whether the published figure represents the amount of money recovered or an estimate of the combined value of corrupt transactions and losses to the state resulting from corruption. Moreover, inflation and rising incomes exert the same distorting effects on bribe size that they do with the threshold value for major designation.

With these caveats in mind, the data suggest that whereas the aggregate incidence of corruption surged during the early reform years, it intensified considerably in the mid-1990s. As a percentage of all economic cases filed by the procuratorate, major cases increased steadily from 1979 to 1991, rising sixfold from 2 percent in 1980 to 12 percent in 1982 and then more than doubling to 28 percent in 1986 (see Figure 4.4). For the next four years, the share hovered around 20 percent. In 1992, however, major cases swelled to 40 percent of the total. Three years later, in 1995, they accounted for half of all cases filed. In 1997, two-thirds of the total caseload involved major cases. By raising the thresholds for major designation, the 1997 revised Criminal Code caused a dramatic drop in the percentage of cases considered major, down to just under a third of the total. But within five years, major cases once again accounted for half the total caseload; by 2007 they represented close to two-thirds of the total.

The amount of money recovered per case filed also grew, doubling from ¥1,200 in 1979 to ¥2,400 in 1980 (see Figure 4.5). During the 1980s, the average climbed from around ¥4,000 in the early 1980s to ¥10,000 in the latter 1980s. In 1993, money recovered suddenly rose to nearly ¥40,000 per case, and by 1999 had increased to nearly ¥140,000. After leveling off for a few years, the average sum shot up again in 2006, surpassing ¥225,000, then hit ¥273,000 in 2007, a sum some 228 times larger than the sum for 1979. Inflation, of course, trimmed the actual magnitude of the increase. Nevertheless, even adjusting for inflation, the

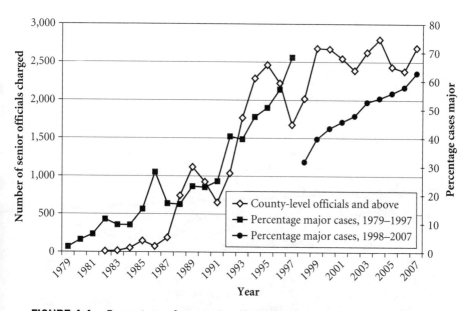

FIGURE 4.4.   Percentage of cases classified as major and number of senior officials charged, 1979–2007
Sources: See Figure 4.3. For a list of sources used to estimate the early period, see Appendix at the end of chapter 4.
Note: At present, data on the number of major cases filed nationally are not available for the early postreform period. I have, therefore, estimated major cases as a percentage of cases filed using an index that combines provincial-level data from Chongqing, Gansu, Guangdong, Guizhou, Hainan, Jiangsu, Jiangxi, Jilin, Qinghai, Shandong, Sichuan, and Tianjin.
In accordance with Chinese legal practice, senior officials are defined as those holding leadership positions at or above the county and department levels (*xianchu ji*).
The available data state that 302 senior officials were charged between 1983 and 1988. For illustrative purposes, I have apportioned these using provincial-level data. Unfortunately, the amount of provincial data is extremely limited, with only Gansu, Hunan, and Shanghai reporting the number of senior officials charged during these early years.

amount of money recovered per case was still more than fifty times larger in real terms in 2007 than it had been in 1979.

Finally, the number of senior officials charged with economic crimes rose from 190 in 1988 to more than 1,100 in 1990, then more than doubled to nearly 2,500 in 1996 (see Figure 4.4). Since then, the average has hovered around 2,500, with the exception of 1997 when the number of senior officials charged dropped to just below 1,700. Relative to the overall number of economic crime cases filed,

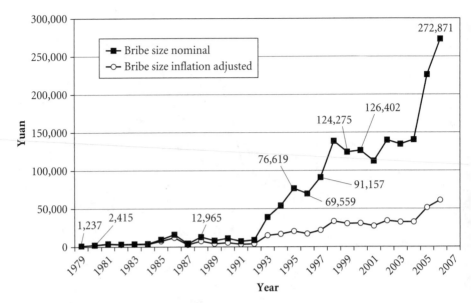

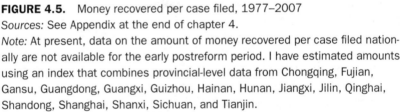

FIGURE 4.5. Money recovered per case filed, 1977–2007

Sources: See Appendix at the end of chapter 4.

Note: At present, data on the amount of money recovered per case filed nationally are not available for the early postreform period. I have estimated amounts using an index that combines provincial-level data from Chongqing, Fujian, Gansu, Guangdong, Guangxi, Guizhou, Hainan, Hunan, Jiangxi, Jilin, Qinghai, Shandong, Shanghai, Shanxi, Sichuan, and Tianjin.

cases involving senior officials climbed from a scant 4 per 10,000 cases filed in 1982, to 277 in 1988, and 313 in 1993. Thereafter, the number doubled to 658 per 10,000 in 1998 and hit more than 1,000 in 2007. In other words, one in ten of those charged held leadership positions at or above the county level. County/department-level officials accounted for the bulk of those charged with corruption (see Table 4.2). This is hardly surprising because this group is far larger than officials at more senior levels.[41] Among senior officials, there do not appear to be significant differences between the three levels (county/departmental, prefecture/bureau, and province/ministry) in terms of when indictments for economic crimes rose significantly.[42]

These three indicators of intensity thus suggest that whereas the aggregate level of corruption began to rise in the years immediately after the advent of the reform period, high-level, high-stakes corruption did not begin to take off until the early 1990s. This is most clearly the case in terms of the amount of money recovered per case, which jumped from ¥9,000 in 1992 to almost ¥38,900 in 1993, then climbed to almost ¥140,000 five years later. The number of senior officials

TABLE 4.2 Senior Chinese officials indicted for economic crimes, 1988–2008

YEAR	COUNTY LEVEL AND ABOVE, TOTAL	COUNTY/DEPARTMENT LEVEL	PREFECTURAL/BUREAU LEVEL	PROVINCE/MINISTRY LEVEL
1988	190	186	4	—
1989	742	701	40	1
1990	1,118	—	—	—
1991	924	889	34	1
1992	652	652	—	—
1993	1,037	972	64	1
1994	1,768	1,680	88	—
1995	2,285	2,146	137	2
1996	2,461	2,313	143	5
1997	2,222	—	—	—
1998	1,674	1,568	103	3
1999	2,019	1,880	136	3
2000	2,680	2,489	184	7
2001	2,670	2,463	201	6
2002	2,546	2,378	163	5
2003	2,389	2,228	157	4
2004	2,626	2,417	198	11
2005	2,799	2,595	196	8
2006	2,435	2,227	202	6
2007	2,380	—	—	—
2008	2,687	2,502	181	4
Total	35,237	29,784	2,050	63

Note: Because of missing data, the sum of the combined totals for County/Department, Prefectural/Bureau, and Province/Ministry columns may not equal the total in the County level and above column.

indicted, on the other hand, began to increase earlier, rising more than fivefold from 190 in 1987 to over 1,100 in 1989. After dipping down in 1990 and 1991, the number of senior officials indicted began to rise rapidly once again in 1992, and by 2000 the number had increased from roughly 1,000 to more than 2,600. The number of major cases, which is probably the least-robust indicator because of inflation, rose steadily during the first decade of reform. By 1991, a quarter of cases filed were considered "major." The following year, the major cases filed jumped to 40 percent of the total caseload. By 1995, more than half of all cases were designated "major." Two years later, nearly 70 percent of cases filed involved sums in excess of ¥10,000. Despite the fivefold upward revision of the threshold for major designation in 1997, by 2006 over 60 percent of indictments involved sums in excess of ¥50,000.

As noted earlier, the data cited in the preceding paragraphs measure changes in the revealed rate of corruption, not the actual rate of corruption. Because the RRC is a measure of enforcement, this means the data might show that it was not until the early 1990s that the regime began cracking down on high-level, high-stakes corruption. It is possible, therefore, that the surge in such corruption occurred earlier. Thus, rather than follow the advent of economic reforms and their incremental deepening, high-level corruption might have worsened before reform had triggered more rapid economic growth.

Absent a means to estimate the ARC, the best way to test if corruption began to rise before enforcement increased is to crudely estimate the ERC using case data to plot when individuals first engaged in corruption and when they were caught. This is an imperfect methodology. First, the volume of case data is a fraction of the overall caseload reflected in the RRC. Second, as noted earlier, as a general rule case data are available only for high-visibility cases because most of the available case data come from either published compilations or, more often, media reports. Third, because the Chinese government exercises considerable control over what cases are reported, we have to assume that stories reported by the Chinese media are subject to politically motivated selection bias and that the media report a subset of those cases the party considered most important and wants to use as a means to demonstrate the government's determination and ability to combat corruption. For cases reported in the international media, many of which originate in the Chinese media, we have to assume there is a secondary filtering process that further selects those cases deemed to show the severity of corruption in China. By assumption, therefore, case data must be viewed as that small subset of the most grievous cases, not a random representative sample of the overall caseload.

Ironically, the unrepresentative nature of the available case data arguably makes them very useful in assessing changes in the most serious forms of corruption. Current economic orthodoxy says little about whether it is volume or severity that drives down economic performance. Probably both will have negative affects. Pervasive low-level corruption can presumably become so encumbering that businesses find it all but impossible to function efficiently if a host of low-level officials continuously demand petty payoffs, throw up administrative roadblocks, and spin endless amounts of red tape as ways to extract bribes. Conversely, whereas low-level officials may bend the rules to extort bribes and may reach into the public till to illicitly grab funds, high-level officials may not only bend the rules, they may write them and can, therefore, tilt the field much more significantly in favor of illicit gain. At the most serious levels, in fact, corrupt senior officials may be able to subvert public policy as a whole to their individual economic interests. Similarly, they are more likely to have access to much larger

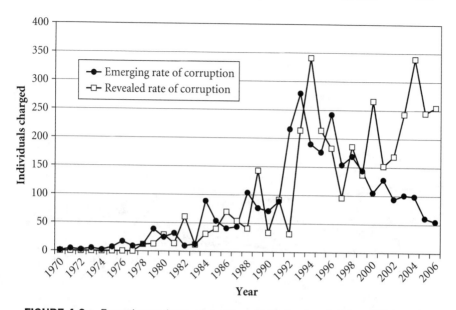

FIGURE 4.6.   Emerging and revealed rates of high-level corruption, 1970–2006
Source: Data were drawn from a search of the LexisNexis database. In total, 3,832 cases were obtained and coded. Out of these, start dates could be determined for 2,589. Arrest dates were determined for all 3,832.

pools of public resources and money from which they can steal. Finally, if corruption spreads from the rank and file to infect more senior ranks, then we may assume this is a sign that corruption has become significantly worse and that serious corruption may be on the verge of morphing into kleptocracy. In sum, even though we lack sufficient case data to estimate the overall ERC, the small subset of case data we have on the most visible high-level corruption provides a means for assessing when corruption began to intensify and the extent to which increased enforcement, as reflected in changes in the RRC, lagged behind changes in the unknowable ARC.

These data suggest that corruption did not begin to intensify until well after the advent of economic reforms. During the 1980s, when the ERC rose, the RRC generally rose in the following year (see Figure 4.6). It was not until 1991 that the ERC spiked dramatically upward. Thus, even though there is a lag between the ERC and the RRC, the overall pattern is essentially similar in that both show a sharp upward movement in high-level corruption in the early 1990s, a decade after the advent of reform. The two trends, however, diverge in the late 1990s, with the ERC falling steadily while the RRC assumes a U-shaped form, falling in the mid-1990s and then rising again in the later 1990s and beyond. In theory,

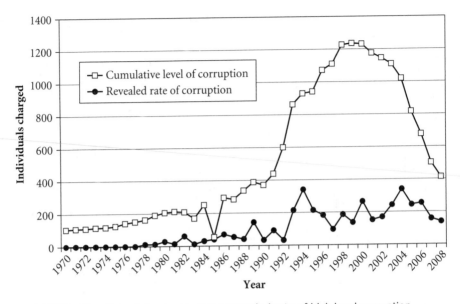

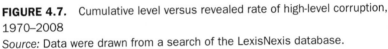

FIGURE 4.7. Cumulative level versus revealed rate of high-level corruption, 1970–2008
Source: Data were drawn from a search of the LexisNexis database.

such a pattern would suggest that the regime's anticorruption effort was making headway against corruption. Such a conclusion must, however, be tempered by recognition that lags between crime and capture will artificially depress the ERC in the most recent years.

The same data set can also be used to crudely calculate the CLC by counting up the years between initial crime and ultimate capture. In key respects, the CLC most closely approximates the ARC because whereas the RRC includes only those officials who get caught and the ERC includes only those who have just turned corrupt, the CLC includes both these groups and those who are actively engaged in corruption but have thus far managed to evade detection. Once again, estimates of the CLC generated by data on the most visible cases of corruption suggest that this form of corruption began to take off in the early 1990s (see Figure 4.7). In turn, these data suggest that high-level corruption reached a peak in the mid- and late 1990s. The CLC strongly suggests that high-level corruption took off after Deng's famous Southern Tour and the decision to move more boldly toward a market economy. As noted before, the downward trend in the CLC in the more recent period is potentially misleading because of lags in capture and reporting.

In sum, a variety of indicators show that while the aggregate RRC rose dramatically in the 1980s, high-level corruption took off in the early 1990s, a decade after the advent of economic reform. This is clearly true for indicators such as the money recovered per case filed, which shot upward in 1992 and 1993. The percentage of cases filed involving in excess of ¥10,000 and the number of cases involving officials holding leadership positions at or above the county level were apparently rising somewhat earlier, with the former climbing steadily from under 2 percent in 1979 to 45 percent in 1991 and the latter rising from perhaps a dozen in 1981–82 to 190 in 1990. In the early 1990s, however, both indicators rose sharply. The share of cases surpassing ¥10,000, for example, jumped from 25 percent in 1991 to 40 percent in 1992 and continued to climb, reaching 68 percent in 1997. Between 1991 and 1993, the number of senior officials indicted for economic crimes jumped from 652 to 1,768 and then rose to 2,285 the following year. Estimates of the emerging rate of corruption and the cumulative level of corruption also point to the early 1990s as the point at which high-level corruption took off. In broad terms, therefore, corruption increased in quantitative terms during the 1980s as the total number of cases rose and qualitatively intensified in the mid-1990s as the stakes involved rose and the number of senior officials involved increased.

Most analyses of corruption in post-Mao China argue that corruption skyrocketed in the years following the advent of economic reform in the last years of the 1970s and increased in an explosive, exponential manner as the reform period progressed. This view is superficially correct. Disaggregating the data, however, suggests a somewhat more complicated picture. The revealed rate of corruption was certainly low before reform. Low levels of prosecution were, however, partially a function of the destruction of the judicial system during the Cultural Revolution. During this period, not only were the courts and the procuratorate in disarray or defunct, corruption was apt to be viewed as a manifestation of ideological revisionism and dealt with in terms of class struggle. Even so, in the later years of the Cultural Revolution, the regime launched a number of new anticorruption campaigns.

A variety of sources make clear that corruption had not been wiped out during the Maoist era. On the contrary, even if the massive anticorruption campaigns during the early 1950s sharply reduced the rampant corruption of the late 1940s, it is clear that corruption flourished during the "three hard years" that followed the collapse of the Great Leap Forward. Facing massive shortages of food and other necessities, cadres not only looked after their families first but also became involved in backdoor relationships through which scarce commodities were traded for gifts and favors. This form of low-level corruption worsened during the Cultural Revolution. During most of this period, cash payments were relatively rare and most transactions were structured around particularistic relations (*guanxi*). Often secured by exchanges of gifts and favors, *guanxi* relationships provided a means of sidestepping official channels and securing access to goods, services, and other opportunities. By the time the worst of the chaos of the Cultural Revolution subsided, the practice of using *guanxi* to "go through the backdoor" had become pervasive within officialdom. Those with connections, those who could "pull *guanxi*" (*la guanxi*) and enter exchange relationships with key cadres were much better positioned than those who lacked connections and who had little to offer. Chronic shortages and a distribution system based on rationing also rendered money of secondary importance. Only after such ties had been formed could money be used to purchase favors, and even then the ability to trade favors was of greater value.[43] In key respects, therefore, the radicalism and chronic shortages characteristic of the Maoist period worked to demonetize corruption rather than to eliminate it. The tight political atmosphere, moreover, pushed those with *guanxi* for obtaining privileges to avoid public displays of their advantages. To a large extent, therefore, corruption took place behind closed doors and was kept hidden. But it was never so hidden that the public did not have a sense that cadres and officials enjoyed advantages they did not. Chronic shortages of consumer goods and rationing created incentives for petty bribery. Gifts, often in the form of cartons of cigarettes or bottles of alcohol, provided a means of jumping the queue and avoiding long waits to obtain items such as bicycles or sewing machines.

Following the first round of reforms, the extent of corruption clearly increased. The available data suggest, however, that the initial surge was primarily in low-level and ordinary corruption. High-level corruption did not begin to increase dramatically until the early 1990s. Viewed in purely quantitative terms, the data show that during the 1990s high-level corruption began to crowd out ordinary corruption. By differentiating between major and ordinary corruption, it becomes clear that corruption, therefore, developed in two distinct movements, with incidence rising in the 1980s and intensity increasing in the 1990s (see Figure 4.8).

That corruption developed in this manner was crucially important to how rising corruption affected economic growth. As I argue in greater detail in chapter 5, China entered the reform period with an economy characterized by chronic shortages, misallocated investment, and prices that that been distorted by administrative fiat during the Maoist era. Given these conditions, a loosening of controls and reform that expanded the number of actors who would legally seek profits and rents created a situation in which would-be entrepreneurs and officials could earn quick and tidy profits by arbitraging between artificially low in-plan prices and much higher black-market prices. The complexities and uncertainties surrounding the emerging rules of the business game also positioned officials in

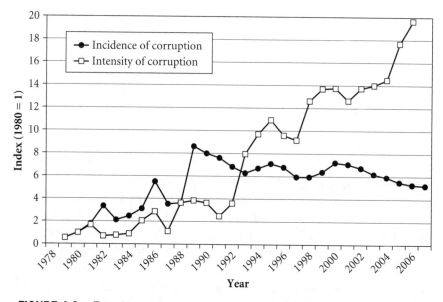

FIGURE 4.8. Two-phased development of corruption, 1976–2007
See Figure 4.3.
Note: In creating the index of intensity, I combined an index of senior (county and above) officials indicted with an index of money recovered per case filed, adjusted for inflation.

areas such as licensing, regulation, and taxation to extract gifts and considerations from private traders and businessmen.

Although conditions were ripe for the explosive spread of corruption in the
early 1980s, corruption did not necessarily pose an insurmountable barrier
to economic growth. On the contrary, because corruption had been reduced
to either relatively petty forms or had been driven underground during the
Maoist era, corrupt interests were not already deeply entrenched, and we have
scant evidence of blocks of officials arrayed to defend corrupted institutions and
systems. Corrupt officials were not, therefore, positioned to essentially stifle the
emerging entrepreneurial economy by smothering it with excessive demands for
illicit payoffs while it was still in its nascent, infant stage. Instead, as corruption
grew apace with the new economy, corrupt officials profited from reforms that
created new opportunities to leverage their authority. Because the new business
activities generated by reform created new opportunities for illicit gain, corrupt
officials had personal and financial reasons to support reform rather than rally in
defense of the old system. In fact, even though the old system gave them privilege
and status, it also created chronic shortages and limited even officials' quality of
life. At the street level, at least, corruption may have arguably greased the wheels

in the sense that the interests of corrupt officials were not at loggerheads with the profit-making interests of China's emerging class of traders, businessmen, and entrepreneurs.

The absence of high-level corruption and entrenched corrupt institutions also reduced the chances that reform would become a guise whereby senior officials used economic policies to strengthen their grip on the economy and bent policies to their selfish, profit-making interests. Arguably, one hallmark of kleptocracy is less a looting rampage than the wholesale perversion of state policy to the private interests of those at the top. State power becomes a means to grab hold of profitable businesses, create rents, and subvert tax and regulations to enhance the profits flowing to officials. In China, by contrast, Deng and his reform coalition were not motivated by corruption. They were driven to reform the economy by a shared perception that, absent growth, the CCP might lose legitimacy. They thus embraced policies that encouraged economic growth rather than served private profit seeking. Individually, some senior officials may have begun cashing in on the opportunities to leverage their authority, but early on, at least, the extent of high-level corruption was likely sufficiently low that the basic integrity of the reform program was not threatened.

In conclusion, I contend that the first key to explaining why worsening corruption did not prevent the Chinese economy from growing rapidly after the adoption of economic reforms in the late 1970s is that when the reforms were adopted, the extent of corruption was sufficiently limited that it was not an a priori barrier to growth. In most of the examples of kleptocratic corruption discussed in chapter 3, corruption had become so deeply entrenched and the weight of corruption so great that it is hard to imagine how these economies ever had a chance. In fact, where kleptocracy came first, it tended to distort and deform the economy so much that growth rates never rose above minimal levels and, in most cases, soon fell into negative numbers. Even in Equatorial Guinea, where the discovery of oil caused growth rates to shoot up to the highest level in the post-1978 period, it is clear that corruption siphoned off wealth as quickly as it poured out of the oil wellheads, with elites either dissipating it on luxurious lifestyles or pumping it straight into foreign safe havens. By contrast, in China the spread of corruption tended to lag slightly behind economic growth, with ordinary corruption spreading first and high-level corruption increasing later. This meant the economy had time to build up a degree of momentum and dynamism before high-level corruption increased the negative, deadweight pressures bearing down on growth. Perhaps even more critically, as discussed in greater depth in the following chapter, the deepening of reform and the advent of a new economic boom following Deng's 1992 Southern Tour triggered the increase in high-level corruption. The intensification of corruption during the 1990s was, in other words, a response to the deepening of reform. Far from stifling growth in the 1990s, corruption fed off the transfer of assets from state control to private and corporate control and siphoned off a share of the windfall profits generated by significant gaps between the state's nominal valuation of assets and prices they could command on the emerging market for commercial, industrial, and real estate assets.

Appendix

PROVINCIAL GAZETTEERS SOURCES FOR FIGURES AND TABLES

Chongqing Shizhi: Gong'an Zhi Jiancha Shenpan Zhi Sifa Xingcheng Zhi, Junshi Zhi, Waishi Zhi [Annals of the Chongqing Municipal Public Security, Procuratorial, Court, Legal, Military Affairs, and Foreign Affairs Systems] (Chongqing: Xi'nan Shefan Daxue Chubanshe, 2005).

Fujian Shengzhi: Jiancha Zhi [Annals of the Fujian Provincial Procuratorate] (Fuzhou: Fangzhi Chubanshe, 1997).

Gansu Shengzhi: Jiancha Zhi [Annals of the Gansu Provincial Procuratorate] (Lanzhou: Gansu Wenhua Chubanshe, 1996).

Guangdong Shengzhi Jijian Jiancha Zhi [Annals of the Guangdong Provincial Disciplinary and Procuratorial Systems] (Guangzhou: Guangdong Renmin Chubanshe, 1999).

Guangxi Tongzhi: Jiancha Zhi [Annals of the Guangxi Regional Procuratorate] (Nanning: Guangxi Renmin Chubanshe, 1996).

Guizhou Shengzhi: Jiancha Zhi [Annals of the Guizhou Provincial Procuratorate] (Guiyang: Guizhou Renmin Chubanshe, 1995).

Hainan Shengzhi: Jiancha Zhi [Annals of the Hainan Provincial Procuratorate] (Haikou: Hainan Chubanshe, 1997).

Hunan Shengzhi: Zhengfa Zhi [Annals of the Hunan Provincial Political-Legal System] (Changsha: Hunan Chubanshe, 1996).

Jiangsu Shengzhi: Jiancha Zhi [Annals of the Jiangsu Provincial Procuratorate] (Nanjing: Jiangsu Renmin Chubanshe, 1997).

Jiangxi Shengzhi Jianzha Zhi [Annals of the Jiangxi Provincial Procuratorate] (Nanchang: Zhonggong Zhongyang Dangxiao Chubanshe, 1995).

Jilin Shengzhi: Sifa Gong'an Jiancha Zhi [Annals of the Jilin Legal, Public Security, and Procuratorial Systems] (Changchun: Jilin Renmin Chubanshe, 1992).

Qinghai Shengzhi: Jiancha Zhi [Annals of the Qinghai Provincial Procuratorate] (Yining: Huangshan Shushe, 2000).

Shandong Shengzhi: Sifa Zhi [Annals of the Shandong Provincial Judicial System] (Jinan: Shandong Renmin Chubanshe, 1998).

Shanxi Shengzhi: Zhengfa Zhi Jiancha Zhi [Annals of the Shanxi Provincial Political-legal and Procuratorial Systems] (Taiyuan: Zhonghua Shuju, 1998).

Sichuan Shengzhi: Jiancha Shenpan Zhi [Annals of the Sichuan Provincial Procuratorial and Court Systems] (Chengdu: Sichuan Renmin Chubanshe, 1996).

Tianjin Tongzhi: Jiancha Zhi [Annals of the Tianjin Procuratorate] (Tianjin: Tianjin Shehui Kexueyuan Chubanshe, 2000).

SYSTEMIC TRANSITION AND CORRUPTION

Economic reforms not only stimulated economic growth but the take off in growth rates was followed by a surge in corruption. The essence of my argument in chapter 4 was that entrenched corruption was not an a priori barrier to growth, nor were economic reforms subverted to corrupt interests (as was arguably the case with the predatory corruption detailed in chapter 3). Because the surge in corruption followed the upward swing in growth rates, I argued that corruption fed off increased growth and was in a sense a byproduct of the economic boom that followed the adoption of economic reforms in the late 1970s and early 1980s. Moreover, I argued that the intensification of corruption in the 1990s occurred after the adoption of new reforms that allowed for the transfer of control rights (though not always outright ownership) of state assets, including land, to corporate managers and even private businessmen.

In this chapter, my focus shifts from changes in the extent and severity of corruption to qualitative changes in the form of corruption. We can link specific forms of corruption to particular phases in the deepening of reform, and new forms of corruption emerged as policy changes created new opportunities for officials to leverage their authority for illicit gain. In this chapter, I seek to demonstrate that as reform deepened, the modal form of corruption shifted from predatory plunder and primarily petty corruption to various forms of transactive corruption wherein corrupt officials "sold" favors to economic interests seeking profit-making opportunities.

My argument has, however, a critical second part. In broad terms, economic reforms in China have entailed the incremental transfer of control over property from the state to nonstate actors. Transfers did not necessarily entail reassignment of full ownership rights but instead could involve transfers of use or control rights, including rights to profits earned from the economic use of resources. Thus, for example, during the early stages of reform, the government approved the establishment of the household responsibility system wherein the land owned by the collectives and worked collectively by brigade members was divided up and individual households were given the right to farm specific plots.

Initially, land was given on a short-term basis and farm households' income rights were sharply limited by the imposition of compulsory sales quotas and restrictions on marketing. Over time, farmers' use rights were extended to longer periods, and the share of farm income to which the state laid prior claim was incrementally reduced, with the result that farm families gained rights to a greater share of their gross income. In the case of industry, the management responsibility system and later enterprise reforms increased the share of profits retained by enterprises and managers' discretion over the allocation of retained profits. In some cases, ownership was transferred from the state to private individuals, but in many more cases the process led to the transformation of state-owned enterprises into "joint stock companies" that remained formally owned by the state. In these companies, either a state-owned holding company or a state asset-management commission controlled all or a majority of the stock, but managers assumed greater control over financial information and, hence, the ability to determine the allocation of income and profits.[1] By the mid-1990s, the state was not only transferring control rights to the managers of state-owned companies, it was beginning to transfer land use rights from the state to developers. Once again, the state retained ultimate ownership rights, and land was leased on a long-term basis rather than sold outright. Nevertheless, the state ceded to nonstate actors the right to develop and earn profits from the use of transferred land.

In many instances, transferring control rights created windfall profits for those who obtained control rights. Windfall profits in state-owned industrial and commercial enterprises could come either from outright takeover of an existing firm, selling off parts of the company, or, in some cases, stripping the original firm of its assets and selling them piecemeal. In other cases, windfall profits might be generated by acquiring underperforming assets, then reorganizing production and operations to quickly increase productivity. Obtaining land at a price determined by the nominal value of the property to the state and then "flipping" the asset by reselling the use rights at market value was a way to earn windfall profits in real estate. Or developers could earn substantial profits by simply acquiring cheap land and developing it for more profitable use. Securing development rights to farmland located on the fringe of China's expanding cities could be particularly profitable. In all such instances, transfers of use rights could be immensely profitable if prices were set by officials absent reliable market valuation or were artificially deflated.

Because officials were often positioned first to set the value of state assets and then to determine who among a set of would-be "bidders" would obtain a particular asset, they could manipulate the transfer process to ensure a considerable gap between an asset's nominal, state-set value and its post-transfer market value. They would then decide who would scrape up the resulting windfall profit. Under these conditions, nonstate bidders had strong incentives to offer officials a share of the resulting windfall profits if they were selected. Moreover, the complexity of the transfer process and the need to obtain the approval of multiple agencies for both the initial transfer and then for development permits, approvals, and financing created a host of additional opportunities for officials to seek a slice of would-be owners' anticipated profits.[2]

The process of transferring control over assets from the state to nonstate actors, in other words, naturally bred new opportunities for high-stakes corruption. Because the value of assets transferred increased over time, the scale of corruption also increased. In the early days, much of what was transferred, principally rights to farmland, were likely of very limited value and hence incentives for bidders to pay large bribes were absent or limited. A farm family might, of course, be willing to give bribes to the cadres overseeing implementation of the household responsibility system and the distribution of collective land in their village; such bribes might take the form of *baijiu*, cigarettes, and perhaps some cash. Even so, only a few families would have accumulated substantial cash assets during the collective era and so most farmers presumably lacked the financial wherewithal to pay more than minimal bribes and were more likely to draw on personal *guanxi* for influence. Certain rural assets, including profitable sideline operations, communal workshops, and rural "factories," may have been of sufficient value to make them worth more substantial bribes, although we have grounds to suspect that many of the more valuable assets found their way into the hands of local cadres and their families instead of being auctioned off to would-be bidders.[3]

As the reform deepened and the scale of assets transferred to de facto nonstate control moved from rural and urban collective enterprises to small state-owned enterprises, and then to larger state corporations, the amounts of money the bidders would have been willing to pay also increased. Arguably, however, the advent of large-scale reassignment of use rights to urban land would have created profit-driven incentives for much larger bribes. By that time, moreover, nonstate actors who had profited during the early stages of reform would have built up the cash resources needed to finance large bribes.

As the value and scale of assets that could be transferred to the control of nonstate bidders increased, so did the seniority of the officials positioned to determine prices and assignment. Whereas decisions regarding the transfers of small assets generally fell within the official purview of local cadres, decisions regarding larger assets (e.g., state-owned factories, blocks of urban and suburban land) were more likely to be controlled by officials at much higher levels. Many of China's largest state-owned industries, for example, were owned by municipal, provincial, or central agencies and hence transfers of control would have required the approval of senior personnel. Transfers of major blocks of urban land to private control were also likely to require approval of senior municipal officials. As a result, as the value of asset transfers increased, we would expect that the seniority of corrupt officials would also have increased.

This does not mean, of course, that lower-level officials might not surreptitiously transfer assets over which they did not have authority. There can be little doubt that in a substantial number of cases, officials "sold" assets behind their superiors' backs. Nor should we forget that even if they did not control the disposition of assets, lower-level officials were often positioned to extract payments for the myriad subordinate approvals needed to complete transfers. Nevertheless, it seems reasonable to assume that with an increase in the value of assets transferred, it was more likely that senior officials would become direct or indirect parties to corrupt transactions. It is also reasonable to assume that as more senior officials became involved in corrupt transfers, the value of illegal payments (e.g., bribes and kickbacks) increased apace. In part, we would expect that the absolute amount of dirty money would increase as the expected value of assets increased. But we also have to assume that because senior officials presumably have more to lose if they get caught and are likely to assess the relative value of illegal income in light of their legal income, they are more likely to demand larger payments. In sum, therefore, we have grounds to assume that as reform deepened and the state transferred control rights, though not necessary ownership rights, to private interests or the managers of state-owned enterprises, the amounts of illegal payments to officials should increase and so should the seniority of those officials involved in corrupt transfers.

Although the preceding assumptions might appear to create a general expectation of an ever-upward spiral in the severity of corruption, as measured in the amount of money and the seniority of corrupt officials involved, corrupt transfers should have been, in theory, one-time transfers. Hypothetically, at least, we might expect that private interests seeking to cash in on gaps between the nominal and market values of assets would be willing to kick back a share of their anticipated windfall profits to the officials responsible for allocating those assets or that officials would demand a share of rents created by transferring assets at artificially low prices. To the extent that private interests obtained secure control rights, this implies that we should see a wave of one-time bribes and kickbacks and that once the bulk of assets had been transferred, corruption would begin to wane.

In fact, most transfers did not ensure secure property rights. Thus, instead of a tidal wave of one-time corruption, we have to anticipate a more sustained period of kickbacks and bribes. We might expect, therefore, that some significant share of corrupt transfers would involve a series of illegal payments, and in some cases buyers might face an open-ended series of demands for bribes and kickbacks. Even so, we might posit that, in most cases, there is likely to be a limit to the period over which the "buyer" will be willing to continue sharing. We might further assume that over time the ability of officials to continue to demand a cut will also decrease. As a result, it seems reasonable to assume that most illegal payments will be linked to the initial windfall profits resulting from transfers of control rights.

Transfers of state assets to private control and windfall profits created by unintentional undervaluation or deliberate underpricing are not, of course, the only sources of corruption. Corruption is also closely associated with regulation and the ability of officials to manipulate rules and regulations in ways that either benefit or threaten to harm economic actors. Complex regulatory structures characterized by high levels of regulatory ambiguity, overlap, and contradiction, combined with high levels of regulatory discretion and lack of transparency, are generally associated with high levels of official corruption. Faced with an ill-defined set of rules and the possibility of unpredictable and arbitrary enforcement, economic actors are likely to have incentives to use bribes to influence regulatory outcomes.[4]

At the beginning of the economic reform period, China had what can best be described as a chronically underdeveloped regulatory system. Regulations were rudimentary and ill adapted to the emerging quasi-marketized economic system. As the reform deepened, regulations were frequently created on the fly, often with little coordination and in an ad hoc manner. A tangled and contradictory web of rules soon evolved in which it was common for multiple agencies, offices, and bureaus, some local and some central, to have a degree of regulatory authority over a single entity or enterprise. Regulations were often byzantine, hidden, or even secret. Recourse was limited or impossible. Conditions were, in short, ripe for widespread bribery and extortion. The regulatory system evolved in ways that, to paraphrase the title of Melanie Manion's book on clean government in Mainland China and Hong Kong, were virtually designed to foster corruption.[5] Over time, conditions improved as regulation became more regularized and transparent and the discretionary power of individual officials was reduced.[6] Even today, however, China's regulatory system is apt to sustain relatively significant levels of corruption.

The final major driver behind high levels of corruption lay in the financial system. Whereas the regime has gradually ceded control over agriculture and much of industry and commerce to private companies or to managerial-controlled state-owned enterprises and hence a new class of "red capitalists," to borrow Bruce Dickson's phrase, it has stubbornly retained a high degree of control over the banking system. Most bank credit flows to state-owned enterprises, with administrative decisions playing a major role in selecting which enterprises get access to credit.[7] For nonstate companies, access to the state banking system remained limited and they were forced to rely on informal capital markets.[8] Under these conditions, most borrowers faced considerable obstacles to obtaining credit, thus giving them incentives to try to influence the officials and bank officers who allocated credit. Capital scarcity also created incentives for officials to use state money to make unauthorized loans and investments and to then skim off interest incomes and profits, an illegal practice which Chinese law defines as "misappropriation" (*nuoyong gongkuan*).

To summarize, if we look at reform as a dynamic process involving reductions in direct state control over the economy and the incremental transfer of assets to either private or managerial control (albeit with the state retaining formal ownership rights), we derive a model wherein gaps between the nominal or pretransfer value of assets and their post-transfer market value creates strong incentives for corruption. Seeking to obtain access to assets at favorable prices, private interests and managers (including those in charge of state-owned companies) had incentives to offer the officials vested with responsibility for asset transfers with an illicit share of the anticipated windfall profits. Officials, having seen their incomes deteriorate relative to members of the emerging entrepreneurial and managerial classes, and presumably having some sense of the gap between pre- and post-transfer values, had complementary incentives to auction off assets to individuals willing to cut them in on the anticipated profits. In theory, the result should have been a wave of corruption followed by a falling off of high-level corruption once most valuable assets had been transferred. Because the transfer process was protracted and began with the transfer of low-value assets (farmland transferred to farm families), the result was actually a long wave. The wave built in size following Deng Xiaoping's 1992 Southern Tour as the volume of transfers increased; it grew to even greater height in the late 1990s when the CCP finally restructured the state sector and transferred real estate to private control.

Other forces contributed to rising corruption. Highly imperfect regulation and restricted access to capital confronted private and managerial interests with incentives and pressures to buy off officials. As a result, we derive a composite model in which basic structural factors—the regulatory and financial systems—are apt to produce high levels of corruption, and transitional factors—the windfall profits generated by the transfer of assets from the state to the market—are apt to fuel a temporary wave of corruption. In theory, within this composite model, the transitional component should yield an initial set of upward pressures followed by a downward trend as the scope and scale of asset transfers decrease, an increasing share of the economy becomes marketized, and hence officials are no longer in a position to leverage a share of profits in the form of bribes and kickbacks. If corruption is in fact fed by reform, we should observe an inverted U-shaped form wherein corruption rises as the reform deepens and the scale of transfers increases, followed by decreasing corruption as the transition process reaches completion. Because regulatory and institutional factors should tend to sustain a relatively high ambient level of corruption and the transfer process has been relatively protracted, however, it seems likely that while the initial upward swing should be rather steep, the secondary downward swing should be much flatter.

There is, however, another factor that affects the dynamic evolution of corruption. As argued in chapter 6, if reform spawned incentives and opportunities for corruption, the regime's decision to fight corruption created disincentives. Even if we assume that the regime was lax in the early days and failed to anticipate that reform would spawn dramatic increases in corruption, we have to recognize that it never ignored signs of worsening corruption. On the contrary, the party launched its first post-1978 attack on corruption in 1982 and followed with anticorruption campaigns in 1986, 1989, and 1993. This is not to say that it did not cover up corruption, particularly at the highest levels, or to imply that it has waged the so-called war on corruption with grim, utter, and unswerving determination. On the contrary, it is clear that China's anticorruption efforts have been imperfect.

While imperfect, China's anticorruption efforts have also been significant in that they created resistance against increases in the level of corruption. If nothing else, they made corruption risky. Officials contemplating corrupt acts face the possibility of severe punishment, including execution, and substantial numbers are punished every year. More broadly, the fact that the Chinese regime has mounted a sustained effort to control corruption stands in rather stark contrast to the more common pattern wherein regimes make little or no attempt to fight corruption or where anticorruption drives are almost entirely driven by political infighting.[9] Once again, this is not to suggest that China's anticorruption campaigns are not tainted by politics. Clearly, local governments and even the CCP itself cover up the most politically sensitive cases of corruption. Nor would I suggest that politics does not play a role in determining who gets prosecuted. Nevertheless, the regime has gone after big political "tigers" including Beijing

Party Secretary Chen Xitong and Shanghai Party Secretary Chen Liangyu, both of whom were members of the CCP Politburo. Even if we assume that in these cases factional politics may have played a role, the fact remains that in both cases very senior members of the party leadership were exposed, prosecuted, and given lengthy prison sentences. In chapter 6, therefore, I contend that at the same time that the deepening of reform and the phased transfer of assets to private and managerial control led to a worsening of corruption, the regime's sustained drive against corruption placed downward pressure on the severity of corruption.

If my argument about the transitional nature of China's surge in corruption is correct, then we ought to see a significant change in the qualitative nature of corruption and shifts in the sectors plagued by corruption. Specifically, we should see a shift in the balance between auto-corruption (the theft of state assets by officials acting largely on their own) and transactive corruption (corrupt exchanges between officials and private interests). In the early days of reform, the state controlled the bulk of potentially profitable assets, and as a result officials seeking to cash in on their authority could most readily do so by looting and plundering the state. The emergence of the private and managerial sectors created new opportunities for officials to sell their authority and to cash in by accepting bribes. We should, therefore, see a distinct shift in the balance between what Chinese law defines as graft (*tanwu*) and bribery (*xinghui*). We should also see a rise in the misappropriation of public funds (*nuoyong gongkuan*), a form of corruption involving the unauthorized lending of public funds and hence a way for officials to cash in on unmet demand for investment capital. In addition to changes in the balance of plunder and bribery, we ought to see a rise in the number of cases involving illegal transfers of assets, corruption linked to financial transactions and land sales, and bribes linked to business more broadly.

My claims that corruption coevolved with reform and that corruption underwent a significant qualitative change after the party leadership accepted Deng's 1992 call for a dramatic deepening of reform is not unique. Most analyses, in fact, articulate a similar dynamic. Yan Sun, for example, differentiates between the "with-in plan phase" of reform (1980–92), during which corruption was characterized by "official profiteering," fraud involving public contracts, and regulatory manipulation, and the "beyond the plan phase" (post-1992), in which corruption spread into public investment, credit allocation, real estate transfers, zoning, and taxation. Sun also points to the significant rise of nepotism and venality of office in the latter period.[10] Ting Gong also uses 1992 as a dividing line, arguing that prior to Deng's Southern Tour corruption was dominated by officials profiting by arbitraging between in-plan prices and market prices and that the "widening and deepening" of reform allowed corruption to spread into new areas including real estate and stock markets, the tax and financial systems, and the business sector.

Increased foreign trade combined with high tariffs, meanwhile, to fuel a surge in smuggling and corruption linked to smuggling.[11] Over time, according to Gong, corrupt officials began to form informal organizations, leading to the emergence of what she terms "collective corruption."[12]

Like Sun and Gong, He Qinglian splits the post-Mao evolution of corruption into two periods but draws the boundary a bit later. Prior to 1995, he argues, corruption was "limited to the venal behavior of individuals." After that year, corruption became "organized" as high-level corruption became "the norm"; state institutions began to engage in routine, illicit exchanges of assets with other state institutions and social organizations; and subordinates became accustomed to bribing their superiors. As a result, China "entered a stage of systemic corruption" in which corruption began to squeeze out honesty in a "Panglossian" manner. He thus concludes that today "all officials are taking kickbacks" and that corruption has spiraled out of control and become "systemic."[13] Like He, Huang Yasheng argues that in the 1990s corruption entered the stage of "grand theft" and "looting" that presages the rise of a degenerate form of "crony capitalism" akin to that found in Latin America.[14]

In many ways, therefore, my assumptions about the evolution of corruption mirror those of Sun, Gong, He, and Huang. My model, however, diverges in a critical manner. Whereas Sun and Gong view the evolutionary process as one of "progressive worsening," I view it as a transitional process wherein qualitative changes in corruption were driven by the deepening of reform and specifically by the redeployment of assets from the state to the market. Because I link corruption to the transfer of assets from the state to markets, my assumption is that while the initial transfer will generate worsening corruption as both officials and private interests seek to capture rents in the form of windfall profits created by significant gaps between the state valuation and ultimate market valuation of assets, once those assets have been moved into the market, the opportunities for continued corruption and rent seeking will diminish. I thus diverge significantly from He, who emphatically rejects the transitional nature of corruption, arguing that the CCP's monopoly on political power lies at the heart of the corruption problem.[15]

My claim is, however, subject to three crucial caveats. First, decreases in corruption depend on the extent to which markets are allowed to function in a reasonably transparent and competitive manner. So long as markets are subject to considerable administrative intervention, opportunities and incentives for corruption will remain significant. Second, decreases in corruption will depend on the establishment of a system of relatively secure property rights. Third, corruption will only decrease if the separation of political and economic power widens; otherwise, marketization will spawn a new system of crony capitalism. The two sections that follow thus examine the changing balance between plunder, bribery, and misappropriation and qualitative shifts in the sectoral distribution of corruption cases.

From Plunder to Transaction

The literature on corruption posits a variety of typologies of corruption. Some of the more widely cited forms differentiate between political or legislative corruption and bureaucratic or administrative corruption depending on whether politicians or bureaucrats are the primary actors; grand or petty depending on the rank of those involved; extraordinary or routine based on the regularity of corrupt acts and the size of corrupt payments[16]; stable or disintegrative based on political consequences[17]; and black or gray or white depending on the degree to which specific types of corrupt acts are seen as illegitimate by society.[18] Others differentiate quid pro quo from diffuse reciprocity depending on whether there is a one for one exchange of illicit gains or illegal payments for favors, or if considerations are given with the expectation of future repayment or in hopes of establishing an ongoing relationship. A number of scholars also distinguish between individual corruption and organizational, collective, or syndicated corruption, with the former involving individual officials or small groups of officials acting in concert. As defined by Xiaobu Lu:

> Organizational corruption refers to the actions of a public agency that, by exploiting its power in regulating the market or its monopoly over vital resources, are aimed at monetary or material gains for the organization.[19]

According to Shawn Shieh, collective corruption differs from organizational corruption because it

> involves collusion within a network spanning multiple departments, enterprises and individuals...not restricted to public units, enterprises and officials... [and] may involve private companies and entrepreneurs, nongovernmental organizations, and organized crime.[20]

As Gong explains, collective corruption is essentially a form of organized crime wherein officials and others conspire to not only extract illegal money from bribery, embezzlement, extortion, smuggling, and other activities but to cover up their illegal activities using protective umbrellas (*baosan*) to thwart external investigations.[21] In a similar vein, Andrei Schleifer and Robert Vishny posit a critically important distinction between anarchic corruption involving a series of uncoordinated "independent" corrupt agencies or actors and "monopolistic" corruption wherein a single agency or even individual is able to control and orchestrate corrupt activities by state officials and agencies.[22]

Syed Hussein Alatas, on the other hand, breaks corruption down into five major forms: transactive, involving mutually beneficial exchanges generally between public and private parties; extortive or defensive, generally involving payments by a private party to a public official designed to avoid some negative outcome; autogenic, involving public officials using insider knowledge and information to earn or obtain illicit gains; nepotistic, revolving around the improper recruitment of generally unqualified but politically loyal friends and relatives into official positions; and supportive, using violence or intrigue to protect corrupt activities.[23] Like Alatas, Donatella della Porta and Alberto Vannucci distinguish illegal exchanges between politicians and state agents (bureaucrats), which they call "institutional exchanges," from illegal exchanges between public agents and private interests (including legitimate businesses, private citizens, and organized crime), which they call "corrupt exchanges."[24] In her analysis of corruption in contemporary China, Sun adopts a similar division between "transactive corruption," exchanges between officials and citizens, and "nontransactive corruption," officials "preying on public resources, rather than private ones."[25] In my own previous work, I drew distinctions between "looting," "rent scraping," and "dividend collecting" based on whether officials (1) directly expropriated public resources for their own benefit; (2) distorted economic policy in ways that enabled them, their families, or their cronies to scrape off rents; or (3) implemented pro-business macroeconomic policies and then collected a share of private-sector profits as a "dividend" for nurturing economic growth.[26]

To briefly reiterate the theoretical discussion in chapter 3, for purposes of analysis I now distinguish between two forms of corruption: plunder and transactive corruption. Plunder involves an official using his public authority to extract state money or assets and appropriate them to his personal control. Plunder thus includes the embezzlement of state funds and the theft of state property by officials. Plunder does not, therefore, involve private parties except to the extent that they might assist officials by, for example, helping them hide stolen wealth. As does Alatas, I define transactive corruption as a form of illicit exchange between corrupt officials and private actors. Transactive corruption may entail either positive-sum or mutually beneficial exchanges wherein the private actor pays the corrupt official to obtain some benefit (e.g., the private actor pays the official a bribe in return for which the official transfers control over a piece of land). Transactive corruption may also involve a negative-sum exchange whereby a private actor pays bribes to the corrupt official to avert some unwanted official action (e.g., pays off a building inspector who has uncovered shoddy or illegal construction). Negative-sum transactions may entail official extortion but can also yield benefits for a private party, particularly if the private party is engaged in illegal or unauthorized activity (as in the preceding example).

My purpose in drawing this distinction between plunder and transactive corruption is that is allows us to map, albeit somewhat imperfectly, plunder to what Chinese law defines as graft (*tanwu*) and transactive corruption to bribery (*huilu*). Herein the key distinction is between corruption that occurs within the party-state and involves officials stealing state assets and corruption that occurs across the divide between the party-state and the economy or, to put it somewhat differently, between the party-state and private actors, with the caveat that "private actors" may include the managers who de facto control state-owned enterprises. Bribery can thus be thought of as fundamentally different from plunder because it involves the commodification of public authority. In the same sense that I describe the reform process as the commodification of state assets and their transfer from a system of allocation and assignment based on authority to a system of allocation based on markets, I assert by commodifying public authority bribery creates a market for public authority in which corrupt officials "sell" their power and unofficial actors "buy" public power. At first blush, this might appear to signal a perverse development. On a deeper level, however, the fact that economic actors are willing to pay officials to manipulate public authority suggests that these private actors are motivated by profit seeking. It is perhaps commonplace to assume that bribery generally involves negative-sum gains or extortion. I do not doubt that in many cases officials do use overt or implied threats to leverage bribes and that bribery frequently involves the payment of protection money. But it is important to keep in mind that not only is there a "supply side" to bribery, there is often a "demand side" and that in many cases bribes are paid willingly because those offering them believe they will profit or because those paying bribes are protecting their own illicit activities. Criminals involved in gambling, prostitution, narcotics trafficking, loan sharking, or private extortion, for example, often willingly pay the police protection money because police protection enables them to earn larger or otherwise unattainable profits.[27] Similarly, a developer who can obtain a piece of land at a cost of $100 million rather than $150 million by paying an official a $5 million "commission" would find herself better off by $45 million, a tidy profit for a small cost (if she does not get caught).

I do not, of course, suggest that the commodification of corruption via the mechanism of bribery creates an efficient or desirable market and is thus an engine of economic growth and development. On the contrary, bribery is likely to come at considerable cost to the public interest and at an economic cost. Construction contracts let at inflated prices that result in shoddy and substandard work, goods and services bought at higher than prevailing prices, the proliferation of vice and criminal activities, and other examples are all clearly bad outcomes. Growth bought by bribery is certainly apt to be, in economic terms, second best. The key point is, however, that compared to plunder, bribery is much more likely to involve profit making and economic activity that generates some amount of net growth. Moreover, in an economy where the state controls assets that are being used inefficiently, bribes that help move those assets from state control and onto the markets may have considerable long-term benefits, even if illicit transfers enable the first buyers to earn windfall profits and enrich dishonest and corrupt officials.[28] More to the point, it is not that bribes stimulate the transfer of underutilized assets to more effective use; the transfer of such assets is apt to generate increased bribery because transfers are apt to involve rents and windfall profits. Increased bribery, in my construct, is not the cause of transfers but the consequence of policy-driven transfers. If we associate plunder with degenerative corruption and kleptocracy and we observe a shift in the plunder-bribery balance toward bribery, this implies a shift toward a more market-driven form of corruption wherein public authority becomes a tradable commodity.

The mid-1990s not only witnessed the commodification of corruption, it also saw the commercialization of corruption.[29] Although it is possible that corrupt officials used dirty money obtained through either plunder or bribery to invest in business or property ventures, such uses of corrupt money are secondary in that they are not the explicit and direct purpose for corrupt acts. Chinese law, however, defines a third major category of economic, misappropriation (*nuoyong gongkuan*) whose direct purpose is the illegal investment of public money in, for the most part, productive activities. Superficially a form of embezzlement, misappropriation involves illegal use of public funds rather than the theft of public funds as in the case of embezzlement. In broad terms, misappropriation occurs when an official or agency privately lends out public funds, fails to return these funds to public accounts within three months, and pockets income earned from such loans. In some cases, loans are made out of official accounts using funds that have been appropriated to a government office or other unit but are not required to cover current expenses. In theory, such idle funds are to be deposited in official bank accounts and held by the bank, which might then use them to make legal loans. Officials may, however, bypass the official banks and misappropriate idle funds to make illegal loans.[30] In other cases, loans may be made using funds accumulated in off-the-books slush funds. Many government agencies and public entities generate a variety of off-budget income from user fees, rents for properties they control, or other sideline business ventures. Some of this income may come from duly authorized fees. Units may also generate illegal income, including income from bribes paid to them by other units or individuals. Off-the-books income is deposited in what is known as the unit's small treasury (*xiaojinku*).[31] Some of these funds are then used to pay unauthorized bonuses, provide various benefits, build housing and other facilities for the use of unit employees, and to make further loans and investments.[32]

The amounts of money that must be diverted in order for an individual or unit to be charged with misappropriation are substantial. According to the 1988 statute that first defined misappropriation as a separate offense, the minimum amount needed to qualify was ¥50,000 (roughly US$13,500 at the then official exchange rate but closer to US$25,000 at the black market rate).[33] In 1998, the threshold for serious misappropriation was increased to ¥150,000 (roughly US$18,000).

Chinese law thus defines three functionally distinct forms of corruption: graft (*tanwu*), which involves the theft of state property and assets by officials and which I define in functional terms to correspond to "auto-corruption" or more simply "plunder"; bribery (*huilu*), which I define in functional terms as a form of transactive corruption involving the commodification and sale of public authority; and misappropriation (*nuoyong gongkuan*), which I define in functional terms as a form of "profit-seeking corruption" involving the illegal lending and investment of public money.[34] There are, of course, other forms and subforms of corruption. Bribery, for example, may entail the purchase and sale of public office (often termed nepotism but more correctly defined as venality of office), which is not limited to transactions between an official and a private actor (one seeking public office) but might involve bribes paid by subordinates seeking promotion or transfer.[35] Moreover, the boundaries between forms are fuzzy, and in some cases officials may engage in multiple forms of corruption (e.g., embezzling public funds, accepting bribes from developers seeking land leases and subordinates seeking promotions, accepting kickbacks from contractors, and extorting protection money from smugglers). The data are thus unlikely to break down into neatly differentiated categories, and trends are apt to be messy.

If measuring corruption in quantitative terms is difficult, describing corruption in qualitative terms is arguably even more difficult. The basic problem is that we have two sets of data with which to describe corruption, neither of which is particularly satisfactory. On the one hand, we have systematic data on the breakdown of corruption into the major legal categories of graft, bribery, and misappropriation. Though systematic, these data are crude in that they do not provide detail as to the nature of the offense or the identity of the offender. They can thus provide only broad descriptors. On the other hand, we have detailed descriptions of individual cases. Although these data provide considerable information on the who, when, and how, at present we have at best a tiny sample compared to the total caseload, not due to a lack of case data (there is in fact a considerable volume of such data available in the Chinese-language press) but rather from the disparity between the number of cases reported and the total number of cases.

Using a sample of cases to describe corruption is, moreover, problematic because by definition any sample, even a very large one, will contain only that subset of corrupt officials who get caught, indicted, prosecuted, and whose cases are publically reported. The latter factor is critical, particularly in the case of a political system such as China's where the regime exercises considerable control over the flow of information and hence has discretion in deciding what cases are swept under the rug, what cases are dealt with quietly and largely behind closed doors, and what cases are publicized. We have to assume that to a considerable extent the state selectively publicizes cases for didactic purposes, including a desire to show its willingness to attack even "big tigers" (senior officials). We also have to assume that the media, both domestic and international, are likely to pick up on cases with a significant scandal factor (sex, debauchery, depravity, notoriety). It thus follows that case-based data likely represent a small, unrepresentative subset of the total caseload and will tend to be biased in favor of high-level, high-visibility cases. Case-based data culled from non-Chinese media are likely to redouble this bias by focusing on the most prominent cases and overlook the more mundane cases reported in the Chinese media.

Though admittedly imperfect, the available data tell an interesting story if we triangulate the macrolevel systematic data with the microlevel case data. Before examining the evolution of corruption during the reform period, it is useful to have a baseline from the prereform period for comparative purposes. Data are spotty. National-level data are not currently available. At the provincial level, detailed data on types of offenses are available for cases handled by the Hunan Procuratorate and the courts in Liaoning, Hainan, Sichuan, and Yunnan. In general, the data show that graft cases accounted for the overwhelming majority of corruption cases. The Hunan Procuratorate data are the most complete and provide data from the years 1950 to 1966. During these years, with the exceptions of 1952, 1953, and 1956, graft constituted over 80 percent of the total.[36] During this period, no bribery cases were reported. The court data are a bit more difficult to deal with because the courts do not aggregate cases in the same manner as the procuratorate. The overall pattern is, nevertheless, similar. The Yunnan Provincial Court data, for example, include only nine bribery cases, all of which involve the paying of bribes (xinghui), compared to 6,041 graft cases.[37] In Liaoning, between 1949 and 1955, provincial courts dealt with 14,102 graft cases and 226 bribery cases.[38] From 1950 to 1969, Sichuan courts tried 30,288 graft cases and only 96 bribery cases, all of them in 1952.[39]

Although the aggregate data seem to suggest that plunder predominated during the prereform period, data culled from individual cases suggest a somewhat more complicated story. The data are, admittedly, limited and include information on a small set of very high-level cases prosecuted in the period before the Great Leap Forward. They suggest that during these early years, when the party was still socializing the economy, over half the cases (55 percent) with charges that would fall under most definitions of corruption involved either embezzlement or graft while just over a tenth (12 percent) involved bribery (see Table 5.1). Profiteering, speculation, and smuggling accounted for close to one third (31 percent). While plunder accounted for the majority of charges and transactive corruption only a small share, the data suggest that corrupt officials were involved in significant amounts of profit-seeking corruption. In most of the charges I have translated into English as "speculation," those involved were said to have collaborated or colluded (*guojie*) with profiteers (*jianshang*), illegal businessmen (*feifa shangren*), or smugglers (*sishang*). In other words, they were involved with private traders operating on the fringes of the increasingly socialized economy and in many cases were presumably trading on the black-market goods that had been designated as state controlled. A number of those charged during this period were accused of selling state secrets (*chumai guojia shangjing mimi*), which in most instances meant they had sold economically valuable information to people engaged in illegal commerce. It is unclear, however, exactly how these corrupt officials colluded with speculators and smugglers. It is quite possible, in fact, that their collusion took the form of bribes or kickbacks. If that were the case, then the line between profit seeking and transactive corruption might be blurred or even nonexistent.

Regardless of whether these cases involved profit seeking or bribery, charges related to speculation and smuggling appear primarily during the period 1950–52 when the regime was struggling to control the economy and to nationalize key economic assets. As the state took control of the economy, both transactive and profit-seeking corruption decreased as private interests willing to collude with corrupt officials and pay bribes were essentially eliminated. Socialization of the economy, in simple terms, eliminated the demand side for corruption by internalizing economic activity inside the state. As such, it is not surprising that transactive and profit-seeking corruption largely disappeared in the mid-1950s.

Data from the Sichuan provincial courts, however, show high levels of speculation not only during 1950–53 but also in 1959–60 and 1963–64.[40] The first period, of course, corresponds to the initial socialization of the economy and hence a time when the private sector was under attack from the state. The second period followed the failure of the Great Leap Forward, the onset of a massive famine, and the so-called 'three hard years.' The third upsurge in speculation charges corresponds to the years of the Socialist Education Movement during which Mao and his leftist allies were struggling to restore the state's grip on the

TABLE 5.1 High-level corruption in the early 1950s (percentage of total charges by year)

CATEGORY	TYPE	1950	1951	1952	1953	1954	ALL YEARS	ECONOMIC CASES ONLY	NUMBER OF CHARGES
Non-economic		16.42	22.22	31.02	84.21	76.92	31.36	—	—
	Degeneracy	7.46	3.70	2.31	—	—	3.07	—	14
	Disciplinary	—	—	5.61	21.05	7.69	4.82	—	22
	Misuse of authority	—	11.11	4.29	36.84	7.69	5.92	—	27
	Political	—	—	4.62	15.79	—	3.73	—	17
	Work style	8.96	7.41	14.19	10.53	61.54	13.82	—	—
Economic		80.60	70.37	65.35	10.53	23.08	64.69	—	—
	Bribery	17.91	7.41	5.94	—	—	7.46	11.53	34
	Embezzlement	23.88	22.22	14.52	10.53	—	16.23	25.09	74
	Fraud	—	1.85	1.65	—	—	1.32	2.04	6
	Graft	17.91	24.07	20.13	—	15.38	19.30	29.83	88
	Profiteering	20.90	12.96	16.50	—	—	15.57	24.07	71
	Smuggling	—	—	1.98	—	—	1.32	2.04	6
	Speculation	—	1.85	3.96	—	7.69	3.07	4.75	14
	Tax	—	—	0.66	—	—	0.44	0.69	2
Crime		2.99	—	2.64	—	—	2.19	—	10
Other		—	7.41	0.99	5.26	—	1.75	—	8
Total		67	54	303	19	13			456

Source: Based on cases reported in Xin Zhongguo Fanfubai Tongjian [Chronicle of Anticorruption in New China] (Tianjin: Renmin Chubanshe, 1993).
Note: Because an individual can be charged with multiple offenses, the data for the number of charges (456) are much greater than the number of cases (149).

economy after Liu Shaoqi, Zhou Enlai, and Deng Xiaoping had relaxed restrictions on market activities during the early 1960s in a desperate attempt to jump start the economy and end the post–Great Leap famine.

Because the Sichuan court data lump together all cases of speculation, including speculation and profiteering by nonstate actors, it is hard to determine the extent to which officials were engaged in profit-seeking corruption during these three periods. The case evidence, however, shows that in the early 1950s there was a fair amount of profit-seeking corruption involving officials and cadres. Anecdotal accounts of the post–Great Leap period would strongly suggest that many officials and cadres did resort to corruption during the latter two periods.[41] One of the core objectives of the 1963–66 Socialist Education Movement was, in fact, to crack down on cadre corruption, including illegal speculation and profiteering.[42] These same data also show a fourth period when the courts dealt with a surge in speculation cases. During 1974–78, the number of speculation cases increased sixfold from 218 in 1974 to 1,258 in 1977. Once again, the data do not indicate the extent to which officials and cadres were engaged in speculation, either on their own or in collusion with private profiteers. Nevertheless, the Sichuan data suggest that a fair amount of profit-seeking corruption occurred during the Maoist period.

On balance, the available evidence seems to show that transactive and profit-seeking corruption occurred with much less frequency than plunder during the Maoist period when China's economy was largely controlled by the state. This is understandable. Transactive corruption and profit-seeking corruption occur along the intersection between the political and the economic. Without a private sector and without private economic actors, the opportunities for and the demand for transactive corruption will be negligible. As a result, to the extent that corruption occurs it will occur within the state as officials and cadres use their authority to appropriate state assets to their private use and control. Bribery diminished during the Maoist era, in other words, because socialization of the economy largely eliminated the private economic actors who would have been the primary source of bribes.

The impact of the marketization of China's economy after 1978 on the qualitative nature of corruption is evident in both the systematic data and the case data. In the early years of the reform period, graft, which I define broadly as a form of plunder, accounted for a sizable majority of economic crime cases filed by the procuratorate (see Figure 5.1). Over time, in relative terms, graft decreased, falling from roughly 70 percent of all cases in 1979–80 to about 40 percent by 1991–92. Bribery, which I equate with transactive corruption, on the other hand, increased from less than 10 percent of the total in 1979–80 to roughly 25 percent by the mid-1990s and then over 40 percent in 2006–7. Legally, profit-seeking

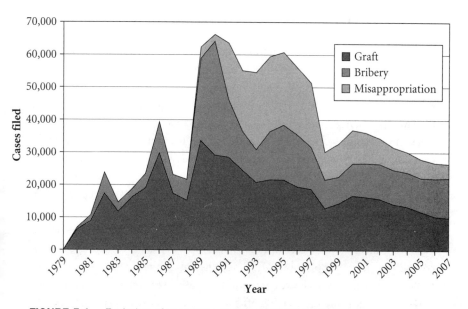

FIGURE 5.1. Evolution of corruption in China, 1979–2007

Sources: Zhongguo Jiancha Nianjian [Procuratorial Yearbook of China] (Beijing: Zhongguo Jiancha Chubanshe, various years); *Tianjin Tongzhi: Jiancha Zhi* [Annals of Tianjin City: Annals of the Procuratorate] (Tianjin: Tianjin Shehui Kexue Chubanshe, 2000), 232–34; *Hebei Shengzhi: Jiancha, di 72 juan: Jiancha Zhi* [Annals of Hebei Province, volume 72: Annals of the Procuratorate] (Shijiazhuang: Zhongguo Shuji Chubanshe, 1991), 240–41; *Jiangsu Shengzhi: Jiancha Zhi* [Annals of Jiangsu Province: Annals of the Procuratorate] (Nanjing: Jiangsu Renmin Chubanshe, 1994), 192; *Fujian Shengzhi: Jiancha Zhi* [Annals of Fujian Province: Annals of the Procuratorate] (Fuzhou: Fangzhi Chubanshe, 1997), 29; *Jiangxi Shengzhi: Jiangxi Sheng Jiancha Zhi* [Annals of the Jiangxi Provincial Procuratorate] (Nanchang: Zhongyang Gongchandang Xuexiao Chubanshe, 1993), 151–53; *Shandong Shengzhi: Sifa Zhi* [Annals of Shandong Province: Annals of the Legal System] (Jinan: Shandong Renmin Chubanshe, 1991), 175; *Guangxi Tongzhi: Jiancha Zhi* [Annals of Guangxi: Annals of the Procuratorate] (Nanning: Jiangxi Renmin Chubanshe, 1996), 128–44; *Hunan Shengzhi: Di liu juan: Zheng-fa Zhi* [Annals of Hunan Province, volume 6: Annals of Politics and Law: Procuratorate] (Changsha: Hunan Chubanshe, 1996), 282; *Chongqing Shi Zhi: Gong'an Zhi, Jiancha Zhi, Sifa Xingzheng Zhi, Junshi Zhi, Waishi Zhi i* [Annals of Chongqing City: Annals of the Public Security, Procuratorial, Legal Administration, Military, and Foreign Affairs Systems] (Chongqing: Xi'nan Shifan Daxue Chubanshe, 2005), 160–61; *Yunnan Shengzhi, Di 54: Jiancha Zhi* [Annals of Yunnan Province, volume 54: Annals of the Procuratorate] (Kunming: Yunnan Renmin Chubanshe, 1989), 140; *Gansu Shengzhi: Jiancha Zhi* [Annals of Gansu Province: Annals of the Procuratorate] (Lanzhou: Gansu Renmin Chubanshe, 1990), 106–16; *Qinghai Shengzhi, 54: Jiancha Zhi* [Annals of Qinghai Province, volume 54: Annals of the Procuratorate] (Lanzhou: Gansu Renmin Chubanshe, 2000), 92–108.

Note: National-level data are available from only 1987 onward. I have, therefore, estimated the earlier years using data from twelve provinces (Tianjin, Hebei, Jiangsu, Fujian, Jiangxi, Shandong, Hunan, Guangxi, Chongqing, Yunnan, Gansu, and Qinghai).

corruption in the form of misappropriation, which I map to profit-seeking corruption, did not exist prior to 1988. Until then, it appears that illegal letting out of public funds was treated as a form of embezzlement or graft. In 1988, in response to evidence that officials were engaged in illegal short-term lending, the law was amended and misappropriation was redefined as a separate and distinct criminal offense.[43] By 1991, misappropriation accounted for a quarter of the caseload, and by the mid 1990s it accounted for between 30 and 40 percent of all economic crime cases. Thereafter, misappropriation declined to less than a quarter of the caseload in 2002 and less than 20 percent in 2005–6. The relative decline in misappropriation was, however, largely the result of a relative increase in bribery. Thus, from 1988 onward, a majority of economic crime cases filed by the procuratorate involved either transactive corruption (bribery) or profit-seeking corruption (misappropriation). Although the data do not allow us to measure the extent to which transactive corruption involved extortion or defensive bribes paid to prevent some undesirable official action, the evidence suggests that, by the early 1990s, corruption was centered along the division between political power and the economy. Most clearly in the case of misappropriation, corruption involved some considerable degree of cooperation, or perhaps more accurately collusion, between those vested with political power and those engaged in profit seeking.

Data culled from a survey of 4,040 high-visibility cases tell a slightly different but not contradictory story.[44] Because individual offenders might be charged with multiple offenses, the database yielded a total of 5,175 charges, of which it was possible to determine the year in which the individual charged first became corrupt in 3,677 instances. According to these data, bribery was more common in the prereform period than the aggregate data suggest, accounting for a fifth of the charges filed prior to 1978 (see Table 5.2).[45] As was true in the aggregate data, bribery became more common as the reform era progressed and by the mid-1990s accounted for nearly 60 percent of all charges. Graft and embezzlement, meanwhile, accounted for half the charges prior to the advent of reform but only a quarter of the charges in more recent years. Misappropriation charges were much less common among these high-visibility cases than in the aggregate data. This may be because Western reporters did not fully appreciate the difference between embezzlement (theft) and misappropriation (temporary embezzlement) and hence reported misappropriation cases as embezzlement. The data reveal a relatively high incidence of profiteering and speculation charges in the early years. During the prereform yeas, profiteering and speculation accounted for nearly a fifth of the charges. In the first part of the reform period, these offenses accounted for about a tenth of the charges. By the early 1990s, however, after the regime had largely eliminated the two-track price system whereby

TABLE 5.2 Charges filed by the procuratorate, by period (based on high-profile cases)

CHARGE	PRE-REFORM	1978–84	1985–88	1989–92	1993–96	1997–2001	2002–9	OVERALL	TOTAL CHARGES
					ALL CHARGES				
Bribery	21.05	38.36	38.17	47.01	49.57	48.65	59.06	47.67	1,753
Graft and embezzlement	49.12	28.93	35.96	36.84	22.11	28.91	22.35	28.12	1,034
Misappropriation	1.75	0.31	3.47	4.54	4.66	6.35	2.35	4.24	156
Misuse of funds	8.77	—	0.32	0.36	1.99	0.24	—	0.90	33
Profiteering and speculation	10.53	14.15	9.78	2.72	0.35	0.12	—	2.77	102
Fraud	1.75	3.77	0.63	0.73	1.99	2.82	2.12	2.04	75
Smuggling	—	4.40	1.26	1.27	9.50	2.00	0.24	4.16	153
Tax evasion	—	0.94	3.47	1.27	1.30	2.00	0.47	1.50	55
Other economic crime	—	0.31	—	—	0.09	0.35	—	0.14	5
Ordinary criminal	1.75	4.72	1.89	3.27	4.58	6.82	6.35	4.84	178
Disciplinary	5.26	3.46	4.42	2.00	3.80	1.76	7.06	3.48	128
Other	—	0.63	0.63	—	0.09	—	—	0.14	5

(Continued)

TABLE 5.2 Charges filed by the procuratorate, by period (based on high-profile cases)—*Continued*

CHARGE	PRE-REFORM	1978-84	1985-88	1989-92	1993-96	1997-2001	2002-9	OVERALL	TOTAL CHARGES
					ECONOMIC CRIME ONLY				
Bribery	22.64	42.07	41.02	49.62	54.15	53.21	68.21	52.08	
Graft and embezzlement	52.83	31.72	38.64	38.89	24.15	31.62	25.82	30.72	
Misappropriation	1.89	0.34	3.73	4.79	5.09	6.94	2.72	4.63	
Misuse of funds	9.43	0.00	0.34	0.38	2.17	0.26	—	0.98	
Profiteering and speculation	11.32	15.52	10.51	2.87	0.38	0.13	—	3.03	
Fraud	1.89	4.14	0.68	0.77	2.17	3.08	2.45	2.23	
Smuggling	—	4.83	1.36	1.34	10.38	2.19	0.27	4.55	
Tax evasion	—	1.03	3.73	1.34	1.42	2.19	0.54	1.63	
Other economic crime	—	0.34	—	—	0.09	0.39	—	0.15	
Total Charges	57	318	317	551	1,158	851	425	—	3,677

Note: Data collected by author from search of the LexisNexis database.

commodities had both low in-plan prices and higher market prices, thus giving officials an easy way to earn illicit profit from arbitrage selling, speculation and profiteering charge dropped to negligible levels.

As the reform process deepened and a new quasi-marketized economy grew up alongside the old command economy, which itself was undergoing corporatization and marketization, the reemergence of economic actors outside the state led to a significant rise in bribery—or, more formally, transactive corruption. During the 1950s and 1960s, this form of corruption had overtly dropped to negligible levels as the state internalized control over the economy and thus largely eliminated the demand side for bribery. But bribery likely never disappeared. Instead, large-scale bribery disappeared while petty bribery continued apace as increasing shortages gave rise to *guanxi* and the practice of going through the backdoor. Reform in effect resurrected the demand side of bribery, and by the mid-1980s, businessmen and others had financial incentives to use money, gifts, and favors to try to influence officials' decisions.

When a new round of reforms in the mid-1990s led to transfers of state assets, including both productive enterprises and real estate, to private or corporate control and created opportunities to earn large windfall profits by manipulating the terms of transfer, the incentives for entrepreneurs, businessmen, developers, and speculators to bribe or otherwise cut officials in on the potential profits were more than redoubled. Not surprisingly, this period saw a surge in high-level, high-stakes bribery. As the economy began to grow rapidly, demand for capital, the supply of which was mostly under the control of the state, also created opportunities for officials responsible for financial management to earn under-the-table income by illegally lending out public funds and pocketing money earned either from interest or investments. As a result, transactive and for-profit corruption proliferated as reform deepened. This does not mean transactive and for-profit corruption crowded out old-fashioned plunder in the form of graft and embezzlement. On the contrary, the data show that Chinese officials and cadres continued to steal from the state. If anything, it appears that the emergence of a new—or perhaps not so new—culture encouraged greater stealing, particularly as mid-ranked officials saw their bosses begin to cash in. In sum, therefore, the 1990s saw a shift in the qualitative nature of corruption as transactive and for-profit corruption reached new levels.

The Commercialization of Corruption

Instead of focusing on the legal charges filed, it is also possible to break down corruption by the area in which corrupt officials worked and the character of the corrupt transaction. Examining corruption in terms of where corrupt officials worked is important in the Chinese case. Whereas in most capitalist economies the boundary between that state and business is relatively well defined, in China the boundary moved dramatically as economic reforms first greatly enlarged the quasi-state collective sector and than spawned a new and rapidly growing private sector. The boundary has also become fuzzy. Prior to reform, the state included not only officials and party cadres but also the managers of state-owned enterprises. By the later 1990s, most state-owned enterprises had been converted to joint stock companies in which the state owned a majority stake and were corporatized in the sense that day-to-day control over the company and access to inside information on its financial condition fell increasingly into the hands of managers who were de facto entrepreneurs even though they nominally continued to work for the state. As a result, people who in a market economy would be called "businessmen" and hence unable to commit violations of public authority (i.e., corruption) were state officials in China and could be charged with public corruption. Overtime, the relative economic weight of the state sector decreased. Nevertheless, that state continued to be a hybrid organization that included both administrative and political elements but still had a considerable foot in the business sector.

Officials and cadres employed in administration and politics, not surprisingly, accounted for the largest block of those charged with corruption during most the reform period (see Table 5.3). Public employees working in what would likely be considered businesses in a market economy, however, accounted for the second-largest cluster of those charged with corruption. As reform progressed and the state began to cede control of a greater share of the economy to the private and managerial sectors, officials working in business declined significantly as a percentage of the total cadres and officials charged with corruption. Finance, which remained dominated by the state-owned banking system rather than private banks as would be the case in a market economy, accounted for a significant share of those charged with corruption. The share increased in the early 1990s as economic reforms deepened and the post-1992 boom fed a growing demand for capital. Combined, officials working in what would be considered business and finance in a market economy, in fact, accounted for approximately half those charged during the first decade of reform, then declined to a third of the total in the early 1990s and a quarter after 2000. A considerable share of those charged in China, in other words, would have been working outside the state in a marketized economy and hence their offenses would have been deemed criminal embezzlement, theft, financial fraud, misdemeanor violations of fiduciary responsibility, or, in not a few cases, legal but perhaps unscrupulous profit making.[46] We might also posit that the apparent decline in corruption charges involving officials in business and finance reflects the fact that marketization and corporatization

TABLE 5.3 Cadres and officials charged, 1970–2007: Functional sector (percentage of those charged in each time period)

SECTOR	PRE-REFORM	1978–84	1985–88	1989–92	1993–96	1997–2001	2002–9	OVERALL	CUMULATIVE	TOTAL INDIVIDUALS
Party and government	37.50	31.36	25.42	29.05	33.10	26.91	27.03	29.58	29.58	833
Business	37.50	47.73	40.42	27.94	17.82	18.04	13.66	23.58	53.16	664
Judicial	10.42	4.55	8.33	9.31	15.75	15.09	17.15	13.14	66.30	370
Financial	4.17	4.55	9.58	16.19	14.48	12.60	10.47	12.46	78.76	351
Infrastructure	8.33	4.55	9.17	8.87	8.39	9.95	7.56	8.49	87.25	239
Private business	—	—	0.42	0.89	2.76	5.44	10.17	3.52	90.77	99
Family	—	1.36	1.25	2.66	1.95	1.71	—	1.63	92.40	46
Medical	—	0.91	2.08		0.23	1.40	4.65	1.21	93.61	34
Power generation	—	—	—	0.89	1.03	2.18	1.74	1.17	94.78	33
Gangster	—	—	0.42	1.11	1.03	1.87	0.87	1.07	95.85	30
Media	—	—	—	0.44	0.46	1.87	3.20	1.03	96.88	29
Other/Unknown	2.08	4.99	2.93	2.66	2.97	2.96	3.48	3.12	100	88
Total individuals	48	220	240	451	870	643	344	—	—	2,816

Source: Data collected by author from search of the LexisNexis database.

moved some of these individuals out of the ranks of officialdom and transformed their offenses from corruption (defined as misuse of authority for personal gain) to business malfeasance (defined as the misuse of fiduciary authority for private gain). Officials in the judiciary, which included court officials and members of the police, accounted for a fourth major block, and it appears that judicial corruption worsened as the reform period progressed.[47]

Based on the preceding, it might seem that we could attribute a considerable share of corruption in post-Mao China to continued state control of a large share of the overall economy and the involvement of many of those charged with official corruption in a variety of business activities, albeit perhaps shady business activities. Breaking down corruption by the purpose of the illegal acts, however, reveals that even though transactive corruption constituted a majority of legal charges, much of what was being transacted may have involved the sorts of transactions we associate with predatory corruption. Corruption linked to construction, real estate development, and commercial activities constituted three of the largest overall corruption categories and combined accounted for a quarter of the total (see Table 5.4). Although high levels of corruption in these areas would be consistent with my argument that the transition from a command to a market economy fed corruption, the other major categories are consistent with plunder. Overtly predatory actions, including embezzlement, protecting criminal activity, and involvement in smuggling, were among the top five categories and combined represented nearly 29 percent of the total. But not all of these actions were necessarily plunder. Smuggling, for example, can be linked to macroeconomic policy and specifically to high import tariffs, which create gaps between world and domestic prices. Bribes paid by smugglers to obtain official protection can, therefore, be seen as a transfer of a share of the rents created by protective tariffs. Moreover, bribes paid by speculators and profiteers may be derived from rents created by administratively imposed prices or contrived shortages. Asset stripping and the diversion of state assets, finally, also involve the transfer of resources from state control to the market and hence may be driven by profit-seeking motives.

If we further disaggregate the data and examine only those cases in which the primary charge was bribery, the nature of transactive corruption is similar. As was true for all cases, bribery linked to construction and real estate development represented the largest block (20 percent), followed by bribes paid for commercial advantage (15 percent). Smuggling, finance, and profiteering accounted for a further 19 percent. A substantial share of bribery cases (54 percent) were thus linked to business activity. Bribery was, however, also linked to non-business-related transactions. Bribes paid to officials by criminals and organized gangs accounted for close to 10 percent of the cases surveyed, as did bribes related to nepotism and venality of office.[48]

TABLE 5.4 Bribery cases classified by purpose or cause of corruption (percentage of total cases in each time period)

TYPE OF CORRUPTION	PRE-REFORM	1978–84	1985–88	1989–92	1993–96	1997–2001	2002–9	OVERALL	CUMULATIVE	TOTAL CASES
Construction and real estate	2.08	5.91	10.00	14.86	20.00	16.33	15.99	15.59	15.59	439
Embezzlement	43.75	13.64	23.75	19.96	7.47	14.00	6.10	13.28	28.87	374
Commerce	—	11.82	13.75	11.75	7.70	7.78	14.53	9.91	38.78	279
Criminal activity	10.42	3.18	2.08	5.76	8.39	12.13	9.30	8.03	46.80	226
Smuggling	—	12.73	10.83	2.22	14.48	2.95	0.29	7.46	54.26	210
Asset stripping and diverting state assets	2.08	10.00	1.67	5.32	6.90	10.11	9.30	7.39	61.65	208
Profiteering and speculation	12.50	21.82	17.92	8.20	3.33	3.89	1.45	6.85	68.50	193
Nepotism	2.08	0.45	0.42	4.88	7.47	5.91	4.94	5.15	73.65	145
Finance	—	—	2.92	5.76	6.78	5.60	2.03	4.79	78.44	135
Bribery (unspecified)	4.17	0.91	2.08	4.43	4.48	3.73	2.33	3.55	82.00	100
Contracting	—	—	0.42	1.77	2.30	3.89	7.56	2.84	84.84	80
Permits	6.25	6.82	3.33	4.88	0.80	0.93	5.52	2.84	87.68	80
Gambling	—	0.45	1.25	2.22	1.26	4.04	6.10	2.56	90.23	72
Fraud	—	3.18	2.92	2.66	1.84	2.64	1.45	2.27	92.51	64
Privilege seeking	16.67	4.09	2.92	0.89	1.61	0.31	0.58	1.63	94.14	46
Taxation	—	—	0.83	—	2.41	2.18	0.29	1.35	95.49	38
Other	—	5.00	2.92	4.43	2.76	3.58	12.21	4.51	100.00	127
Total cases	48	220	240	451	870	643	344	—		2,816

Source: Data collected by author from search of the LexisNexis database.

Note: The number of "other" cases is much higher in the 2002–9 period because of a substantial increase in the number of cases linked to health care (2.33 percent of the total in that period versus 0.43 percent overall) and village elections (3.20 percent overall versus 0.57 percent).

Temporally, the data break down in a manner generally consistent with my argument that corruption and reform coevolved. Corruption linked to profiteering and speculation, for example, was most common during the 1980s when the two-track price system gave officials opportunities to scrape off rents created by gaps between in-plan and market prices but then diminished as most commodity prices were set by the market rather than by administrative fiat. By the same token, corruption linked to construction and real estate development increased as public works spending increased and the state began transferring control over land to developers. Smuggling-related corruption fell sharply after China's entry into the World Trade Organization brought down the tariffs that created rent-bearing gaps between domestic prices and world prices. Corruption related to criminal activity also increased as the loosening of state control created new opportunities for illicit activities and space for the growth of organized crime. Similarly, the loosening of political controls and the weakening of party discipline opened up new opportunities for venality and a market for official positions and promotions, with the result that what has often been described in the literature as "nepotism" worsened as the reform period progressed.[49]

On balance, the data do not yield a crisp picture in which transactive corruption supplanted plunder. The lack of a crisp picture should not be surprising. After all, as noted earlier, so long as we cannot accurately measure the rate of corruption, we are forced to use imperfect proxies and hence are likely to get a fuzzy sense of reality. Nevertheless, the data suggest that as economic reforms progressed, the plunder-transactive corruption mix skewed more toward transactive corruption, particularly in the 1990s. Plunder, in the form of graft and embezzlement, continued at relatively high levels and increased during the first decade of reform. It was, however, growth in transactive corruption in the form of bribery and misappropriation that pushed the overall level of corruption upward in the later 1980s and 1990s. Based on the case data, it appears that some of the increase in bribery and misappropriation was linked to predation and extortion.

The line between willing and coerced bribery is not, however, always clear. Bribery, after all, can have both a supply side (corrupt officials) and a demand side (private interests). In some instances, businessmen and the managers of corporatized state-owned enterprises undoubtedly have had to pay bribes to avoid official harassment or to prevent officials from using their authority to harm a company's business activities. But it would be wrong to assume that private actors are axiomatically the victims of corruption. On the contrary, businessmen may well be willing participants or even the initiators of corrupt exchanges or, as Douglas Beets argues, businesses may be victims, participants, or perpetrators.[50] Bribery may well be a means to maximize profits. A highway contractor, for example, might be quite happy to pay a contract administrator bribes of $1 million if the result is a contract inflated by $2 million, thus yielding the businessman a

$1 million bribe-derived profit. Similarly, a shipping firm is apt to prefer slipping customs inspectors a couple bottles of scotch and a few cartons of expensive cigarettes if that means its goods clear customs faster than those of its more honest competitors. Businesses can, as Schleifer points out, bribe officials to obtain tax relief or low-tariff charges or to affect policy and regulatory decisions in ways that advance their corporate interests or perhaps even harm their competitors.[51]

Businesses may also pay bribes to protect profitable but shady business activities from unwanted official scrutiny or control. A bank manager, for instance, might find that payoffs to state auditors are desirable if they would mean that serious problems with his balance sheets remain hidden from depositors who might want to pull their funds out if they knew the bank was carrying so many nonperforming loans that it was on the verge of insolvency. Individuals involved in illegal activity, be it narcotics trafficking, prostitution, loan sharking, labor racketeering, or counterfeiting, all have strong incentives to pay bribes to protect themselves from arrest and punishment. There is also a demand side to misappropriation, and would-be borrowers are often willing to offer officials high rates—and perhaps bribes and kickbacks—in return for obtaining illegal loans. The initiative for misappropriation may thus come from businessmen, entrepreneurs, and speculators rather than officials seeking to make predatory short-term loans. In looking at the surge in transactive and profit-seeking corruption, therefore, it is critically important to recognize that the deepening of reform not only created new opportunities for officials to engage in corruption, it also spawned and enlarged the demand for corruption.

In sum, both the case data and the aggregated data show corruption coevolving with reform. Reform clearly led to the worsening of corruption, both in terms of the overall number of officials engaged in corruption and in terms of the intensity of corruption. Herein lies the key to at least partially unlocking the paradox of corruption and rapid growth in China. Although there can be little doubt that corruption negatively affected economic performance and induced significant distortions, corruption was not an a priori barrier to rapid growth. At the outset, corruption was, quite simply, not sufficiently serious or entrenched within the state to stifle economic growth. This is not to imply that corruption was absent. We have clear evidence of corruption in prereform China. By and large, corruption in prereform China and even in the early reform period seems to have been primarily in the form of petty corruption—small bribes to help one get in the backdoor and build connections. In the mid-1980s, the two-track price system produced a surge in official profiteering as corrupt officials reaped quick profits by arbitraging between low in-plan prices and higher market prices. Just as price reforms largely eliminated the two-track price system, the deepening of reform in the mid-1990s and the advent of large-scale transfers of assets from the state to the market stimulated the rise of high-level, high-stakes corruption. In the process, not only did corruption worsen and intensify as reform deepened, the balance between plunder and transactive corruption shifted in the direction of transactive corruption.

In a fundamental sense, reform spawned increased corruption by loosening state controls and hence affording officials new opportunities to use their authority for illicit personal gain and by creating a new differentiation between the state and the economy, thereby expanding the demand for corrupt transactions. Whereas control over most significant economic assets was internalized to the state prior to the reform period, as reform progressed, more and more of these assets came under the formal or de facto control of new actors. Although some of these new economic actors were private businessmen, many were part of a gray sector that included state officials assigned to economic and commercial enterprises, officials who had given up their formal state jobs and "taken the plunge" (*xia hai*) into the business world but without necessarily shedding their connections with their former employers and colleagues, officials who were moonlighting in the private sector, and, as time went on, a complex set of shady operators and outright gangsters. The children of senior officials, the so-called "princelings" (*taizi*), found themselves positioned to cash in on their inside knowledge of how that party-state system worked and their ties to kin, classmates, and friends, often by gaming the system. The emergence of this new economic sector, or more properly its enlargement because illegal black and gray markets predated the advent of reform,[52] significantly enlarged the range of actors willing to use bribes, kickbacks, commissions, gifts, and favors to manipulate officials and authority. As a result, whereas corruption had primarily taken the form of plunder prior to reform, with corrupt officials preying on the state and its assets, in the reform period transactive corruption become increasingly common. In broad terms, whereas the majority of corruption cases involved graft in the prereform period, by the 1990s bribery accounted for a substantial share of the total. During the mid-1990s, as the economy roared into high gear and pushed the demand for capital to unprecedented levels, profit-seeking corruption in the form of misappropriation also increased. By the mid-1990s, transactive and profit-seeking corruption accounted for a majority of the cases filed by the procuratorate.

Increases in transactive and profit-seeking corruption morphed corruption. Other analysts have argued that corruption moved into new areas as the reform period progressed and have also posited that corruption changed shape. Sun, for example, argues that corruption became increasingly marketized and commercialized during the first two decades of reform while also spiraling upward to include senior officials with control over the allocation of property rights, investment resources, infrastructural contracting, commercial and legal enforcement, tax assessment and collection, and personnel appointments.[53] Similarly, Gong concludes that reforms enacted in the early 1990s bred new opportunities for corruption linked to stock markets, real estate, financial transactions, taxation, smuggling, and what she labels "cadre entrepreneurship."[54] Guo, finally, postulates a phased model wherein he sees China's economic transition as breeding new forms of corruption.[55] My argument goes further, asserting that not only did corruption spread into new areas and intensify as the reform period advanced, it also changed shape, becoming less based on plunder and more based on the buying and selling of public authority. In a sense, therefore, the marketization of the Chinese economy also led to the marketization of corruption as corrupt activity shifted outside the state apparatus and moved increasingly to the boundary between the market and the state. Corruption in China became less kleptocratic and more oriented toward manipulating public authority for the joint benefit of corrupt officials and unscrupulous business interests. Predatory corruption continued and in some areas and at some points constituted the sorts of pure plunder witnessed in places such as Equatorial Guinea.[56] The evidence, however, suggests that the new corruption was more parasitic than predatory in the sense that it fed off the growing economy rather than on the economy's vitals.

To say that corruption was parasitic begs a critical question: Why did it not reach the point where it became debilitating? It is widely assumed that worsening corruption has a propensity to spiral out of control as it moves from being infectious, reaches epidemic levels, and finally worsens into an endemic or perhaps even pandemic and economically fatal disease.[57] In one line of argument, it is said that this occurs because worsening corruption breeds a culture of corruption in which corruption becomes informally and quasi-acceptable because officials come to believe that "everybody else does it, so why shouldn't I cash in and grab my piece of the pie as well?"[58] A second argument holds that once corruption reaches a certain level, it swamps a regime's ability to resist and that once the tipping point has been passed, corruption will increase at exponential rates as the odds of detection rapidly diminish.[59]

As argued in chapter 6, even though corruption intensified as the deepening of reform progressively loosened controls and spawned new opportunities for illicit activity, corruption never really spiraled out of control. On the contrary, as corruption worsened, the regime responded first with a series of short-term bursts of hyper enforcement ("campaigns") designed to wipe out corruption. When these failed to dramatically reduce the level of corruption, the regime launched a sustained war of attrition. Unlike the stereotypical kleptocracy where corruption is allowed to fester and metastasize, the CCP has tried to fight the rot. And while its efforts may not have been entirely or perhaps even largely successful in dramatically reducing corruption, the mere fact that the regime battled corruption prevented it from spiraling out of control. The regime's sustained war on corruption has thus acted as a governor, albeit an imperfect one, that has at least kept corruption in check.

ANTICORRUPTION AND CORRUPTION

Now over a quarter-century old, the Chinese Communist Party's battle against corruption has often been dismissed as either a farce or a failure. To many observers, the CCP's endless verbal attacks on corruption and its occasional campaigns are little more than carefully scripted and staged political theater designed to create an illusion of a determination to fight the problem but in reality achieving little. Many thus dismiss China's anticorruption fight as a joke. Others believe that although the top leadership may be sincere in calling for vigorous action, it has consistently shied away from a true war of annihilation. To combine an increasingly popular saying and a paraphrase of words attributed to former KMT Chairman Jiang Jieshi, the leadership fears that if it were to kill corruption, it would lose political power because corruption has become an illness of the CCP's political heart.[1]

By and large, critics of China's ongoing war on corruption point to what they see as low rates of detection, lax punishments, and the assumption that the guilty are often protected by powerful patrons as evidence that the war has been largely ineffectual. As noted earlier, for instance, Qinglian He asserts that corruption has become a social "norm," that "all officials are taking kickbacks," and that honest officials are being "squeezed out" by dishonest officials.[2] Chengze Simon Fan and Herschel Grossman go much further, suggesting that the regime has adopted an informal policy of "selective toleration" and "selective enforcement." Corruption, they argue, provides local officials with illicit incentives to promote local economic development because they can skim off a share of the profits, and the regime tolerates corruption where it yields economic results. Tolerance, however, also gives the regime leverage over local officials because, according to Fan and Grossman, as long as the regime has "dirt" on all of them, it can selectively target officials who become too independent or whose political loyalty becomes suspect.[3]

An examination of the raw data on indictments reveals a potential complication. Whereas critics of China's anticorruption efforts suggest that corruption is spiraling out of control, the trend in the revealed rate of corruption (RRC) has been downward since 2000, and outside experts' estimates of the perceived level of corruption have hovered at about the same level since 1996, which seems to suggest that perhaps corruption is not getting worse as is often asserted. The upward spike in the total number of senior officials, however, suggests that even though the total number of cases has not risen, the perceived worsening over the last decade and a half is perhaps a function of a strong sense that at the senior levels the war on corruption is faltering as deterrents to corruption break down.

Minxin Pei dismisses the drop-off in indictments, arguing that if anything it reflects a failing anticorruption effort. He points to data showing that only one in four tips from the public about corruption is ever investigated. When allegations are investigated, he continues, formal charges are filed less than 40 percent of the time. Punishment rates are lower still. As a result, according to Pei, only 5 to 6 percent of CCP members accused of corruption are actually convicted.[4] Officials, he concludes, face a "negligible probability" of punishment, thus "making corruption a high-return, low-risk activity."[5] Moreover, according to Pei, the probability of punishment has decreased significantly since the mid-1990s. During the preceding decade, he argues, even though the number of officials assigned to the procuratorate increased significantly, the number of cases it accepted for investigation declined 50 percent between 1990 and 2003, with the implication that the intensity of enforcement has become more lax.[6] China's "lagging enforcement efforts" are so ineffectual, he concludes, that the Chinese state has degenerated into a decentralized collection of "predatory...local mafia states" and is in danger of becoming "incapacitated."[7]

Pei, in broad terms, implies that the gap between the actual rate of corruption (ARC) and the RRC has widened in the last decade and that by the mid-2000s the RRC represented perhaps as little as 1 percent of the ARC or even less.[8] If Pei is correct, the risk associated with corruption is indeed so low that it is hard to imagine that any but the most timid, the most severely risk-averse individuals would be scared off by the threat of punishment. Absent even some rough indication of the ARC, it is, however, impossible to know if Pei is right. In fact, Pei's claim rests on assumptions about something that is not only unmeasured but for all intents and purposes cannot be measured. Essentially, the validity of Pei's argument requires that we assume the observable measure (the RRC) is diverging from the unobservable measure (the ARC). Not only does Pei's claim, and, by extension, the general belief that China's anticorruption effort has been ineffectual, require that we assume something rather than observe it; the method Pei uses to derive it is questionable. A careful reexamination of the data reveals that while China's war on corruption may not have made dramatic inroads, and corruption remains at a relatively high level, it has succeeded in the sense that it has very likely controlled growth in corruption.

To understand why this might be the case, it is first necessary to break down the incentives for officials to either embrace or eschew corruption. As argued by Gary Becker and others, an individual's choice to engage in an illegal act is heavily influenced by the expected value of committing the crime versus the expected value of remaining honest, wherein the expected value of committing the crime is the payoff from the crime, minus the expected value of punishment, which is determined by the probability of getting caught and the severity of the punishment. Thus, for example, if a clerk in a liquor store is contemplating slipping a twenty-dollar bill out of the cash register, if he is a true rational actor he will have to weigh the benefit of twenty dollars against the chances he will be caught, lose his job and hence his wages, and possibly face jail time and then decide if given the risks it might be better not to steal the money and simply keep his job.[9] From this rather simple construct flow a variety of arguments highlighting other effects. For example, if the number of officials who become corrupt increases and enforcement resources remain constant, presumably the odds of getting caught will decrease because there is safety in a crowd. Risk aversion plays a role because a would-be corrupt official cannot precisely measure the odds of getting caught and must guess instead. Cautious officials are thus presumably more likely to fear they will get caught than risk takers who are much more apt to believe they are invincible and will never get caught.

Based on this rational choice model of the decision to remain honest or become corrupt, a government or agency seeking to reduce or control corruption has a wide range of options.

- It can seek to improve the aggregate level of honesty by educating officials and the public on the negative consequences of corruption, try to convince them that corruption is morally wrong, and signal that those subject to official extortion or witnesses to corruption that they should report illegal demands.
- It can reduce the opportunities for corruption by tightening controls and internal oversight over officials' actions by reducing officials' discretionary authority and regularizing how policies and regulations are implemented and enforced.
- It can make governmental functions more transparent and thus make it harder for corrupt officials and would-be corruptors to conceal their dirty work.

- It can reduce the power and autonomy of officials by giving the public democratic powers, strengthening public accountability, and allowing the press to aggressive report alleged corruption as well as setting up mechanisms (e.g., tip lines, websites, complaint boxes) through which the public can anonymously report corruption.
- It can reduce and rationalize regulations and procedures, thus reducing the red tape that affords officials opportunities to extract speed money and extort considerations from those having to do business with the government.
- It can tighten budgetary controls and conduct audits aimed at detecting fiscal irregularities.
- It can require officials to disclose all of their assets and punish those found with unexplainable assets.
- It can intensify policing by establishing new anticorruption agencies or increasing the resources and independence of existing agencies with the aim of increasing the odds of detections.
- It can conduct periodic crackdowns during which it initially offers those involved in corruption some sort of full or limited amnesty if they come clean and then shifts to a policy of hyper enforcement during which scrutiny is ramped up, the thresholds for indictment are lowered, and maximal punishments are imposed.
- It can send out undercover agents to offer bribes and kickbacks to officials in an effort to entrap corrupt officials.
- It can mandate stiffer punishments for those involved in corruption and adopt a zero-tolerance policy.

And, of course, it can do all of the above, which are only some of the most common and obvious measures. Regardless of what set of measures a regime adopts, the ultimate objective is to decrease the net expected value of engaging in corruption by increasing the perceived risk of detection and the negative payoffs, including criminal punishment, associated with getting caught. The goal of an effective anticorruption effort is thus only partly to punish those who have turned to corruption but more critically to convince those who have not that honesty is the better choice. Fighting corruption, in other words, is one part combat and two parts psychological warfare because the ultimate goal is to reduce corruption in the present by intensified enforcement and reductions in the opportunities for officials to misuse their authority while deterring corruption in the future.

The CCP has done many of the things the various anticorruption prescriptions suggest. This is not to say that it has done everything it should or that the steps it took were all properly and vigorously executed. The regime has, nevertheless, sought to create disincentives by increasing risk and consequences. In the conventional wisdom, the continued worsening of corruption is generally attributed to either insincerity or incompetence. But we have to remember that as the regime tried to fight corruption, as argued in chapter 5, the deepening of reform was vastly increasing the gains officials could obtain from abusing their ability to commodify and transfer state assets to the control of the emerging business sector. Given these cross pressures, in the pages that follow, I focus first on the issue of punishment in an attempt to assess the severity of the penalties corrupt officials might suffer and then on the more complicated task of trying to determine if the risk of getting caught has changed.

Punishment

Most critics of China's war on corruption advance an argument that combines risk and punishment rather than carefully disaggregating them and treating them as two distinct parts of the basic expected value model. In what is likely the most systematic examination of the various data, Pei seeks to show that corrupt officials face an extremely low risk or probability of prosecution and punishment by focusing on the rate at which the party's Discipline Inspection Commission (DIC) remands cases to the judicial system for criminal investigation and prosecution. Three major agencies are involved in the war on corruption. The DIC is tasked with investigating allegations of malfeasance by party members and has the authority to impose a variety of disciplinary measures ranging from issuing warnings and placing an individual on party probation up to expulsion from the party. As a nonjudicial organ, it does not have prosecutorial authority and cannot therefore inflict criminal punishments. The Ministry of Supervision has similar jurisdiction and authority in cases involving state officials. It also lacks judicial authority and is limited to the imposition of various administrative sanctions, with dismissal from office being the harshest. The procuratorate, which is part of the judicial system, does have legal authority to indict individuals on criminal charges and prosecute cases in a court of law. As a result, if either the DIC or the Ministry of Supervision believes that one of its cases warrants criminal charges, the case must be remanded to the procuratorate, which then conducts an investigation and, if warranted, issues an indictment. The case is then forwarded to the court system for trial, with the procuratorate acting as the prosecutor. According to Pei, only about one in twenty of those accused of malfeasance is ever prosecuted.

Pei's figure of a 5 to 6 percent remand rate is based on the best available data. I thus do not dispute his figure, but I believe his implicit suggestion that this means that the 94 to 95 percent of those investigated and let off were guilty of corruption is misleading. To begin with, the DIC's jurisdiction covers a much wider range of offenses than what is conventionally considered corruption. It is responsible for enforcing party discipline in general. The best available estimates suggest that only about a third of the alleged offenses the DIC deals with involve economic crimes and that about half of those do not involve corruption as conventionally defined.[10] Moreover, even though we do not have a breakdown of the severity of these cases, it seems likely that many of these economic cases may not have met the criteria for criminal investigation but may have instead involved petty offenses.[11] As such, two-thirds of DIC cases were likely not remanded because they involved various types of disciplinary infractions and some substantial, but unknown, share of the remaining third involved economic crimes that did not involve criminal offenses. If the preceding is true, then the percentage of serious corruption cases that the DIC remands to the judicial system would be several times the 5 to 6 percent that Pei cites. Absent better data, however, what that percentage might be cannot be estimated with precision.[12]

Although Pei may be correct that the number of cases the DIC remanded to the judicial system for criminal investigation might seem inordinately low,[13] the number of economic crime cases investigated and prosecuted by the judicial system was substantial. Between 2001 and 2006, the procuratorate accepted (shou'an) an average of approximately 58,000 cases of alleged corruption per year (see Table 6.1).[14] Of these, it conducted a preliminary investigation (chucha) in an average of 49,000 cases and terminated 9,000 (15 percent). Out of those it carried forward, prosecutors filed (li'an) an average of 31,500 cases involving 35,600 individuals for formal criminal investigation. An average of 17,400 cases accepted were conversely not filed (35 percent). Exactly what happened in these cases is not well documented. In some instances, investigators may have decided that the allegations were not supported and the accused was innocent. A substantial number of cases likely involved sums that did not reach the legal threshold for criminality and hence resulted in administrative punishments (xingzheng chufen) such as dismissal from office or demotion. In some share of these "dropped" cases, prosecutors presumably opted to exempt the accused from criminal indictment because they expressed repentance, handed over all their illegal gains, or provided information on others.

Among the cases it filed, the procuratorate concluded (yi zhencha zhongjie) an average of 29,600 cases, involving 33,400 individuals, of whom it bound over an average of 24,500 (90 percent) for trial (yisong shencha qisu). It closed the cases of 1,500 individuals (chexiao anjian), thus releasing the accused. In addition, an average of 1,400 individuals were bound over for trial but were not prosecuted (yisong bu qisu).[15] A residual group averaging 2,200 individuals was apparently left in some sort of legal limbo, having had their cases concluded but with no final decision on the disposition of their cases. In all likelihood, most of this

TABLE 6.1 Disposition of procuratorate case load, 2001–6

YEAR	ACCEPTED ALLEGATIONS, CASES	PRELIMINARY INVESTIGATIONS, CASES	NOT INVESTIGATED, CASES	PERCENTAGE NOT INVESTIGATED, CASES (%)	FILED FOR INVESTIGATION, CASES	NOT FILED, CASES	PERCENTAGE INVESTIGATED NOT FILED, CASES (%)	FILED FOR INVESTIGATION, INDIVIDUALS
2001	76,533	59,451	17,082	22.32	36,447	23,004	38.69	40,195
2002	67,935	56,642	11,293	16.62	34,716	21,926	38.71	38,022
2003	55,333	48,101	7,232	13.07	31,953	16,148	33.57	34,922
2004	53,418	46,391	7,027	13.15	30,548	15,843	34.15	35,031
2005	48,722	42,730	5,992	12.30	28,322	14,408	33.72	33,366
2006	45,057	39,975	5,082	11.28	27,119	12,856	32.16	31,949
Average	57,833	48,882	8,951	14.79	31,518	17,364	35.17	35,581

YEAR	CONCLUDED INVESTIGATIONS, CASES	CONCLUDED INVESTIGATIONS, INDIVIDUALS	FILED – CONCLUDED, INDIVIDUALS	PERCENTAGE CONCLUDED/FILED, INDIVIDUALS	REMANDED FOR PROSECUTION, CASES	PROSECUTED + CLOSED + NOT PROSECUTED, INDIVIDUALS	PERCENTAGE PROS + CLOSED + NOT PROS/ COMPLETED, INDIVIDUALS	COMPLETED – PROSECUTED + CLOSED + NOT PROSECUTED, CASES
2001	33,900	37,401	2,794	93.05	21,782	29,137	77.90	8,264
2002	33,085	36,142	1,880	95.06	19,980	27,032	74.79	9,110
2003	29,986	32,707	2,215	93.66	19,848	25,586	78.23	7,121
2004	28,525	32,493	2,538	92.75	22,178	28,405	87.42	4,088
2005	26,492	31,109	2,257	93.24	21,146	27,257	87.62	3,852
2006	25,697	30,256	1,693	94.70	20,711	26,754	88.43	3,502
Average	29,614	33,351	2,230	93.74	20,941	27,362	82.40	5,990

YEAR	REMANDED FOR PROSECUTION, INDIVIDUALS	PERCENTAGE INDIVIDUALS PROSECUTED (%)	CASE CLOSED, INDIVIDUALS	PERCENTAGE INDIVIDUALS CASE CLOSED (%)	MOVED NOT TO PROSECUTE, INDIVIDUALS	PERCENTAGE INDIVIDUALS MOVED NOT TO PROSECUTE (%)
2001	24,909	85.49	2,098	7.20	2,130	7.31
2002	22,676	83.89	2,342	8.66	2,014	7.45
2003	22,631	88.45	1,576	6.16	1,379	5.39
2004	26,131	91.99	1,106	3.89	1,168	4.11
2005	25,530	93.66	876	3.21	851	3.12
2006	25,115	93.87	743	2.78	896	3.35
Average	24,499	89.56	1,457	5.32	1,406	5.12

Source: Zhongguo Jiancha Nianjian [Procuratorial Yearbook of China] (Beijing: Zhongguo Jiancha Chubanshe, various years).

residual group included cases that initiated in one year but were not concluded until the following year (or even later).

Between 2001 and 2004, the court system accepted an average of 20,900 corruption cases for adjudication and handed down sentences in an average of 18,200 cases (87 percent). Although specific sentencing data for corruption trials are not currently available, data for the broader category of economic crime likely provide a reasonable guide.[16] Of those convicted of economic crimes, 21 percent received prison sentences in excess of five years (including life, death with two-year suspension,[17] and death), 31 percent were sentenced to five or fewer years, 36 percent received probation, and 6 percent were exempted (*mianxing*) from criminal punishment. Only 1 percent of those tried were found innocent.[18] In broad terms, therefore, of the approximately 50,000 individuals on whom the procuratorate conducted preliminary investigations each year, about one in five (roughly 9,500) ended up in prison, one in ten received probation, and close to 20,000 received lesser, nonjudicial, administrative punishments.

Because the Chinese government does not publish systematic data on capital punishment or detailed sentencing data, it is difficult to ascertain the extent to which those convicted on corruption-related charges face death or long prison terms. The number of documented death sentences is, however, considerable. The "Peoples Republic of China: The Death Penalty Log" compiled by Amnesty International (AI) identifies 350 death sentences for economic crimes between the summer of 1995 and the end of 2000, including 139 in which the accused was listed as having been executed, 65 in which the accused received the death penalty but AI could not confirm that the sentence had been carried out, and 146 (42 percent) cases where the defendant was granted a suspended death sentence.[19] My database of 4,200 high-profile cases yielded 645 cases involving capital punishment, of which 409 (63 percent) involved death sentences and 236 (37 percent) involved suspended death. Even if they avoided capital punishment, officials convicted on corruption-related charges faced stiff punishment. Among the 2,400 officials in my database for whom I was able to locate sentencing data, 30 percent were sentenced to over ten years, with an additional 11 percent serving five to ten years (see Table 6.2).

It is sometimes asserted that even though the penalties for corruption may appear harsh, only the small fry end up being punished while the big tigers—those with power and political connections—escape or get off with a slap on the wrist. Once again, the data suggest otherwise. Politics undoubtedly plays a role in China's anticorruption effort, and there can be little question that powerful officials escape prosecution because of their protective umbrellas (*baohusan*). Nevertheless, 40,304 senior officials were charged with corruption between 1988 and 2008, including two members of the Politburo (Chen Xitong and Chen Liangyu);

TABLE 6.2 Sentencing in high-profile cases

SENTENCE	NUMBER OF SENTENCES	PERCENTAGE SPECIFIED SENTENCES (%)
Death	409	16.71
Death w/two year reprieve	236	9.64
Subtotal	645	26.35
Life	262	10.70
Sixteen or more years	138	5.64
Ten to fifteen years	348	14.22
Five to ten years	280	11.44
One to five years	267	10.91
Subtotal	1,295	52.90
Administrative or disciplinary punishment	445	18.18
Other	63	2.57
Known sentences	2,448	
Total cases	4,040	

Source: Data collected by author from search of the LexisNexis database.

65 other officials holding ministerial or provincial leadership positions; 2,231 holding senior positions at the bureau or prefectural levels; and 32,286 holding senior positions at the department and county levels.[20] Out of these, between 1992 and 2008, at least 7,070 stood trial, including 47 senior ministerial and provincial officials, 927 bureau and prefecture officials, and 6,096 departmental and county-level leaders.[21]

The available data also show that it is not the case that the big tigers always get off with a mere slap on the paw while the small fry receive stiff sentences. At least eighteen senior officials have been executed, eighteen received suspended death sentences, and twenty were sentenced to life. In all, in a quarter of the cases covered in my database for which sentences were specified, those convicted received very stiff sentences (see Table 6.3). An additional 42 percent of senior officials were sent to prison after being convicted. Among lower-ranked officials, 18 percent of those sentenced were executed or given suspended death sentences, 10 percent were given life sentences, and 46 percent went to prison. Punishment was even harsher for the managers of industrial, financial, and commercial enterprises, with 32 percent receiving capital punishment, while 37 percent of bank officers and over 40 percent of managers and bankers convicted ended up with prison sentences. Assuming that the aggregate statistics on economic crime cases handled by the courts are a reasonable guide, only a tiny fraction (1 to 2 percent) walked away scot-free. At least for those corrupt officials who get caught and prosecuted, therefore, the consequences can be dire, including a bullet to the back of the head. We cannot therefore dismiss corruption as essentially risk free or conclude that China's anticorruption drive is some sort of sham paper tiger. The waves of panic and fear that were evident in the wake of the fall of Politburo members Chen Xitong in Beijing in 1995 and Chen Liangyu in Shanghai in 2006, in fact, imply that even very powerful officials fear that they can get caught and that if they do, they are likely to face harsh justice.[22]

In sum, the data on cases handled by the judicial system reveal that on average 20,000 individuals are convicted on corruption-related charges each year and that about half of these go to prison. Furthermore, we have evidence that hundreds of officials have either been executed or sent to prison for life after being convicted of corruption. The claim that corrupt officials get off with a mere slap on the wrist is thus unsustainable. Sentences handed down in China were much harsher than those given to U.S. officials prosecuted in federal courts in the United States.[23] To begin with, no official in the United States was executed or given a suspended death sentence whereas, among the 2,400 senior officials included in my database, 645 Chinese officials did. Nor was a single U.S. official sentenced to life, a sentence given to 262 out of 2,400 Chinese officials in my database. Among my sample alone, therefore, nearly a thousand Chinese convicted on corruption charges received penalties exponentially harsher than those handed down in the United States.

A comparison of average sentences also shows that senior Chinese officials who received lesser sentences faced much stiffer penalties. Using a sample of 116 high-profile cases prosecuted by the U.S. Department of Justice's Public Integrity Section in 2005 as a baseline, the average sentence in the United States was thirty-one months, just under three years.[24] Among the cases I analyzed, the average sentence in China was just over ten years—four times as long.[25] In the United States, ten of the 116 prosecuted in 2005 received sentences of more than five years. Thus, whereas 8.5 percent of Americans convicted for corruption went to prison for five or more years, 85 percent of those convicted in China and sent to prison went to prison for more than five years. Sixty-two percent of those convicted in the United States, by contrast, were sentenced to less than five years, and 24 percent were either remanded to house arrest or given probation. Compared with their U.S. counterparts, therefore, Chinese officials faced much harsher punishments.

Analysis of the penalties handed down to Chinese officials convicted of corruption makes it clear that the law is not a toothless tiger in China. A careful

TABLE 6.3 Sentencing high-profile cases, by rank (selected ranks)

RANK	NOT SPECIFIED	DEATH	SUSPENDED DEATH SENTENCE	CAPITAL PUNISHMENT AS A PERCENTAGE OF KNOWN SENTENCES (%)	LIFE	TEN YEARS TO LIFE	FIVE TO TEN YEARS	ONE TO FIVE YEARS	LESS THAN A YEAR OR NON-PRISON SENTENCE	TOTAL
Minister	6	1	1	11.11	2	3	—	2	9	24
Provincial secretary	4	—	—	—	1	4	—	—	1	10
Governor	2	4	3	25.93	—	4	2	2	12	29
Municipal party secretary	3	—	—	—	—	—	—	—	3	6
Mayor	57	7	11	19.78	7	20	15	3	28	148
Prefecture secretary	5	—	1	9.09	1	4	—	2	3	16
Prefecture chief	1	—	—	—	—	1	—	0	1	3
County secretary	23	5	1	12.77	8	12	7	3	11	70
County magistrate	24	1	1	7.14	1	5	4	5	11	52
Leading cadres	125	18	18	15.45	20	53	28	17	79	358
Ministerial officials	31	5	3	19.51	5	11	11	4	2	72
Provincial officials	103	18	16	14.53	30	51	24	22	73	337
Municipal officials	197	22	20	17.50	18	51	44	24	61	437
County officials	57	14	4	28.57	6	10	4	11	14	120
District officials	26	5	4	20.93	6	8	5	6	9	69
Ordinary cadres	414	64	47	17.87	65	131	88	67	159	1,035
Managers	435	107	75	31.99	74	109	53	64	87	1,004
Bank officers	103	36	13	37.12	17	26	17	13	10	235
Total	1,077	225	153	24.31	176	319	186	161	335	2,632

Source: Data collected by author from search of the LexisNexis database.

accounting shows that contrary to Pei's claim that most of the guilty walk free, the progressive decreases in the number of corruption cases from the stage of preliminary investigation to formal investigation, indictment, trial, and sentencing are largely due to the fact that many of the cases are deemed not to warrant formal criminal prosecution. Moreover, it would be wrong to assume that those who do not end up on trial get off scot-free. Administrative penalties might not sound bad compared to death, but they can devastate careers, ruin reputations, and lead to disgrace. Officials can lose their jobs and find themselves unemployable pariahs. Even if an official avoids getting sacked, she faces the possibility of demotion and reassignment to dead-end jobs. To make matters even worse, administrative sanctions are generally handed out for relatively minor infractions. According to the 1997 Criminal Code, an official can be sacked for taking bribes totaling less than ¥5,000, the equivalent of about US$650 based on an average exchange rate between 2005 and 2010.

An important caveat is in order before I proceed with the analysis. The data I use in this section to calculate the severity of punishments comes from an admittedly unrepresentative sample of cases. By and large, the cases I use involve high-level, high stakes corruption. As a result, the penalties handed down are very likely, almost certainly, much harsher than those handed down in ordinary cases. Recall, however, that what has driven the qualitative evolution of corruption is the worsening not of corruption as a whole but significant increases in high-level, high-stakes corruption. Thus, even though the sample is obviously unrepresentative, it applies directly to the sort of corruption I associate with the deepening of reform. As such, even though Pei and He may assume that only the small fry and the chumps end up getting punished, in actuality even a senior official contemplating a bribe or other corrupt act faces a punitive regime that includes the possibility of a bullet in the back of the head or, short of that, a lengthy spell in a Chinese prison.

The severity of punishments, however, only matters if the risk of getting caught is non-negligible. If an official expects that his or her chances of getting caught are minimal, then harsh penalties are essentially irrelevant. In the following section, therefore, I turn to the most difficult part of the analysis: assessing risk.

Risk

Risk—the probability that a corrupt official gets caught—is the devil in the details of all work on corruption. So long as we cannot measure the actual rate of corruption, we cannot calculate what percentage of the total we observe in hard measures such as the revealed rate of corruption. Thus, although we know how many corrupt officials were caught, we cannot know how many corrupt officials were not caught. Do half of corrupt officials get caught? One in ten? We cannot tell. Nor can we determine if the ARC:RRC ratio is constant over time, whether it varies randomly, or if there are important secular trends. If the RRC goes up, does that mean more officials are corrupt, or does it mean the regime ordered a crackdown? If the RRC goes down, are fewer officials corrupt or has enforcement slacked off and fewer are getting caught? Sometimes we know the RRC spikes upward because the regime announces an anticorruption campaign (as it did in 1982, 1986, 1989, and 1993). By assumption, during these periods the percentage of corrupt officials caught up in the dragnet increases. But so long as we cannot compare the RRC to the ARC, we have no grounds for assuming that the RRC is a constant linear function of the ARC and hence that movements in the RRC mirror movements in the ARC.

More critically, we have no way of knowing if the share of corrupt officials indicted represents a significant share of the total or an inconsequential fraction of the total. Using experts to estimate the perceived level of corruption does little to get us around the underlying trap because at the end of the day most of the so-called experts must themselves derive their assessments from the observable but unreliable hard data.[26] The RRC, in short, records the "body count" without providing information on risk. Without some sense of risk, it is impossible to determine if the odds of capture are sufficient that the relatively harsh punishments described in the previous section are meaningful. On a gut level, of course, we cannot discount the fact that tens of thousands of Chinese officials are punished, with some 10,000 going to prison each year. But to more fully appreciate the efficacy of the CCP's protracted war against corruption, at least a broad sense of risk, and particularly changes in risk, is required.

Although we are unable to estimate aggregate risk by comparing the RRC to the ARC, we can examine risk on an individual level. Mathematically, the RRC is the fraction of all cases in which corrupt officials get caught and hence also represents the "risk" of getting caught. That is:

$$\text{ARC} = \frac{\text{Corrupt Officials}}{\text{Total Officials}}$$

$$\text{RRC} = \frac{\text{Officials Prosecuted}}{\text{Total Officials}}$$

$$\frac{\text{RRC}}{\text{ARC}} = \text{Percentage of Corrupt Officials Prosecuted}$$

$$\frac{\text{RRC}}{\text{ARC}} \approx \text{Odds of Prosecution}$$

Thus, if the RRC is a quarter of the ARC and one in four corrupt officials gets caught, then a corrupt official has a one-in-four chance of getting caught. Similarly, if one in ten officials is corrupt but only one in fifty is prosecuted, the odds of prosecution will be 20 percent. If five in ten are corrupt and one in fifty is prosecuted, the odds of prosecution will be 4 percent.

Because we can restate the RRC-ARC gap in terms of risk, it is possible to shift from aggregate measures of the level of corruption to data on individuals charged with corruption and specifically the length of time between when they become corrupt and when they get caught. To do so, we must conceive of corruption as a form of iterated game wherein once officials commit a corrupt act, they face a series of lotteries (games of chance) in which they may either evade capture and punishment or may get caught.[27] Each lottery is governed by a set of odds determined largely by the RRC-ARC gap—which we cannot determine. We can, however, begin to make some inferences about variations in risk over time by examining differences in distribution of when corrupt officials first engage in corruption and when they get caught.

The analysis begins with the simple observation that if the odds of getting caught are high, it is likely that corrupt officials will be caught in the first few lotteries and that as the game progresses more and more corrupt officials will be caught, albeit at a decreasing rate. Thus, for example, if the probability of getting caught in any round is 50 percent, according to a simple chained probability model, in a repeated lottery the chances a corrupt official will be caught within two rounds is 75 percent, and after six rounds 98 percent will have been caught. If, however, the probability is 10 percent in each round, a corrupt official would have a greater than 53 percent change of avoiding detection after six rounds and after ten rounds would still have a 38.7 percent chance of getting away with his or her crimes.[28] In slightly different terms, if we begin with a group of 100 corrupt officials, if the odds of getting caught are 10 percent, a total of 47 will be caught in six rounds whereas 99 will be caught in six rounds if the odds are 50 percent.

Using this method to first estimate the number of officials who will be caught in each successive round and then using some arbitrarily selected round as the last round, we can calculate what percentage of all of those who get caught will be caught in each round. Thus, in the example used above, if the odds of getting caught are 10 percent after six rounds, a total of 47 out of the hypothetical group of 100 corrupt officials will get caught. Based on that figure, we can then determine that 21 percent of those who will be get caught will be caught in the first round (10/47), 19 percent in the second round (9/47), etc. By contrast, if the probability of getting caught is 50 percent, then half of those who will get caught will get caught in the first round, 76 percent will have been caught by the second round, etc. Comparative statics modeling can then be used to calculate a hypothetical set of lag distributions based on alternative probabilities of capture.

From this simple one-group model, it is possible to develop a more complicated model that better mimics the real world using a dynamic generation model which begins with a group of 1,000 officials, some of whom become corrupt and some whom remain honest. It subjects the group of corrupt officials to a lottery, factoring out that proportion who get caught, and then passes both the honest officials and the corrupt officials who escaped capture to the next round where those who escaped capture continue to face the possibility of getting caught for their previous crimes. If we wish to assume that corrupt officials will continue to commit new crimes until they get caught, the model can be structured to subject those engaged in serial corruption to multiple lotteries in each round, with the odds of capture for past crimes being discounted compared to the odds for new crimes.[29] In each successive round, a share of those officials who were honest in the previous round can be assumed to "go bad," in which case they must face the capture lottery. Finally, in each round new officials replace the corrupt officials who get caught and they are in turn plugged into a corruption lottery in which some remain honest and others turn corrupt. Those who turn corrupt then face the capture lottery, etc. Regardless of how simple or complex we make the analysis, ultimately what we find is that when the hypothetical probability of capture is high, then the crime-capture lag distribution will be "steep" and fall off rapidly. As the probability falls, the distribution will become progressively flatter, with a smaller percentage of those who ultimately get caught being captured in the first rounds of the game. Even without complex modeling, intuition implies that if the percentage of those captured soon after their first offense is much higher in a particular year than in another, then the odds of capture were presumably higher in that year than in the other.

Before examining the data, it is important to reiterate that crime-capture lags do not allow us to calculate the probability of capture or estimate what percentage of corrupt officials get caught. Instead, these data allow us to indirectly compare the odds in one year or time period to another and assess whether the distribution of crime-capture lags is associated with a different probability of capture in the other.

Data on the lag between first offense (crime) and indictment (capture) were drawn from a database of approximately 4,300 high-profile cases, of which data on both crime and capture were available in 3,037 cases. According to the data on indictments by year, during the 1980s, about half of those indicted in any given year had been engaged in corruption for two years or less and nearly 90 percent had been engaged in corruption for five years or less (see Figure 6.1). Over the

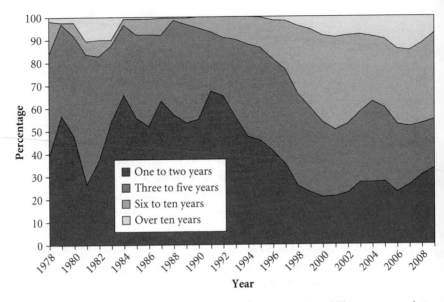

FIGURE 6.1. Crime-capture lag distribution by year captured (three-year moving average), 1978–2008

Source: Author's database.

Note: The sharp upward movement in the share of those caught within two years, or what we might term "short-timers," in the post-2006 years is misleading. The lag between crime and capture ensures that as the data get closer to the present, more of those who will eventually get caught have not yet been caught, thus reducing the number of longer duration cases.

next decade, the proportion of "short timers" (one to two years) fell by about half, and by the early 2000s only about 25 percent of those indicted had been corrupt for two years or less.[30] The number of "long timers," those who managed to evade capture for more than five years, meanwhile, increased dramatically, and from about 2000 on this group accounted for about half of those indicted. Looking at the data in terms of when those indicated first engaged in corruption suggests that about a third of corrupt officials got caught within two years. This has remained pretty much constant, while the proportion of long timers increased from about 20 percent in the early 1980s to about 35 percent in the late 1990s.

Interpreting the data is complicated by several factors. First, as argued in chapter 4, the data suggest that the real explosion in the sort of high-level corruption associated with the cases in this database occurred during the mid-1990s, as evidenced by the sharp rise in the cumulative rate of corruption and its divergence from the RRC (see Figure 4.7). Clearly, enforcement lagged behind the growth in corruption during that period. In this same period, we see the number of short timers drop by half. Second, because the data examined in chapter 4 show that over time, high-level corruption, as evidenced in both the aggregate data on indictments by the procuratorate and convictions by the courts, has apparently steadily and significantly increased, there is a natural aging process at work. Quite simply, over time, not only has the number of corrupt officials increased, the pool of those who have escaped capture in the past has also increased. The growth in the number of long timers thus reflects the fact that many of those indicted in the first decade of the 2000s were part of the new wave of corrupt officials that formed in the mid-1990s when the deepening of reform created a host of new opportunities for corruption. Third, the fact that investigators are now catching more officials who have been engaged in long-term serial corruption can be interpreted as evidence not of a faltering anticorruption effort but of one that is increasingly effective at cracking complex cases and breaking down the protective umbrellas that facilitate sustained corruption. Similarly, even if the odds of capture never change, the more times corrupt officials play the capture lottery and accept new bribes or embezzle more public money, the odds of getting caught increases. In very simple terms, if the capture lottery is nothing more than a flip of the coin in which heads you win, tails you lose, if you flip the coin enough times you are going to get tails. I might also suggest that over time corrupt officials are apt to get sloppy and leave more and more telltale signs of wrongdoing. Thus, as China's post-Mao corruption problem has aged, it is natural that the pool of long-timers has increased, and as that pool has grown, long-timers as a percentage of those caught would have also increased.

With these considerations in mind, the data are consistent with a relatively stable crime-capture lag structure but one in which the maturing of corruption— that is, the increased distance between the onset of increased corruption in the 1980s and the intensification of corruption during the 1990s—has led to an increase in the number of officials who have been involved in corruption for extended periods. It is particularly striking that the shift in the lag structures from one in which most of those indicted were caught within five years to one in which only about half of those indicted were caught within five years can be connected to the rise in both the number of indictments of senior officials (county level and above) and the cumulative level of corruption, both of which occurred in the 1990s. If we understand that period to have been one of qualitative changes in the nature of corruption and one in which the emergence of a form of corruption that, because of its nature (high-level, high-stakes), is likely to have been much more deeply hidden, then it makes sense that we should find a significant shift in the lag distribution. Once that qualitative shift had taken place, the lag structure remained relatively stable. This suggests that the risk of capture was also relatively stable during most of the 1990s. This, in turn, suggests that the RRC-ARC ratio also remained relatively stable. If that is the case, then the downward trending of the RRC evident in recent years would suggest that the ARC has been falling or that the trend in the ARC is not diverging from the RRC and is not rising rapidly. The most prudent interpretation is thus that corruption has remained at about the same level for nearly a decade.

But if risks have remained stable and there is no definitive evidence in the data on the lag between crime and capture, is risk credible? That is, does an official involved in corruption stand a reasonable chance of getting caught? As argued repeatedly, there is no way to estimate the ARC, and so long as the ARC is unknowable there is no way to estimate the probability that a corrupt official will get caught. We can, however, derive some sort of notion of what risk might look like by comparing the cumulative level of corruption (CLC) to the RRC for the sample of officials contained in the database on high-level, high-visibility cases. Dividing the number of indictments (i.e., the RRC) in a particular year by the total number of officials who were corrupt that year (i.e., the CLC) yields the percentage of corrupt officials caught that year. The results of this exercise suggest that about 10 percent of those involved in corruption get caught each year (see Figure 6.2). That is, of course, 10 percent of the officials who ultimately got caught. Ten percent is, therefore, a minimal estimate of the risk of capture.

To some, a 10 percent chance of getting caught might seem miniscule, so low that the risk of capture could hardly serve as a check on corruption, even when tied to the risk of the relatively harsh punishments discussed in the preceding section. Recall, however, that 10 percent is the risk of getting caught in each successive round of the capture lottery. Because corrupt officials remain legally liable for punishment after they have committed a corrupt offense and because it is clear from the case evidence that once officials become corrupt they are likely to engage in new acts of corruption, having ducked punishment once, corrupt officials still have to hope they will be as lucky the next time. Given that the database shows that corrupt officials do in fact get caught years, even decades after they first "went bad," the evidence suggests that in the end many find that their luck runs out. Moreover, if an official engages in repeated acts of corruption and then gets caught, the severity of the offense will presumably be greater than for a first time offender. There is, therefore, something of a ladder effect that ratchets up the severity of the punishment and those who find themselves in the "lucky 90" repeatedly can find themselves in the "unlucky 10." In this light, the fact that less than 10 percent of those involved in corruption get caught each year might appear rather less inconsequential.

The relatively stable risk of capture is also noteworthy. As noted in this and the previous chapter, the literature on anticorruption stresses the importance of systematic reductions in the opportunities for corruption, improvement in the moral fiber of public officials, and keeping corruption at some controlled level.

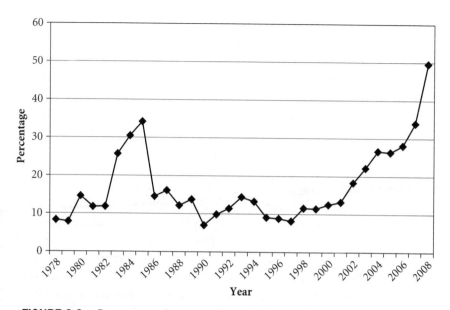

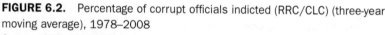

FIGURE 6.2.   Percentage of corrupt officials indicted (RRC/CLC) (three-year moving average), 1978–2008
Source: Author's database.
Note: Once again, the upward swing in the indictment-corruption ratio in recent years is an artifact of the cumulative level of corruption becoming less complete as it gets close to the present because long-duration cases are not included.

In particular, the literature points to the danger that rising levels of corruption will swamp a government's anticorruption resources, leading to a sharp downturn in the risk of capture and a flood of new corruption as officials see that others are getting away with it and decide to grab a piece of the action. In the mid-1990s when awareness of corruption grew, many of those writing on the topic talked about an accelerating spiral and suggested corruption was on the verge of becoming a rapidly metastasizing cancer. In many ways, the data examined in this and the two preceding chapters suggest they were not entirely wrong. Corruption was clearly intensifying in the mid-1990s and morphing from a combination of low-level bribery and official profiteering into new forms in which senior officials were beginning to rake in huge sums as economic assets and property were transferred from the state to the market. Data on the CLC derived from cases of high-level, high-stakes corruption clearly show a rapid rise in the total number of officials engaged in corruption and a widening gap between the CLC and the RRC. The data on crime-capture lag distributions also show a marked decrease during this period in the percentage of corrupt officials captured soon after they first became corrupt and within five years of their first offense. But by the early 2000s, the pattern had stabilized and the shape of crime-capture lags remained relatively constant. (The apparent increase in the percentage of officials caught within the first two years in Figure 6.1 is misleading because the percentage of long-timers who ultimately get caught naturally decreases as the data approach the present.) Overall, therefore, the data suggest a crisis in corruption in the mid-1990s. They do not suggest that corruption then spiraled out of control. On the contrary, they would seem to indicate that intensified anticorruption efforts succeeded in keeping corruption at a high but relatively stable level between 2000 and 2010.

Large n-samples of cases provide one way of trying to assess the extent of risk. There is, however, another simpler and more straightforward method. To many observers, each new revelation of corruption in high places, each new scandal involving senior officials and huge sums of money, is evidence of worsening corruption. In reality, however, each new scandal can be interpreted as evidence that the regime's anticorruption efforts are working. In China, rumors of corruption in high places abound. But almost without exception the big cases that tend to shape our thinking about the severity of corruption are those in which the authorities have already cracked the case and publicized it. Looking at some of the most visible and notorious cases, in fact, shows not so much that corruption has run wild but that the authorities are willing to attack corruption in high places.

It is no doubt true, of course, that some corruption in high places remains covered up and that some corrupt officials escape punishment because of their political clout and connections. It would also be wrong to assume that politics does not play a role in determining who gets prosecuted and that some prosecutions are not driven by factional infighting. An examination of four major scandals, nevertheless, shows that even the most powerful and politically entrenched officials are not immune to the risk of prosecution and harsh punishment. In the pages that follow, I discuss the case of Chen Xitong, the Xiamen Smuggling Ring case, the Chen Liangyu case, and the Chongqing Organized Crime case. All have been discussed elsewhere. My point is thus not so much to reveal anything new about these cases but to reinforce the point that even though the data suggest that the risk of capture may be low, it is far from negligible, even for those with deep political connections.

The case involving CCP Politburo member and First Secretary of the Beijing Municipal Party Committee Chen Xitong broke in early April 1995 when Beijing Vice Mayor Wang Baosen killed himself two days after being questioned by a party committee about his involvement with a company based in Wuxi (Jiangsu).[31] In early 1995, local investigators in Wuxi had begun looking into the financial dealings of a bankrupt investment company named Xinxing. Xinxing, they quickly discovered, was a massive Ponzi scheme in which investors were promised fat returns on their investments. In short order, Xinxing had taken in an estimated ¥3.2 billion (US$383 million) from nearly four hundred state enterprises and offices in twelve provinces. Rather than investing, however, Xinxing was paying its early investors out of the income from new investors. As is inevitably true, ultimately the income from new investors proved insufficient to meet previous obligations, and the scheme collapsed overnight leaving behind a mountain of debt. As they began to unravel Xinxing's finances, the investigators detained two officials from Beijing, Li Min and Chen Jian, who admitted they had been serving as bagmen for Wang Baosen and bringing down suitcases of cash drawn from the Beijing municipal "small treasury" (*xiaojinku*). This was a slush fund in which Wang and others had deposited funds obtained from a variety of sources, including commissions paid to the city by developers, irregular fees, and the profits from businesses the city owned under the table. Li, a deputy secretary in the Beijing Municipal Public Security Bureau, and Chen, who was Chen Xitong's secretary, also admitted to having taken bribes from Zhou Beifang, the head of the powerful Capital Steel Group (Shougang), and other businessmen seeking access to the municipal slush fund for investment purposes as well as help arranging permission to travel to Hong Kong and other overseas destinations. During a meeting with Wang on April 2, the party investigatory committee—which included Chen Xitong—asked him about his role in a number of development projects. One of these involved rumors that Hong Kong developer Li Ka-shing had paid bribes to officials for revoking a twenty-year lease granted to McDonald's for a property located at the corner of Wangfujing Street and Chang'an Boulevard and then leasing the property to Li.[32] Wang apparently did not reveal much and was allowed to return home. He then traveled to a luxury villa he had built in Huirou, a town outside Beijing, and put a pistol to his head. In the weeks the followed his suicide, investigators discovered that Wang had not only been sending money down to Xinxing in Wuxi, he had also been channeling money from the municipal slush fund into investment schemes run by his brother (Wang Baochuan), his mistress, and a number of his cronies. Thereafter, they determined that both Wang and Chen had routinely collected commissions from developers seeking leases for prime real estate in downtown Beijing and that Chen had accepted ¥200 million (US$24 million).[33] They found that Chen's wife and his son Chen Xiaotong been heavily involved in the solicitation of commissions from real estate developers and others.[34] Chen was detained, and a wave of arrests followed during the summer. After two years in party detention, Chen was handed over to prosecutors, tried, convicted on charges of corruption and dereliction of duty in 1998, and given a thirteen-year sentence.[35] His son received a twelve-year sentence for bribery and misuse of public funds.[36]

Like Chen Xitong, Politiburo member and Secretary of the Shanghai Municipal CCP Committee Chen Liangyu (no relation to Chen Xitong) was caught
diverting funds into illegal investments. Chen authorized his lieutenants to lend
money from the municipal pension fund to a number of investors and businessmen rather than depositing it in the Pudong Development Bank as required by
law. Loans were made to Yu Zhifei, a businessman who was seeking to develop
a Formula One race track in the city; Zhang Rongkun, the owner of Shanghai
Electric, a major telecommunications firm, and director of Fuxi Investments,
a construction firm involved in the construction of the Shanghai-Hangzhou,
Jiading-Jinshan, and Suzhou-Hangzhou expressways; and Han Fanghe, the
manager of Hua An Investments, one of the largest investment firms in China.[37]
According to investigators, close to ¥33.9 billion (UDS\$4.9 billion) was diverted
out of the pension fund, most of which apparently went to either Yu's racing
venture or Zhang's highway projects.[38] Zhang, for example, reportedly obtained
loans totaling ¥3.45 billion (US\$496 million) from the pension fund.[39] Chen also
arranged the 2002 sale of the city government's stake in the Shanghai Road and
Bridge Development Corporation to Zhang's Shanghai Fuxi Investment Holdings Corporation at a very low price.[40] In return, Zhang financed Chen's flamboyant lifestyle, including the cost of maintaining a string of mistresses.

Chen used his position first as mayor and then party secretary to help his
brother Chen Liangjun obtain a large parcel of land at a price of ¥344 million
(US\$50 million), considerably less than its real value. His brother quickly resold
the land and made a fast profit of ¥118 million (US\$17 million).[41] Chen's son
Chen Weili was hired by Huawen Investments at a salary in excess of ¥300,000
(US\$43,000) a year, presumably with an eye to gaining influence with his father.[42]
Chen's wife Wang Yiling, who held the post of president of the Shanghai Charity
Foundation, was charged with accepting bribes on his behalf and speculating in
stocks with the help of Zhou Zhengyi, a local developer who had been convicted
on fraud charges in 2003 but was then released after serving only part of his sentence. Chen's brother-in-law Zhu Wenjin, a section chief in the Shanghai Municipal Housing, Land, and Resources Bureau, was also arrested on bribery charges.

By the time the investigation was complete, more than three dozen individuals had been charged with wrongdoing, including fourteen municipal officials
and Qiu Xiaohua, the Director of the National Bureau of Statistics. Chen was
sentenced to eighteen years in prison for his role in diverting pension funds and
accepting ¥2.39 million (US\$344,000) in bribes from Yu, Zhang, Han, and other
real estate developers.[43] Zhang Rongkun received nineteen years, three others
were given suspended death sentences, and five were sentenced to life in prison.

There can be little doubt that both the Chen Xitong and Chen Liangyu cases
were highly political. It is widely assumed that the fall of Chen Xitong, who had

played a central role in the suppression of antigovernment demonstrations in 1989, was part of an effort by Jiang Zemin's "Shanghai Gang" to consolidate its grip on power by seizing control of the Beijing party apparatus. Chen Liangyu, conversely, is said to have been the victim of Hu Jintao's effort to leverage members of Jiang's Shanghai Gang out of key positions of power, including control over China's economic capital, and replace them with loyalists from his Communist Youth League faction.[44] Politics does not, however, appear to have been the primary trigger in either case. Chen Xitong was caught in a cascading scandal that began with the collapse of the Wuxi pyramid scheme and the arrest of the two bagmen from the Beijing municipal apparatus. The case then exploded after Wang Baosen put a pistol to his head and killed himself. The genesis of the Chen Liangyu scandal is less clear but it appears that investigators had been looking into the murky world of Shanghai business, including rumors that funds from the pension fund were being loaned out illegally, for some time before Chen was detained in Beijing after attending a meeting of the Politburo.

The duration of the two cases was quite different. Both Chens reportedly turned corrupt in 1990. At that time, Chen Xitong was mayor of Beijing. He was promoted to secretary in 1992, just before the beginning of the post–Southern Tour boom. Less than three years later, he was in detention. Chen Liangyu, by contrast, was still climbing up through the ranks, serving as a district magistrate in Shanghai in the early 1990s. In 1996, he was appointed deputy mayor and then took over as mayor in late 2001. Two years later, he was selected as secretary of the Municipal CCP Committee. Chen Liangyu was clearly much more successful than Chen Xitong in evading detection, even though he was rumored to have led a playboy lifestyle that was not compatible with his official salary for years before he was detained in 2006. (While Chen Xitong apparently did not flout his illegal wealth, his son reportedly did.) Times had, of course changed. Whereas private cars, luxury condominiums, and flashy nightclubs were rare in China in 1995, by 2006 they had become commonplace in Shanghai and other major cities. The wealth of China's elites, moreover, had grown exponentially during the intervening decade. Chen Liangyu could thus more easily get away with a sort of flamboyant lifestyle that would have been unimaginable in 1995. Nevertheless, in the end both were caught and, while their political connections may have kept investigators at bay for a while, in the end they were not sufficient to protect them from prosecution and conviction.

The size of the corrupt rings tied to the two Chens pales in comparison to those associated with the Xiamen smuggling case. In the fall of 1999, several hundred investigators from Beijing and elsewhere descended on the port city of Xiamen where a ring of smugglers led by a man named Lai Changxing had reportedly smuggled in a total of ¥53 billion (US$6.4 billion) worth of petroleum, edible oil, cigarettes, automobiles, electronics, pharmaceuticals, and other goods between 1996 and 1999. In the process, they managed to evade ¥30 billion (US$3.6 billion) in customs duties.[45] Lai's operation was not an isolated phenomenon. Quite the contrary, during the mid-1990s there was widespread smuggling, including smuggling orchestrated by the People's Liberation Army, due to high tariffs and large gaps between high domestic prices for a wide range of products and lower global prices.[46] Lai's operation was, on the other hand, on an unprecedented scale. He and his confederates were not smuggling in a few cases of cigarettes stashed in the bilges of fishing boats or a couple of stolen cars tucked away in a shipping container. They were bringing in entire tankers full of petroleum and container ships filled with other goods, often using state-owned trading and shipping companies to move, store, and distribute the goods. Nor was the ring running their goods in over the beaches in the dark of night. On the contrary, they were moving the goods in broad daylight through the port of Xiamen.[47]

Since it was obviously impossible to disguise the scope of his operations, Lai built a protective web of officials at the municipal, provincial, and national levels. Working out of a club/hotel/massage parlor/bordello known as the Red Mansion and using the Yuanhua Group as a front for his operations, Lai cultivated the senior members of the Xiamen party and state administrations, the heads of the municipal customs administration, senior officials in the local public security bureau, members of the tax bureau, and managers of major state-owned corporations and banks.[48] His network also included Li Jizhou, a deputy minister of Public Security, and General Ji Shengde, the director of the PLA General Staff's Military Intelligence Department and deputy director of China's antismuggling effort.[49] In all, Lai's operation is thought to have involved at least 600 people, including 360 officials who not only protected Lai and helped move goods through the port of Xiamen but also laundered Yuanhua's profits through a series of underground banks in Fujian Province where the funds were converted into hard currency and then transferred to Hong Kong, where they were used to finance further smuggling, buy real estate, or were "round tripped" back into China as foreign investment.

By 1999, Yuanhua and other smuggling operations had become so brazen that there was little hiding their operations. According to James Mulvenon, in 1998 smugglers brought in 42 million barrels of oil, and smuggled oil accounted for one-quarter to one-third of the petroleum sold in China. Legal imports were down 100 percent and the domestic oil industry was losing ¥10–20 billion a year because it could not compete with smugglers who could buy oil on the international spot market at ¥900 a ton, 60 percent of the official domestic price of ¥1,500 a ton.[50] Faced with evidence of sharply increased smuggling, Beijing ordered a crackdown in July 1998. The first major break in the Xiamen case came from the exposure of another large smuggling ring in Zhanjiang, Guangdong, in September of that year.[51] Like Lai, the man at the center of the Zhanjiang ring, Chen Lisheng, had forged illicit ties with General Ji, and when these came to light so too did Ji's connection to Yuanhua.[52] At about the same time, the Ministry of Supervision reportedly received a lengthy letter detailing Yuanhua's operation and implicating Li Jizhou.[53] Soon thereafter, Beijing dispatched a team of investigators to Fujian and began arresting the smugglers and their official confederates, making arrests in Fujian, Guangdong, Hainan, Shandong, Zhejiang, Shaanxi, and Shanghai. In all, investigators reported that between the summer of 1998 and the end of 1999 they solved over 25,000 smuggling cases, arrested thousands of smugglers, and seized goods valued at ¥32.5 billion (US$3.9 billion).[54]

The 1998–99 antismuggling campaign and cases such as Yuanhua present an analytical dilemma: which is more significant, the fact that smuggling reached epidemic levels in the mid-1990s or the fact that when it did the government cracked down hard? For many, the failure to control smuggling in the first place represents a major governmental failure. Yet I would argue that the fact that the regime ultimately responded forcefully and sent a bevy of senior officials to prison, including General Ji (sentenced to life in prison), Vice Minister Li (death with two year reprieve), and the head of the Deputy General Manager General of the Customs Administration Wang Leyi (13 years), shows a willingness and capacity to fight back with relatively decisive results. It is noteworthy that in both the cases of the two Chens and the antismuggling campaign, Beijing found it necessary to deploy teams from the outside to attack entrenched corruption, which strongly suggests that in localities infected by corruption involving senior local officials and rings of corrupt officials, routine local enforcement is likely to break down and become an ineffectual check. The combination of failed local anticorruption work and the success of outside intervention thus reveals the complex nature of China's still imperfect capabilities. The fact Chen Liangyu was not deterred from resorting to massive corruption by the imprisonment of Chen Xitong or the harsh punishments handed down to senior officials in the 1998–99 antismuggling campaign or other contemporary cases also shows that even though senior officials face a tangible combination of risk and possibly severe punishment, the fear of getting caught remains an incomplete and imperfect hedge against corruption. Pei and others may thus be correct that the perceived risk of getting caught may not deter officials from resorting to corruption but that does not necessarily mean that they will not get caught.

The 2009 crackdown on organized crime in Chongqing revealed a web of crime and corruption that was arguably the equal of the Yuanhua case in scope. As with other high-profile cases, the Chongqing scandal was precipitated by three seemingly random and unrelated events. First, in December 2007, Beijing reshuffled the provincial leadership and transferred Bo Xilai from Liaoning to Chongqing, where he assumed the post of secretary of the Municipal Party Committee in November. Second, in November 2008 the city was hit by a massive taxi strike, in response to which Bo held a televised meeting with drivers, who complained about high management fees, fuel shortages, and competition from illegal "black cabs" but also told Bo that Li Qiang, a billionaire businessman and one-time delegate to the Chongqing Municipal People's Congress, had hired thugs to pressure them into joining the strike.[55] Third, in June 2009 police reportedly conducted a raid on an illegal gun factory, finding 1,700 firearms and sending something of a shockwave through Beijing.[56]

The son of Bo Yibo, one of the "eight immortals" who constituted Deng's inner circle during the late 1980s and a member of the "princeling" class made up of the sons and daughters of senior political leaders, Bo Xilai was widely believed to have political ambitions that extended beyond his twin posts as secretary of the Chongqing Municipal Party Committee and member of the Politburo, to which he had been elected in 2007. It was speculated that Bo had his sights on a seat on the Politburo Standing Committee and possibly the chair of the National People's Congress. His major rival for these two posts was reportedly former Chongqing Secretary Wang Yang, who was identified with Hu Jintao's Communist Youth League faction and had been promoted to the post of secretary of the Guangdong Provincial Party Committee in 2007.[57] Although Bo has denied that his decision to launch an assault on organized crime was politically motivated, he nevertheless moved quickly. He first ordered the local police to conduct a crackdown on illegal guns and then in March 2008 arranged the transfer of Jinzhou police chief Wang Lijun from Liaoning, where Bo had been mayor of Dalian and later governor. Wang had built a reputation as a tough cop who was particularly hard on organized crime (and was said to have the scars to prove it) while police chief of Jinzhou.[58] Wang replaced Wen Qiang, who had gained local fame for busting a major bank robber, as the head of the Chongqing Public Security Bureau and ordered a massive strike against organized crime in the city in June 2008.[59] The crackdown took a significant turn in August 2008 when investigators arrested Wen Qiang. Wen, prosecutors charged, had provided protection to a string of Chongqing's gangs in return for massive bribes.

In key respects, Wen's arrest transformed the Chongqing crackdown on organized crime into a much larger corruption scandal. His arrest made clear that the proliferation of organized crime in Chongqing was due to collaboration between the gangsters and the police, with the latter providing the former with protective umbrellas (*baosan*). As the scandal deepened, it became apparent that not only were the police working with organized crime, a whole host of municipal officials, including senior members of the local courts, were also colluding with the gangsters. Moreover, many of the "gangsters" arrested were major figures in Chongqing's business circles. Li Qiang, for example, controlled a fleet of one thousand buses operating on fifty separate bus lines and a number of companies involved in transport. According to prosecutors, Li had bought the help of Xiao Qinglong, the director of the Communication and Transportation Administration of Shapingba District; Jiang Hong, the director of the Road Transport Administration of Ba'nan District of Chongqing; and Jiang Chunyan, the director of the municipal complaints department.[60] After his arrest, prosecutors reportedly found cell phone messages from numerous officials and policemen warning Li that investigators were about to detain him and urging him to flee the city.[61] Li and his confederates went on trial on charges of leading an organized crime syndicate, disturbing public order, disrupting public transportation, bribery, financial fraud, and tax evasion. Li was convicted and sentenced to twenty years in prison.[62]

Wen was ultimately executed after the courts found him guilty of accepting ¥12 million (US$1.7 million) in bribes for protecting criminals and from subordinates seeking promotions; he was also found guilty of rape and engaging prostitutes. He was said to possess upward of ¥400 million (US$58 million) worth of luxury villas, art, expensive wines, and other goods. Wen's wife reportedly turned state's evidence and led investigators to a pond where Wen had stashed ¥20 million (US$2.9 million) in cash after she was told about Wen's sexual escapades, which included maintaining a stable of mistresses and several rapes. She went to prison for eight years after the court convicted her of acting as a go-between for her husband.[63] Wen's sister-in-law Xie Caiping, whom the media quickly dubbed the "godmother" of Chongqing, received an eighteen-year sentence after she was convicted on gambling, prostitution, drug-dealing, and arms-trafficking charges.[64]

Deputy Police Chief Peng Changjian, who had ironically directed the crackdown on illegal arms trafficking that was the prelude for the larger antiorganized crime crackdown, received a life sentence after he was convicted of accepting ¥4.7 million (US$680,000) in bribes from gangsters and having ¥4.6 million (US$670,000) in unexplained assets.[65] Mao Jianping, the deputy director of the municipal procuratorate, and Zhao Wenrui, the head of the Beibei district, were detained at the same time on suspicion of conspiring to protect Chongqing's network of gangsters.[66]

Wen and Li proved to be the tip of an iceberg of crime and corruption that included a cast of shady businessmen (known locally as "black bosses with red hats" [heiban hongmao] because of their political connections), gangsters, small-time hooligans, ex-cons, crooked officials, and dirty cops.[67] Wang Neng, a member of the Chongqing Municipal People's Congress like Li Qiang, was charged

with assault, extortion, illegal firearms possession, and leading a criminal organization.[68] One-time member of the municipal Chinese People's Political Con-
sultative Conference Wang Tianlun received a suspended death sentence after
being convicted of using gangsters in an attempt to gain control of the city's
wholesale pork market.[69] The major shareholder in the Chongqing Hilton and
prominent property mogul Peng Zhimin was shown to have used the hotel as a
front for a high-priced brothel and casino, in addition to engaging in loan sharking, illegal land dealings, and illegal logging.[70] Chen Mingliang, a former district
legislator and the CEO of a billion-yuan real estate development company, allegedly headed a gang that earned ¥26 million (US$3.8 million) from prostitution,
received ¥7.6 million (US$1.1 million) for arranging illegal gambling trips to
Macau, and used strong-arm tactics to "settle" ¥60 million (US$8.7 million) in
debts for various businesses who paid the gang a percentage. Chen and his hench-
man Ma Dang were also charged with giving deputy police chief Peng Changjian
¥130,000 (US$19,000) in return for his protection.[71] Former police officer Yue
Cun, who ran a string of pawn shops and detective agencies, was sentenced to
death after being convicted of heading an organized crime ring that engaged
in murder, assault, abduction, racketeering, and arms trafficking. Yue's various
operations were said to have generated ¥200 million (US$29 million).[72] A former
tax official, Deng Yuping, was tried on charges that he and his partner in a gambling and loan sharking ring took in ¥30 million (US$4.3 million) from casinos
with a turnover of ¥1 billion (US$145 million) and earned ¥15 million (US$2.7
million) from ¥500 million (US$72 million) in illegal loans. The operation was
allegedly protected by the former head of the Yubei district, Liu Xinyong, and
other officials.[73] Two police officers from that district, Guo Sheng and Gan Yong,
were prosecuted for protecting criminal activities.[74] Chen Kunzhi, a one-time
policeman with a record of bribery and violence who had become a real estate
speculator, was charged with using his connections to prevent other developers
from bidding on several prime lots.[75]

A host of other police and judicial officers were also involved with the so-
called "black society" (*heishe*) of the criminal underworld. The deputy chief
of the municipal antidrug brigade Luo Li was convicted of accepting ¥1.2 million (US$174,000) from narcotics traffickers and conspiring to murder a drug
dealer.[76] The former vice president of the municipal high court Zhang Tao was
convicted of accepting ¥9.02 million (US$1.30) million in protection money.[77]
Four policemen were convicted of accepting bribes from a pair of businessmen
who ran four companies that served as a front for a ¥100 million (US$14.5 mil-
lion) string of brothels.[78] Another officer was charged with conspiring with Wang
Xingqiang, the head of a violent extortion and money-laundering ring who was
sentenced to death in late 2008, before the crackdown began.[79] Investigators

charged the police chief of Dangjiang County, Xu Qiang, with accepting bribes, including a car, from subordinates seeking promotions and with offering Wen Qiang a ¥280,000 (US$41,000) bribe.[80] Wu Xiaoqing, a former judge, allegedly committed suicide after his detention on bribery charges. Prosecutors reportedly believed he had taken ¥3.5 million (US$500,000) in bribes over a ten-year period and had an additional ¥5 million (US$725,000) in unexplained assets.[81]

Corruption extended beyond the judiciary. The head of the Chongqing Coal Mine Safety Supervision Bureau Wang Xiping, the director of the municipal equipment department Wu Jungen, and the deputy head of the Chongqing Public Security Bureau's anticrime squad Chen Hongqiang were charged with accepting ¥13.34 million (US$1.9 million) from coal mine operators seeking to cover up accidents and obtain improper safety certifications. Chen was also charged with forcing other operators to give him shares in their mines.[82] Liu Jianchun, the deputy director of the municipal publicity office was convicted of taking ¥1.01 million (US$146,000) in bribes in return for arranging jobs and government contracts.[83]

By the time the investigation reached its finale, the evidence suggested that corruption in Chongqing had reached the proportions of a Hollywood gangster movie. Investigators estimated that loan sharking alone was a ¥30 billion (US$4.3 billion) operation.[84] As of late 2009, investigators had frozen ¥1 billion (US$145 million) in what they believed were illegal assets control by organized crime.[85] By the end of 2010, prosecutors in Chongqing had arrested 920 in the antigang crackdown, including 177 officials, of whom 87 were members of the judicial system, and had adjudicated over 1,300 other cases related to organized crime.[86] Dozens of gang members were executed.

From one perspective, the Chongqing Black Society case represents one more shocking example of corruption run wild in post-Mao China. To an extent this is true. Corruption and organized crime clearly flourished in the city, particularly after it was separated from Sichuan Province and made an independent provincial-level municipality in 1997. By 2008, corruption infected not only the police, who were in direct contact with the city's gangsters, but a range of other departments, including those that had contract with the front companies behind which the gangs increasingly operated. As with the other major cases discussed in the preceding pages, in the end a change in political leadership and a series of almost random events led to a massive crackdown and hence the revelation of the extent of corruption. The Chongqing scandal, in other words, looks particularly bad because so many officials and gangsters were caught. Some undoubtedly got away and to some extent organized crime surely survived the crackdown, but it seems clear that the authorities led by Bo Xilai made a concerted effort to break up the web of corruption and organized crime in the city.

Random events, the beating of the antismuggling officers in Zhanjiang, and the raid on illegal arms factories in Chongqing, may have triggered crackdowns in the Yuanhua Smuggling Ring and the Chongqing Black Society cases. But by the time these cases, and that of Chen Liangyu, broke, corruption had become so large scale and blatant that it is hard to imagine how things could have continued apace. Corruption thrives in secret, and, properly conducted, as Li Ling insightfully writes, corruption is a subtle art. Exchanges are never direct, and when money changes hands it is exchanged discreetly.[87] Favors are given but never as a result of an explicit quid pro quo agreement. More critically, dirty money must be kept hidden, and corrupt officials must avoid engaging in flamboyant displays of wealth. Thus, in many cases corrupt payoffs are not channeled directly to an official but are instead made to intermediaries including wives, children, relatives, or mistresses and are made in the form of business opportunities, consulting fees, or commissions. Paying the tuition and living expenses of children attending expensive private school in the United States, Britain, Australia, and elsewhere is said to have become an increasingly popular method of channeling money to senior officials. If payments are made in cash, large-scale corruption can become cumbersome because the largest unit of currency is the RMB100 bill, worth about US$14. Large cash payoffs, therefore, require bulky transfers of cash. Unless the money is then laundered by being deposited in a series of false name bank accounts, moved offshore through the underground banking system, or transformed into investment capital, over time a corrupt official is apt to find himself having to store and hide boxes of cash. Wen Qiang, for example, is said to have sealed ¥20 million (US$2.8 million) in a waterproof container and thrown it into a pond in an attempt to hide his ill-gotten gains. (Wen's attempt failed, however, after his angry wife led investigators to his stash.) Another Chongqing official, Yan Dabin, the head of Wushan County's transportation department, was caught after his neighbors complained about water leaking from a flat he owned.[88] When police opened the door for the plumber, who called them after nobody answered the door, they found a leaking toilet and nine cartons containing almost ¥10 million (US$1.4 million) of wet money. Yan was subsequently found guilty of accepting over ¥22 million (US$3.14 million) from companies seeking road and bridge contracts and was executed. Other officials have been exposed by wearing expensive Rolex watches or by being photographed smoking expensive imported cigarettes. Others have gotten caught when they started driving expensive sedans or moved into luxury villas.

Herein we confront a key point. To be "successful," a corrupt official must never appear to be corrupt, and yet corruption often seems to become a form of addiction. As officials become more corrupt and start raking in large amounts of cash, they let their guard down and start openly enjoying the fruits of their abuse of power. Once they start living beyond their means and engaging flashy displays of wealth, corrupt officials become vulnerable and are apt to survive only so long as their colleagues and outside investigators turn a blind eye. Very often, they become sloppy and begin to get too close to those who are buying them off. Once corrupt officials begin to let their guard down, they are likely to last only so long as the regime is very half-heartedly committed to controlling corruption. If the regime stops turning a blind eye to evidence of corruption, in many cases it then becomes more a matter of time before their misdeeds catch up to them. For a regime looking for ways to show the public it is determined to fight corruption, officials living flamboyant, high-flying lifestyles complete with multiple mistresses, a taste for expensive liquor, fine dining, expensive cars, and luxurious flats make very tempting targets.

Such was the case in all four of the major cases reviewed here. By the time Wang Baosen shot himself, rumors of high-level corruption involving land leasing in downtown Beijing were common. The scale and scope of the Yuanhua operation, as well as that in Zhanjiang, were so large it would have been hard to miss them. The amount of money diverted from the Shanghai Pension Fund was so large that it would be difficult to imagine that officials at the Pudong Development Bank, which was supposed to manage the fund's cash, were not aware of what was going on. Chongqing had long "enjoyed" a reputation for its steamy weather and seedy—sometimes violent—underworld. These cases therefore suggest that even if the chances of getting caught appear low and even if it may be true that some officials may escape punishment for political reason, many of the "high rollers" who engage in repeated acts of corruption are apt to find that odds eventually catch up with them.

In the end, the most important factor is less whether China's anticorruption effort has achieved some abstract threshold of effectiveness. Instead, the key factor is that the Chinese government has mounted a sustained fight against corruption. In most of the cases of hyper-corruption and kleptocracy, either the regime fails to take action or attacks corruption for purely political reasons, targeting its political enemies, including erstwhile allies turned foes or underlings who have "muscled" in on their superiors' "loot," while ignoring or even openly tolerating blatant and outrageous plundering by members of the regime's inner circle.

To a certain extent, therefore, Pei is correct in criticizing China's anticorruption efforts. Ultimately, there is little evidence that Chinese authorities have succeeded in bringing down the overall level of corruption. In fact, the evidence is mixed. On the one hand, there is little to show that the extent of corruption has dramatically increased since the year 2000. But there is also little sign that corruption has decreased in recent years. By the same token, there is evidence that the risk of getting caught has decreased but also evidence to suggest that even though the one-time odds of getting caught are low, over time the odds are against those engaged in corruption.[89] And when they do get caught, the odds of punishment are high and, for those engaged in high-stakes corruption, the result can be death.

Despite the emergence of new opportunities for corruption and its spread into the more senior ranks of the state and party apparatus during the early 1990s, the overall level of corruption, as imperfectly captured by the RRC and the PLC, remained roughly constant over the decade from 2000 to 2010. In part, this may have been because, in theory, as reform evolved it not only created new avenues for corruption but also closed off others. There seems to be a general consensus, for example, that as production of consumer goods increased and rationing became less common, much of the petty corruption that ordinary citizens faced in trying to get permission to buy goods during the 1970s and early 1980s largely disappeared. It also seems clear that as the range of commodities subject to the two-track price system decreased, official profiteering in the form of arbitrage between the plan and the market decreased. Corruption related to smuggling also appears to have waned after China entered the World Trade Organization and the import tariffs that created substantial gaps between the world market price for commodities such as petroleum and products such as automobiles were substantially lowered and even eliminated. Recent tightening of administrative regulations and efforts to increase transparency in public contracting, the leasing of land, and the sale of state assets have also likely helped decrease the extent of backroom dealings and corruption.

I believe, however, that the leveling off of corruption beginning in the mid-1990s was only partly due to the elimination or diminution of the incentives for certain types of corruption. Credit must also be given to China's oft-maligned war on corruption. In a sense, reform, corruption, and anticorruption coevolved. The advent of reform created new opportunities for corruption and hence resulted in significant increases in bribery, misappropriation, and graft. Faced with evidence of rising corruption and fearful of the political fallout, the regime—which had to write and enact a criminal code and rehabilitate the disciplinary, supervisory, and judicial institutions responsible for combating corruption at the same time it was implementing reform—responded by progressively augmenting its anticorruption capabilities in the 1980s. It launched highly visible anticorruption campaigns in 1982, 1986, and 1989. When the deepening of reform in the early 1990s intensified high-level, high-stakes corruption and pushed it into new areas (including upward within party and state ranks), the regime responded by shifting its focus from broad-based anticorruption drives to a less visible but sustained effort targeting corruption among senior officials, the officers of the state-controlled banks, and the managers of state-owned enterprises. Along the way, the regime has tried to improve its institutional capacities. In recent years, for example, the government has established a new National Corruption Prevention Bureau and intensified its attack on the demand side for corruption—business interests willing to bribe officials for favorable treatment.[90] It has implemented new regulations that allow for the prosecution of officials for the possession of unexplained assets (*ju'e caichan laiyuan buming*) and cracked down on the use of false name bank accounts that allow corrupt officials to hide their ill-gotten gains.[91] The regime has intensified auditing of government and public institutions by strengthening the authority of the National Audit Office and its ability to detect improper activities.[92] Administrative procedures have been changed in ways that reduce officials' discretionary power, impose more regularized budgeting and account procedures, and limit officials' access to cash transactions involving the public. A concerted effort has also been made to eliminate the unauthorized slush funds in which state and other public institutions stash illegally obtained money. A series of university-based anticorruption centers have been established, in part to increase the academic study of corruption and in part to provide enhanced training of civil servants and to help local governments tighten control of the allocation and disposition of public money.[93]

In conclusion, as reform spawned corruption, the regime's anticorruption efforts proved insufficient to substantially reduce corruption, but they appear to have been more minimally successful in the sense that they kept corruption under control. Even though it is impossible to infer the aggregate efficacy of China's war on corruption in terms of what percentage of corrupt officials get caught, data on cases investigated and prosecuted by the procuratorate and sentences handed down by the courts make clear that a substantial number of corrupt officials were caught each year and many of them harshly punished. The partial data drawn from my database of over four thousand high-profile cases make clear that it was not just the unlucky small fry who faced punishment. Senior officials, cadres, managers, and bank officers were sent to prison in substantial numbers. Hundreds were executed. Even very senior officials found themselves behind bars or facing the executioner. Thus, unlike the prototypical kleptocracy where corruption is allowed to spread unchecked and only those corrupt officials who fall afoul of the kleptocrat-in-chief are punished, in contemporary China officials contemplating corruption face a very real prospect that they may have to pay the ultimate price for their misdeeds.[94] China's anticorruption efforts have, therefore, created a check on corruption that was presumably lacking or substantially less credible in other cases of rampant corruption. The concurrence of intensifying corruption and sustained rapid growth in China can thus be explained in part by the fact that corruption fed off economic reform, evolving as reform evolved, and was sustained by the high rates of growth generated by the reforms. The concurrence can also be explained in part because even though corruption worsened, the existence of an at least partially effective anticorruption effort prevented corruption from spiraling out of control and reaching levels that might have had a far worse and visible impact on the economy's vitality.

CONTROLLING CORRUPTION
AND SUSTAINING RAPID GROWTH

As I argued in the opening paragraphs of this book, there are two distinct images of post-Mao China: one of the economic miracle, the other of corruption gone wild. Neither of these images is false. On the contrary, it is clear that the Chinese economy has grown tremendously. It is also clear that the low-level, almost subterranean corruption of the later Maoist period has morphed into often flagrant high-level corruption. Because economists have argued that there is a negative correlation between corruption and growth rates, the two images appear to be contradictory. If the economists are right, how could the Chinese economy grow so fast, even as corruption exploded and intensified?

The easy answer is that although econometric studies show that, in aggregate, higher levels of corruption correlate with lower rates of growth, more finely grained case studies suggest that developmental corruption in the form of coalition-building machine politics lay at the heart of some economic successes, including the so-called developmental states of East Asia. Because developmental corruption tends to be structural in nature and hence deeply embedded in the political process, it is less visible than the smash-and-grab corruption associated with kleptocracy. As a result, it is quite likely that the perceptual estimates of levels of corruption employed by most econometric analyses underestimated corruption in these cases.[1] Strong economic performance and subterranean corruption are also likely to mask the presence of corruption or convince outside observers that corruption is benign or tangential. Moreover, because the combination of developmental corruption and rapid growth is presumably much less common than the combination of kleptocracy and economic decline, the negative correlation between corruption and growth is not particularly surprising. In this understanding, the concurrence of worsening corruption and rapid growth in China might be deemed an "outlier" to the negative correlation between corruption and growth. And in a sense, China does, in fact, appear to be an outlier having a much higher annual growth rate than other countries with similar levels of corruption (see Figure 7.1).

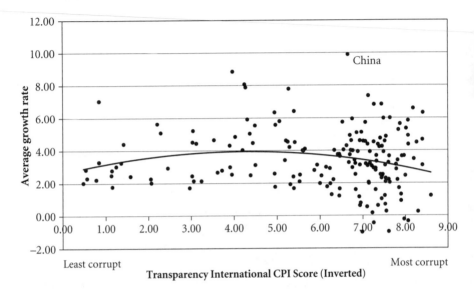

FIGURE 7.1. National corruption and average growth, 1992–2008
Sources: Corruption measured by each country's average score in Transparency International's annual "Corruption Perceptions Index," available at http://www.transparency.org/policy_research/surveys_indices/cpi/2009, accessed May 1, 2010. Average annual growth rates (1978 to 2008) from World Bank, *World Development Indicators* database, available at http://0-data.worldbank.org.library.unl.edu, accessed July 22, 2011 (World Bank, Development Data Group, Washington, DC: The World Bank).
Note: All countries included in TI's CPI are plotted. I have, however, opted to remove several cases from this chart, including Afghanistan, Bosnia, and Cambodia, each of which experienced short bursts of very high post-conflict growth, which combined with missing data for conflict periods, creates what I deem to be inflated average growth rates. I also opted not to plot Equatorial Guinea, whose oil-driven average growth rate of over 17 percent tends to visually distort the picture by compressing the Y-axis. I have added a trend line primarily for visual reference and do not wish to suggest that this particular simple bivariate trend line represents a statistically derived estimate of the correlation of corruption and growth. Obviously calculating such a correlation requires a far more complicated multivariate model that fully accounts for other factors that affect growth rates.

But it is not as much an outlier as it might appear at first glance. For all the hype about China's descent into endemic corruption, in relative terms corruption in China is not remarkably bad. Between 1992 and 2009, Transparency International's Corruption Perceptions Index gave the country an average score of 6.66 out of a possible 10, with 10 being the worst (most corrupt) score. At that level, corruption in China was worse than the global average of 6.01 but better than the median of 6.81. In fact, China's average score placed it in the second-most corrupt quartile, where scores ranged from 5.06 to 6.81. It's true, of course, that China was located close to the upper quartile boundary. Nevertheless, in simple terms, Transparency International's "poll of polls" methodology estimated that corruption in more than half of the 183 countries it ranked annually was worse than in China. Moreover, China's annual score declined from a peak of 7.57 in 1995 and 1996 to 6.40 in 2009 and 6.50 in 2010. In the process, its score regressed toward the mean (see Figure 7.2).[2] Thus, while corruption certainly worsened in the 1980s and 1990s, it essentially rose to levels that are relatively normal, particularly among rapidly developing economies.[3] If China is an outlier, it is perhaps primarily due to its very high rate of growth rather than an exceptionally high corruption score.

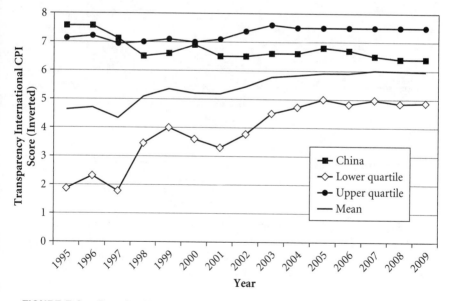

FIGURE 7.2.   Perceived level of corruption in China versus international mean, 1995–2009

Source: Based on data from Transparency International's annual "Corruption Perceptions Index," available at http://www.transparency.org/policy_research/ surveys_ indices/cpi/2009, accessed May 1, 2010.

The TI scores, however, tell only part of the story. Estimates of the business risk associated with corruption generated by the Political Risk Services (PRS) Group show that China made a dramatic shift in the mid-1990s, moving from below the mean to above it (see Figure 7.3).[4] Thus, even if corruption in China did not reach the levels often assumed, the fact remains that corruption dramatically worsened after the advent of reform and remained at significant levels as reform deepened. We need to explain why high levels of corruption and rapid growth coexisted in the 1990s and beyond, and also why corruption worsened in the early 1990s and why its worsening did not have negative consequences.

Superficially, the first part of the question might be answered by referencing other examples of rapid growth, including first and foremost the developmental states of South Korea and Taiwan. Although the literature on the developmental state may have downplayed the extent of corruption in the East Asian

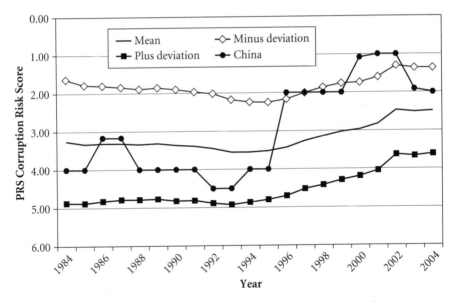

FIGURE 7.3. Perceived business risk of corruption in China versus international mean, 1984–2004

Source: Based on data from Political Risk Service Group, *International Country Risk Guide,* available at http://www.prsgroup.com/ICRG.aspx, accessed July 22, 2011.

Note: Like Transparency International, the PRS Group uses a scale of decreasing risk in which higher scores denote lower levels of risk and lower scores denote higher levels of risk. For consistency, I have simply inverted the Y-axis: zero denotes the highest possible risk and 6 denotes the lowest possible risk.

economic miracles, it is clear that corruption, primarily in the form of political or structural corruption and machine politics, played a central role by laying the political foundations for economic development. Confronted by political fragmentation and instability, conservative politicians in South Korea and Taiwan used money politics financed by big business to buy off and bind together the right. In return, they repaid their business clientele with pro-growth macroeconomic policy regimes. The marriage of conservative politics and big business in these two cases was never prefect, in large part because exchanges of dirty money lay at the heart of the relationship. Over time, the political partners tended to become increasingly self-serving, while the business partners found that they needed the policy support of the state less and less. But, even though the relationship might have gradually cooled, the arrangement was strong enough in the early years to allow these economies to overcome a variety of start-up costs and begin to develop rapidly.

In China, the political functions I ascribe to structural corruption in South Korea and Taiwan were performed by the Communist Party. The party was, after all, in a fundamental sense a massive political machine that bound together a diverse set of political interests in the common pursuit of political hegemony. Moreover, legacies from events such as the disastrous Great Leap Forward, the massive famine it produced, the chaotic Cultural Revolution, and a twenty-year legacy of stunted growth, helped make rapid economic growth and rising standards of living a political imperative for the party. As a result, there was no need for money politics to bind together a developmental coalition and give it political reasons to adopt a new pro-growth policy regime. This does not mean the developmental state examples are irrelevant to explaining the Chinese case. Rapid economic growth in China required the formation of the same sort of developmental alliance, and without the core of the CCP political machine and its politically derived drive to grow the economy, the Chinese economy might have remained a chronic underperformer. Nevertheless, structural corruption was not a necessary precondition for rapid growth in China because the CCP performed its functions.

Even though a new marriage between money and power was unnecessary in the Chinese case, corruption surged and intensified after the adoption of economic reforms. Prior to that, China had a low-grade form of petty corruption involving lots of tiny bribes and exchange of small favors. In the mid-1980s, first the scope and then the scale of corruption exploded, and by the early 1990s huge sums of money were changing hands in deals involving major assets and increasingly senior officials and party cadres. As a result, corruption in China rapidly increased from below-average levels to levels that put it close to, if not among, the most corrupt countries.

On the surface, this shift could be interpreted as a slide into kleptocracy and degenerative corruption. Whereas the developmental corruption found in South Korea and Taiwan involved a conclusive partnership between political and economic power, kleptocracy is characterized by the plundering of economic interests by the politically powerful. Far from building up an economy, kleptocracy assaults and destroys the business sector, wreaks havoc on vitally important property rights, and triggers the flight of liquid capital, either abroad or into an underground economy where it can be more easily hidden from the regime and its looters. Although in key respects corrupt officials and cadres in China turned to plunder, the worsening of corruption in the late 1980s and early 1990s did not give birth to kleptocracy. In large part, China avoided kleptocracy because at the same time that corruption began to take off, the regime launched a counterattack. As should be evident from the cases discussed in chapter 3, although it might appear to be anarchic, kleptocracy is generally a top-down form of corruption in which the political leader acts as kleptocrat-in-chief and the state becomes an instrument for private plunder. In China, the CCP never became an institution for plunder. Nor did the leadership as a collective become corrupted. Individual cadres and officials, including some at the highest levels, turned to corruption, and segments of the party and state were converted into mini-kleptocracies. As a political institution, however, the party remained uncorrupted and fought back, albeit imperfectly, against the spread of corruption within its ranks. Thus, unlike a classic kleptocracy where corruption spirals out of control because the entire political system becomes a mechanism for plunder by those in power, in China worsening corruption was met with anticorruption. At this juncture, it is unclear whether the CCP is winning its now nearly three-decade war on corruption. The available indicators (a flat revealed rate of corruption and a slighting falling perceived level of corruption) suggest nevertheless that at a minimum the war has succeeded in the sense that it prevented corruption from running out of control.

More critically, I contend, the surge in corruption witnessed between roughly 1985 and 1995 was a byproduct of the reform, not an attack on it. First, as argued in chapter 4, the worsening and intensification of corruption occurred after the first rounds of reform had laid the foundations for a burst of economic activity. The intensification of corruption during the 1990s was, as argued in chapter 5, driven to an important extent by reforms that transferred undervalued state-assets to managerial and private control. Shifting undervalued assets from state control to market control created tremendous windfall profits that could be earned by whomever was able to buy them at prices that approximated their state-set nominal value and then arbitrage them onto emerging markets. The size of these windfall profits was so great in many instances that officials and cadres either tried to arrogate the assets to their private control or to extract a share of the anticipated profits in the form of bribes and kickbacks, which many buyers were apparently willing to pay because they anticipated they would reap the lion's share.

Second, as reform deepened, the boundary between public and private and between the state and business shifted. In the beginning, the state largely controlled services, commerce, industry, and banking. As the reforms unfolded, economic administrators became managers and businessmen. Cadres became investors and capitalists. Party cadres, state officials, and even academics took the plunge into business. In the process, many of the economic functions that had been internal to the state during the prereform period were externalized and shifted to the emerging market economy. In the transition from the plan to the market, the line between corruption and business was often ill defined. The rules of the market game were new and evolving; the regulatory system was chaotic, incomplete, and often contradictory; and business ethics were rudimentary and emerging. Even the laws and regulations defining corruption had only been recently drawn up, and the institutions tasked with detecting, investigating, and prosecuting official wrongdoing were being hastily reconstituted at the same time that reforms were dramatically changing the economic system. In short, reform not only spawned new opportunities for corruption, institutional flux and change created an environment in which it was easy for officials to cross the line and use their authority for illicit purposes.

Third, not only were valuable assets being transferred from state to private control, the economy was booming and a great deal of new wealth was being created. In the early years, it was private entrepreneurs who got rich quick.[5] In the 1990s, it was the managers of state-owned firms partnered with foreign investors and the managers of corporatized state-owned enterprises whose incomes and assets grew to unheard-of levels. With so much new money being made, a form of boom corruption emerged in which newly rich businessmen were often prepared to pay for official favors, and officials, seeing their relative income and social status fall rapidly, were often eager to get a slice of the pie. Under this combination of conditions, a surge in corruption should not have come as a surprise. In fact, it would have been more surprising if corruption had not increased. Reform was creating a host of new opportunities for officials to parley their authority into private gain, and many of them, as George Washington Plunkitt put it, "seen [their] opportunities and...took 'em."[6]

To an extent, corruption linked the private interests of cadres and officials to the profit-making interests of those in business. Profits, after all, formed the basis for payoffs. New businesses and ventures created opportunities for bribes to "facilitate" licenses and to "insure" against overly "aggressive" regulation and oversight, as well as opportunities for "silent partnerships." An expanding local economy also created new opportunities for local governments to dream up new and irregular "surtaxes" and fees that could be pocketed or used to pay for new benefits. Promoting growth, in short, could be made very profitable for officials or cadres willing to play a bit wild and loose with their authority. And corruption could be very profitable for businessmen willing to "entertain" officials with wine, women, song, and cash. In this sense, corruption bound together officials and businesses in the sorts of developmental alliances found in South Korea and Taiwan. To the extent this occurred, it was not at the national or regime level, however, but at the local and informal level.

This is not to say, and I cannot stress this point enough, that corruption led to rapid growth. On the contrary, although corruption fed off rapid growth, the causes of rapid growth were exogenous to corruption. It is also very important to stress that while some officials may have engaged in a form of developmental corruption, others looted and plundered. Post-Mao China did not lack for kleptocrats. It is, I conclude, wrong to argue that corruption in China was distinct from corruption in postcommunist Russia because of greater levels of profit-sharing corruption versus greater levels of looting, as Sun argues.[7] China had plenty of both. The key in China was that the "chicken" of rapid growth came before the foxes began stealing its golden "eggs." Thus, corrupt officials in China were really no different from their "fox in the henhouse" cousins in other corrupt systems, but whereas the foxes in most kleptocracies prey on a scrawny hen that can lay only a few small eggs, in China the hen was increasingly robust and capable of laying more eggs than the Chinese foxes could grab. Moreover, whereas the "farmer" (i.e., the regime) in most kleptocracies either turned a blind eye to the foxes and their thieving or was himself engaged in the plunder, in China the regime made an attempt to catch at least some of the foxes and punish them. The CCP and the judicial system do, as shown in chapter 6, catch more than a few of those who turn to corruption; many end up with harsh punishments, including a bullet to the back of the head. And it is not just the little foxes that are getting caught; some very big tigers have also ended up serving lengthy prison terms or facing execution.

In sum, there is nothing "special" or "miraculous" about Chinese corruption. Although the particular ways and means through which officials illicitly use their authority to channel dirty money into their pockets obviously vary by country, ultimately Chinese corruption is much like corruption everywhere else. What sets China apart from other countries with relatively serious corruption problems is that corruption was mostly petty when the economy began to take off; corruption fed off the deepening of reform, with high-level corruption in particular being driven by the transfer of valuable assets from state control to the emerging market economy; and as corruption increased, the regime fought back.

In certain abstract ways, in fact, the political economy of corruption in contemporary China bears a resemblance to corruption in the United States during the Gilded Age.

Corruption with U.S. Characteristics

Although the United States sits far on the other side of the mean level from China in most indices of corruption today, it is not a shining example of good government as a necessary precondition for successful development. In the nineteenth century, the United States suffered from extensive corruption, not only at the local and state levels but on occasion even at the highest levels of government.[8] During this same period, however, the United States transformed itself from a peripheral agrarian society into what would in 1945 become the most advanced industrial power in the world.

As the title of Mark Summers's history of the Gilded Age describes it, the latter half of the nineteenth century was an "era of good stealing,"[9] during which the political system was populated by venal bosses and politicos whose "machines" milked the economy and stole from the honest and upright citizenry.[10] Although the best-known machines, such as New York's Tammany Hall, operated at the municipal level, elements of machine-style politics could be found at the state and federal levels as well.[11] Unlike the centralized developmental machines in South Korea and Taiwan, machine politics in the United States was fragmented, with most machines largely independent and local. Nevertheless, the political economy of decentralized U.S. machine politics conformed to the general pattern I describe in chapter 2.

The political machine grew out of increasingly competitive electoral pressures and hence contenders' need to build organizations that could mobilize popular support, deliver voters to the polling stations, and suppress opposition voters. At the time, elections were frequently rough and tumble, with both sides relying on street toughs, vote buying, voter intimidation, vote fraud, and occasional electoral violence.[12] Electoral success depended not only on a candidate's ability to mobilize support during the campaign but on a politician's ability to sustain his campaign organization between elections. The temporary, ad hoc campaign organization thus evolved into a permanent machine as politicians—turned bosses—used patronage to secure government jobs for their key stalwarts: those who had served as precinct captains, ward heelers, and street walkers during the campaign.[13] To fund his machine's operations, the boss relied in large part on local government coffers and contributions from public employees.[14] Not only were government jobs filled on the basis of political loyalty, thus burdening taxpayers with the cost of paying the machine's core cadre, government procurement and public works contracts were steered into the hands of political loyalists, as were franchises for local utilities and transport systems. Local government was thus suborned to sustaining the boss's electoral machine and consolidating his political control.

In most cases, machines were not wholly dependent on municipal coffers for funds but instead drew in political monies from businesses and, in many cities, criminal organizations.[15] Like the individual stalwarts who staffed the machine's political organization, businessmen and gang leaders assumed their support would be repaid in public works contracts, favorable zoning, tax relief, better regulatory treatment, and police protection. Their political support was thus premised on the prospect of private profit making.[16]

Once in office, finally, politicians expected to reap the rewards of victory by cashing in through a bit of "honest graft." After all, according to George Washington Plunkitt, a major operative in the Tammany Hall machine, why should a capable and hardworking individual invest his time in public service if he could not profit from his work?[17] In a crude but surprisingly appropriate application of the economic concept of opportunity cost, Plunkitt went on to ask: If there was no profit from public service, why should that individual not go into the business sector where profit was not only considered legitimate but outright honorable? And why should politicians work hard to create profitable opportunities for the business community, if all the profits were reserved for private interests and they were barred from enjoying the fruits of their public toil? Why should a politician work night and day serving the public and taking care of his constituents without receiving full compensation? Certainly, he concluded, a politician who served his community well deserved just reward for his efforts, and there was nothing wrong with him making a profit from his service.[18]

The U.S. political machine was, in short, a political-business alliance aimed at winning control over local government and then to use that control to advance the political and economic interests of the organization and its stalwarts. At a fundamental level, the machine was a form of for-profit politics. Politicians sought both power and "honest graft," as did the ward heelers and precinct captains responsible for marshalling the rank and file, who in turn expected to receive benefits in the form of public jobs, the occasional raucous summer picnic complete with beer and whiskey, the proverbial Christmas turkey, and, when times were hard, a bucket of coal to ward off the cold of winter. Businesses allied to the machine sought favorable and preferential treatment, while criminals tied to it sought protection, often in the form a blind eye turned their way. Politics, in short, was all about the spoils of power and making sure that your side got the right to claim the spoils.

In abstract, the machine might not appear to be radically different from a plunder-based kleptocracy, and it was often portrayed as such by its enemies.[19] In reality, the efficacy of machine politics depended in large part on the ability of the boss to negotiate and coordinate the interests of those seeking to gain and retain political power and those seeking economic gains. The political machine was an organization predicated on maximizing its chances of long-term survival. The fact that it was organized, according to Schleifer and Vishny, implies it had a much better capacity to regulate the extent of corruption than a stereotypical anarchic kleptocracy populated by roving bandits and to ensure that the aggregate burden of corruption did not become unbearable.[20] Moreover, like Mancur Olson's "stationary bandit," the bosses should have seen utility not only in maintaining the underlying health of their revenue base but also in expanding it to maximize the long-term income stream while seeking to limit freelance predation and prevent roving bandits from plundering their turf.[21] In addition, the bosses should have faced pressures from their allies in the business community to limit the extent of plunder and to bend public policy to serve their profit-making interests.

In all likelihood, of course, business interests would also demand that policy be bent to create rents which they could capture and then seek to minimize the amount they share with the bosses. Political considerations, however, would act as a counterweight to the rent-seeking demands of the machine's business wing because excessive rent seeking could create a political backlash that would tip the balance against the machine in the next election. The boss would thus face a juggling act wherein he needed to keep his stalwarts happy while also preventing spoils politics from getting out of hand. The result was not, therefore, an "efficient" economic regime but one that skews benefits toward particular companies and interests while imposing costs on the economy as a whole in the form of rents and inflated costs. "Pay to play" politics could also damage property rights by leaving those who would not or could not "pay" vulnerable to retaliation and harassment at the hands of the machine, its henchmen, its business cronies, and even organized crime groups aligned with the machine. More critically, the ultimate safeguard against a descent into plunder was the boss and his willingness and ability to recognize the need to limit plunder and to keep his more rapacious underlings at bay. Absent a boss who could and would control the machine's urge to plunder, machine politics could quickly morph into kleptocracy or trigger a voter revolt that would "throw the bums" out of office. As such, the machine was at best an imperfect political institution and vulnerable to rapid decay.

Although undoubtedly flawed both abstractly and in reality, machine politics was nevertheless integral to the rise of the U.S. economy, particularly after the Civil War. At one level, the machine was itself very much a byproduct of growth; extensive infrastructure development and public works created the resources need to sustain machine politics, both by creating opportunities for politicians to "auction" off projects to the "highest bidders" and, perhaps even more important, by creating stet government jobs that could be staffed with political stalwarts.[22] At the state and federal levels, the construction of new canals, turnpikes, and railroads generally required enabling legislation, and hence presented additional opportunities for politicians to leverage contributions and commissions.[23] The state, in fact, played a major role in economic development during this period. Governmental financial guarantees and intervention, including land grants for rights-of-way and condemnation of properties along rights-of-way, were often critical to large-scale infrastructural developments, as were government programs that helped fund construction or abated financial risks.[24] In most states, the incorporation of companies generally required specific enabling legislation, and so entrepreneurs seeking to establish new joint stock companies or to transform privately held companies into joint stock companies were dependent on action by state legislatures.[25] The federal government was also making extensive land grants for ranching and mining in the newly acquired western territories. The outbreak of the Civil War in 1861, finally, caused a surge in federal spending on war materials and supplies.[26]

Machine politics in the United States during the Gilded Age thus provides a contrasting example of the relationship between corruption and growth to that of the stylized kleptocracy. Corruption in a kleptocracy strikes at the economic vitals, siphoning off public revenues and economic capital into the pockets of corrupt politicians, bureaucrats, and others while rendering property rights insecure and driving economic activity into flight abroad or retreat into the underground economy. Machine politics generally rests on a much more symbiotic relationship between political and economic power. At the local level, the bosses were more often than not allied with at least a substantial portion of the business community and were engaged in a form of pay-to-play politics wherein businesses seeking access to public contracts and favorable treatment had to support the boss and his machine in its fight for political power and were rewarded for their support with sweetheart deals. Individuals within the community who supported the machine by "turning out" the vote could hope to obtain steady work on the city payroll. In a sense, supporting the boss and his machine was a form of investment that paid off if the boss won election.

At the state and federal levels, the same sort of system ensured that the political interests of politicians were linked to the profit-making interests of those constituents who stood behind them during elections. But whereas the city boss might dole out contracts and patronage to repay his supporters, the "millionaires' club," as the Senate was branded by its critics, provided few private goods but instead doled out public goods in the form of a stable and predictable macroeconomic policy, a hard currency backed by the gold standard, open domestic markets, and a protective tariff.[27] In this system, corruption in its purest form (the use of public authority for private gain) was intermingled with a much more political form of corruption wherein politicians used public authority to obtain political advantage, along with perhaps a bit of "honest graft."[28]

By linking the political interests of the bosses and the profit-making interests of their business (and criminal) supporters, machine politics provided the basis for what I described in chapter 2 as developmental corruption. Herein the notion is not that corruption fosters development. Rather, unlike the degenerative corruption associated with kleptocracy, machine politics creates a situation wherein corruption and development cannot only coexist but may, in fact, feed off each other. By providing individuals and groups with selective incentives, generally in the form of tangible private goods (such as contracts and patronage), machine politics can generate centripetal political forces capable of pulling together disparate, and perhaps even rival or hostile, political groups by showing that if they unite and win, they stand to profit, both politically and personally. The result may be a largely mercenary ruling political coalition but one which has at least some interest the profit-making interests of its business allies. And so long as the machine benefits at least some powerful economic interests, they will, in turn, have incentives to contribute (or perhaps, to put it more bluntly, kick back) that share of their profits needed to keep the machine in power. The machine thus has a parasite-like relationship with the private sector, drawing its sustenance from its economic host, and yet too has an interest in the survival of the host.

At some very minimalist level, therefore, machine politics might be more developmentalist than kleptocracy because whereas the latter is apt to degenerate into blind plunder, the former is likely to make some effort to protect the private economy, albeit so long as the private sector contributes to the political coffers of the bosses. As such, mercenary machine politics is likely preferable to kleptocracy. The machine is also likely preferable to anarchy and the predatory corruption and plunder that usually accompanies a breakdown in political order or sustained political instability since neither is particularly conducive to investment and sustained economic growth. Such low expectations notwithstanding, it is also possible that machine politics could give rise to a political-business partnership that would be conducive to economic growth. In fact, if the business community is relatively strong but power is not concentrated in the hands of a few robber barons who can extort rents from the bosses as a quid pro quo for political support, the result well may be a stable, pro-business political machine whose core ideology boils down to a belief in "GNP-ism": growth that not only benefits its business allies but also causes the economic pie to grow and provide new treats and spoils with which the boss can buy friends and influence people.

China's Gilded Age?

On a very broad level, post-Mao China would seem to mirror the United States during the Gilded Age more closely than it does either the developmental machines of South Korea and Taiwan or the kleptocracies of Equatorial Guinea, Zaire, and Haiti. First, in the United States and China, we have evidence of extensive but disorganized corruption coexisting with rapid economic development. Despite major differences, both kleptocracy and developmental corruption are essentially top-down systems of organized corruption: both regimes are based on systematic corruption, albeit with corruption focusing on plunder in the kleptocracies and coalition building in the developmental states. In the case of the United States, despite the popular image of a political system dominated by corrupt politicos and robber barons, corruption was never systematic. Instead, corruption was organized into discrete nodes and focused on the struggle to control particular governments, most often at the municipal level but also to a certain extent at the state level. Local machines might form temporary alliances at the state level and through these alliances forge ties with politicians at the national level since the latter largely controlled federal employment within each state. Senators, in turn, might form temporary alliances and thus informally link machines in different states together, but there is no evidence of anything approaching the highly centralized machines found in places such as South Korea and Taiwan. Moreover, whereas the centralized machines in South Korea and Taiwan enjoyed considerable political hegemony, most machines in the United States had to perpetually battle for political power. In some localities, machines managed to entrench themselves. By and large, however, machine domination was surprisingly short-lived, and in many localities machines were apt to find themselves alternating between periods in office and periods in the political wilderness.[29]

China displays a very similar pattern of disorganized corruption. Although some, such as Hilton Root, have suggested that corruption is evolving toward some sort of systematic corruption, the evidence reveals that corruption in China involves individual officials, small cliques of officials, individual state and public institutions, and even collusive rings of officials, businessmen, and gangsters operating largely on their own.[30] In other words, individual parts and segments of the party-state apparatus have usurped their authority for illicit gain. The regime as a whole, as an institution, has not, thus far, degenerated into an instrument of plunder. Corruption remains a fragmentary problem. At the same time, while there is evidence to suggest that corruption has become the glue for local corporatism in some localities, there is no evidence that national economic policy is predicated on the CCP's dependence on the business sector. The party-state is unquestionably biased in favor of state-owned corporations, particularly the very large ones, and, as Yasheng Huang argues, economic policies frequently give the state sector an unfair advantage over the private sector.[31] The state is not, however, a hostage of the business sector in the manner that David Kang sees the South Korean state locked into a collusive and ultimately corrupt relationship with the *chaebol*.[32] Corruption in China, therefore, has much more in common with the disorganized, localized machine politics found in the United States during the Gilded Age (and later) than it does with either a classical kleptocracy or a stylized developmental state.

Second, like the United States during the Gilded Age, the spread of corruption in post-Mao China bred anticorruption. In the United States anticorruption pressures were largely driven by electoral politics. Evidence of widespread vote buying, ballot-box stuffing, and even political violence notwithstanding, elections were vigorous and wide open political fights in which charges and countercharges of corruption flew freely. Incumbents were relentlessly attacked as corrupt thieves. Challengers were accused of seeking plunder. A highly partisan free press also ensured that allegations of corruption and dirty deals were constantly put before the electorate. In China, on the other hand, anticorruption was a top-down affair, with the central leadership acting as the primary driving force. The public played an important but indirect role in the sense that fear of a popular backlash was a major motivating force behind the leadership's attack on corruption. Even though the modalities may have been radically different, the reality was not. In both instances the corrupt constantly feared punishment. In China the corrupt had to fear the wrath of the party disciplinary commission and the procuratorate. In the United States, the corrupt had to fear the wrath of the voter and crusading district attorneys. Even though some, perhaps even most, of those involved in corruption may well have escaped punishment, in neither case could the wicked go about their dirty work without worrying that their luck might suddenly run out and they would find themselves facing judgment. In both cases, therefore, anticorruption acted as a check on corruption and hence helped ensure that corruption did not spiral out of control as was the case in a kleptocracy.

Third, both the U.S. and Chinese economies were undergoing major structural transformations. The change in China is obvious and the connection to corruption overt. As argued in chapter 5, stripped to its barest essentials, economic reform in China entailed the transfer of control of valuable economic assets from the state to private or corporate control. In the process, tremendous windfall profits could be made by arbitraging between the nominal value of assets and economic opportunities in the new profit-based marketized economy. Windfall profits, I thus assert, bred corruption because corrupt officials were positioned to leverage their authority and would-be entrepreneurs were equally willing to pay for privileged access. Reform, structural transformation, and windfall profits, combined with an underdeveloped and struggling legal system, thus created a wide array of opportunities for corruption in post-Mao China.

The U.S. economy was, of course, not transitioning from the plan to the market. As such, there were no obvious windfall profits to drive corruption. And yet, the U.S. economy was undergoing a dramatic change that in scale, if not detail, was as dramatic as that which took place in post-Mao China. Prior to the Gilded Age, most companies were small, local, proprietor-owned and -managed firms. As the U.S. Industrial Revolution progressed, an entirely new form of capitalism emerged. With the changing scale and scope of U.S. business, the economy moved from a form of early capitalism to a more advanced industrial capitalism in which business became increasingly political business.[33] In this transition, the relationship between the state and business deepened as the extent of regulation increased and the state became an important economic actor, as well as playing its traditional role as tax collector and tariff setter. Public works spending was on the rise, as was government involvement in infrastructural development. Business itself was undergoing a tremendous transformation and consolidation as numerous localized firms were either being absorbed into larger corporations or, in many cases, forced out of business by firms whose size enabled them to achieve much higher economies of scale, cut costs, and undercut their competitors.[34] The rules of the game in this period were changing fast and were often ill defined or subject to political manipulation. And new fortunes were being made—and lost. Municipal government too exercised considerable local regulatory authority, including the granting of licenses and franchises, which positioned local politicians to exert influence.[35]

The parallels between contemporary China and the United States in its Gilded Age are perhaps a bit broad, but they are, I believe, significant. In both cases, corruption grew apace with the economy, and yet in neither case did corruption degenerate into uncontrolled kleptocracy. Given the parallels between post-Mao China and the U.S. Gilded Age, it is possible that the end of the Gilded Age may provide insight into the future of corruption in China. As noted earlier, popular pressure for an end to bossism and corruption was ever-present, and beginning in the 1870s attempts were made to reduce corruption, first by creating a new professional civil service and reducing the scope of patronage and its maxim of "to the winner go the spoils" of political warfare. Eliminating the spoils system took time, but by the beginning of the twentieth century, during what is generally called the Progressive Era, many public-sector jobs had been professionalized.[36] In the process, many bureaucratic positions that had been held by politicians and political loyalists were taken over by nonpolitical managers and technocrats. Fast and loose systems for collecting taxes and spending public monies were replaced by regularized budgeting and systems of accounting that made it much more difficult for politicians to steer funds to their political and business allies or into their own pockets. Businesses, meanwhile, were being professionalized as white-collar salaried workers replaced the entrepreneurial captains of industry and the swashbuckling robber barons at the helms of major corporations. Professionalization of the state and corporatization of business tended to work toward decreases in the use of irregular means as both bureaucrats and salary men looked more toward long-term job security than short-term payoffs. The process took considerable time, and political machines remained entrenched in many places well into the 1940s or even later.

In some sense, China is now slowly moving toward a type of progressive era. In the last decade, considerable strides have been made to reduce the opportunities for corruption by establishing more regular and transparent governmental processes, including systematic auditing, requirements that public officials disclose their assets, and efforts to root out false-named bank accounts used to hide officials' ill-gotten gains. The leadership has also faced pressure from within the political establishment. In 1996 and again in 1997, for example, the State Council faced what is in Chinese politics the equivalent of a parliamentary revolt when large numbers of delegates to the National People's Congress either abstained or voted against approving the annual work report of the Supreme People's Procuratorate and the Supreme People's Court, the governmental agencies that play the leading role in investigating and prosecuting corruption.[37]

More important, perhaps, both hard and soft measures of corruption seem to suggest that after worsening in the 1980s and intensifying in the 1990s, the severity of corruption has leveled off. As argued in chapter 4, for close to a decade the broad RRC has been declining. Whereas on average between 1996 and 2002, the procuratorate filed 32,000 economic crime cases, between 2003 and 2007 it filed an average of 29,000, a 10 percent decrease. Similarly, as noted earlier in this chapter, Transparency International's Corruption Perceptions Index score for China decreased from 7.57 in 1995 and 1996 to 6.50 in 2010, bringing it closer to the global mean.[38] Because the RRC is a partial and imperfect proxy for the ARC, and the PLC is likely a partial function of the RRC, changes in these measures do not reliably reflect changes in the actual rate of corruption. Attempts to measure variations in the gap between the RRC and the ARC using changes in risk, as derived from examination of changes in the lag between when an individual first engages in corruption and when he or she is caught, yield mixed results. The results do, however, suggest there has not been decisive movement toward either a marked decrease in the ARC or a significant increase.[39] By extension, this implies that after over a quarter-century of fighting corruption, the CCP has at least managed to head off the trend toward steady increases in the incidence of corruption, as had occurred in the late 1980s, and this has helped keep the incidence of corruption from moving beyond some ill-defined tipping point where it could swamp the regime.[40]

The evidence on trends in intensity suggests that the regime has been less successful in controlling high-level, high-stakes corruption. Nevertheless, in the last few years the rate of intensification seems to have decreased as the number of senior officials charged with corruption has been relatively constant at about 2,500. The average amount of money recovered per case, however, continued to rise, though not as rapidly as in the past. In sum, the evidence suggests that China's war on corruption has reached a stalemate. If this is the case, then we would date China's "crisis of corruption" to a period between roughly 1985 and 1995 and categorize the last decade and a half as one of "steady state" corruption in which the economy has been able to withstand the negative effects of corruption and continue to grow at a healthy pace.

Skeptics of my claim that China has sustained rapid growth despite a marked worsening and intensification of corruption will likely find the chicken analogy used earlier an apt opportunity to attack my arguments. To critics such as Gordon Chang and Minxin Pei, the lack of apparent negative effects of corruption is a case of the chickens having yet to come home to roost.[41] From this point of view, corruption is a ticking time-bomb, a delayed disaster. To this view, the so-called Chinese Economic Miracle[42] is thus nothing more than the world's most incredible bubble. And just as all bubble economies heretofore have burst, often with devastating economic consequences, ultimately the albatross of corruption will catch up with the "liar's poker" of China's boom. Huang also suggests that the overt economic success since 1990 has been the result of the growth not of dynamic entrepreneurial capitalism but of a form of state-sponsored capitalism in which state-owned enterprises have turned the economy into something resembling the crony capitalism found in places such as pre-1997 Indonesia.[43] On one level, Pei and others are correct. There is certainly a danger that China will become trapped in some sort of corrupt crony capitalism with Chinese characteristics.

Rather than seeing the worsening of corruption as largely a function of institutional decay, my argument asserts that we have witnessed concurrent increases in corruption and high growth rates because the transition from the old, planned economy to a more marketized economy and the transfer of control rights from the state to private economic interests created new opportunities for corruption, including a wave of windfall profits generated by the transfer of assets from the state to the economy. In theory, the opportunities and incentives for windfall-driven corruption should diminish once assets have been transferred from the state to the market. In reality, conditions will only change dramatically if such transfers are complemented by the establishment of secure property rights. So long as transfers remain incomplete and property rights stet tentative, corrupt officials will be able to extract bribes and kickbacks from would-be buyers. If the sale of these assets is complete in the sense that the buyers receive unfettered control rights, then officials will be less able to lay claim to them and through such claims demand further payments. If, on the other hand, the sale is incomplete, conditional, or can be abruptly and arbitrarily revoked, the door remains open for an ongoing series of demands for illicit payments. In this latter scenario, corrupt officials are positioned to demand a share of the initial windfall profits created by the difference between the state's nominal valuation of an asset and its de facto market value, and they can continue to demand a share of the profits generated by the asset by threatening to re-expropriate it from its initial purchaser and resell it to another would-be buyer. An incomplete and insecure set of post-transfer property rights, in other words, creates conditions favorable for an extended period of extortionary corruption and could, in my view, become a considerable drag on the economy. It is quite possible, therefore, that over time corruption in China could come to act much more in the manner described by the conventional wisdom in economics. In this sense, corruption would remain the sort of ticking time bomb described by Pei and others.

Heretofore, property rights have not been firmly established in China. As a result, corrupt officials remain positioned to extract illicit payments from those who obtain control over former state assets. In many cases, rights bought from one seller prove to be incomplete because the seller had only partial control rights and once the asset is sold, other claimants emerge to demand additional payments once the new owner begins to profit from the asset. In other instances, once profits begin to flow, the original seller will revoke the sale and reclaim the asset. In still other cases, buyers will quickly flip an asset by reselling it without fully transferring right to the asset to the secondary buyer, who then finds that once profits begin to flow claimants unbeknownst to them suddenly appear.

Problems in the regulatory and legal system have also contributed to ongoing corruption. Both the regulatory and legal systems have been works in progress since the advent of economic reforms, and neither has reached the point of impartiality or predictability. Regulations are often incomplete, reduplicative, contradictory, and arbitrary. The courts and legal system are similarly imperfect and subject to manipulation. Combined with insecure property rights, regulatory and legal deficiencies create additional opportunities for corruption and hence help ensure that rather than a single wave of windfall-driven corruption, China has faced a prolonged high tide of corruption.

A final factor that has, in my view, contributed to sustained high levels of corruption in post-Mao China is a distinct urban-rural gap. Perhaps inadequately articulated, my analysis in this book has a strong urban bias, particularly in chapter 5 where I point to the transitioning of assets from the state to the emerging private and semiprivate corporate sector as fueling a wave of windfall-driven corruption. Corruption is not, however, a purely urban phenomenon associated with the commercial and industrial sectors. Corruption is also a very serious and ongoing problem in the countryside. Although for purposes of brevity I have not delved into the unfolding dynamics of corruption in the countryside, it appears that a very different logic applies. The work of Thomas Bernstein and Lu Xiaobo, for example, strongly suggests that corruption in the countryside and in the less developed regions of China's hinterland is much more predatory that that found in the rapidly growing cities and regions along the eastern seaboard.[44] Presumably, if the aggregate data I present in this study were broken down into urban and rural subcategories, the contrast between city and countryside would not only be stark but the extent to which urban corruption has been more developmental in nature would also be accentuated. Moreover, if we posit that corruption was more predatory in the countryside and hence more developmental in the cities, the overt second paradox of high levels of predatory corruption and rapid growth in post-Mao China would be decreased because growth rates in rural areas have been much lower than in major cities. In other words, the tale of two post-Mao Chinas I raise in my introduction, the China of the economic miracle and the China with out-of-control corruption, needs to be conjoined with an additional tale of a rapidly developing urban China and a lagging hinterland. That analysis must, however, be deferred to future work.

Despite the lack of a demonstrated contrast between corruption in the cities and corruption in the countryside, if corruption in the countryside is not linked to the transfer of assets from the state to private and semiprivate control but rather to the largely arbitrary and unchecked power of rural cadres, then decreases in corruption there depend much more heavily on political reforms exogenous to the transitional dynamics I focus on in this book. Absent such reforms, the prospect is for ongoing high levels of predatory corruption in the countryside, which will tend to keep the aggregate level of corruption high.

So long as corruption remains a serious aggregate problem, even if we do not see dramatic increases, there is a danger that corruption will produce the extreme negative consequences predicted by Chang, Pei, and others. That high levels of corruption have not been directly associated with retarded growth heretofore is no guarantee that they will not in the future. I would not, therefore, entirely rule out a future crisis of corruption along the lines they suggest. Even so, I do not think the possibility of such a crisis contradicts my finding that heretofore the dynamic relationship between corruption and growth has been positive in that growth rates have remained high even as corruption worsened and intensified.

In conclusion, China appears to present students of the political economy of corruption with a double paradox, the primary paradox of a worsening corruption and sustained rapid economic growth and the secondary paradox of a worsening of predatory corruption and sustained rapid economic growth. As such, it seems to provide a unique example of a country that has not only flipped on its head the otherwise general rule that corruption is negatively correlated with growth but has managed to sustain high rates of growth even in the face of what appears to be a particularly bad form of corruption. Although corruption may be defined broadly as the misuse of public authority for private advantage, not all forms of corruption are equally damaging to an economy. I have endeavored to show that although some forms of corruption (degenerative corruption or what is also called kleptocracy) are certainly the cause of poor economic performance if not economic collapse, there are other instances in which corruption binds together the profit-making interests of business and the political interests of politicians through the nexus of politicians' need for political money and business interests' desire for favorable policy treatment to form developmental alliances. In chapter 2, I argue that the latter form of corruption, which I term "developmental corruption," was foundational to the economic success of South Korea and Taiwan. But when I turn my attention to China, the evidence clearly shows that dirty money and its use to create a developmental machine was not a necessary precondition for the adoption of pro-growth macroeconomic policies. On the contrary, the form of corruption most common in China at the advent of economic reforms was much closer to the predatory corruption associated with kleptocracy. Resolving the first paradox by showing why South Korea and Taiwan managed to grow rapidly even though corruption was deeply embedding in their political systems, thus called forth the needed for a much deeper explanation of China's ability to defy conventional wisdom and grow rapidly despite experiencing the growth of a form of corruption that more closely resembled that found in Zaire or Sierra Leone than that in the South Korea or Taiwan.

In chapters 4 and 5, I attempt to resolve the second paradox by first demonstrating that although corruption existed prior to reforms, it was not until the adoption of reforms spurred a burst of growth that the incidence of corruption began to rise significantly. More critically, it was not until the deepening of reforms and the adoption of policies that transferred control over key economic assets from the state to economic actors that corruption began to intensify. The shift from rising, low-level corruption to increasingly high-stakes, high-level corruption, I assert, occurred only after the economy was already in high gear. As a result, corruption fed off growth rather than acting as an a priori barrier to accelerated economic development. Moreover, as argued in chapter 6, when corruption first began to worsen and then intensify, the CCP-dominated state was perhaps slow to respond. But after corruption helped fuel major antigovernment demonstrations in the spring of 1989, the party leadership stepped up its so-called "war on corruption." Rising corruption was thus met with anticorruption, and although it would be hard to argue that the regime's war on corruption has been successful in reducing corruption, the evidence suggests that regardless of its deficiencies, the effort has kept corruption from spiraling out of control.

The double paradox of high levels of predatory corruption and rapid growth in China is thus a tale of a massive transfer of wealth in which officials were able to siphon off a share of the resulting windfall profits. Not all the surge in corruption during the reform period was, of course, linked to this transfer. A general loosening of bureaucratic controls and lack of constraints on officials' authority also fueled the worsening of corruption. Reform thus caused an increase in what we might call the ambient level of corruption. The surge in corruption that became evident in the years after Tiananmen can, however, be directly linked with the deepening of reform in the early 1990s. Transferring state assets to the private and semiprivate sectors fueled a high growth rate as these assets were put to more efficient use, while at the same time generating a burst of corruption as officials sought to cash in on both the windfall profits generated by the immediate transfer and the profits that began to flow to the new buyers afterward. The result was a combination of rapid growth and intensified corruption. Corruption was not, it must be emphasized once again, the cause of rapid growth. Corruption in China was not, therefore, some sort of growth-generating phenomenon. On the contrary, the evidence shows that corruption in China was no different from corruption elsewhere. But the surge in corruption in China took place in the context of a powerful economic boom. In theory, because the surge was a function of the transfer of assets from the state to the private and semiprivate sectors, the surge should slacken as the transfer process reaches completion. But this is only likely if a system of secure property rights is put in place and the new owners of these assets become less vulnerable to officials seeking to use their authority for private gain. It is thus possible that in the long run China's surge of corruption may become a heavy drag on its economy. The evidence suggests, however, that the surge of the early 1990s has been brought under a semblance of control, which may foretell a continuation of the present pattern of corruption plus growth for some time to come.

Notes

1. Ivan Tang, "Corruption 'Boosts Economic Growth,'" *South China Morning Post,* June 7, 1997.

CHAPTER 1

1. See Justin Yifu Lin, *The China Miracle: Development Strategy and Economic Reform* (Hong Kong: Chinese University Press, 1996).

2. Based on data from the International Monetary Fund, World Economic Outlook Database, October 2010, available at http://www.imf.org/external/pubs/ft/weo/2010/02/weodata/index.aspx, accessed January 12, 2011. Data for 1979 and 1980 from the World Economic Outlook Database, October 2002.

3. Ibid.

4. See Gordon G. Chang, *The Coming Collapse of China* (New York: Random House, 2001).

5. Based on data in *Zhongguo Jiancha Nianjian* [Procuratorial Yearbook of China] (Beijing: Zhongguo Jiancha Chubanshe, various years).

6. As used here, "bribe size" is derived by dividing the total amount of money that the procuratorate reported it recovered from prosecuting economic crimes by the total number of cases filed. Because it is not entirely clear how the procuratorate calculates the amount of money it recovers and whether the percentage of all corrupt money it "recovers" varies significantly between years, the result is at best a crude estimate of bribe size.

7. See Political Risk Services, *International Country Risk Guide;* Transparency International, Corruption Perceptions Index, available at http://www.transparency.org/policy_research/surveys_indices/cpi, accessed September 12, 2008; and Political and Economic Risk Consultancy (http://www.asiarisk.com).

8. See inter alia Paolo Mauro, "Corruption and Growth," *Quarterly Journal of Economics* 111:3 (1995): 681–712; Kwabena Gyimah-Brempong, "Corruption, Economic Growth, and Income Inequality in Africa," *Economics of Governance* 3:3 (2002): 183–209; Sanjeev Gupta, Hamid Davoodi, and Rosa Alonso-Terme, "Does Corruption Affect Income Inequality?" *Economics of Governance* 3:1 (2002): 3: 23–45; Pak Hung Mo, "Corruption and Economic Growth," *Journal of Comparative Economics* 29:1 (2001): 66–79; Shang-Jin Wei, "Bribery in the Economies: Grease or Sand?" *Economic Survey of Europe 2001* (New York: United Nations, 2001), 101–12; Axel Dreher and Thomas Herzfeld, "The Economic Costs of Corruption: A Survey and New Evidence," mimeo 2005, available at http://ideas.repec.org/p/wpa/wuwppe/0506001.html, accessed January 27, 2006; Alberto Ades and Rafael Di Tella, "The New Economics of Corruption: A Survey and Some New Results," *Political Studies* 55:3 (1997): 496–515; and Daniel Kaufmann and Aart Kraay, "Growth without Governance," *Economia* 3:1 (2002), available at http://www.worldbank.org/wbi/governance/wp-corruption.html, accessed September 15, 2007.

9. Hamid Davoodi, "IMF Research on Corruption," in Transparency International, *Global Corruption Report 2001*, available at http://www.transparency.org/publications/gcr/gcr_2001, accessed May 29, 2007. Growth rate data based on data in IMF's World Economic Outlook 2004 database.

10. Transparency International index available at http://www.transparency.org/policy_research/surveys_indices/cpi, accessed April 4, 2011. TI uses a "poll of polls" method to aggregate expert estimates of the relative level of corruption in each country. This yields a "soft" measure of corruption because it is ultimately based on each individual's subjective sense of how bad corruption is in a particular country.

11. The conventional wisdom is not without its economic critics. In contrast to other economists, for instance, Barreto finds a positive correlation between corruption and growth. Raul A. Barreto, "Endogenous Corruption, Inequality and Growth," mimeo, University of Colorado Boulder, available at http://www.economics.adelaide.edu.au/staff/barreto/research.html, accessed May 18, 2000; and Raul A. Barreto, "Institutional Corruption, the Public Sector, and Economic Development: Institutional Corruption and Paraguayan Economic Development; Corruption in a Simple Endogenous Growth Model; and Endogenous Corruption, Income Inequality, and Growth: Econometric Evidence" (PhD diss., Department of Economics, University of Colorado Boulder, 1996), available at http://www.economics.adelaide.edu.au/staff/barreto/html, accessed January 28, 2006. Elsewhere, however, Barreto hedges his claim, concluding that the effects of corruption on growth appear "neither efficiency enhancing nor efficiency detracting with respect to growth." Raul A. Barreto, "Endogenous Corruption in a Neoclassical Growth Model," *European Economic Review* 44 (2000): 35–60. Meon and Weill find that although corruption is negatively correlated with growth in cases where institutions are effective, it can have a positive effect where institutions are defective. Pierre-Guillaume and Khalid Sekkat, "Does Corruption Grease or Sand the Wheels of Growth?" *Public Choice* 122:1–2 (2005): 69–97. Pellegrini and Gerlagh, on the other hand, suggest that corruption has a marginal and ambiguous impact on growth rates. Lorenzo Pellegrini and Reyer Gerlagh, "Corruption's Effect on Growth and its Transmission Channels," *Kyklos* 57:3 (2004): 457–70. Mendez and Sepulveda also find an ambiguous relationship, with low levels of corruption having an apparent positive effect on growth in free countries but an indeterminate effect on growth in nonfree countries. Fabio Mendez and Facundo Sepulveda, "Corruption, Growth, and Political Regimes: Cross Country Evidence," *European Journal of Political Economy* 22:1 (2005): 82–98. Also see Francis T. Lui, "Three Aspects of Corruption," *Contemporary Economic Policy* 14:3 (1996): 26–29. Political scientists have questioned the validity of indices based on expert polls, arguing that better governance, including lower levels of corruption, is a consequence of economic development, which implies that the correlation between higher levels of corruption and lower rate of growth is spurious. Marcus J. Kurtz and Andrew Schrank, "Growth and Governance: Model, Measures, and Mechanisms," *Journal of Politics* 69:2 (2007): 538–54.

12. Chalmers Johnson, "Tanaka Kakuei, Structural Corruption, and the Advent of Machine Politics in Japan," *Annuals of Japanese Studies* 12:1 (1986): 1–28.

13. Ting Gong, "Forms and Characteristics of China's Corruption in the 1990s: Change with Continuity," *Communist and Post-Communist Studies* 30:3 (1997): 277–88.

14. For a more in-depth discussion of corruption involving the real estate market, see Ting Gong, "Corruption and Local Governance: The Double Identity of Chinese Local Government in Market Reform," *Pacific Review* 19:1 (2006): 85–102.

15. Ting Gong, "Dangerous Collusion: Corruption as a Collective Venture in Contemporary China," *Communist and Post-Communist Studies* 35:1 (2002): 85–103.

16. See also Guo Yong, "How Does Economic Transition Breed Corruption?" *China Economic Journal* 1:2 (2008): 227–36.

17. See Mayfair Mei-hua Yang, *Gifts, Favors, and Banquets: The Art of Social Relationships in China* (Ithaca, N.Y.: Cornell University Press, 1994). Also see Julia Kwong, *The Political Economy of Corruption in China* (Armonk, N.Y.: M. E. Sharpe, 1997).

18. See Lu Xiaobo, *Cadres and Corruption: The Organizational Involution of the Chinese Communist Party* (Stanford: Stanford University Press, 2000).

19. Yan Sun, *Corruption and Market in Contemporary China* (Ithaca, N.Y.: Cornell University Press, 2004): 192–215.

20. Sun Yan, "Reform, State, and Post-Communist Corruption: Is Corruption Less Destructive in China than in Russia?" *Comparative Politics* 32:1 (1999): 1–20. In 1997, I proposed a tripartite model of corruption that distinguished between looting, rent scraping, and dividend collecting. In that model, I used the term "dividend collecting" to describe a form of collusion between big businesses and ruling parties, wherein a ruling party enacted pro-growth macroeconomic policies that favored big business. In return, the beneficiaries of these policies were expected and required to provide the political capital necessary to maintain the ruling party's grip on power. I subsumed dividend collecting under a more general model that I termed "developmental corruption." In contrast to what I described as "degenerative corruption" where some combination of kleptocracy, plunder, and crony capitalism predominates, developmental corruption describes cases in which politicians and big business reached a tacit modus vivendi: the politicians supported profitmaking by big business, and big business agreed to render the financial support required for political purposes—but also provided politicians with personal financial rewards. See Andrew Wedeman, "Looters, Rent-Scrapers, and Dividend Collectors: Corruption and Growth in Zaire, South Korea, and the Philippines," *Journal of Developing Areas* 31:4 (1997); and Andrew Wedeman, "Development and Corruption: The East Asian Paradox," in Edmund Terence Gomez, ed., *Political Business in East Asia* (New York: Routledge, 2002), 34–61. In her 1999 comparison of the contrasting effects of corruption in China and Russia, Sun repackaged the dividend-collecting model using the title of "profit sharing" without substantially altering the original model. Sun, "Reform, State, and Post-Communist Corruption."

21. Jane Duckett, "The Emergence of the Entrepreneurial State in Contemporary China," *Pacific Review* 9 (1996): 180–98; Jane Duckett, "Bureaucrats in Business, Chinese Style: The Lessons of Market Reform and State Entrepreneurialism in the People's Republic of China," *World Development* 29:1 (2001): 23–37; Chengze Simon Fan and Herschel I. Grossman, "Incentives and Corruption in Chinese Economic Reform," *Policy Reform* 4 (2001): 195–206; Jean C. Oi, "The Role of the Local State in China's Transitional Economy," *China Quarterly* 144 (1995): 1132–49; Jean C. Oi, "The Evolution of Local State Corporatism," in Andrew G. Walder, *Zouping in Transition: The Process of Reform in Rural North China* (Cambridge, Mass.: Harvard University Press, 1998), 35–61; and Andrew G. Walder, "Local Governments as Industrial Firms: An Organizational Analysis of China's Transitional Economy," *American Journal of Sociology* 101:2 (1995): 263–301.

22. Sun, *Corruption and Market*, 203–8.

23. Gong, "Forms and Characteristics of China's Corruption in the 1990s," 277–88.

24. Minxin Pei, "Will China Become Another Indonesia," *Foreign Policy* 116 (1999): 94–119; Minxin Pei, "The Dark Side of China's Rise," *Foreign Policy* 153 (2006); 32–40; and Minxin Pei, *China's Trapped Transition: The Limits of Developmental Autocracy* (Cambridge, Mass.: Harvard University Press, 2006), 209.

25. Hilton Root, "Corruption in China: Has It Become Systemic?" *Asian Survey* 36:8 (1996): 741–57.

26. Melanie Manion, *Corruption by Design: Building Clean Government in Mainland China and Hong Kong* (Cambridge, Mass.: Harvard University Press, 2004), 114–15.

27. Estimates of the costs imposed on the Chinese economy by corruption vary. Manion, for example, cites estimates of between 2 and 4 percent. Ibid., 113. Pei derives an estimate of the direct cost of corruption at around US$86 billion (¥712 billion) a year in 2003, or about 3 percent of GDP. Minxin Pei, "Corruption Threatens China's Future," Carnegie Endowment for International Peace, Policy Brief 55 (2007). Chinese economist Hu Angang, on the other hand, argues that in the late 1990s corruption absorbed 13–17

percent of GDP, siphoned off 15–20 percent of public expenditures, and cost the government ¥150 billion (US$18 billion) in lost tax revenues. Hu's estimates quoted in June Teufel Dreyer, "The Limits to China's Growth," *Orbis* 48:2 (2002): 243.

28. *Zhongguo Tongji Nianjian* [Statistical Yearbook of China] (Beijing: Zhongguo Tongji Chubanshe, various years). In China, the "budget" includes all revenues and expenditures from the unitary budget and includes spending by the central, provincial, and subprovincial budget. The "extra budget" includes revenues and expenditures by governments that are not included in the unitary budget. The figure of ¥15.2 trillion in extrabudgetary expenditures for capital construction must be treated with caution because, prior to 1993, extrabudgetary expenditures included capital investment by state-owned industries, whose profits were classified as extra budgetary funds. After 1993, the profits of state-owned industries were moved off the extra budget and reclassified as enterprise funds. Hence, after 1993 capital construction expenditures by state-owned enterprises were no longer included in the data of extrabudgetary spending.

29. Geoff Dwyer, "China Embarks on Infrastructure Spending Spree," *Financial Times*, June 6, 2010; and Glenn Pew, "Infrastructure Spending, China-Style," AVweb, March 3, 2011, available at http://www.avweb.com/avwebflash/news/china_infrastructure_spending_airports_aircraft_airliner_204211–1.html, accessed March 10, 2011.

30. Based on data in *Zhongguo Jiancha Nianjian,* various years. Chinese law categorizes "graft" (*tanwu*), bribery (*xinghui*), and "misappropriation" (*nuoyong gongkuan*) as "economic crimes" (*jingji fanzui*). *Tanwu* is conventionally translated as "corruption." To distinguish it from the more general term for corruption (*fubai*), I translate it as graft. "Misappropriation" differs from embezzlement (*daoyong* or *qintun*), which is considered to be a form of graft. Misappropriation involves the use of public funds to make unauthorized investments or deposits and then skimming off the interest or profits. The difference between embezzlement and misappropriation is that embezzlement involves the outright theft of public funds whereas misappropriation involves the misuse of funds. Over the years, a number of other offenses have been included under the rubric of economic crime, including tax evasion, tax resistance, and copyright infringement. More recently, the offenses of asset stripping and possession of unexplained assets have been added. Chinese law also defines a secondary form of misuse of authority as disciplinary (*faji*) offenses, which includes dereliction of duty, negligence, abuse of prisoners and detainees, and violations of citizens' civil or religious rights. The difference between economic crime and disciplinary offense is that the former involves the misuse of authority for personal gain and the latter involves the abuse of authority. In this book, I focus on economic crime and do not delve into the question of disciplinary offenses, which remain a largely unexplored area of official malfeasance.

31. Based on data in *Zhongguo Falu Nianjian* [China Legal Yearbook] (Beijing: Zhongguo Falu Nianjian Chubanshe, various years).

32. Between 1995 and 2000, Amnesty International compiled reports of death sentences handed down by Chinese courts gleaned from both the Western and Chinese press in its annual "China Death Penalty Log" (both the 1995 and 1996 logs, however, contained only partial year data). (Death Penalty Logs available at http://www.amnesty.org/en/library, accessed August 12, 2002.) In all, Amnesty International documented 350 death sentences for bribery, graft, and embezzlement during these years. Searches conducted by the author for the years prior to 1996 and after 2000 using the LexisNexis system produce an additional 496 cases. My estimate of 1,000 death sentences should, therefore, be considered a conservative minimum. A suspended death sentence is normally commuted to life after two years.

33. On the complicated relationship between the disciplinary actions by the Discipline Inspection Commission, criminal investigations by the procuratorate, and court

prosecutions, see Andrew Wedeman, "Guilt and Punishment in China's War on Corruption," in Jean C. Oi, Scott Rozelle, and Xueguang Zhou, eds., *Growing Pains: Tension and Opportunity in Contemporary China* (Stanford, Calif.: Walter H. Shorenstein Asia-Pacific Research Center, 2010), 117–42.

34. Mark R. Kleiman, "Enforcement Swamping: A Positive Feedback Mechanism in Rates of Illicit Activity," *Mathematical Computer Modeling* 17:2 (1993): 65–75; and Francis T. Lui, "A Dynamic Model of Corruption Deterrence," *Journal of Public Economics* 31:2 (1986): 215–26.

35. The government's main anticorruption agency, the procuratorate, had been disbanded prior to the Cultural Revolution and was not resurrected in 1978. The party's Discipline Inspection Commission, which is charged with internal policing (but lacks judicial authority) had also been defunct and was not reestablished until the late 1970s. Moreover, until 1979 the PRC had no criminal code and hence no formal legal definition of what constituted corruption. In the early 1980s, the regime thus had to scramble to build its anticorruption agencies.

36. Also see Andrew Wedeman, "Win, Lose, or Draw? China's War on Corruption," *Crime, Law and Social Change* 49:1 (2008): 7–26.

37. Andrew Wedeman, "Anticorruption Campaigns and the Intensification of Corruption in China," *Journal of Contemporary China* 14:41 (2005): 93–107.

38. Andrei Schleifer and Robert W. Vishny, "Corruption," *Quarterly Journal of Economics* 108:3 (1993): 599–617.

CHAPTER 2

1. Chalmers Johnson, *MITI and the Japanese Miracle: The Growth of Industrial Policy, 1925–1975* (Stanford, Calif.: Stanford University Press, 1982), 34; and Chalmers Johnson, "Tanaka Kakuei, Structural Corruption, and the Advent of Machine Politics in Japan," *Journal of Japanese Studies* 12:1 (1986): 1–28.

2. Ezra F. Vogel, *Japan as Number One: Lessons for America* (New York: Harper & Row, 1979), 126.

3. Richard H. Mitchell, *Political Bribery in Japan* (Honolulu: University of Hawaii Press, 1996), 157.

4. Robert Wade, *Governing the Market: Economic Theory and the Role of the Government in East Asian Industrialization* (Princeton, N.J.: Princeton University Press, 1990), 287–89.

5. Beatrice Weder, *Model, Myth, or Miracle: Reassessing the Role of Governments in the East Asian Experience* (New York: United Nations University Press, 1999).

6. Asian Development Bank, *Emerging Asia Changes and Challenges* (Manila: Asian Development Bank, 1997), 75. Transparency International's annual corruption rankings show that corruption was not lower in East Asia as a whole. Compared with other developing regions, the average perceived level of corruption in East Asia was fairly high, particularly when Hong Kong, Japan, and Singapore are treated separately:

Average Regional Corruption Perceptions Index Scores, 1992–2009, calculated by Transparency International (inverted so that 10 equals the worst possible corruption and 1 the least possible corruption)

Hong Kong, Japan, and Singapore	2.03
Advanced Industrial Democracies	2.35
Eastern Europe	5.96
Latin America	6.17
Middle East and North Africa	6.42

East Asia	6.67
Sub-Saharan Africa	7.05
South Asia	7.28
Former Soviet Union	7.31

Because the Transparency International data extend back only to the 1990s, and the putative heyday of the developmental state in Japan, South Korea, and Taiwan predated that time, their utility in comparing levels of corruption is obviously somewhat limited. Data from Transparency International, "Corruption Perceptions Index," 1992 to 2009, available at http://www.transparency.org, accessed June 15, 2010. Rock and Bonnett, however, find that statistically corruption had less of a negative impact on economic performance in East Asia. Michael T. Rock and Heidi Bonnett, "The Comparative Politics of Corruption: Accounting for the East Asian Paradox in Empirical Studies of Corruption, Growth and Investment," *World Development* 32:6 (2004): 999–1017.

7. I am not the first to come to this conclusion. Corruption was so blatant in South Korea during the 1980s that one critic described it as a degenerate "racketeering state." Martin Hart-Landsberg, *The Rush to Development: Economic Change and Political Struggle in South Korea* (New York: Monthly Review Press, 1993), 235. Looking back at the history of political scandals involving the "shadow shoguns" that ran the Liberal Democratic Party during its heyday, Schlesinger concluded that the Japanese developmental state was "rotten to the core." Jacob M. Schlesinger, *Shadow Shoguns: The Rise of Japan's Postwar Political Machine* (New York: Simon & Schuster, 1997), 88.

8. Johnson, *MITI and the Japanese Miracle,* 314–15.

9. Peter Evans, *Embedded Autonomy: States and Industrial Transformation* (Princeton, N.J.: Princeton University Press, 1995).

10. Johnson, "Tanaka Kakuei."

11. The model outlined in this paragraph imperfectly fits the Taiwanese case because for much of the developmentalist era, the Republic of China government was controlled by an authoritarian regime. As a result, the ruling Kuomintang was not dependent on elections to maintain its grip on power. As I argue, however, the KMT embraced machine-style politics because it afforded it a way to forge political alliances with local political factions and thereby mitigate "ethnic" conflicts between the mainlander-dominated KMT and the native Taiwanese.

12. David C. Kang, *Crony Capitalism: Corruption and Development in South Korea and the Philippines* (New York: Cambridge University Press, 2002).

13. Geddes argues that successful politicians combine expertise and patronage, using technocrats to create public goods such as economic growth and while using private goods in the form of patronage to secure political support. Political leaders who pursue public goods alone are apt to face stiff political opposition from within their own base which will prefer the generation of private goods. Political leaders who ignore the pursuit of public goods and focus on private benefits for their supporters will likely face mounting political pressure from opposition groups due in part to poor economic performance. Successful politicians, she concludes, are those who can bifurcate the state in ways that give experts and technocrats control over macroeconomic policy while also bestowing patronage and rents on their political loyalists. See Barbara Geddes, *Politician's Dilemma: Building State Capacity in Latin America* (Berkeley: University of California Press, 1994).

14. In a survey of corruption in resource-rich countries in Africa, McFerson uses the term "hyper-corruption," which might be a better descriptor of the extreme levels of corruption I lumped under the term "kleptocracy." Unfortunately, she does not offer sufficient definition in qualitative terms to render it a clearly better descriptor. Hazel McFerson,

"Governance and Hyper-Corruption in Resource-rich African Countries," *Third World Quarterly* 30:8 (2009): 1529–48.

15. Benjamin Nyblade and Steven R. Reed, "Who Cheats? Who Loots? Political Competition and Corruption in Japan, 1947–1993," *American Journal of Political Science* 52:4 (2008): 926–41.

16. Quee-young Kim, *The Fall of Syngman Rhee* (Berkeley: Institute of East Asian Studies, University of California, 1983), 22.

17. Ki-shik Hahn, "Underlying Factors in Political Party Organization and Elections," in Edward Reynolds Wright, ed., *Korean Politics in Transition* (Seattle: University of Washington Press, 1975), 87–88.

18. Based on data in Han Ki-shik, "Development of Parties and Politics in Korea," Part 1, *Korea Journal* 14:8 (1974): 46–47.

19. In 1960, surveys revealed that over half of voters replied "don't know" when asked about their partisan identification. Lee Joung-sik, "Voting Behavior in Korea," *Korean Affairs* 2:3–4 (1963): 353.

20. Kim, *The Fall of Syngman Rhee.*

21. Gregory Henderson, *Korea: The Politics of the Vortex* (Cambridge, Mass.: Harvard University Press, 1968), 288–89.

22. Han Tae-soo, "A Review of Political Party Activities in Korea (1945–1954)," *Korean Affairs* 1:4 (1962): 414.

23. In 1950, Rhee had organized the Daehan National Party but it captured only twenty-four seats in the May 1950 National Assembly elections, just one more that the main opposition party (the Democratic Nationalist Party). In late 1951, Rhee reorganized that party and established the Liberal Party, which would become the dominant party during the 1950s. Ibid., 425.

24. Han, "Development of Parties and Politics in Korea," Part 2, *Korea Journal* 14:10 (1974): 44.

25. Edward C. Keefer, "The Truman Administration and the South Korean Political Crisis of 1952: Democracy's Failure?" *Pacific Historical Review* 60:2 (1991): 148–52. Soon after the formation of the Liberal Party, Rhee purged its ranks in an effort to prevent the formations of factions loyal to other political leaders. Han T'ae-soo, "A Review of Political Party Activities in Korea (1955–60)," *Korean Affairs* 2:4 (1963): 320–21.

26. Jong Yil Ra, "Political Crisis in Korea, 1952: The Administration, Legislature, Military and Foreign Powers," *Journal of Contemporary History* 27:2 (1992): 301–18.

27. Se-Jin Kim, *The Politics of Military Revolution in Korea* (Chapel Hill: University of North Carolina Press, 1971), 21.

28. Kim, *The Fall of Syngman Rhee*, 17–18. Six years later in 1958, when the opposition Democratic Party threatened to block a bill that would have allowed the police greater leeway in charging individuals with subversion, government thugs stormed the National Assembly and violently ousted the opposition parliamentarians, thus allowing the Liberals to ram the law through. David M. Earl, "Korea: The Meaning of the Second Republic," *Far Eastern Survey* 29:11 (1960): 172. During this period, local police chiefs were expected to ensure that Liberal Party candidates won elections and were often demoted or sacked if they failed. Kim Kyu-taik, "The Behavior Patterns of Rulers and Ruled in Korean Politics," *Korean Affairs* 1:3 (1963): 324–25.

29. Ibid., 20.

30. Hahn, "Underlying Factors in Political Party Organization and Elections," 93. Ballot-rigging practices included the classic "rely method" in which a voter enters the voting both, marks the ballot, but then exits without casting it. The ballot is then passed to a party activist, who hands it to a second voter, who casts it and returns with an unmarked ballot. The "rely" ensures that bought voters vote as agreed. There was also the "piano"

method wherein election officials used ink-soaked fingers to soil opposition ballots, thus invalidating them. A third method was the "owl vote" wherein the lights would be shut off during the vote count so the ruling party's vote counters could "properly adjust" the vote tally. See Han, "Development of Parties and Politics in Korea," Part 2, *Korea Journal* 14:10 (1974): 56 (note 65).

31. William A. Douglas, "South Korea's Search for Leadership," *Pacific Affairs* 37:1 (1964): 23; Kyong-Dong Kim, "Political Factors in the Formation of the Entrepreneurial Elite in South Korea," *Asian Survey* 16:5 (1976): 465–77; Jung-en Woo, *Race to the Swift: State and Finance in Korean Industrialization* (New York: Columbia University Press, 1991), 65–69; Kim, *Politics of Military Revolution in Korea*, 24; and Mark L. Clifford, *Troubled Tiger: Businessmen, Bureaucrats, and Generals in South Korea* (Armonk, N.Y.: M. E. Sharpe, 1994), 93.

32. Kim, *Politics of Military Revolution in Korea*, 75–76, 83.

33. Ibid., 75.

34. W. D. Reeve, *The Republic of Korea: A Political and Economic Study* (New York: Oxford University Press, 1963), 97–100; and Kim, *The Fall of Syngman Rhee*, 19–20.

35. Jung Ku-hyun, "Business-Government Relations in the Growth of Korean Business Groups," *Korean Social Science Journal* 14 (1988): 67–82; Stephan Haggard, *Pathways from the Periphery: The Political of Growth in Newly Industrializing Countries* (Ithaca, N.Y.: Cornell University Press, 1990), 61; and Stephan Haggard, Byung-kook Kim, and Chung-in Moon, "The Transition to Export-Led Growth in South Korea, 1954–1966," *Journal of Asian Studies* 50:4 (1991): 850–73.

36. Earl, "Korea," 171.

37. Quee-young Kim, "From Protest to Change of Regime: The 4–19 Revolt and the Fall of the Rhee Regime in South Korea," *Social Forces* 74:4 (1996): 1179–1208. Also see Kim, *The Fall of Syngman Rhee*, for a more exhaustive account.

38. The South Korean military was under the formal control of the United Nations command, which was headed by the commander of the U.S. Eighth Army. In theory, South Korean military units could not leave their posts without the approval of the U.S. Army.

39. Immediately after Rhee's departure, a caretaker government headed by Ho Chong took over. Ho was, however, a transitional figure and his regime was soon swept out of power.

40. Choi Yearn H., "Failure of Democracy in Legislative Process: The Case of South Korea, 1960," *World Affairs* 140:4 (1978): 331–40; and Kim, *Politics of Military Revolution in Korea*, 27.

41. William A. Douglas, "Korean Students and Politics," *Asian Survey* 3:12 (1963): 584–95; and C. I. Eugene Kim and Ke-soo Kim, "The April 1960 Korean Student Movement," *Western Political Quarterly* 17:1 (1964): 83–92.

42. Henderson, *Korea*, 178.

43. Kim, *Politics of Military Revolution in Korea*, 27; and Kyung Cho Chung, *Korea: The Third Republic* (New York: Macmillan, 1971).

44. Anti-Japanese nationalism ran deep in post-1945 South Korea and the Rhee government banned virtually all imports from Japan, ostensibly because impoverished postwar South Korea had to conserve its small stocks of foreign currency. Joungwon Alexander Kim, *Divided Korea: The Politics of Development, 1945–1972* (Cambridge, Mass.: Harvard University Press, 1975), 213.

45. John Kie-chiang Oh, *Korea: Democracy on Trial* (Ithaca, N.Y.: Cornell University Press, 1968), 91.

46. Kim, *Politics of Military Revolution in Korea*, 83; and Sungjoo Han, *The Failure of Democracy in South Korea* (Berkeley: University of California Press, 1974).

47. Y. C. Han, "Political Parties and Political Development in South Korea," *Pacific Affairs* 42:4 (1969–70): 448; and Kim, *Divided Korea*, 231.

48. Kim, *Politics of Military Revolution in Korea,* 101.

49. Even before the coup, the military had been embroiled in a bitter fight between corrupt senior officers, some of whom were also clearly involved in the massive vote fraud that resulted in Rhee's reelection in February 1960, and a cadre of "young Turks" who unsuccessfully attempted to stage an intra-army coup in the form of a "purification movement" immediately after the April 1960 revolution. Ibid., 76–81.

50. Kim, *Divided Korea,* 235.

51. Quoted in Kim, *Politics of Military Revolution in Korea,* 108. Also see Kim, *Divided Korea,* 235; and Soon Sung Cho, "Korea: Election Year," *Asian Survey* 8:1 (1968): 33–34.

52. Eun Mee Kim, *Big Business, Strong State: Collusion and Conflict in South Korean Development, 1960–1990* (Albany: State University of New York Press, 1997), 114–15. The attack on profiteering had begun in April 1960 during the short-lived Ho Chong government, which announced it would investigate illegal purchases of confiscated Japanese property, cut-rate bank loans, illegal foreign currency trading, smuggling, bribery, and tax evasion. Twenty-five individuals were identified representing seventy-one organizations which had evaded ₩5 billion (US$7.7 million at the de facto exchange rate of ₩642:US$1) in taxes. The Ho government subsequently charged that sixteen of the largest corporations had failed to pay ₩5.8 billion (US$7 million) and then revised the figure up to ₩9 billion (US$14 million). After the collapse of the Ho government, the Chang government raised the total to ₩19 billion and identified major corporations in a wide range of sectors as tax evaders. Chang, however, took no decisive action because, his critics charged, the corporations involved agreed to fund his political activities, a charge Chang later admitted, saying he had indeed accepted ₩200 million in contributions from those charged with tax evasion. Sungjoo Han, *The Failure of Democracy in South Korea* (Berkeley: University of California Press, 1974), 62–63, 165–69.

53. Kim, *Politics of Military Revolution in Korea,* 105; and Kim, *Divided Korea,* 232.

54. Kim, *Politics of Military Revolution in Korea,* 110.

55. Shong-Sik Lee, "Korea: In Search of Stability," *Asian Survey* 4:1 (1964): 565; and Glenn D. Paige, "1966: Korea Creates the Future," *Asian Survey* 7:1 (1967): 23.

56. Kim, *Divided Korea,* 279; and Joungwon Alexander Kim, "The Republic of Korea: A Quest for New Directions," *Asian Survey* 11:1 (1971): 98.

57. Chae-Jin Lee, "South Korea: Political Competition and Government Adaptation," *Asian Survey* 12:1 (1972): 43.

58. Sungjoo Han, "South Korea in 1974: The 'Korean Democracy' on Trial," *Asian Survey* 15:1 (1975): 35–42.

59. Clifford, *Troubled Tiger,* 131.

60. Clifford, *Troubled Tiger,* 84. It was believed, for instance, that the waitresses in *kisaeng* houses and the girls who worked the bars were all KCIA informants. *Kisaeng* (or what is known in Japan as *geisha*) were women who worked as entertainers in the high-class clubs used by powerful officials and businessmen to host banquets.

61. John Lie, *Han Unbound: The Political Economy of South Korea* (Stanford, Calif.: Stanford University Press, 2000), 96. A total of 265 officials were implicated, including five cabinet members, eight members of the National Assembly, and two dozen judges and prosecutors. William Chapman, "Seoul Officials Probed over Housing Scandal," *Washington Post,* July 7, 1978; and Koon Woo Nam, *South Korean Politics: The Search for Political Consensus and Stability* (Lanham, Md.: University Press of America, 1989), 142–43.

62. Han, "Political Parties and Political Development in South Korea," 449.

63. Jae-on Kim and D. C. Kim, "The Dynamics of Electoral Politics: Social Development, Political Participation, and Manipulation of Electoral Laws," in Chong Lim Kim, ed., *Political Participation in Korea: Democracy, Mobilization and Stability* (Santa Barbara, Calif.: Clio Books, 1980), 74; and Henderson, *Korea,* 289.

64. Kim, *Divided Korea*, 243, 265.

65. Han, "Political Parties and Political Development in South Korea," 450; and Henderson, *Korea*, 307.

66. The sedans were sold as taxis at a 100 percent markup.

67. See Kim, *Divided Korea*, 241. The Walker Hill scheme faltered after U.S. Eighth Army Command placed it off limits to U.S. military personnel.

68. In the 1963 Three Flours Scandal, for example, it was said that industrialists involved in black-market sales of sugar, flour, and cement allegedly earned the DRP ₩4.94 billion (US$38 million) in illicit income. Kim, *Divided Korea*, 241.

69. The DRP allegedly accepted ₩4.94 billion (US$38 million) for allowing illegal imports of Japanese goods and capital in 1963. Kim, *Divided Korea*, 253. Based on CIA documents, Woo asserts that Japanese firms "donated" US$66 million (over ₩12 billion based on the average exchange rate) to the DRP between 1961 and 1965, providing two-thirds of its funding. Woo cites statements that Kim Jong-pil told Japanese sources that the DRP would need US$26 million to contest the 1967 National Assembly elections and that he hoped to raise the money by selling monopoly rights to Japanese companies. Woo, *Race to the Swift*, 107. Hart-Landsberg writes that Gulf Oil illegally donated US$1 million to the party in 1966, and in 1971 U.S. firms handed over US$8.5 million. Hart-Landsberg, *Rush to Development*, 169.

70. Kim, *Divided Korea*, 242.

71. Jung, "Business-Government Relations," 67–82.

72. Russell Mardon, "The State and the Effective Control of Foreign Capital: The Case of South Korea," *World Politics* 43:1 (1990): 111–38.

73. The presidential residence in Seoul is known as the Blue House because of the color of its tile roof.

74. When adjusted for inflation, the interest rates paid by the *chaebol* were negative from the 1950s through 1980, with the result that the receipt of a loan automatically yielded the borrower a net profit. Ku Hyun Jung, "Business-Government Relations in Korea," in Kao H. Chung and Hak Chong Lee, eds., *Korean Managerial Dynamics* (Westport, Conn.: Praeger, 1989), 11–26.

75. During the early 1960s, firms that received low-interest loans from the banks were allowed to relend the money out at the high kerb market rate. They had to then kick back a percentage of the profits generated by this arbitrage lending to the DRP. This practice was discontinued in 1964–65. The practice of collecting kickbacks from import licensing was also ended at this time. Kim, *Divided Korea*, 266–67.

76. David C. Kang, "Bad Loans to Good Friends: Money Politics and the Developmental State in South Korea," *International Organization* 56:1 (2002): 185–86. Although efforts had been made to improve rural conditions during the 1960s, the Saemaul was reinvigorated after the DRP saw its share of the rural vote diminish in the 1967 and 1972 elections. In theory a community driven, self-help movement aimed at building rural roads, replacing old thatched roofs with tile or slate roofing, expanding rural electrification, improving local irrigation networks, and installing rural water and sanitation systems, the Saemaul program was financed by a combination of public funds and private donations under the administrative supervision of the Ministry of Home Affairs, which was also in charge of the national police. Because funds were provided to selected villages, it would seem likely that villages that voted for the DRP were favored while those that voted for the opposition were apt to be ignored. I am not, however, aware of a systematic study of the allocation of Saemaul funds and have been told that the disaggregated data needed to determine if Saemaul funds were politically targeted have not been made available. Japan was reportedly pressure to help fund the movement with a US$1 billion loan. After Chun took over in the 1980s, the movement came under the control of his brother, who systematically plundered much of the ₩150 billion in funds allocated to it. Vincent

S. R. Brandt, "Rural Development in South Korea," *Asian Affairs* 6:3 (1979): 148–63; Clifford, *Troubled Tiger*, 94–96, 212; Seung-Mi Han, "The New Community Movement: Park Chung-hee and the Making of State Populism in Korea," *Pacific Affairs* 77:1 (2004): 69–93; Chae-Jin Lee, "South Korea: The Politics of Domestic-Foreign Linkage," *Asian Survey* 13:1 (1973): 98; and Mick Moore, "Mobilization and Disillusion in Rural Korea: The Saemaul Movement in Retrospect," *Pacific Affairs* 57:4 (1984–85): 577–98.

77. Kang, "Bad Loans to Good Friends," 185–86.

78. Although how much money was needed to sustain the DRP and fend off the opposition is necessarily unclear, the limited evidence suggests that it was considerable. In the 1960s, according to Han, routine upkeep cost the DRP somewhere in the area of ₩340 million (approximately US$100 million) per year. Of this amount, less than 2 percent came from publicly reported sources. The 1967 National Assembly election reportedly cost the DRP a minimum of ₩1 million for each of the 150 candidates it fielded, with races in areas of opposition strength costing considerably more. To these costs must be added the cost of under-the-table payoffs to opposition politicians. The DRP was supposedly prepared to pay upward of ₩30 to ₩50 million to members of the New Democratic Party if they would bolt that party and join the DRP. Han, "Development of Parties and Politics in Korea," Part 2, 49–50; and Hahn, "Underlying Factors in Political Party Organization and Elections," 97. Even leading members of the opposition, including Kim Daehung, were rumored to have accepted funds from Park.

79. See Han, "Development of Parties and Politics in Korea," Part 1, 43. Kim returned from exile within a few months and stood for election in the fall of 1963 as a DRP candidate. After winning a resounding victory, he was then elected chairman of the DRP. C. I. Eugene Kim, "Significance of the 1963 Korean Elections," *Asian Survey* 4:3 (1964): 722. Kim again fell afoul of Park in 1969 when he overplayed his hand on the question of whether the constitution should be amended to allow Park to run for a third term as president. Kim had assumed that he would succeed Park and opposed the change. Kim was once again thrown into the political wilderness and a number of his allies were purged from the party. Kim nevertheless survived and returned to become prime minister in 1971.

80. Chan Wook Park, "Home Style in a Developing Polity: How Korean Legislators Communicate with Their Constituents," *Korea Journal* 30:5 (1990): 5.

81. Ibid., 6–7; and Young Whan Kihl, "Political Roles and Participation of Community Notables: A Study of *Yuji* in Korea," in Kim, ed., *Political Participation in Korea*, 85–117.

82. Park, "Home Style," 7.

83. Chan Wook Park, "Financing Political Parties in South Korea: 1988–1881," in Herbert E. Alexander and Rei Shiratori, eds., *Comparative Political Finance among the Democracies* (Boulder, Colo.: Westview Press, 1994), 135–36.

84. Chan Wook Park, "Legislators and Their Constituents in South Korea: The Patterns of District Representation," *Asian Survey* 28:10 (1988): 1049. During the 1980s, Presidents Chun Doo-wan and Roh Tae-woo both established power using presidential *sa choji* (also transliterated as *sajojic*).

85. Park, "Home Style," 7; and Park, "Legislators and their Constituents," 1053.

86. According to Kang, the DRP spent ₩5.6 billion (US$40 million) buying votes in 1967, a sum almost equal to its legally reported administrative costs. Kang, *Crony Capitalism*, 100.

87. Park, "Legislators and Their Constituents," 1052.

88. Henderson, *Korea*, 306–7.

89. Soohyun Chon, "The Election Process and Informal Politics in South Korea," in Lowell Dittmer, Haruhiro Fukui, and Peter N. S. Lee, eds., *Informal Politics in East Asia* (New York: Cambridge University Press, 2000), 69.

90. Cho, "Korea," 36. Neither positive inducements nor negative disincentives were, however, sufficient to ensure tight discipline. In 1969, for example, thirty-seven members of the DRP defected to join the opposition in bringing down the Minister of Education.

Five of the rebels were later expelled by the DRP. Joungwon Alexander Kim, "Divided Korea 1969: Consolidating for Transition," *Asian Survey* 10:1 (1970): 30–42.

91. The continuing strength of the opposition New Democratic Party is remarkable. The opposition not only had to deal with the natural fractionalism characteristic of Korean politics, it had to face the well-financed DRP on a political starvation diet. Unlike their DRP rivals, opposition politicians could not bring home pork-barrel money (districts that voted for the opposition were, in fact, likely to be deprived of government aid), fund large local political machines, or pump money into the pockets of their supporters, and they lacked the leverage with state officials that made businessmen willing to contribute to politicians' coffers. As poor men in a money-driven political system, the opposition should have crumbled, leaving only a hard core of idealists to continue challenging the ruling party. The opposition, however, managed not only to survive but, given the adverse conditions facing it, might be said to have thrived.

92. Soon Sung Cho, "Korea: Election Year," *Asian Survey* 8:1 (1968): 29–42; C. I. Eugene Kim, "Significance of the 1963 Korean Elections," *Asian Survey* 4:3 (1964): 765–73; Chae-Jin Lee, "South Korea: Political Competition and Government Adaptation," *Asian Survey* 12:1 (1972): 38–45; and Chong-Sik Lee, "Korea: In Search of Stability," *Asian Survey* 4:1 (1964): 656–65.

93. Under the Yushin Constitution, the president appointed 73 out of 219 members of the National Assembly, thus ensuring that ruling party would control a parliamentary majority even if the opposition were to win 109 out of the 146 elected seats.

94. When he needed political money, Park's practice was to call in the head of the KFI and simply tell him how much money he wanted. The head of the KFI took the total and allocated it to peak business associations based on the value of the sectors they represented. The associations, in turn, assessed individual *chaebol* based on their capitalization and profits. Although the KFI and other associations were originally formed to act as a way for Park to control the business community, over time they evolved into de facto defensive alliances which relied on their power in numbers to negotiate with Park. Kim, *Big Business, Strong State*, ch. 5; Clifford, *Troubled Tiger*, 91–93; and Jones and Il, *Government, Business, and Entrepreneurship in Economic Development*, 70.

95. Like DRP politicians, most Korean industrialists routinely violated financial regulations and restrictions on political donations. Many engaged in a pattern of gift giving that amounted to tacit bribery. Park took advantage of their vulnerability to squeeze them, with the implied threat that if they did not comply with his demands, he would unleash the legal system on them.

96. Park apparently did, however, turn a blind eye to the skimming off of considerable sums of money by his lieutenants. After Park's assassination, for example, Kim Jong-pil was charged with accumulating a fortune worth US$45 million, while Lee Hu-rak, Park's chief of staff, allegedly raked in US$40 million and Oh Won-chul, who orchestrated Park's heavy industrial and chemical strategy, took in US$4.5 million. David Kang, "Policies, Pork, and Regionalism in Korean Politics," paper presented at the American Political Science Annual Meeting (Boston, Mass.), August 25, 1998, 10–12. These charges should be viewed with a degree of caution because Park's successor Chun Doo-wan had political incentives to level charges of personal corruption against Park's aides. It is possible, therefore, that some of the funds Kim, Lee, and Oh held were in fact party funds. Nevertheless, it is not unreasonable to assume that members of Park's inner circle took advantage of their roles as intermediaries between the *chaebol* and Park to extort bribes.

97. Jung Ku-hyun, "Business-Government Relations in the Growth of Korean Business Groups," *Korean Social Sciences Journal* 14 (1988): 67–82. In 1974, Park had also responded to the growing power and independence of the *chaebol* with a program of deconcentration. Unlike Chun, however, Park also tightened state control over the financial

sector by cracking down on the kerb market. Fields, *Enterprise and State in Korea and Taiwan*, 53–54.

98. Yung Chul Park and Dong Won Kim, "Korea: Development and Structural Change in the Banking System," in Hugh T. Patrick and Yung Chul Park, eds., *The Financial Development of Japan, Korea, and Taiwan: Growth, Repression, and Liberalization* (New York: Oxford University Press, 1994), 129–87.

99. Gary G. Hamilton, "The Organization of Capitalism in South Korea and Taiwan," in A. E. Safarian and Wendy Dobson, eds., *East Asian Capitalism: Diversity and Dynamism* (Toronto: University of Toronto Press, 1997), 27.

100. Haggard and Moon, "Institutions and Economic Policy," 220–21.

101. Chung-in Moon, "The Demise of a Developmentalist State: Neoconservative Reforms and the Political Consequences in South Korea," *Journal of Developing Societies* 4 (1988): 67–84.

102. Ingyu Oh and Recep Varcin, "The Mafioso State: State-led Market Bypassing in South Korea and Turkey," *Third World Quarterly* 23:4 (2002): 711–23; Yeam-Hong Choi and Yeam-Ho; Lee, "Political Reform and the Government-Business (Chaebol) Relationship in South Korea," *Korea Observer* 26:1 (1995): 39–61; Chang-Hee Nam, "South Korea's Big Business Clientalism in Democratic Reform," *Korea Observer* 25:2 (1994): 357–66; James C. Schopf, "An Explanation for the End of Political Bank Robbery in the Republic of Korea: The T + T Model," *Asian Survey* 41:5 (2001): 693–715; and Kang, "Bad Loans to Good Friends," 187–88.

103. George H. Kerr, *Formosa Betrayed* (New York: Da Capo, 1976).

104. Douglas Mendal, *The Politics of Formosan Nationalism* (Berkeley: University of California Press, 1970), 28.

105. Stephan Haggard and Chien-kuo Pang, "The Transition to Export-Led Growth in Taiwan," in Joel D. Aberbach, David Dollar, and Kenneth L. Sokoloff, eds., *The Role of the State in Taiwan's Development* (Armonk, N.Y.: M. E. Sharpe, 1994), 53.

106. Lai Tse-han, Ramon H. Myers, and Wei Wou, *A Tragic Beginning: The Taiwan Uprising of February 28, 1947* (Stanford, Calif.: Stanford University Press, 1991).

107. Denny Roy, *Taiwan: A Political History* (Ithaca, N.Y.: Cornell University Press, 2003), 76.

108. See Suzanne Pepper, *Civil War in China: The Political Struggle, 1945–1949* (Berkeley: University of California Press, 1978). Although the pre-1949 Nationalist regime is widely seen as a paragon of corruption, there is little evidence that either Chiang Kai-shek or his son and successor Chiang Ch'ing-kuo were personally corrupt. Even though he was clearly surrounded by corruption, turned a blind eye to the greed of members of his wife's family during his years on the mainland, and was likely involved in criminal activity in the days before he joined the KMT, it appears that Chiang Kai-shek did not use his office to enrich himself, at least during the post-1949 period. See Jonathan Fenby, *Chiang Kai-shek: China's Generalissimo and the Nation He Lost* (New York: Carrol & Graf, 2003). His son appears to have been quite uncorrupt. Chiang Ch'ing-kuo explicitly forbade his legitimate sons from becoming businessmen so that there could be no appearance that they were cashing in on their father's power. His two illegitimate sons had to work their way through college because he was unwilling to provide them more than very modest financial support. See Jay Taylor, *The Generalissimo's Son: Chiang Ch'ing-kuo and the Revolutions in China and Taiwan* (Cambridge, Mass.: Harvard University Press, 2000), 276–82. Chiang Kai-shek's wife, Soong Mei-ling, however, was a wealthy woman and it seems likely that some of her wealth was obtained from the crooked business dealings of her brother (T. V. Soong), who controlled ROC finances during the pre-1949 period, and her brother-in-law (H. H. Kung), who was one of China's wealthiest bankers. See Laura Tyson Li, *Madame Chiang Kai-shek: China's Eternal First Lady* (New York: Grove Press, 2007). Neither Soong

nor Kung was a major factor after 1949 as both decided not accompany the retreat to Taiwan, opting instead to move to the United States.

109. The use of the term "Taiwanese" is politically complex. On the island, a distinction is drawn between those "of the province" (*ben sheng*) and those from "outside the province" (*wai sheng*), with the line generally drawn between those who were resident prior to the retreat and those who came in 1949. But even that line is not precise or hard. As used herein, "Taiwanese" refers to ethnic Chinese who immigrated to the island prior to 1895. For an in-depth analysis of identify politics on Taiwan, see Alan M. Wachman, *Taiwan: National Identity and Democratization* (Armonk, N.Y.: M. E. Sharpe, 1994).

110. Bruce J. Dickson, "The Lessons of Defeat: The Reorganization of the Kuomintang on Taiwan, 1950–52," *China Quarterly* 133 (1993): 56–84.

111. According to Dickson, mainlanders, who accounted for only about 10 percent of the total population, made up half the party membership. Bruce J. Dickson, *Democratization in China and Taiwan: The Adaptability of Leninist Parties* (New York: Oxford University Press, 1997), 59–61. As a percentage of the total population, party members represented 5.39 percent in 1961. At that time, however, 40.0 percent of the population was under age 15. Based on data in *Republic of China Yearbook, 2008*, available at http://www.gio.gov.tw/taiwan-website/5-gp/yearbook/ch2.html#PopulationTrends, accessed March 29, 2009.

112. Jing-lung Jiang and Wen-cheng Wu, "The Changing Role of the KMT in Taiwan's Political System," in Tun-jen Cheng and Stephan Haggard, eds., *Political Change in Taiwan* (Boulder, Colo.: Lynne Rienner, 1992), 76–78; and Bernard Gallin, "Political Factionalism and Its Impact on Chinese Village School Organizations," in Marc J. Swartz, ed., *Local-level Politics: Social and Cultural Perspectives* (Chicago: Aldine, 1968), 383.

113. Edwin A. Winkler, "Roles Linking State and Society," in Emily Martin Ahern and Hill Gates, eds., *The Anthropology of Taiwanese Society* (Stanford, Calif.: Stanford University Press, 1981), 54.

114. Karl J. Fields, *Enterprise and the State in Korea and Taiwan* (Ithaca, N.Y.: Cornell University Press, 1995), 135.

115. Joyce K. Kallgren, "Nationalist China: The Continuing Dilemma of the 'Mainland' Philosophy," *Asian Survey* 3:1 (1962): 11–16; Joyce K. Kallgren, "Nationalist China: Political Inflexibility and Economic Accommodation," *Asian Survey* 4:1 (1964): 638–45; Melvin Gurtov, "Taiwan in 1966: Political Rigidity, Economic Growth," *Asian Survey* 7:1 (1967): 40–45; Robert Payne, *Chiang Kai-shek* (New York: Weybright and Talley, 1969), 301; and Mendal, *The Politics of Formosan Nationalism*, 29.

116. Allan B. Cole, "Political Roles of Taiwanese Enterprisers," *Asian Survey* 7:9 (1967): 645–54.

117. Haggard and Pang, "The Transition to Export-led Growth in Taiwan," 71–72.

118. Mark Plummer, "Taiwan: Toward a Second Generation of Mainland Rule," *Asian Survey* 10:1 (1970): 18–24; J. Bruce Jacobs, "Taiwan 1973: Consolidation of the Succession," *Asian Survey,* 14:1 (1974): 22–29; and J. Bruce Jacobs, "Recent Leadership and Political Trends in Taiwan," *China Quarterly* 45 (1971): 129–54. Fifty officials and businessmen ultimately went to prison for their involvement in the Banana Scandal.

119. Fields, *Enterprise and the State in Korea and Taiwan*, 87.

120. J. Bruce Jacobs, "Taiwan 1972: Political Season," *Asian Survey* 13:1 (1973): 102–12.

121. Roy, *Taiwan*, 157. Critics claim, with some justification, that Chiang Ch'ing-kuo occasionally used charges of corruption as a way of destroying his political rivals. Edwin A. Winkler, "Elite Political Struggle 1945–1985," in Edwin A. Winkler and Susan Greenhalgh, eds., *Contending Approaches to the Political Economy of Taiwan* (Armonk, N.Y.: M. E. Sharpe, 1988), 158–60; and Linda Chao and Ramon H. Myers, *The First Chinese Democracy: Political Life in the Republic of China on Taiwan* (Baltimore: Johns Hopkins University Press, 1998), 107.

122. Wade, *Governing the Market,* 286–88. According to Wade, businessmen were most likely to have to hand over "gifts" when dealing with officials in public works, urban planning, tax, customs, and traffic police departments.

123. Gerald McBeath, "Taiwan in 1976: Chiang in the Saddle," *Asian Survey* 17:1 (1977): 18–26; Gerald McBeath, "Taiwan in 1977: Holding the Reins," *Asian Survey* 18:1 (1978): 17–28; and J. Bruce Jacobs, "Taiwan 1979: 'Normalcy' after 'Normalization,'" *Asian Survey* 20:1 (1980): 84–93.

124. See Wade, *Governing the Market;* and Evans, *Embedded Autonomy.*

125. See Geddes, *Politician's Dilemma.*

126. Martin M. C. Yang, *Socio-Economic Results of Land Reform in Taiwan* (Honolulu: East-West Center Press, 1970), 21–34.

127. The regime also sponsored the formation of women's association, teachers' associations, small business owners' associations, and a variety of other occupation-based groups.

128. Yang, *Socio-Economic Results of Land Reform in Taiwan,* 308–410. From the 1950s up to the 1970s, the Taiwan Provincial Food Bureau bought about 60 percent of farmers' rice production. Part of the value of such purchases was applied to farmers' tax liabilities and part was paid for in kind with chemical fertilizer. Licensed rice dealers or the Farmers' Associations controlled the purchase and resale of the remainder. Ronald G. Knapp, "Marketing and Social Patterns in Rural Taiwan," *Annals of the Association of American Geographers* 64:1 (March 1971): 131–55.

129. J. Alexander Caldwell, "The Financial System in Taiwan: Structure, Functions and Issues for the Future," *Asian Survey* 16:8 (1976): 733.

130. Chyuan-Jenq Shiau, "Elections and the Changing State-Business Relationship," in Tien, ed., *Taiwan's Electoral Politics and Democratic Transition,* 217.

131. See Chao Yongmao and Huang Qiongwen, "Taiwan wenquan zhi zhuanxing qianhou nonghui paixi tezhi bianqian yanjiu: Yunlin Xian Shuili Xiang 1970 weiji 1990 niandai weili zhi bijiao fenxi" [The Changing Characteristics of Farmers Associations and Faction in Taiwan: Analysis of the case of Shuilin Township, Yunlin County, 1970–1990], *Zhengji yu Xuecong* [Political Science Forum] 13 (1990): 165–200; Wang Zhenhuan and Shen Guoping, "Difang paixi, fandui shili yu difang zhengzhi de zhuanxing: Kaoshiung Xian ge an yenjiu" [Local Factions, Opposition and the Transformation of Local Politics: A Case Study of Kaohsiung County], *Donghai Xuebao* 36 (1995): 1–34; Wang Minghui, "Cong wangluo guanxi tantao nonghui xingyongbu zhi gongzou: Yi Daya xiang nonghui weili" [From Networks to Relationships: The Operations of the Credit Department of Farmers' Associations using the example of Daya Township], *Yi yu yan* 31:2 (1993): 115–40; Huang Defu and Liu Huazong, "Nonghui yu difang zhengzhi: Yi Taizhong yu Kaoshiung Xian Weili" [Farmers' Associations and Local Politics: The Cases of Taichung and Kaohsiung Counties], *Xuanju Yankiu* 2:2 (1994): 63–82; and Joseph Bosco, "Taiwan Factions: *Guanxi,* Patronage, and the State in Local Politics," *Ethnology* 31:2 (1992): 157–83. Because less has been written on them, I am not clear to what extent the fishermen's and water conservancy associations mirrored the farmers' associations in terms of their role in redistributive politics.

132. Zhang Kunshan and Huang Zhengxiong, *Difang Paixi yu Taiwan Zhengzhi* [Local factions and Taiwanese Politics] (Taipei: Lianhe Baoshe, 1996), 12.

133. See Qingshan Tan, Peter Kien-hong Yu, and Wen-chun Chen, "Local Politics in Taiwan: Democratic Consolidation," *Asian Survey* 36:5 (1996): 485–86.

134. Shiau, "Elections and the Changing State-Business Relationship," in Tien, ed., *Taiwan's Electoral Politics and Democratic Transition,* 217.

135. Hung-mao Tien, "Elections and Taiwan's Democratic Development," in Hungmao Tien, ed., *Taiwan's Electoral Politics and Democratic Transition: Riding the Third Wave* (Armonk, N.Y.: M. E. Sharpe, 1996), 19; and Chung-li Wu, "Taiwan's Local Factions and American Political Machines in Comparative Perspective," *China Report* 37:1 (2001): 56.

136. Although factions tended to exist over long periods, their membership could vary over time as subgroups, including clans and families as well as individuals, shifted their allegiances between different factions. Factions also endured because Taiwan's multimember district system for electing members of local legislative bodies and the existence of multiple elected executive positions meant that even losing factions often retained some access to patronage. For its own political purposes, the KMT had a vested interest in protecting weak factions so that they could be used as a counterweight against stronger factions. The literature on local factions is extensive. See inter alia, Chen Mingtan, *Paixi zhengzhi yu Taiwan shengzhi bianqian* [Factional Politics and the Evolution of Taiwanese Politics] (Taipei: Xin Ziranzhuyi Fuwu Xian Gongsi, 1995); Liao Zhongjun, *Taiwan difang paixi de xingcheng fazhan yu zhibian* [The Formation, Development, and Evolution of Taiwan's Local Factions] (Taipei: Yun Chen Wenhua Shiyu Fuwu Youxiangongxi, 1997); Cai Minghui, *Taiwan xianzhen paixi yu zhengzhi bianqian: Hekou zhen. "Shanding" yu "Jiez" de zhengzhou* [Taiwan's Village-Township Factions and Political Change: The Struggle between the "the Peak" and "the Street" in Hekou Township] (Taipei: Hongyeye Wenhua Shiye Youxian Gongsi, 1998); Huang Jiashu and He Chengrui, *Taiwan zhengzhi gu xuanju wenhua* [Taiwanese Politics and Electoral Culture] (Taipei: Boyang Wenhua, 2001); and Ming-tong Chen, "Local Factions and Elections in Taiwan's Democratization," in Tien, ed., *Taiwan's Electoral Politics and Democratic Transition*, 174–92.

137. According to Gallin, prior to the late 1950s local politics was based primarily on kinship groups and was notably nonpartisan, at least in the localities where he conducted his fieldwork. In 1957–58, the traditional village elders found themselves pushed aside by a new class of politicians who saw political power as a means of obtaining both prestige and wealth and who many older villagers described as being part of an emerging "black society" (*heishe*). Changes in the organization of local elections enacted at roughly the same time also sharply reduced the electoral viability of candidates who grounded themselves solely in kinship organizations and created incentives to form political organizations that spanned multiple kinship groups. Gallin, "Factionalism and Its Impact on Chinese Village Organization," 385–89.

138. The-fu Huang, "Elections and the Evolution of the Kuomintang," in Tien, ed., *Taiwan's Electoral Politics and Democratic Transition*, 130–31.

139. In many elections, the number of seats was sufficiently large and the minimum winning threshold was so low that candidates could expect to win with a 10 percent vote share. In many districts, therefore, the KMT employed a system of "responsibility zones" whereby individual candidates were assigned particular geographic areas or functional groups on which they were to concentrate their campaigns. I-Chou Liu, "Campaigning in an SNTV System: The Case of the Kuomintang," in Bernard Grofman et al., eds., *Elections in Japan, Korea, and Taiwan under the Single Non-transferable Vote: The Comparative Study of an Embedded Institution* (Ann Arbor: University of Michigan Press, 1999), 181–208; and Edwin A. Winkler, "Institutionalization and Participation on Taiwan: From Hard to Soft Authoritarianism?" *China Quarterly* 99 (1984): 497.

140. Hung-mao Tien, *The Great Transition: Political and Social Change in the Republic of China* (Stanford: Calif.: Hoover Institution Press, 1989), 132. According to Tien, over half of local governments' budgetary funds were derived from subsidies.

141. On the politics of budgetary subsides and grants, see Luo Qingjun, *Taiwan fenpei zhengzhi* [Distributive Politics in Taiwan] (Taipei: Qianwei Chubanshe, 2001).

142. Rigger, for instance, declares: "For many *tiau-a-ka* [vote brokers], their only connection with the KMT is the party pin on their preferred candidate." Shelly Rigger, "Machine Politics and Protracted Transition in Taiwan," *Democratization* 7:3 (2000): 144.

143. Shelly Rigger, *Politics in Taiwan: Voting for Democracy* (New York: Routledge, 1999): 84–86. At the local level, the KMT party secretary, who was often an outsider and

perhaps even a mainlander, remained independent of any particular factions. Joseph Bosco, "Factions versus Ideology: Mobilization Strategies in Taiwan's Elections," *China Quarterly* 137 (1994): 37–38.

144. Wu, "Taiwan's Local Faction and American Political Machines," 57–58.

145. Wu identifies over one hundred local factions during the period 1951–2001 and asserts that they were present at the county and city levels in fifteen out of twenty-two localities. Six of the remaining localities had no county-level factions but had township and district-level factions. Only the Taipei municipality lacked identifiable factions. Chung-li Wu, "Local Factions and the Kuomintang in Taiwan's Electoral Politics," *International Relations of the Asia-Pacific* 3:1 (2003): 109–11.

146. Bosco, "Factions versus Ideology," 35.

147. The literal meaning of *tiau-a-ka* is, more or less, a base that supports a set of piles or pillars. The term is generally translated as either "pillar," which is perhaps the more direct rendering, or "ward heeler," which perhaps better captures the implied political meaning of the term but also carries with it connotations from U.S. politics that distort the impression of Western readers. In Taiwan, the term can have very negative connotations, with some viewing them as little more than political gangsters or perhaps gangsters who involve themselves in politics. They may also be presented in a more positive light, which would imply they were men who took responsibility for mobilizing the local community.

148. Lawrence W. Crissman, "The Structure of Local and Regional Systems," in Emily Martin Ahern and Hill Gates, ed., *The Anthropology of Taiwanese Society* (Stanford, Calif.: Stanford University Press, 1981), 107–8.

149. Payments were never large. In the late 1960s, according to Lerman, voters received NT$40 (US$1). Crissman, however, reports being told that payments could vary from NT$10 (US$0.25), the cost of a pack of cigarettes, in "safe" neighborhoods to NTS$100 (US$4) in hotly contested areas. Two decades later, Wang and Kurzman report that the amount had "swelled" to NT$300 (US$10), just enough, they observe, to buy two dinners at a cheap restaurant. In the early days, voters were often given soap and hand towels instead of cash. Estimates of the percentage of voters accepting payments vary from 20–25 percent to 40 percent. Most studies concluded, however, that a significant share of those who accepted money did not alter their vote choice and simply pocketed the cash not, in many cases, because they wanted it but rather because refusing it was socially awkward. Research also suggests that money was most often given to existing supporters and that the primary purpose of the payment was not to buy a vote per se but rather to reinforce the *guanxi* ties between voters and the *tiau-a-ka*. In some instances, votes were bought from nonallies, in which case the price was reportedly double the payment given to supporters. Even then, the sums were far from princely. Moreover, it appears that while a candidate could buy the votes of his supporters and perhaps some noncommitted voters, he could not expect to buy the votes of voters with pre-existing ties to his opponents. Bosco, "Faction versus Ideology," 39. Also see Rigger, *Politics in Taiwan,* 96; Chin-shou Wang and Charles Kurzman, "The Logistics: How to Buy Votes," in Frederic Charles Schaffer, ed., *Elections for Sale: The Causes and Consequences of Vote Buying* (Boulder, Colo.: Lynne Rienner, 2007), 61–78; Crissman, "The Structure of Local and Regional Systems," 110; He Jinming, "Huixuan xianxiang yu huixuan xiaoguo: Kaohsiung shi er jie liwei xuanju de ge'an fenxi" [The Vote-buying Problem and the Impact of Vote Buying: A Case Study of the Kaohsiong Second Legislative Committee Election], *Zhengzhi kexue luncong* 6 (1995): 109–44; J. Bruce Jacobs, *Local Politics in a Rural Chinese Cultural Setting: A Field Study of Mazu Township, Taiwan* (Canberra: Australian National University, 1980), 147; Arthur J. Lerman, *Taiwan's Politics: The Provincial Assemblyman's World* (Washington: University Press of America, 1978), 112; and Chin-shou Wang and Charles Kurzman, "Dilemmas of Electoral Clientelism: Taiwan, 1993," *International Political Science Review* 28:2 (2007): 225–45.

150. Gallin, "Factionalism and Its Impact on Chinese Village Organization," 387. In the late 1950s, according to Jacobs, candidates for county assembly speaker were expected to give the party NT$300,000–500,000 (US$12–20,000) to secure their nomination. Jacobs, *Local Politics in a Rural Chinese Cultural Setting,* 127.

151. Jacobs, *Local Politics in a Rural Chinese Cultural Setting,* 130, 137.

152. Bosco, "Factions versus Ideology," 40.

153. Lerman, *Taiwan's Politics,* 111–16.

154. Crissman, "The Structure of Local and Regional Systems," 107.

155. Lerman, *Taiwanese Politics,* 130–31.

156. Fred Riggs, *Formosa under Chinese Nationalist Rule* (New York: Macmillan, 1952), 90.

157. Ming-sho Ho, "Manufacturing Loyalty: Political Mobilization of Labor in Taiwan (1950–1986)," unpublished paper, provided by the author and used with permission.

158. The data on the number of workers are spotty. In his *China Quarterly* article, Ho reports a figure of 13.5 percent, which he took from Liu Jinqing, *Taiwan zhen hou fenxi* [An Analysis of Taiwan's Postwar Economy] (Taipei: Renjian, 1992), 111. He subsequently examined Liu's sources and recalculated the total at 11.41 percent (personal communication, April 21, 2009). Based on Ho's estimate and data on total industrial employment from the ROC statistical yearbook, I extrapolate the figure of 72,000. Directorate General of Budget, Accounting, and Statistics, Executive Yuan, Republic of China, *Statistical Yearbook of the Republic of China, 1994,* 54.

159. Within SOEs, the regime maintained a secret police system staffed by retired members of the Security Police, which had unrestricted authority to conduct searches, supplemented by a network of party agents and informants. Ho, "Manufacturing Loyalty," 19.

160. Even the children of employees were under pressure to demonstrate their political reliability because the children of party stalwarts could fall back on the company if they found better employment elsewhere. Ibid.

161. Ming-sho Ho, "Challenging State Corporatism: The Politics of Taiwan's Labor Federation Movement," *China Journal* 56 (2006): 109–10.

162. Like their counterparts on the mainland, Taiwan-based state-owned enterprises (SOEs) provided employees with a variety of recreational facilities, canteens, and other services. These were generally owned and operated by the union, which might also own other businesses either linked to the company or independent of it. Profits from these activities were supposed to accrue to the union's welfare fund. In many cases, according to Ho, union officers skimmed off the profits and pocketed them. Union officers also reportedly took kickbacks from businesses supplying the union with various goods (including annual gifts for employees) and services. See Ming-sho Ho, "The Rise and Fall of Leninist Control in Taiwan's Industry," *China Quarterly* 89 (2007): 162–79.

163. Only about half of the delegates to the Legislative Yuan elected in the 1948 general election retreated to Taiwan. Faced with declining numbers due to retirements and deaths, in 1969 Chiang Kai-shek approved the addition of new supplemental seats. The number rose from 8 in 1969 to 98 in 1983. Because these legislators were de facto elected by Taiwanese voters, they served to progressively increase Taiwanese representation to the point that by the mid-1980s legislators representing Taiwanese voters dominated the active membership of the Legislative Yuan.

164. See Douglas Mendal, *The Politics of Formosan Nationalism* (Berkeley: University of California Press, 1970), 119; Ming-min Peng, "Political Offences in Taiwan: Laws and Problems," *China Quarterly* 47 (1971): 471–93; and Winkler, "Elite Political Struggle, 1945–1985," 156–58.

165. See Christian Schafferer, *The Power of the Ballot Box: Political Development and Election Campaigning in Taiwan* (New York: Lexington Books, 2003), 120–21; and Feiling Lui, "The Electoral System and Voting Behavior in Taiwan," in Tun-jen Cheng and

Stephan Haggard, eds., *Political Change in Taiwan* (Boulder, Colo.: Lynne Rienner, 1992), 155–58.

166. Chao Yongmao, *Taiwan difang heidao zhi xingcheng Beijing ji qi xuangju zhi guanxi* [The Background and Form of the "Black Way" and Its Effect on Elections in Taiwan], *Lilun yu zhengce* 7:2 (1993): 24. U.S. dollar amounts based on the average exchange rate for the period 1980 to 1989. Exchange rate data from Center for International Comparison, University of Pennsylvania, "Penn World Table version 7.0," June 2011, available at http://pwt.econ.upenn.edu, accessed July 15, 2011.

167. Chao Yongmao, *Difang zhengzhi shengtai yu difang zingcheng de guanxi* [The Relationship between Local Political Ecology and Local Administration], *Zhengzhi kexue lilun* 9 (1997): 312.

168. Chao Yongmao, "Fei duhui qu heidao yu xuanju zhi guanxi" [Organized Crime and Elections in Rural Areas], *Lilun yu zhengzho* (1994): 84–86; and Sonny Shiu-hing Lo, "The Politics of Controlling *Heidao* and Corruption in Taiwan," *Asian Affairs* 35:2 (2008): 62.

169. In 1996, the minister of justice estimated that one-third of city and county councilors, one-quarter of the members of the Taiwan Provincial Assembly, and 5 percent of the members of the Legislative Yuan were either gangsters or had ties to organized crime. Ko-lin Chin, "Black Gold Politics: Organized Crime, Business, and Politics in Taiwan," in Roy Godson, ed., *Menace to Society: Political-Criminal Collaboration Around the World* (New Brunswick, N.J.: Transaction Books, 2003), 266–67.

170. On the rise of organized crime and the development of "black gold" politics, see Ko-lin Chin, *Heijin: Organized Crime, Business, and Politics in Taiwan* (Armonk, N.Y.: M. E. Sharpe, 2003).

171. Rigger, "Machine Politics and Protracted Transition in Taiwan," 146–47.

172. Roy, *Taiwan*, 63–64. Chen Yi's policy of socializing the major means of production was in line with the KMT founding ideology as laid down in Sun Yatsen's Three People's Principles (*San Min Zhuyi*) which called for a form of socialism in which the state would control capitalism though a combination of state-ownership of key industries and "strict regulation of private capital." Fields, *Enterprise and the State in Korea and Taiwan,* 84–85. Even before the retreat to Taiwan in 1949, the ROC government had been heavily involved in the economy and exercised monopoly control over certain sectors. Chen Han-seng, "Monopoly and Civil War in China," *Far Eastern Survey* 15:20 (1946): 305–10. The tobacco and alcohol monopoly was a major source of state tax revenues for many decades. Gerald A. McBeath, "Taiwan Privatizes by Fits and Starts," *Asian Survey* 37:12 (1997): 1147.

173. Calculating the value of confiscated properties is complicated by the lack of reliable exchange rate data prior to 1949, at which point the Nationalist government fixed the value of the Old Taiwan Dollar at OT$40,000 to NT$1 and the exchange rate for the New Taiwan Dollar to the U.S. dollar at 5:1. At those rates, the OT$9.5 billion confiscated would have been worth US$1.2 million (in 1949 dollars). The island had, however, experienced hyperinflation between 1945 and 1949, which cut the value of the Old Taiwan Dollar to a fraction of its 1945–46 value. The value of confiscated properties was thus many times the nominal value of US$1.2 million. See Gail E. Makinen and G. Thomas Woodward, "The Taiwanese Hyperinflation and Stabilization of 1945–1952," *Journal of Money, Credit and Banking* 21:1 (1989): 90–105.

174. Yongping Wu, *A Political Explanation of Economic Growth: State Survival, Bureaucratic Politics, and Private Enterprises in the Making of Taiwan's Economy, 1950–1985* (Cambridge, Mass.: Harvard University Press, 2005), 39–46; and Huang Huangxiong, Zhang Qingxin, and Huang Shixin, *Hai cai yu min: Guomingdang chan hequ he cong* [Give the Wealth Back to the People: What Course for the Kuomintang's Estate?] (Taipei: Shangzhou Chuban, 2000), 16–18. Prior to the establishment of Nationalist control in October 1945, Japanese citizens sold two-thirds of the estimated value of private property

to Taiwanese interests at fire-sale prices, thus creating a new class of Taiwanese capitalists overnight. Nationalist authorities voided all sales made after the Japanese surrender of August 15 and confiscated these properties. See Hong-zen Wang, "Class Structures and Social Mobility in Taiwan in the Initial Post-War Period," *China Journal* 48 (2002): 58–59. Confiscation and nationalization, therefore, forestalled the rapid emergence of a large and autonomous Taiwanese industrial-commercial sector.

175. Roy, *Taiwan*, 64.

176. Ibid., 77.

177. Wu Ruoyi, *Zhanhou Taiwan gongying Shiye zhi zhengjing fenxi* [An Analysis of the State Sector in Taiwan's Postwar Political Economy] (Taipei: Yeqiang, 1992), 86.

178. In 1990, the total book value of private enterprises was NT$9.5 trillion (US$352 billion) while the total book value of state-owned enterprises was NT$2.4 trillion (US$89 billion). In this definition, however, the private sector includes enterprises owned by the KMT, which had a total book value of about NT$1 trillion (US$37 billion). Xu Dianqing, "The KMT Party's Enterprises in Taiwan," *Modern Asian Studies* 31:2 (1997): 399–400. Figures in New Taiwan dollars are as quoted by Xu.

179. Ibid., 402, and Yun-han Chu, "The Realignment of Business-Government Relations and Regime Transition in Taiwan," in Andrew MacIntyre, ed., *Business and Government in Industrializing Asia* (Ithaca, N.Y.: Cornell University Press, 1994): 118.

180. McBeath, "Taiwan Privatizes by Fits and Starts," 1148.

181. Many of VAR's enterprises were hospitals and nursing homes for retired soldiers. The commission also owned a variety of factories. Most were small enterprises producing goods for the agricultural sector. The VAR did, however, own more substantial enterprises, including a major pharmaceutical maker. Ibid., 1149, 1158.

182. Karl J. Fields, "KMT, Inc.: Liberalization, Democratization, and the Future of Politics in Business," in Edmund Terrence Gomez, ed., *Political Business in East Asia* (New York: Rutledge, 2002), 119.

183. Wu, *A Political Explanation of Economic Growth*, 111.

184. Fields, *Enterprise and the State in Korea and Taiwan*, 149.

185. Hong-zen Wang, "Class Structures and Social Mobility in Taiwan in the Initial Post-War Period," *China Journal* 48 (2002): 58–59.

186. Ichiro Numazaki, "Networks of Taiwanese Big Business: A Preliminary Analysis," *Modern China* 12:4 (1986): 490. The "five big families" included the Lin clan of northern Taiwan, the Gu clan in Lugang, the Yan clan in Keelong, the Chen clan in Tainan, and the Lin clan in Wufeng. Large landowners, these families also operated rice mills and rice trading companies and engaged in money lending.

187. This is hardly surprising since industrialists and capitalists who were not hardcore loyalists were more likely to relocate to British-controlled Hong Kong, Southeast Asia, or the United States.

188. Chu, "Realignment and Transition in Taiwan," 116–17.

189. Wang, "Class Structures and Social Mobility in Taiwan in the Initial Post-War Period," 79.

190. Ibid., 80.

191. Winkler, "Institutionalization and Participation on Taiwan," 492–93.

192. Hsin-huang Michael Hsiao, "Formation and Transformation of Taiwan's State-Business Relations: A Critical Analysis," *Zhongyang Yenjiu Yuan Minxu Xue Yanjiusuo Jikan* 74 (1992): 17.

193. Wade, *Governing the Market*, 280–83; and Chu, "Realignment and Transition in Taiwan," 118–19.

194. Wu, *A Political Explanation of Economic Growth*, 116; and Fields, *Enterprise and the State in Korea and Taiwan*, 87–88.

195. Chu, "Realignment and Transition in Taiwan," 119–20.

196. Wu, *A Political Explanation of Economic Growth*, 222; and Fields, *Enterprise and the State in Korea and Taiwan*, 64.

197. Fields, "KMT, Inc.," 141–49; and Xu, "The KMT Party's Enterprises in Taiwan," 399–413.

198. Wu, *A Political Explanation of Economic Growth*, 156–64.

199. Xu, "The KMT Party's Enterprises in Taiwan," 401.

200. For specific data on the companies the party owned, see Fields, "KMT, Inc.," 141–49; and Xu, "The KMT Party's Enterprises in Taiwan," 399–413.

201. Karl Fields, "KMT Inc. and the Taiwan Miracle," paper presented at the Western Conference of the Association for Asian Studies (WCAAS) (Portland), 2004; and Liang Yonghuang and Tian Xiru, *Paimai Guomintang: Dangchan da qingsuan* [Auction Off the Kuomintang: An Accounting of the Party's Assets] (Taipei: Caxun Chubanshe, 2000), 206.

202. Ibid., 232.

203. Ibid., 138, 145, 151–56; Mitsutoyo Masumoto, "Political Democratization and the KMT Party-owned Enterprises in Taiwan," *The Developing Economies* 40:3 (2002): 364; Huang, Zhang, and Huang, *Hai cai yu min*, 63–67. All NT$ values converted to U.S. dollars at the average exchange rate for the period 1994–96.

204. Kingdom had a net negative value of NT$400 million (US$15 million) at the time these estimates were compiled due to financial reversals.

205. Fields, "KMT, Inc.," 123.

206. Until 1994, the party hid its business investments. Fields, "KMT, Inc.," 123.

207. Liang and Tian, *Paimai Guomintang*, 241.

208. Frank Norris, *The Octopus: A Story of California* (Garden City, N.Y.: Doubleday, 1901).

209. Evans, *Embedded Autonomy*.

210. Kang, *Crony Capitalism*.

211. In Japan, the pattern was different. Big business played a much more active and assertive role, particularly in urging the Liberal and Democratic parties to merge and after the formation of the Liberal Democratic Party by pumping money into the party through a variety of channels in ways that bound together the LDP's factions and individual politicians. Thus, whereas power in the developmental alliances of South Korea and Taiwan tended to flow downward from a strong political leadership, the Japanese alliance was more organic and lacked a central strongman. In many other ways, however, the system was the same, with the ruling party using its control of the state to repay its business benefactors with pro-growth macro-economic policies (and a fair share of rents in the form of trade protectionism and a tolerance for cartelization) while using the resources of the state to dole out pork for LDP politicians to take back home to their supporters.

212. It is often said that the problem with buying political loyalty is that you never finish paying for it and that once bought, corrupt politicians have to be bought and rebought over and over again.

213. Mancur Olson, "Dictatorship, Democracy, and Development," *American Political Science Review* 87:3 (1993): 567–76.

214. Ting Gong, "Dangerous Collusion: Corruption as a Collective Venture in Contemporary China," *Communist and Post-Communist Studies* 35:1 (2002): 85–103; Shawn Shieh, "The Rise of Collective Corruption in China: The Xiamen Smuggling Case," *Journal of Contemporary China* 14:42 (2005): 67–91; Lu Xiaobo, "Booty Socialism, Bureau-Preneurs, and the State in Transition: Organizational Corruption in China," *Comparative Politics* 32:3 (2000): 273–94; Thomas J. Bickford, "The Chinese Military and Its Business Operations: The PLA as Entrepreneur," *Asian Survey* 34:5 (1994): 460–74; and James C. Mulvenon, *Soldiers of Fortune: The Rise and Fall of the Chinese Military-Business Complex, 1978–1998* (Armonk, N.Y.: M. E. Sharpe, 2001).

CHAPTER 3

1. In thinking about profits and gains, it is important to recognize that some profits and gains may appear to be negative costs. In the case of a protection racket, for example, a shopkeeper may have to hand over a fee each week to ensure that fires do not mysteriously break out in the middle of the night or bricks do not accidentally come crashing through his windows. If we assume that the shopkeeper's protector would become the agent whereby these unfortunate events might come to pass, then the payment of protection money would be a cost. If, on the other hand, the police cannot or will not stop arson and brick throwing by teenage hooligans but the local wise guys can, then paying protection money might benefit the shopkeeper. Similarly, if the shopkeeper is selling narcotics under the counter and paying the local wise guys to warn him when the cops are nosing around—or perhaps to convince them not to nose around—paying protection money may be profitable.

2. The term "auto-corruption" seems to originate with Robert Brooks who used it in 1909 to describe a form of corruption wherein legislators would vote for legislation from which they stood to profit without having been bribed by outside interests who might also profit. See Robert C. Brooks, "The Nature of Corruption," *Political Science Quarterly* 24:1 (1909): 4. Subsequently, V. O. Key defined auto-corruption as a method by which an official "secures for himself the administrative privilege which would be [otherwise] secured by an outsider by bribery" and "appropriates public property." V. O. Key, Jr., "Techniques of Political Graft," in Arnold J. Heidenheimer, ed., *Political Corruption: Readings in Comparative Analysis* (New Brunswick, N.J.: Transaction Books, 1970), 48. Key's work originally appeared in V. O. Key, Jr., *The Technique of Political Graft in the United States* (Chicago: University of Chicago Libraries, 1936).

3. Early on, a number of scholars argued that corruption might facilitate economic growth by greasing the wheels of inefficient bureaucracies and enabling entrepreneurs to purchase favorable treatment from politicians. See Nathaniel H. Leff, "Economic Development through Bureaucratic Corruption," and David H. Bayley, "The Effects of Corruption in a Developing Nation," in Arnold J. Heidenheimer, ed., *Political Corruption: Readings in Comparative Analysis* (New Brunswick, N.J.: Transaction Books, 1978), 510–20, and 521–33, respectively. There is, however, scant if any hard evidence for the existence of growth-enhancing corruption. Houston provides some evidence that in certain cases, corruption can provide an alternative to weak legal institutions and insecure property rights, but that this is only true in countries with very low GDP which have also suffered from high levels of protracted instability. Even in these cases it would seem that corruption is only better than anarchy and chaos. Douglas A. Houston, "Can Corruption Ever Improve an Economy?" *Cato Journal* 27:3 (2007): 325–42.

4. J. S. Nye, "Corruption and Political Development: A Cost-Benefit Analysis," *American Political Science Review* 61:2 (1967): 419.

5. Syed Hussein Alatas, *Political Corruption: Its Nature, Causes, and Consequences* (Aldershot: Avesbury, 1990), chapter 1.

6. On the concept of structural corruption see Chalmers Johnson, "Tanaka Kakuei, Structural Corruption, and the Advent of Machine Politics in Japan," *Annuals of Japanese Studies* 12:1 (1986): 1–28.

7. Sinnathamby Rajaratnam, "Bureaucracy versus Kleptocracy," in Heidenheimer, ed., *Political Corruption*, 547.

8. Stanislav Andreski, "Kleptocracy as a System of Government in Africa," in Heidenheimer, ed., *Political Corruption*, 346–57.

9. Mats Lundahl, "History as an Obstacle to Change: The Case of Haiti," *Journal of Interamerican Studies and World Affairs* 31:1–2 (1989): 16.

10. Mancur Olson, "Dictatorship, Democracy, and Development," *American Political Science Review* 87:3 (1993): 567–76. As Acemgolu et al. point out, Mobutu held on to power in Zaire for thirty-two years and fought to the bitter end to retain power. The reigns of Trujillo, who dominated the Dominican Republic for thirty-one years, and the Somoza family, which ruled Nicaragua for forty-two years, were ended by were assassination and revolution respectively. Daron Acemoglu, James A. Robinson, and Thierry Verdier, "Kleptocracy and Divide-and-Rule: A Model of Personal Rule," *Journal of the European Economic Association* 2:2–3 (2004): 163. Also see M. H. Khalil Timany, "African Leaders and Corruption," *Review of African Political Economy* 32:104–105 (2005): 383–93.

11. H. E. Chehabi and Juan J. Linz, "A Theory of Sultanism 1: A Type of Nondemocratic Rule" and "A Theory of Sultanism 2: Genesis and Demise of Sultanistic Regimes," in H. E. Chehabi and Juan J. Linz, eds., *Sultanistic Regimes* (Baltimore, Md.: Johns Hopkins University Press, 1998), 3–25 and 26–48. Chehabi and Linz make only a passing distinction between kleptocracy and sultanism. In fact, most of the case studies contained in their edited volume are the same as those cited in the literature on kleptocracy, which would suggest that the two terms are synonymous or that sultanism represents that subset of kleptocracy in which plunder is organized in a hierarchical, top-down manner and assumes a quasi-institutional form.

12. See William Reno, *Warlord Politics and African States* (Boulder, Colo.: Rienner, 1998); and Jean-Francois Bayant, Stephen Ellis, and Beatrice Hibou, *The Criminalization of the State in Africa* (Bloomington: University of Indiana Press, 1999). Although evocative, the mafia state appears to be a little-used model, at least in academia, where its use has been largely limited to the case of Italy. The term appears widely outside of academia but tends to be used as metaphor for a combination of high levels of corruption and organized crime without a clear definition of what constitutes a mafia state. In theory, a mafia or criminal state would be a state whose controllers operate the state as an instrument of organized crime or a state controlled by organized crime.

13. The concept of the captive state was first applied to the United Kingdom and used to describe how the state had become captive to corporate interests. George Monbiot, *Captive State: The Corporate Takeover of Britain* (London: Pan Books, 2001). It has since been applied to a number of cases in the former Soviet Union. In general, state capture in these analyses describes instances where private parties, including criminal organizations, have gained full or at least partial control over segments of the state, though not the state as a whole. See Joel S. Hellman and Mark Schanlerman, "Intervention, Corruption, and State Capture: The Nexus between Enterprises and the State," *Economics of Transition* 8:3 (2000): 545–76; Joel S. Hellman, Geraint Jones, and Daniel Kaufmann, "'Seize the State, Seize the Day': State Capture, Corruption, and Influence in Transition," World Bank Policy Research Working Paper no. 2444 (2000), available at http://papers.ssrn.com, accessed March 11, 2010; Ichiro Iwasaki and Taku Suzuki, "Transition Strategy, Corporate Exploitation, and State Capture: An Empirical Analysis of the Former Soviet State," *Communist and Post-Communist Studies* 40:4 (2007): 392–422; and Joanna Szalacha, "Poland as a Captive State?" *Slovo* 16:2 (2004): 143–51. There are relatively few clear-cut examples of a true captive state, one in which private interests have converted the state into a mechanism for private plunder. Perhaps the closest examples of colonized states were putatively found in Central America where the powerful United Fruit Corporation was said to have transformed a number of states into "banana republics". In Honduras, Guatemala, and Costa Rica, United Fruit dominated the national governments by its sheer economic weight and by the economies' dependence on it and its subsidiaries, including most critically its control over these nations' rail systems. At the peak of its power, United Fruit's corporate resources were greater than those of these states. This enabled the company to hold the economy hostage while at the same time it built up a core of political supporters. It financed various political

parties and individuals and allowed key politicians to become shareholders in various corporate ventures and to thereby extract a wide range of concessions from the local government, including monopoly rights over a variety of key sectors. Gaining monopoly rights, in turn, allowed United Fruit to redouble its grip on the economy and hence on the state. Even at the zenith of its power, however, United Fruit never really owned any of the governments of the so-called Central American banana republics and instead had to fight a series of political battles to maintain a position of power over indigenous political elites. Thus, while United Fruit was arguably sufficiently powerful to force local governments to grant it monopoly rights on concessionary terms and hence capture of lion's share of the resulting political rents, local political elites were still able to wrest a share. Moreover, even in its heyday, United Fruit never controlled the entire economies of the so-called banana republics. See Charles David Kepner, Jr., and Jay Henry Soothill, *The Banana Empire: A Case of Economic Imperialism* (New York: Vanguard Press, 1935), chapter 8; Mark Moberg, "Crown Colony as Banana Republic: The United Fruit Company in British Honduras, 1900–1920," *Journal of Latin American Studies* 28:2 (1996): 357–81; Vilma Lainez and Victor Meza, "The Banana Enclave," in Nancy Perkenham and Annie Street, eds., *Honduras: Portrait of a Captive Nation* (New York: Praeger, 1985): 34–37; Edward Boatman-Guillan, "'In Honduras a Mule is Worth More than a Congressman,'" ibid., 38–43; and Paul J. Doral, *Doing Business with the Dictators: A Political History of United Front in Guatemala, 1899–1944* (Wilmington, Del.: Scholarly Books, 1993), chapters 1 and 2.

14. The term "vampire state" has been used to describe Ghana, Kenya, and Zimbabwe. See Jonathan H. Frimpong-Ansah, *The Vampire State in Africa: The Political Economy of Decline in Africa* (Trenton, N.J.: Africa World Press, 1992); Robert Osei, "A Growth Collapse with Diffuse Resources: Ghana," in R. M. Auty, ed., *Resource Abundance and Economic Development* (New York: Oxford University Press, 2001), 165–78; Parselelo Kantai, "In the Grip of the Vampire State: Maasai Land Struggles in Kenyan Politics," *Journal of Eastern African Studies* 1:1 (2007): 107–22; and Robert Guest, *The Shackled Continent: Power, Corruption, and African Lives* (Washington: Smithsonian Books, 2004).

15. For an enlightening and entertaining example of the complexity of this sort of corruption, see Mark Stanton, *The Prince of Providence: The True Story of Buddy Cianci, America's Most Notorious Mayor, Some Wiseguys, and the Feds* (New York: Random House, 2003). Despite leading a flamboyant lifestyle that his critics said made him get rich while serving multiple terms as mayor of the struggling city of Providence, Rhode Island, Cianci was apparently a skilled practitioner of the art of corruption. He is supposed to have lived by the rules of (1) no checks, cash only; (2) never discuss payments or what they might be for; and (3) make sure that if you took money to never commit yourself to anything in return. When tried on federal corruption charges, Cianci beat all but one of over two dozen charges. He was convicted on one count of racketeering, a conspiracy charge based primarily on his demonstrated association with others who either had pleaded guilty to corruption-related charges or had been convicted on similar charges. Earlier in his political career, he was convicted a beating a man he accused of having an affair with his wife and forced from office. Cianci, however, managed a political comeback and returned to the mayor's office after seven years in the political wilderness.

16. In many legal systems, in fact, the definition of bribery is such that a legal violation only occurs when there is a quid pro quo expectation and both parties understand that one party is paying a bribe and that the other party will provide an illicit service in return and when the person being bribed has the authority to directly provide the illicit service. Thus, if a businessman hands a politician an envelope full of cash and talks about how much he would like to get a particular public works contract, and then several days later the politician votes in favor of awarding the contract to the same businessman, bribery may not have occurred. The politician could have believed the cash was a political contribution offered independent of the discussion that followed, or even though the politician voted

in favor of the contract award, he may not have not had the authority himself to award the contract and even without his vote the company might have won it anyway. For an interesting discussion of this problem, see David T. Johnson, "Why the Wicked Sleep: The Prosecution of Political Corruption in Postwar Japan," *Asian Perspective* 24:4 (2000): 59–77.

17. Tullock observed that in the 1970s the U.S. automotive industry was able to buy what he guessed was "billions" in profits by spending a mere faction of that amount lobbying Congress to restrict imports of Japanese cars. Gordon Tullock, "Where Is the Rectangle?" *Public Choice* 91:2 (1997): 149–59.

18. The Tullock Paradox can, in fact, be resolved by recognizing that the appropriate metric for judging the value of payoffs from corrupt transactions is in comparing not the relative gain of each party to such transactions, but the payoff of each party relative to the payoff from honesty. In other words, the value of the bribe to the official is relative to the opportunity cost of not accepting the bribe and not providing the favor, or what we might call his "honest wage." From that perspective, a bribe might appear large relative to the official's honest wage, even though it might represent a tiny fraction of the value of the favor he provided. Thus, for example, if a procurement officer making $50,000 steers a contract worth $50 million to a company in return for a $50,000 bribe, the bribe is worth 100 percent of his honest wage, an obviously large sum, not a tenth of a percent of $50 million, which would certainly appear to be very tiny faction. Hypothetically, a shrewd official might "shop" the contract award out, seeking larger bribes from other companies. In reality, however, this is a recipe for disaster because the losers will have incentives, and perhaps evidence, to expose the corrupt official. The need for secrecy, therefore, helps depress the value of bribes and contributes to the Tullock Paradox.

19. It is important to keep in mind that a clear distinction exists between the so-called mafia state discussed earlier in which corrupt officials use the state to engage in what amounts to an organized crime racket and cases where criminal organizations use bribes to buy protection from the law.

20. Beginning in the late nineteenth century, police units in Hong Kong operated protection rackets wherein beat officers collected money from the operators of illegal nightclubs, brothels, massage parlors, and gambling dens, a percentage of which they handed over to the precinct sergeants, who in turn paid a share to their supervisors. Under this arrangement, the police effectively received a cut of the profits from illegal activity, profits the criminal underworld could not have earned if the police had enforced the law. As such, it would be hard to see these criminals as victims of police corruption but more correct to recognize that they and the corrupt police were partners in crime. Beat officers also squeezed the operators of legitimate businesses, forcing them to hand over a share of their profits to avoid unwarranted police harassment. Syndicated police corruption in Hong Kong was thus a mixed form of corruption, having elements of both predatory plunder and mutual benefit-seeking transactive corruption. See T. S. Cheung, "A Profile of Syndicated Corruption in the Police Force," in Jamil M. Abun-Nasr, ed., *Corruption and Its Control in Hong Kong* (Hong Kong: Chinese University Press, 1981); H. J. Lethbridge, *Hard Graft in Hong Kong: Scandal, Corruption, and the ICAC* (Hong Kong: Oxford University Press, 1985); and Ying Shang, "Corruption Control in Hong Kong," in Nicholas Tarling, *Corruption and Good Government in Asia* (New York: Routledge, 2005), 121–44.

21. I take the term "true pillage" from comments made by Placido Mico Abogo, a leading member of the opposition to a reporter for the *Washington Post* who described President Obiang as engaging in "true pillaging." Douglas Farah, "Oil Gives African National a Chance for Change; Despite Leader's Promises, Many Fear People of Equatorial Guinea Will Not Benefit From Windfall," *Washington Post* May 13, 2001.

22. See Laurence Whitehead, "On Presidential Graft: The Latin American Evidence," in Arnold. J. Heidenheimer, Michael Johnston, and Victor T. Levine, eds., *Political Corruption: A Handbook* (New Brunswick, N.J.: Transaction Books, 1989), 781–800.

23. See John Waterbury, "Endemic and Planned Corruption in a Monarchical Regime," in Monday V. Ekpo, ed., *Bureaucratic Corruption in Sub-Saharan Africa: Toward a Search for Causes and Consequences* (Washington: University Press of America, 1979), 355–80.

24. On the link between regime insecurity, corruption, and the politics of survival, see Joel Migdal, *Strong Societies and Weak States: State-Society Relations and State Capabilities in the Third World* (Princeton, N.J.: Princeton University Press, 1988).

25. At one point, Mobutu tried to ban private trading in gold and diamonds by mandating that all gold and diamonds be sold to officially designated stores, owned by his family and members of his inner circle. The attempt ended up stimulating smuggling as sellers sought higher prices outside the country. Kisangani N. F. Emizet, "Confronting Leaders at the Apex of the State: The Growth of the Unofficial Economy in Congo," *African Studies Review* 41:1 (1998): 99–137.

26. Taxi and truck drivers, for example, had to pay a daily tax to the police and gendarmes who controlled specific sections of major roads. The street cops had to purchase their assigned section of roadway from their supervisors. Emizet, "Confronting Leaders at the Apex of Power," 117.

27. Andrew Wedeman, "Looters, Rent-Scrapers, and Dividend Collectors: Corruption and Growth in Zaire, South Korea, and the Philippines," *Journal of Developing Areas* 31:4 (1997), 462–65. In the last years of his regime, Mobutu was accused of either participating in or at least abetting a series of massive Ponzi schemes whereby thousands lost their savings, orchestrating the violence which followed their collapse, and then using state funds to compensate members of the ruling elite for fictitious losses suffered during the looting. The collapse of theses funds in May 1991 proved to be a major factor in Mobutu's fall. Emizet, "Confronting Leaders at the Apex of Power," 108.

28. See Morton Boas, "Liberia and Sierra Leone: Dead Ringers? The Logic of Neopatrimonial Rule," *Third World Quarterly* 22:5 (2001): 697–723; Earl Conteh-Morgan and Mac Dixon-Fyle, *Sierra Leone at the End of the Twentieth Century: History, Politics, and Society* (New York: Peter Lang, 1999); Jimmy D. Kandeh, "Sierra Leone: Contradictory Class Functionality of the 'Soft' State," *Review of African Political Economy* 20:55 (1992): 30–43; Jimmy D. Kandeh, "Ransoming the State: Elite Origins of Subaltern Terrorism in Sierra Leone," *Review of African Political Economy* 26:81 (1999): 349–66; Sahr John Kpundeh, "Limiting Administrative Corruption in Sierra Leone," *Journal of Modern African Studies* 32:1 (1994): 139–57; Sahr John Kpundeh, *Politics and Corruption in Africa: A Case Study of Sierra Leone* (Lanham, Md.: University Press of America, 1995); Neil O. Leighton, "The Lebanese in Sierra Leone," *Transition* 44 (1974): 23–29; Migdal, *Strong Societies and Weak States;* William Reno, *Corruption and State Politics in Sierra Leone* (New York: Cambridge University Press, 1995); David Fasole Luke and Stephan P. Riley, "The Politics of Economic Decline in Sierra Leone," *Journal of Modern African Studies* 27:1 (1989): 133–41; and Gerald H. Smith, "The Dichotomy of Politics and Corruption in a Neopatrimonial State: Evidence from Sierra Leone," *Journal of Opinion* 25:1 (1997): 58–62.

29. Originally a benefice (a grant of income rights from a specific area) awarded to members of the church, as used herein a prebend is a grant that allows an official holder to exploit his authority for personal gain. In a prebendal state, the ruler parcels out segments of the state to individuals who "reciprocate by giving the ruler absolute loyalty and a share of 'the rent'" they squeeze from their office. Hazel M. McFerson, "Democracy and Development in Africa," *Journal of Peace Research* 29:3 (1992): 243. Also see Richard A. Joseph, "Class, State, and Prebendal Politics in Nigeria," *Journal of Commonwealth and Comparative Politics* 21:3 (1983): 21–38.

30. As Landahl points out, Duvalier did not introduce kleptocracy to Haiti. He argues that "brigandage" had been the defining characteristic of Haitian politics since 1843, with a brief respite in the years following the U.S. occupation. What set Papa Doc apart from his predecessors was, Landahl assets, the sheer brazenness of his plunder, which he argues was

a function of Papa Doc's ability to quickly and totally eliminate internal security threats. Mats Lundahl, "Papa Doc: Innovator in the Predatory State," *Scandia* 50:1 (1984): 39–78.

31. Bernard Diederich and Al Burt, *Papa Doc: The Truth about Haiti Today* (New York: Avon Book, 1969), chapter 12.

32. Michel-Rolph Trouillot, *Haiti: State Against Nation. The Origins and Legacy of Duvalierism* (New York: Monthly Review Press, 1990), 176; and Yolaine Armand, "Democracy in Haiti: The Legacy of Anti-Democratic Political and Social Traditions," *International Journal of Politics, Culture, and Society* 2:4 (1989): 555.

33. Lundahl, "Papa Doc," 64; Robert I. Rotberg, with Christopher K. Clague, *Haiti: The Politics of Squalor* (Boston: Houghton Mifflin, 1971), 223–57; and Robert Debs Heinl, Jr., and Nancy Gordon Heinl, *Written in Blood: The Story of the Haitian People, 1492–1971* (Boston: Houghton Mifflin, 1978), chapter 14.

34. Elizabeth Abbott, *Haiti: The Duvaliers and Their Legacy* (New York: McGraw-Hill, 1988), 138.

35. Alex Dupuy, *Haiti in the World Economy: Class, Race, and Underdevelopment since 1700* (Boulder, Colo.: Westview Press, 1989), 161–67.

36. Ibid., 172.

37. Simon M. Fass, *The Political Economy in Haiti: The Drama of Survival* (New Brunswick, N.J.: Transaction Books, 1988), chapter 1; and Trouillot, *Haiti: State against Nation,* 192–93.

38. David Nichols, "The Duvalier Regime in Haiti," in Chehabi and Linz, eds., *Sultanistic Regimes,* 163.

39. Anastasio Somoza and his two sons, Luis Somoza Debayle and Anastasio Somoza Debayle, controlled Nicaragua from mid-1935 when the elder Somoza forced the president to resign, thus clearing the way for his election. In 1944, the U.S. government forced him to step aside. Somoza, however, staged a coup in 1947 and installed his uncle as president while retaining de facto control. He was elected president again in 1950. After Anastasio Somoza was assassinated in 1956, his eldest son, Luis, assumed the presidency until 1963, when he left office, turning it over to a newly elected family loyalist. From the mid-1950s onward real power was, however, held by Anastasio Somoza's younger son, Anastasio Somoza Debayle, who commanded the National Guard. Anastasio Somoza Debayle assumed the presidency in 1967 and remained in power until the revolution of 1979. See Eduardo Crawley, *Dictators Never Die: A Portrait of Nicaragua and the Somoza Family* (London: C. Hurst, 1979); and Knut Walter, *The Regime of Anastasio Somoza, 1936–1956* (Chapel Hill: University of North Carolina Press, 1993).

40. Robert D. Crassweller, *Trujillo: The Life and Times of a Caribbean Dictator* (New York: Macmillan, 1966), 125–29; and Jesus de Galindez, *The Era of Trujillo: Dominican Dictator* (Tucson: University of Arizona Press, 1973), 186–93.

41. Stanislav Andreski, *Parasitism and Subversion: The Case of Latin America* (New York: Schocken Books, 1996), 66.

42. Frank Moya Pons, "The Dominican Republic since 1930," in Leslie Bethell, ed., *The Cambridge History of Latin American,* Volume VII: *Latin America since 1930: Mexico, Central America and the Caribbean* (New York: Cambridge University Press, 1990), 511–21.

43. Jonathan Hartlyn, "The Trujillo Regime in the Dominican Republic," in Chehabi and Linz, eds., *Sultanistic Regimes,* 95.

44. Pons, "The Dominican Republic since 1930," 515.

45. Ibid., 521.

46. Crassweller, *Trujillo,* 347. In 1959, Trujillo announced that the Dominican Navy had repelled an attempted invasion by Cuban-backed revolutionaries and warned that Castro and the exiles were plotting further attacks. Michael Becker and Jonathan Wilkenfeld, *A Study of Crisis* (Ann Arbor: University of Michigan Press, 1997), 505.

47. Crawley, *Dictators Never Die,* 141–42; and John A. Booth, "The Somoza Regime in Nicaragua," in Chehabi and Linz, eds., *Sultanistic Regime,* 131–52.

48. John A. Booth, *The End and the Beginning: The Nicaraguan Revolution* (Boulder, Colo.: Westview Press, 1982), 65–69, 80–81.

49. Ibid., 69, 78.

50. Venezuelan President Juan Vicente Gomez constructed a similar system. He used his public authority to arrogate valuable properties and enterprises to his personal control and form a sprawling business empire that penetrated into virtually every sector of the economy. He also entered a complex series of business partnerships with regional and military power holders that secured his dictatorship. See Doug Yarrington, "Cattle, Corruption, and Venezuelan State Formation During the Regime of Juan Vicente Gomez, 1908–35," *Latin American Research Review* 38:2 (2003): 9–33.

51. Brian Titley, *Dark Age: The Political Odyssey of Emperor Bokassa* (Montreal: McGill University Press, 1997), chapters 5 and 13.

52. In 1990, Equatorial Guinea's population was estimated at 450,000. As of 2007, the population had reportedly more than doubled to 1.2 million. International Monetary Fund, *World Economic Outlook Database,* October 2008, available at http://imf.org/external/pubs/ft/weo/2008/02/weodata/index.aspx, accessed November 10, 2008.

53. Total reserves of oil are currently estimated at 1.1 billion barrels. Natural gas reserves are estimated at 1.3 trillion cubic feet. U.S. Department of Energy, Energy Information Administration, *Country Analysis Briefs: Equatorial Guinea,* October 2007, available at http://www.eia.doe.gov/cabs/Equatorial_Guinea/pdf.pdf, accessed November 10, 2008.

54. Ibid.

55. McFerson, "Governance and Hyper-corruption," 1538.

56. IMF, *World Economic Outlook Database,* October 2008; and *Business Day* (South Africa), September 8, 1999.

57. Data available at http://www.transparency.org/policy_research/surveys_indices/cpi, accessed November 10, 2008.

58. For illustrative purposes, I have rescaled the World Bank's Worldwide Governance Indicators, which rely on a five-point range from –2.5 to +2.5 with a midpoint of 0 in which –2.5 represents the worst possible score for "control of corruption" and +2.5 the best possible score. In order to make governance scores dovetail more easily with the system used by Transparency International and others, I have rescaled them using the same five-point range but setting the highest score of 5 to correspond to the worst possible corruption. Data available at http://info.worldbank.org/governance/wgi/sc_country.asp, accessed November 10, 2008.

59. *Sunday Telegraph* (London), August 29, 2004.

60. *Washington Post,* May 13, 2001.

61. Dan Gardner, "Our Friend, the Ruthless African Dictator," *Montreal Gazette,* June 28, 2008; *Africa News,* October 6, 2008; and *The Times* (London), August 26, 2004.

62. McFerson, "Governance and Hyper-corruption," 1538.

63. Ibid.

64. Samuel Decalo, *Psychoses of Power: African Personal Dictatorships* (Boulder, Colo.: Westview Press, 1989), 57.

65. Equatorial Guinea consists of the major island of Fernando Po which lies roughly 20 miles off the west coast of Cameroon, the much larger enclave of Rio Muni located on the African mainland about 100 miles south of Fernando Po, and a number of smaller islands off the coast of Rio Muni. Originally established as a base for operations in the Bight of Benin by the Portuguese in the late fifteenth century, Fernando Po (originally named Formosa by the Portuguese) was transferred to Spanish control in 1777–78. For much of the nineteenth century, the island served as base for British Royal Navy ships involved in antislaving operations and until the late 1850s the Spanish maintained no meaningful political presence on the island. Spanish control was not extended to Rio

Muni until the 1920s, and the enclave was brought under effective Spanish control only after World War II. Randall Fegley, *Equatorial Guinea: An African Tragedy* (New York: Peter Lang, 1989), chapter 1; Barry E. Miller, "Spanish Guinea: Evolution or Revolution?" *African Today* 12:3 (1965): 8–11; and Suzanne Cronje, *Equatorial Guinea: The Forgotten Dictatorship* (London: Anti-Slavery Society, 1976), 8.

66. Ibrahim K. Sundiata, "The Roots of African Despotism: The Question of Political Culture," *African Studies Review* 31:1 (1988): 13.

67. Ibid., 12.

68. Per capita income on Fernando Po was reportedly nearly US$500 in 1965, which would have made it the highest in West Africa. Fegley, *Equatorial Guinea,* 59.

69. Decalo, *Psychoses of Power,* 49.

70. Ibid.

71. Conje, *Equatorial Guinea,* 17. This was not the first time that such charges had been leveled about working conditions in Fernando Po. In the 1920s, the League of Nations initiated an investigation into charges that Liberian workers on the island were being held as slaves.

72. Rene Pelessier, "Autopsy of a Miracle," *Africa Report,* May–June 1980: 10–14.

73. In all, an estimated 50,000 to 80,000 Equatorial Guineans died as a result of the terror. Pelessier, "Autopsy of a Miracle," 14; and Decalo, *Psychoses of Power,* 58.

74. Macias was said to have been mentally deranged and a heavy user of narcotics.

75. Decalo, *Psychoses of Power,* 63.

76. Sundiata, "Roots of African Despotism," 26.

77. *Deutsche Presse-Agentur,* April 20, 1995.

78. See Robert Klitgaard, *Tropical Gangsters: One Man's Experience with Development and Decadence in Deepest Africa* (New York: Basic Books, 1990). Klitgaard, who was hired by the World Bank to oversee its operations in Equatorial Guinea in the early 1980s, provides a rollicking account of his experiences in dealing with Obiang's corrupt regime.

79. *Boston Globe,* June 15, 1993.

80. *Agence France Presse,* October 15, 2003.

81. Equatorial Guinea was among a number of what might be termed "petro-kleptocracies" in West Africa, including Nigeria, Cameroon, Congo-Brazzaville, Gabon, and Angola. In all these cases, political leaders have siphoned off large sums of their country's income from oil production while using oil revenues to fund corruption-driven neo-patrimonial political machines and finance bloated security forces, often staffed by imported mercenaries. See Nicholas Shaxson, *Poisoned Wells: The Dirty Politics of African Oil* (New York: Palgrave Macmillan, 2008); Ricardo Soares de Oliveria, *Oil and Politics in the Gulf of New Guinea* (New York: Columbia University Press, 2007); and John Ghazvinian, *Untapped: The Scramble for Africa's Oil* (New York: Mariner Books, 2008).

82. Like his uncle, Obiang believed he was divinely anointed. The government radio described him as "the god of Equatorial Guinea" and asserted that he was "in permanent contract with the Almighty." Also like Macias, Obiang blamed the country's problems on the "diabolical, prejudicial, and destructive machinations of foreign enemies." According to Obiang, foreign businessmen were responsible for corruption. *British Broadcasting Corporation,* June 14, 2005; *Agence France Presse,* July 8, 2006; *Radio Nacional de Guinea Ecuatorial,* October 10, 2003, in *British Broadcast Service Worldwide Monitoring,* October 17, 2003; and *Africa News,* April 25, 2004. Obiang's charges that outsiders are plotting against him are not entirely unfounded. In 2004 a group of white mercenaries and demobilized black South African soldiers were arrested in Zimbabwe as they attempted to load a Boeing 727 with arms in what prosecutors say was the opening move of an attempted invasion of Equatorial Guinea. Backers of the coup allegedly included the son of former British Prime Minister Margaret Thatcher. See Adam Roberts, *The Wonga Coup: Guns, Thugs,*

and a Ruthless Determination to Create Mayhem in an Oil-Rich Corner of Africa (New York: Public Affairs, 2006).

83. Riggs Bank, based in Washington, played a central role in Obiang's efforts to siphon off oil royalties from government accounts. At one point, the Equatorial Guinea government and various senior officials were major customers of Riggs Bank. Exposure of the bank's role in laundering money for Obiang and his henchmen almost led to its collapse. On this role and for a telling description of how money was moved from official accounts in the hands of corrupt officials, see U.S. Senate Permanent Subcommittee on Investigations, Committee on Governmental Affairs, "Money Laundering and Foreign Corruption: Enforcement and Effectiveness of the Patriot Act Case Study Involving Riggs Bank," July 15, 2004, available at http://hsgac.senate.gov/public/_files/ACF5F8.pdf, accessed March 17, 2011. Much of what is known about corruption in Equatorial Guinea comes from this investigation.

84. Jedrqej George Frynas, "The Oil Boom in Equatorial Guinea," *African Affairs* 103:413 (2004): 527–46; and Shaxson, *Poisoned Well*, 36–38.

85. The following paragraphs are based on newspaper reports including *UN Integrated Regional Information News*, July 16, 2004; *Washington Post*, September 7, 2004; *The Independent* (London), September 5, 2004, and March 16, 2004; *Africa Research Bulletin*, February 1, 2003; *Oilgram News*, August 5, 2004; *The Guardian* (London), October 9, 2004; *Africa News*, November 6, 2002; and Peter Maass, "A Touch of Crude," *Mother Jones*, January 2005, available at http://www.petermaass.com/articles/a touch of crude/, accessed July 16, 2011.

86. Maass, "A Touch of Crude."

87. *The Guardian* (London), June 2, 2005.

88. Geoffrey Wood, "Business and Politics in a Criminal State: The Case of Equatorial Guinea," *African Affairs* 103:413 (2004): 547–67.

89. *Agence France Press*, January 30, 2005, and December 13, 1999.

90. Maass, "A Touch of Crude."

91. *Deutsche Presse-Agentur*, August 11, 2006, and July 24–25, 2001; *Agence France Presse*, April 17, 2002, December 13, and November 26, 1999; and November 28, 1989.

92. *Associated Press*, March 27, 2006. TRACE's mission statement is available at http://www.secure.traceinternational.org, accessed November 15, 2008.

93. McFerson, "Governance and Hyper-corruption," 1538.

94. The dark and foreboding atmosphere of fear that accompanied Haiti's descent into kleptocracy has been captured by Graham Greene in the novel *The Comedians* (New York: Viking, 1966). In the Dominican Republic, Trujillo's secret police were so dreaded that an "asphyxiating … culture of fear" took hold. Lauren Derby, "In the Shadow of the State: The Politics of Denunciation and Panegyric during the Trujillo Regime in the Dominican Republic, 1940–1958," *Hispanic American Historical Review* 83:2 (2003): 295–344.

CHAPTER 4

1. See Andrew Wedeman, *From Mao to Market: Rent Seeking, Local Protectionism, and Marketization in China* (New York: Cambridge University Press, 2003).

2. See Barry Naughton, *Growing Out of the Plan: Chinese Economic Reform, 1978–1993* (New York: Cambridge University Press, 1996).

3. In broad terms, local protectionism refers to local governments' use of irregular and often unauthorized means to block the flow of goods and to protect local interests, including local companies, from outside competition. During the 1980s and 1990s, financially hard-pressed local governments frequently resorted to local protectionism to capture rents embedded in the price system rather than allow them to be captured by other

localities. They therefore restricted exports of undervalued goods (generally raw materials and other commodities) and imports of goods (generally finished products) that would compete with local products, thereby allowing local producers to charge inflated prices. In this context, local protectionism can be defined as a form of institutional corruption in that it involves the improper use of public authority by local governments to obtain illicit financial advantages.

4. Prices were driven toward market-clearing levels because rising prices for heretofore undervalued commodities stimulated a surge in production that culminated in glut conditions in which black market prices fell either to the point where they were equal to the administratively set price or below it. In the case of overpriced goods, inflated profits stimulated a surge in production that also led to glut conditions and hence a regression of prices toward market-clearing levels.

5. Although the state retains formal ownership of most land, property developers are granted long-term use right leases (generally 70 to 90 years) that essentially grant them de facto ownership rights, including the right to sell or transfer their use rights to others.

6. As Tanzi and Davoodi point out, the large monetary value of many public works contracts, particularly those involving infrastructure construction, makes them prone to corruption because not only does the company that wins the contract stand to make large profits, skimming even a percentage or two off the top can yield large payoffs. Bidders have strong incentives and the capability, therefore, to offer bribes to officials responsible for awarding contracts. Vito Tanzi and Hamid Davoodi, "Corruption, Public Investment, and Growth," International Monetary Fund Working Paper, WP/97/139 (1997), available at http://www.imf.org/external/pubs/ft/wp/wp97139.pdf, accessed May 20, 2009.

7. According to Kenny, between 5 and 25 percent of the value of infrastructural spending in the developing world is siphoned off by corruption. Charles Kenny, "Measuring and Reducing the Impact of Corruption in Infrastructure," World Bank Policy Research Working Paper 4099 (2006), available at http://papers.ssrn.com/sol3/papers.cfm?abstract_id=952071#, accessed May 20, 2009; and Charles Kenny, "Transport Construction, Corruption, and Developing Countries," *Transportation Review* 29:1 (2009): 21–41.

8. Over the past twenty years, IFA jumped 315 fold, rising from ¥96 billion in 1981 to ¥452 billion in 1990, then jumped to ¥2,025 billion five years later. In 1995 annual spending hit ¥3.31 trillion. The greatest increases were in the first decade of the 2000s, during which IFA rose to ¥9.46 trillion in 2005 and an estimated ¥30.29 trillion in 2010. Spending on construction rose at a similar rate, increasing from ¥35 billion in 1980 to ¥5.10 trillion in 2007. *China Statistical Yearbook,* various years.

9. See Shawn Shieh, "The Rise of Collective Corruption in China: The Xiamen Smuggling Case," *Journal of Contemporary China* 14:42 (2005): 67–91.

10. According to Lu, between 1979 and 1996, the regime launched nine distinct anticorruption campaigns, one every two years. Lu Xiaobo, *Cadres and Corruption: The Organizational Involution of the Chinese Communist Party* (Stanford, Calif.: Stanford University Press, 2000), 223. During the 1980s, anticorruption campaigns produced very visible increases in the number of cases filed. In the 1990s, campaigns tended to produce no visible spikes in the total number of indictments because they generally targeted specific types of corruption and concentrated increasingly on senior officials, whose smaller number made the impact of campaigns much less visible, at least in the aggregate data.

11. Guo Yong, "Corruption in Transitional China: An Empirical Analysis," *China Quarterly* 194 (2008): 349–64.

12. In recent years, a number of public opinion polls have asked ordinary Chinese about corruption. Most tend to indicate that a majority of Chinese consider corruption a major problem. Unfortunately, these sorts of data do not track corruption over time and hence provide only snapshot measures. Moreover, we have no polling data for the early 1980s.

13. During this period, for example, the enjoyment of material comforts, an unwillingness to engage in manual labor, and simple laziness could be construed as a form of corruption. In other instances, corruption was equated with forms of moral decadence associated with an urbane, bourgeois lifestyle and mindset. It is not clear, however, if people accused of such offenses were criminally prosecuted or were instead subject to political denunciation. Albert James Bergesen, "A Durkheimian Theory of 'Witch-Hunts' with the Chinese Cultural Revolution of 1966–1969 as an Example," *Journal for the Scientific Study of Religion* 17:1 (1978): 19–29; Yomi Braester, "'A Big Dying Vat': The Vilifying of Shanghai during the Good Eighth Company Campaign," *Modern China* 31:4 (2005): 411–47; and Rensselaer W. Lee III, "The Hsia Fang System: Marxism and Modernisation," *China Quarterly* 28 (1966): 40–62.

14. The National Audit Office also plays a role in helping to detect corruption and financial irregularities involving government agencies, state-owned enterprises, and other public agencies. In 2007, the State Council established a new National Corruption Prevention Bureau and tasked it with implementing measures designed to prevent corruption, improve interagency cooperation, and increase monitoring of corrupt practices in the private sector and among nongovernmental organizations. See Yuan Baishun, *Shenji Zhidu yu Zhongguo Dalu de Lianzheng Jianshe* [The Role of the Audit System in China's Building of Clean Government], paper presented at the workshop "Toward a Clean Government: Institutional Design and Policy Capacity," City University of Hong Kong, May 2007; and Jeffrey Becker, "Tackling Corruption at Its Source: The National Corruption Prevention Bureau," *Journal of Chinese Political Science* 13:3 (2008): 287–303.

15. After its establishment in 1988, the Ministry of Supervision initially operated independently from the DIC. Because many state officials are party members, and in practice the DIC has prior jurisdiction in all cases involving party members, it soon became apparent that concurrent, independent investigations were impractical. As a result, in 1993 the DIC and Ministry of Supervision merged their investigative efforts, with the supervisory system assuming a subordinate role. Depending on the outcome of joint investigations, the DIC may impose party disciplinary measures (including expulsion from the party), the Ministry of Supervision may impose administrative sanctions (such as dismissal from office and demotion), or the individual may receive concurrent party and administrative sanctions. The ministry also appears to take the lead in investigating institutional misconduct, including problems associated with the three disorders (*san luan*)—illegal taxation and fee collection, arbitrary imposition of fines, and improper imposition of costs—and the related problem of excessive burdens imposed on rural residents (*nongmin fudan*).

16. Based on data from Anhui (1992–95), Beijing (1989–93), Chongqing (1989–96), Fujian (1994–95, 1999, and 2003), Guangdong (1987–88), Guangxi (1989–93 and 1999–2000), Guizhou (1997–98), Hainan (1990–99 and 2005–7), Hebei (1992–95), Henan (1994–96), Hubei (1988–99, 2001, and 2003), Hunan (1989–93), Jiangsu (1994–96), Jilin (1992), Liaoning (1992), Shaanxi (1992), Shandong (1986–93, 1997–98, and 2003), Shanxi (1989–90), Yunnan (1989–92, 1994, and 1997–98), and Zhejiang (1991–95). Data from various provincial yearbooks.

17. The courts, for instance, define smuggling as a form of economic crime while the procuratorate does not.

18. For a more detailed discussion of corruption in the 1950s, see Lu, *Cadres and Corruption*, chapter 2.

19. For a detailed discussion of these campaigns and information on major cases, see *Xin Zhongguo Fanfubai Tongjian* [Chronicle of Anticorruption in New China] (Tianjin: Renmin Chubanshe, 1993). Also see Theodore His-En Chen and Wen-Hui C. Chen, "The 'Three Anti' and the 'Five Anti' Movements in China," *Pacific Affairs* 26:1 (1953): 3–23.

20. Lu, *Cadres and Corruption*, 55–57. Average wage data from *Quanguo Ge Sheng, Zizhiqu, Zhenxia Shi Lishi Tongji Ziliao Huiban* (1949–89) [Compilation of Historical Statistics for All Provinces, Autonomous Regions, and Cities under the Direct Jurisdiction of the Central Government (1949–89)] (Beijing: Zhongguo Tongji Chubanshe, 1990), 34.

21. Lu, *Cadres and Corruption*, 55–57; and *Xin Zhongguo Fanfubai Tongjian*, 32.

22. *Xin Zhongguo Fanfubai Tongjian*, 104.

23. *Hunan Shengzhi, Di liu juan: Zhengfa Zhi* [Hunan Provincial Gazetteer, volume 6: Political and Legal Affairs] (Changsha: Hunan Chubanshe, 1996), 276.

24. *Jiangxi Sheng Jiancha Zhi* [Gazetteer of the Jiangxi Provincial Procuratorate] (Beijing: Zhongyang Zhonggongdang Chubanshe, 1995), 159–61. For a discussion of the Twenty Three Points and the Socialist Education Movement, see Richard Baum, "Revolution and Reaction in the Chinese Countryside: The Socialist Education Movement in Cultural Revolution Perspective," *China Quarterly* 38 (1969): 92–119; and Richard Baum and Frederick C. Teiwes, *Ssu-ch'ing: The Socialist Education Movement of 1962–1966* (Berkeley: Center For Chinese Studies, University of California, 1968).

25. Based on information on county-level procuratorates published in *Zhongguo Renmin Gongheguo Renmin Jianchayuan Gailian* [An Overview of the Peoples Procuratorate of the People's Republic of China] (Beijing: Zhongguo Jiancha Chubanshe, 1995). This multivolume work provides data on each county-level procuratorate, including a thumbnail history.

26. *Xin Zhongguo Fanfubai Tongjian*, 116.

27. Dennis Woodward, "Rural Campaigns: Continuity and Change in the Chinese Countryside—The Early Post-Cultural Revolution Experience (1969–1972)," *Australian Journal of Chinese Affairs* 6 (1981): 97–124.

28. Lu, *Cadres and Corruption*, 129.

29. Ibid.

30. On the emergence of *guanxi* during the Cultural Revolution period and its development, see Mayfair Mei-hua Yang, *Gifts, Favors, and Banquets: The Art of Social Relationships in China* (Ithaca, N.Y.: Cornell University Press, 1994). Gold, however, argues that *guanxi* draws on traditional cultural institutions wherein individuals build relationships as a form of "social investment." Thomas B. Gold, "After Comradeship: Personal Relations in China since the Cultural Revolution," *China Quarterly* 104 (1985): 657–75.

31. See Lu, *Cadres and Corruption*, 130–37, for a more complete discussion of the backdoor *guanxi* phenomenon.

32. The social practice of *guanxi* and its connection with corruption has received a great deal of attention in the both the scholarly and the popular literature. In broad terms, *guanxi* refers to set of connections linking individuals either directly or though networks of intermediary ties. In the main, *guanxi* involves social connections that imply some degree of mutual obligation and is often reinforced by the exchanges of gifts and favors. *Guanxi* is not, however, synonymous with bribery. As Yang argues, *guanxi* involves an emotional connection whereas bribery implies a more overtly instrumental transaction. *Guanxi* relationships can, of course, serve as a precursor for bribery, but *guanxi* and the gift-giving relationships that may accompany it are not necessarily premised on the expectation that a gift or favor will yield material advantage. See, *inter alia*, Lowell Dittmer and Lu Xiaobo, "Personal Politics in the Chinese *Danwei* under Reform," *Asian Survey* 36:3 (1996): 246–67; Douglas Guthrie, "The Declining Significance of Guanxi in China's Economic Transition," *China Quarterly* 154 (1998): 254–82; Andrew B. Kipnis, "The Language of Gifts: Managing Guanxi in a North China Village," *Modern China* 22:3 (1996): 285–314; Jean C. Oi, "Communism and Clientalism: Rural Politics in China," *World Politics* 37:2 (1985): 238–66; Alan Smart, "Gifts, Bribes, and Guanxi: A Reconsideration of Bourdieu's Social Capital," *Cultural Anthropology* 8:3 (1993): 388–408; Yunxiang Yun, "The Cultural

of Guanxi in a North China Village," *China Journal* 35 (1996): 1–25; Yang, *Gifts, Favors, and Banquets;* Mayfair Mei-hui Yang, "The Resilience of *Guanxi* and Its New Development: A Critique of Some New *Guanxi* Scholarship," *China Quarterly* 170 (2002): 459–76; and Mayfair Mei-hui Yang, "The Gift Economy and State Power in China," *Comparative Studies in Society and History* 31:1 (1989): 25–54.

33. Lu, *Cadres and Corruption,* 144–53.

34. Ibid., 141–44.

35. According to a sample containing data on 175 city- and county-level bureaus, the process of reconstituting the procuratorate began in early 1978, with a majority of local bureaus being reestablished in the fall of 1978. In some areas, however, they were not set up until the summer of 1979. Based on data in *Zhongguo Renmin Gongheguo Renmin Jianchayuan Gailian.* On the party disciplinary system, see Graham Young, "Control and Style: Discipline Inspection Commissions since the 11th Congress," *China Quarterly* 97 (1984): 30.

36. Arrests in 1989 accounted for over 60 percent of all arrests of senior officials prior to 1990.

37. In 416 major cases reported between 1979 and 1989, only 13 percent of those arrested had been engaged in corruption prior to 1979. Most of those who had been involved in the Maoist era were arrested early on, and by 1984 virtually all those arrested had turned corrupt after 1979. Based on author's database of cases drawn from LexisNexis.

38. Inflation and wage data from *Zhongguo Tongji Nianjian* [Statistical Yearbook of China] (Beijing: Zhongguo Tongji Chubanshe, various years). Volumes for 1996 to 2008 available at http://www.stats.gov.cn/, accessed October 12, 2009.

39. In fact, the ¥2,400 inflation-adjusted real value of the threshold would have dropped the threshold to just about the lower threshold for criminal culpability of ¥2,000.

40. Such cases are considered to fall below the level of criminality and hence carry administrative penalties (e.g., dismissal from office, demotion, etc.). See Gao Gezhao, *Dingzui yu Liangxing* [Conviction and Penalty Measuring] (Beijing: Zhongguo Fangzheng Chubanshe, 2001), 984–95; and Meng Qinghua, *Shouhui Zui Yanjiu Xin Dongxiang* [New Trends in Research on the Crime of Accepting Bribes] (Beijing: Zhongguo Fangzheng Chubanshe, 2005), 4–5.

41. Among regional governments, for instance, county governments accounted for roughly 90 percent of the total, with prefectural governments accounting for 10 percent and provincial governments just 1 percent.

42. The top (provincial/ministry) level shows much higher volatility in the number of indictments, but this is due to the relatively small number of officials and hence indictments at the highest levels of the official hierarchy. In China's unitary governmental system, regional governments—or as they are known in China "horizontal" (*kuai*) administrations—(counties, prefectures, and provinces) are considered the functional equivalent of the "vertical" (*tiao*) agencies of the central government. Thus, a province is considered of equal bureaucratic rank to the ministry.

43. Ironically, even though wages were generally very low during the 1970s, many people ended up accumulating substantial amounts of savings because there was so little to buy.

CHAPTER 5

1. In key respects, the process can be mapped to what has been called the "managerial" or "corporate" revolution in the United States. Companies were originally proprietary, owned and managed by the same individual. As they grew in size, not only did increasing capital requirements necessitate the formation of partnerships and then sale of partial

ownership rights to outside investors, the increasing complexity of operations made it difficult for a single individual to effectively manage an entire company. A new class of managers possessing technical skills began to assume responsibility for coordinating production and operations while owners retreated from day-to-day operations. Further growth in the size of major companies led to the dissipation of ownership as the number of investors, many of whom invested for the short term by trading stocks, increased to the point that even the largest shareholders owned a fraction of total equity. Because managers had firsthand access to financial information and fractional owners had weak incentives to actively monitor the company's performance, information asymmetries grew. Power ultimately shifted from owners to managers, who were often positioned to control the selection of the corporate boards, which were established to monitor managers on behalf of the shareholders at large. The rise of the so-called public corporation in the United States thus has surprising parallels to the transformation of China's state-owned companies from the proprietary property of specific government agencies to joint stock companies nominally owned by the state but actually controlled by their managers. On the managerial and corporate revolutions, see Adolf A. Berle and Gardiner C. Means, *The Modern Corporation and Private Property* (New York: Harcourt, Brace & World, 1968); and Alfred D. Chandler, Jr., *The Visible Hand: The Managerial Revolution in American Business* (Cambridge, Mass.: Belknap Press, 1977).

2. In Shaanxi, for example, condominium developers had to obtain upward of 150 different "chops" between the time they acquired a piece of property and when they finally sold units. Anonymous interview, Xi'an, May 18, 2010.

3. See Susan Whiting, *Power and Wealth in Rural China: The Political Economy of Institutional Change* (New York: Cambridge University Press, 2001).

4. See Melanie Manion, "Corruption by Design: Bribery in Chinese Enterprise Licensing," *Journal of Law, Economics & Organization* 12:1 (1996): 167–95; Dali Yang, *Remaking the Chinese Leviathan: Market Transition and the Politics of Governance in China* (Stanford, Calif.: Stanford University Press, 2004); and Yasheng Huang, *Selling China: Foreign Direct Investment in the Reform Era* (New York: Cambridge University Press, 2003).

5. Manion, "Corruption by Design."

6. A degree of temperance is perhaps warranted when describing the quality of China's regulatory system. There are endless tales of regulatory nightmares involving webs of red tape, arbitrary rules, and stone-faced bureaucrats who can only be warmed up and animated by the applications of *baijiu*, banquets, and cigarettes. When compared to the rest of the world, however, regulatory irrationalities in China might not appear so bad. The World Bank's Governance Index, for example, scores the quality of China's regulatory system as only slightly worse than the global average, giving it an average score of –0.27 on a scale with an average of 0, a maximum of 2.11, a minimum of –2.61, and a lower quartile of –0.66. China, in other words, is pretty much in the middle of the pack in terms of quality of regulation. If we compare the earliest score (1996) to the most recent (2008), there would appear to have been slippage from a slightly above average score (+0.15) to a slightly below average score (–0.22). It would be hard, however, to say that there has been a clear trend because China's score has bounced around, dropping from +0.15 in 1996 to –0.26 in 1998, then sinking to –0.52 in 2002, at which point it began to approach the lower quartile bound of –0.71. China's score improved, however, to –0.39 in 2003 and continued to improve in subsequent years, with the exception of 2006 when it declined from –0.26 in 2005 to –0.33 in 2006. Thereafter, it bounded back up to –0.24 in 2007 and improved to –0.22 in 2008. Data available at http://web.worldbank.org/. WBSITE/EXTERNAL/WBI/EXTWBIGOVANTCOR/0,contentMDK:20673879~menu PK:1742423~pagePK:64168445~piPK:64168309~theSitePK:1740530,00.html, accessed January 25, 2010.

7. Victor C. Shih, *Factions and Finance in China: Elite Conflict and Inflation* (New York: Cambridge University Press, 2008), chapter 3; and Bruce J. Dickson, *Red Capitalists in China: The Party, Private Entrepreneurs, and the Prospects for Political Change* (New York: Cambridge University Press, 2003).

8. See Kellee S. Tsai, *Back-Alley Banking: Private Entrepreneurs in China* (Ithaca, N.Y.: Cornell University Press, 2002); and Whiting, *Power and Wealth in Rural China.*

9. See Kate Gillespie and Gwenn Okruhlik, "The Political Dimensions of Corruption Cleanups: a Framework for Analysis," *Comparative Politics* 24:1 (1991): 77–95.

10. Yan Sun, *Corruption and Market in Contemporary China* (Ithaca, N.Y.: Cornell University Press, 2004), 55–68.

11. Ting Gong, "Forms and Characteristics of China's Corruption in the 1990s: Change with Continuity," *Communist and Post-Communist Studies* 30:3 (1997): 277–88.

12. Ting Gong, "Dangerous Collusion: Corruption as a Collective Venture in Contemporary China," *Communist and Post-Communist Studies* 35:1 (2002).

13. He Qinglian, "On Systemic Corruption in China and its Influence," in William C. Heffernan and John Kleinin, eds., *Private and Public Corruption* (New York: Rowman & Littlefield, 2004), 240–41.

14. Huang Yasheng, *Capitalism with Chinese Characteristics: Entrepreneurship and the State* (New York: Cambridge University Press, 2008), 285.

15. He, "On Systemic Corruption in China and Its Influence," 242.

16. Michael Johnston, "The Political Consequences of Corruption: A Reassessment," *Comparative Politics* 18:4 (1986): 465.

17. Ibid., 464.

18. Arnold J. Heidenheimer, "Introduction," in Arnold J. Heidenheimer, ed., *Political Corruption: Readings in Comparative Analysis* (New Brunswick, N.J.: Transaction Books, 1970), 26–27.

19. Xiaobo Lu, "Booty Socialism, Bureau-Preneurs, and the State in Transition: Organizational Corruption in China," *Comparative Politics* 32:3 (2000): 275. On institutional corruption see Andrew Wedeman, "Stealing From the Farmers: Institutional Corruption and the 1992 IOU Crisis," *China Quarterly* 152 (1997): 81–107. On collective corruption, see Shawn Shieh, "The Rise of Collective Corruption in China: The Xiamen Smuggling Case," *Journal of Contemporary China* 14:42 (2005): 67–69.

20. Shieh, "The Rise of Collective Corruption," 69.

21. Gong, "Dangerous Collusion," 87–89.

22. Andrei Schleifer and Robert W. Vishny, "Corruption," *Quarterly Journal of Economics,* 108:3 (1993): 599–617.

23. Syed Hussein Alatas, *Corruption: Its Nature, Causes, and Functions* (Hants, UK: Avebury, 1990). Also see Paul Heywood, "Political Corruption: Problems and Perspectives," *Political Studies* 45 (1997): 417–35.

24. Donatella della Porta and Alberto Vannucci, *Corrupt Exchanges: Actors, Resources, and Mechanisms of Political Corruption* (New York: Aldine de Gruyter, 1999), 20–24.

25. Sun, *Corruption and Market in Contemporary China,* 23–24.

26. Andrew Wedeman, "Looters, Rent-Scrapers, and Dividend-Collectors: Corruption and Growth in Zaire, South Korea, and the Philippines," *Journal of Developing Areas* 31:4 (1997): 457–78. In her comparative analysis of the differing consequences of corruption in China and Russia, Sun appropriates my tripartite model but uses the term "profit sharing" instead of "dividend collecting." Yan Sun, "Reform, State, and Corruption: Is Corruption Less Destructive in China than in Russia?" *Comparative Politics* 32:1 (1999): 1–20.

27. According to Becker, in contemporary China the demand side of corruption is much more loosely policed than the supply side, and bribe-paying businessmen are much less likely to be prosecuted than bribe-taking officials and cadres. Jeffrey Becker, "Tackling

Corruption at Its Source: The National Corruption Prevention Bureau," *Journal of Chinese Political Science* 13:3 (2008): 292.

28. The claim that corruption yields positive economic benefits by enabling potential users of inefficiently employed state assets to use bribes to bid for them is, of course, an old claim and widely disputed, in large part because Leff seems to imply that red tape is exogenously created whereas, as Banerjee and others have pointed out, it is more often an endogenous bureaucratic creation designed to generate the need for bribes and "speed money." I thus invoke it with trepidation. I do not believe that in general corruption will stimulate growth by creating an efficient allocation of resource. On the contrary, as argued in chapters 1 and 2, I accept the conventional wisdom that corruption is negatively correlated with growth rates and is detrimental to economic development. Thus, I see these sorts of transactions as transfer payments without necessarily seeing them as efficiency-increasing payments. On the alleged efficiency-increasing affects of corruption, see Nathaniel H. Leff, "Economic Development through Bureaucratic Corruption," in Heidenheimer, ed., *Political Corruption*, 510–20; and Abhijit V. Banerjee, "A Theory of Misgovernance," *Quarterly Journal of Economics* 112:4 (1997): 1289–1332.

29. As used herein "commercialized corruption" is different from what is called "commercial bribery" (*shangye huilu*). In Chinese legal terms, commercial bribery refers to cases in which at least one of the parties is in the business sector and can include not only private-to-public bribery but also private-to-private bribery, in which case neither party need be an official. Rather than involving the misuse of public authority for private gain, "private corruption" involves the misuse of corporate authority (or what is known as fiduciary responsibility). See Andrew Wedeman, "The Challenge of Commercial Bribery and Organized Crime in China," *Journal of Contemporary China*, forthcoming.

30. Perhaps the best-known example of misappropriation was the Chen Liangyu case in Shanghai. Chen, the municipal party secretary, allowed or ordered his subordinates to use money belonging to the Shanghai Municipal Pension fund to make speculative loans to some of the city's leading property developers. For a detailed discussion of this case, see chapter 6.

31. The Chen Xitong case is a good example of this. Chen accumulated a slush fund of ¥200 million, much of it apparently obtained from commissions paid by real estate developers to the Beijing party apparatus. Deputy Mayor Wang Baosen used part of this money to invest in the Xinxing Industrial Corporation, a firm based in Wuxi (Jiangsu) that offered investors monthly returns of between 5 and 10 percent. Xinxing was, however, a pyramid scheme, and in July 1994 it collapsed, leaving debts of ¥3.2 billion, much of it owed to nearly four hundred state enterprises and units. Investigators in Wuxi discovered that two members of the Beijing municipal apparatus, one of whom was Chen Xitong's secretary, were acting as "bag men," bringing large sums of cash down from Beijing to invest in the Xinxing scheme. When questioned, they implicated Wang Baosen as the man responsible for putting out the Beijing party's slush funds. After being confronted by investigators in Beijing, Wang committed suicide. Shortly thereafter, Chen—who was a member of the panel that questioned Wang the day before his suicide—was detained and eventually charged. In his defense, he claimed he had done nothing wrong because it was common practice for developers to pay agencies commissions and for the money to be used to make investments, the profits of which he claimed were then used to provide benefits and bonuses. See Andrew Wedeman, "Corruption and Politics," in Maurice Brosseau, Suzanne Pepper, and Tsang Shu-ki, eds., *China Review 1996* (Hong Kong: Chinese University Press, 1996), 61–94.

32. See Andrew Wedeman, "Budgets, Extra-budgets, and Small Treasuries: The Utility of Illegal Monies," *Journal of Contemporary China* 9:25 (2000): 489–511.

33. "Zuigao Renmin Fayuan, Zuigao Renmin Jiancha Yuan Yuanyi zhengque zhi xing liang ge Buchong de Tongzh" [Notice of the Supreme Peoples Court and Supreme Peoples

Procuratorate Regarding Proper Implementation of the Two Supplemental Regulations], in *Zhongguo Chengzhi Jingji Fanzui Quanshu* [Comprehensive Guide to the Punishment of Economic Crimes in China] (Beijing: Zhongguo Zhengfa Daxue Chubanshe, 1995), 1029–31.

34. As used herein, "profit-seeking corruption" is not the same as "commercial brib- ery" (*shangye huilu*), which refers to bribes accepted by corporate managers and officers. Although largely unstudied, private-to-private corruption is likely widespread in China and elsewhere. See Antonio Argandona, "Private-to-Private Corruption," IESE Business School, University of Navarra, Working Paper No. 531 (2003), available at http://papers. ssrn.com/sol3/cf_dev/AbsAyAuth.cfm?per_id=293156, accessed February 12, 2010.

35. Technically, nepotism refers to the favoring of relatives or protégés. Venality of office, on the other hand, refers to the practice of selling appointments to office, including the sale of promotions and transfers. Venality was common in early modern Europe. Brit- ish military officers, for example, continued to buy their commissions well into the mid- nineteenth century. It was also a feature of the pre-1911 imperial system in China according to Marsh. See James Eastgate Brink, "The Estates General of Languedoc: Struggles for Pro- vincial Autonomy in Early 16th Century France," *Legislative Studies Quarterly* 5:3 (1980): 437–46; William Doyle, "The Price of Offices in Pre-Revolutionary France," *Historical Journal* 27:4 (1984): 831–60; John J. Hurt, III, "The Parlement of Brittany and the Crown: 1665–1675," *French Historical Studies* 4:4 (1966): 411–33; Robert M. Marsh, "The Venal- ity of Provincial Office in China and in Comparative Perspective," *Comparative Studies in Society and History* 4:4 (1962): 454–66; Jeffrey K. Sawyer, "Judicial Corruption and Legal Reform in Early Seventeenth-Century France," *Law and History Review* 6:1 (1988): 95–117; Christopher Stocker, "Public and Private Enterprise in the Administration of a Renaissance Monarchy: The First Sales of Office in the Parlement of Paris (1512–1524)," *Sixteenth Century Journal* 9:2 (1978): 4–29; and H. C. Tomlinson, "Place and Profit: An Examination of the Ordnance Office, 1660–1714: The Alexander Prize Essay," *Transactions of the Royal Historical Society* 25 (1975): 55–75.

36. *Hunan Shengzhi di liu juan: Zhengfa Zhi Jiancha* [Annals of Hunan Province, vol- ume 6: Politics and Law Annals: Procuratorate] (Changsha: Hunan Chubanshe, 1996): 281, 324–27.

37. *Yunnan Shengzhi Wushiwu Juan: Shenpan Zhi* [Annals of Yunnan Province, volume 55: Annals of the Criminal Justice System] (Kunming: Yunnan Renmin Chubanshe, 1999).

38. *Liaoning Shengzhi: Shenpan Zhi* [Annals of Liaoning Province: Annals of the Crim- inal Justice System (Shenyang: Liaoning Minzu Chubanshe, 2003).

39. *Sichuan Shengzhi: Di Sanshiwu Juan: Jiancha Shenpan Zhi* [Annals of Sichuan Prov- ince, volume 35: Annuals of the Procuratorial and Criminal Justices Systems] (Chengdu: Sichuan Renmin Chubanshe, 1996), 265.

40. *Sichuan Shenpan Zhi* [Annuals of the Sichuan Province Judiciary] (Chengdu: Dianzi Kexue Daxue Chubanshe, 2003), 365–66.

41. According to Dikotter, corruption, speculation, pilferage, and theft ran rampant during the Great Leap and the famine years. Frank Dikotter, *Mao's Great Famine: The History of China's Most Devastating Famine, 1958–1962* (New York: Walker & Company, 2010), chapters 22–24. Also see Jasper Becker, *Hungry Ghosts: China's Secret Famine* (Lon- don: J. Murray, 1996); and Ralph A. Thaxton, *Catastrophe and Contention in Rural China: Mao's Great Leap Forward Famine and the Origins of Righteous Resistance in Da Fo Village* (New York: Cambridge University Press, 2008).

42. See Richard Baum, *Prelude to Revolution: Mao, the Party, and the Peasant Question, 1962–66* (New York: Columbia University Press, 1975).

43. Prior to 1985, cases involving the diversion of funds were treated as embezzlement (*qintun*) and classified as graft (*tanwu*). That year, legal experts convinced the Supreme

Court to issue new regulations stipulating that if money were returned within six months, the case would be classified as a violation of financial discipline (*waifan caijing jilu xinwei*) and only warrant administrative sanctions (*xingzheng chufen*). If the funds were not returned to the state within six months or the amount diverted for less than six months was significant, the offense would be considered to constitute graft. In 1988, the Supreme Court again revised the statutes by cutting the time limit for the return of diverted funds from six to three months and classifying misappropriation as a separate offense with a standard sentence of five years' imprisonment. If, however, the sum was deemed to be large, the charge could be changed to graft and a longer prison sentence handed down. As such, the rise in misappropriation after 1988 resulted in part from legal reclassification. See Gao Mingxuan and Wan Zuofu, eds., *Zhongguo Chengzhi Jingji Fanzui Quanshu* [A Comprehensive Guide to the Punishment of Economic Crimes] (Beijing: Zhongguo Zhengfa Daxue, 1995); and Meng Qinghu, *Nuoyong Gongkuan Zui Yanjiu Dongixang* [Research on New Tendencies in the Crime of Misappropriation] (Beijing: Beijing Daxue Chubanshe, 2006).

44. Cases were located using the LexisNexis database. They include only cases reported by the Western media, and my assumption is that they represent the most visible cases. That is, they represent the cases prominently reported in the Chinese media (and hence were cases the government decided to publicize), and the Western press likely filtered out "minor" cases because reporters and editors would have considered them of little interest to readers. I thus conclude that the cases in my database were likely selected because they involved senior officials, involved large sums of money, resulted in harsh punishments, and involved a heavy element of scandal. That said, the database does include a surprising number of relatively mundane cases.

45. For analytical purposes, I have divided the data into periods. The first period encompasses all cases before 1979. The second period includes the early reform period during which the emphasis was on rural reform and limited industrial reform. The third period is defined by the adoption of the dual-track price system in 1984 and the 1988 retrenchment. The fourth period covers the recessionary years of 1989 and 1990 plus the two years of drift prior Deng's Southern Tour. The fifth period encompasses the boom years that followed Deng's Southern Tour. The sixth period is that of the deflationary years of the later 1990s, when the regime restructured the state sector and forced the closure of money-losing SOEs. The final period covers the years 2001 to 2007 during which the economy grew at a steady pace.

46. In recent years, Chinese prosecutors have focused more attention on what is called "commercial corruption," which includes bribery within the business sector. They have also at least threatened to more vigorously prosecute those private bribe payers rather than focus only on officials who accepted bribes.

47. On judicial corruption, see Ting Gong, "Dependent Judiciary and Unaccountable Judges: Judicial Corruption in Contemporary China," *China Review* 4:2 (Fall 2004): 33–44.

48. On the revival of organized crime in China in the post-Mao period, see Ko-lin Chin and Roy Godson, "Organized Crime and the Political-Criminal Nexus in China," *Trends in Organized Crime* 9:2 (Spring 2006): 5–44.

49. See Sun Yan, "Cadre Recruitment and Corruption: What Goes Wrong?" *Crime, Law, and Social Change* 49:1 (2008): 61–79.

50. S. Douglas Beets, "Understanding the Demand-Side Issue of International Corruption," *Journal of Business Ethics* 57:1 (2005): 65.

51. Andrei Schleifer, "Does Competition Destroy Ethical Behavior?" *American Economic Review* 94:2 (2004): 415. Also see Schleifer and Vishny, "Corruption," 599–617.

52. See Anita Chan and Jonathan Unger, "Grey and Black: The Hidden Economy of Rural China," *Pacific Affairs* 55:3 (1982): 452–71.

53. Sun, *Corruption and Market in Contemporary China*, 195–96.

54. Gong, "Forms and Characteristics of China's Corruption in the 1990s."

55. Guo Yong, "How Does Economic Transition Breed Corruption?" *China Economic Journal* 1:2 (2008): 227–36.

56. It is widely assumed that corruption in rural and poor localities is much more predatory in nature than in urban and rich areas. In very simple terms, it is said that cadres and officials in rapidly developing areas are able to slice off a share of the gains from growth while cadres and officials in poor areas have no alternative but to plunder what scarce resources are available locally.

57. Li Fang, "Fubai Wenhua de Weihai yu Zhili" [The Danger of a Culture of Corruption and Its Control], *Zhonngwai Qiyi Jia*, December 2009, available at http://www.chinaqking.com/content/show.aspx?newsid=66837, accessed February 12, 2010.

58. On the concept of a culture of corruption, see *inter alia* Alan P. L. Liu, "The Politics of Corruption in the People's Republic of China," *American Political Science Review* 77:3 (1983): 618; Pranab Bardhan, "Corruption and Development: A Review of the Literature," *Journal of Economic Literature* 35:3 (1997): 1320–46; Martin Stuart-Fox, "The Political Culture of Corruption in the Lao PDR," *Asian Studies Review* 30 (2006): 59–75; Rasma Karklins, "Typologies of Post-Communist Corruption," *Problems of Post-Communism* 49:4 (2002): 22–32; Richard C. LaMagna, "Changing a Culture of Corruption: How Hong Kong's Independent Commission against Corruption Succeeded in Furthering a Culture of Lawfulness," *Trends in Organized Crime* 5:1 (1999): 121–37; Thomas Li-Ping Tang and Randy K. Chiu, "Income, Money Ethnic, Pay Satisfaction, Commitment, and Unethical Behavior: Is the Love of Money the Root of Evil for Hong Kong Employees?" *Journal of Business Ethics* 46:1 (2003): 13–30; and Stephen P. Morris, "Corruption and the Mexican Political System: Continuity and Change," *Third World Quarterly* 20:3 (1999): 623–43.

59. See Mark R. Kleiman, "Enforcement Swamping: A Positive Feedback Mechanism in Rates of Illicit Activity," *Mathematical Computer Modeling* 17:2 (1993): 65–75; Francis T. Lui, "A Dynamic Model of Corruption Deterrence," *Journal of Public Economics* 31:2 (1986): 215–26; Jeans Christopher Andvig, "The Economics of Corruption: A Survey," *Studi Economici* 46:43 (1991): 70–75; Jens Christopher Andvig and Karl Ove Moene, "How Corruption May Corrupt," *Journal of Economic Behavior and Organization* 13 (1990): 63–76; and Olivier Cadot, "Corruption as a Gamble," *Journal of Public Economics* 33:2 (1987): 223–44.

CHAPTER 6

1. He Qinglian, "On Systemic Corruption in China and Its Influence," in William C. Heffernan and John Kleinin, eds., *Private and Public Corruption* (New York: Rowman & Littlefield, 2004), 267.

2. Ibid., 240–41.

3. Chengze Simon Fan and Herschel I. Grossman, "Incentives and Corruption in Chinese Economic Reform," *Policy Reform* 4 (2001): 195–206.

4. Minxin Pei, *China's Trapped Transition: The Limits of Developmental Autocracy* (Cambridge, Mass.: Harvard University Press, 2006), 150–53.

5. Minxin Pei, "Corruption Threatens China's Future," Carnegie Endowment for International Peace, Policy Brief 55 (2007), 4.

6. Ibid., 151. Between 1986 and 2000, the total number of procuratorial personnel increased from 140,000 to 228,000. After 2000 the number fell, and as of 2005, the number of procuratorial personnel totaled 214,000. *Zhongguo Jiancha Nianjian* [Procuratorial Yearbook of China] (Beijing: Zhongguo Jiancha Chubanshe, various years).

7. Ibid., 150 and 159–66.

8. I derive this 1 percent estimate from Pei's assertion that only 3 to 6 percent of those caught are prosecuted and then assuming that the detection rate must be less than one in three. If the RRC was 1 percent of the ARC, then in this implies that roughly one in four public employees is actively engaged in corruption. (In recent years the procuratorate has indicted about 35,000 officials, of which 20,000 were prosecuted in court, while about 12 million individuals have been employed by the state and other public agencies. Hence, 35,000*100=3.5 million corrupt officials, out of 12 million total ≈ 30 percent.) See Pei, *China's Trapped Transition*, 150–53.

9. See *inter alia* Gary Becker, "Crime and Punishment: An Economic Approach," *Journal of Political Economy* 76:2 (1968): 69–217; Bruce L. Benson and John Baden, "The Political Economy of Governmental Corruption: The Logic of Underground Government," *Journal of Legal Studies* 14:2 (1985): 391–410; Jin-Wook Choi, "Institutional Structures and Effectiveness of Anticorruption Agencies: A Comparative Analysis of South Korea and Hong Kong," *Asian Journal of Political Science* 14:2 (1985): 195–214; Isaac Ehrlich, "Participation in Illegitimate Activities: A Theoretical and Empirical Investigation," *Journal of Political Economy* 81:3 (1973): 521–65; Philip A. Neber, "A Pure Theory of Muggery," *American Economic Review* 68:3 (1978): 437–45; A. Mitchell Polinsky and Steven Shavell, "The Economic Theory of Public Enforcement of Law," *Journal of Economic Literature* 38 (2000): 45–76; B. Peter Pashigian, "On the Control of Crime and Bribery," *Journal of Legal Studies* 4:2 (1975): 311–26; and Zoltan Szanto, "Principals, Agents, and Clients: Review of the Modern Corruption," *Innovation* 12:4 (1999): 629–32.

10. Chinese officials and cadres are notorious for taking advantage of their authority to create perks. Excessive banqueting at public expense or at the expense of private citizens is one such example. Accepting gifts is another. In many such instances, officials do not accept cash. Nor do they provide a quid pro quo favor. Banqueting and gifts are used instead to build *guanxi* ties that are repaid through a process of diffuse reciprocity most often in the form of help at some point in the future. Relationships may also be built indirectly, with a private citizen lending a hand to an official's relatives, friends, or spouse. In other cases, assistance may be rendered to an official organization rather than to a specific individual. In fact, savvy officials are apt to be very careful not to engage in quid pro quo exchanges. This not only allows them to reduce the possibility of prosecution, it also allows them to avoid becoming trapped in relationships with specific individuals. The DIC system also adjudicates a set of offenses frequently described as "degeneracy" (*fuhua duoluo daode baihuai*), an ill-defined and probably largely subjective category which includes drunkenness, womanizing, gambling, drug use, and whoring. While unquestionably disgraceful forms of behavior, most of these offenses do not necessarily involve abuse of power or even (with the obvious exceptions of whoring and drug use) criminal activity. They may be construed, however, as violating the rules governing proper conduct and thus warranting disciplinary action. Finally, sketchy provincial-level data suggest that in the past about a third of the DIC caseload involved violations of the one-child policy. Between 1978 and 1995, for example, 30 percent of the Guangdong Provincial Discipline Inspection Commission's cases involved alleged violations of the one-child policy, 18 percent involved corruption, 14 percent involved other economic offenses (e.g., speculation, violations of financial regulations, illegal logging), and 18 percent were various forms of degeneracy (e.g., improper sexual relations, gambling, drug possession). *Guangdong Jijian Jiancha Zhi: (1950–1995 Nian)* [Annuals of the Guangdong Provincial Discipline Inspection Commission] (Guangzhou: Guangdong Renmin Chubanshe, 2009). Data from various provincial yearbooks suggest that economic cases (including both corruption and other financial misconduct) account for between one-third and one-half of the party's disciplinary caseload, while violations of the one-child policy account for 20–30 percent. Data from Beijing, Hebei, Shanxi, Jiangsu, Zhejiang, Fujian, Jiangxi, Shandong, Henan, Hubei, Hunan, Guangxi, Hainan, Chongqing, and Yunnan.

11. Gao Gezhu, *Dingzui yu Liangxing* [Conviction and Penalty Measuring] (Beijing: Zhongguo Fangzheng Chubanshe, 2001), 984–95. In the case of bribery, prior to 1997 cases involving sums of less than ¥2,000 were considered to fall below the level of criminality and hence were normally dealt with administratively. In 1997 the revised criminal code raised the threshold to ¥5,000. Meng Qinghua, *Shouhui Zui Yanjiu Xin Dongxiang* [New Trends in Research on the Crime of Accepting Bribes] (Beijing: Zhongguo Fangzheng Chubanshe, 2005), 4–5. Also see *Criminal Law of the People's Republic China* (March 1997), available at http://www.colaw.cn/findlaw/crime/criminallaw3.html, accessed February 23, 2010.

12. If we assume two-thirds of the cases involved disciplinary issues and further assume that half of the remaining third did not rise to the level of criminality, then the remand rate for corruption cases would work out to 25–30 percent. Estimating the remand rate is further complicated by the fact that there is no limitation on the time that the DIC may continue a case. Under party regulations, it can hold an individual for investigation indefinitely using a provision known as the "double regulation" or "dual designation" (*shuanggui*). This provision also shifts the burden of proof onto the suspect. See Jerome A. Cohen, "Human Rights and the Rule of Law in China," testimony before the Congressional-Executive Commission on China, September 20, 2006, available at http://www.cfr.org/china/human-rights-rule-law-china/p11521 l, accessed July 16, 2011.

13. The remand rate, according to available data, varied considerably year to year. In 2003, the DIC/Ministry of Supervision systems disciplined 174,507 individuals of whom 8,691 (4.9 percent) were remanded for criminal investigation. The following year, the DIC/Supervision disciplined 164,831 individuals and forwarded 4,775 cases (2.9 percent) to the judicial system. In 2005, however, they disciplined 147,539 individuals and remanded 15,177 (10.2 percent). In 2006, the number of party members disciplined fell to 123,489 and the number of individuals remanded dropped to 3,530 (2.8 percent). *Zhongguo Renmin Gongheguo Nianjian* [Yearbook of the People's Republic of China] (Beijing: Zhongguo Gongheguo Nianjian Chubanshe, various years) and Xinhua News Agency, February 13, 2007. Because neither the DIC nor the Ministry of Supervision publishes a yearbook containing standardized reporting categories, there is some question about the consistency of these data.

14. During this same period, the DIC remanded an average of approximately 6,100 cases to the judicial system. It thus seems obvious that most corruption cases originate in the procuratorate, not the DIC or Ministry of Supervision. This does not mean the party does not play a role. Cases involving party members are normally vetted through the appropriate discipline inspection office or a party committee.

15. According to the Criminal Procedure Law, the procuratorate may terminate a case (*chexiao anjian*) if it determines the offense does not constitute a crime, the offense is covered by an amnesty, or the statute of limitations has expired. After the procuratorate has forwarded a case to the courts, the case may be closed without prosecution for similar reasons. See *Zhongguo Renmin Gongheguo Xingshi Susongfa* [Code of Criminal Procedure of the People's Republic China] available at http://www.gov.cn/banshi/2005–05/25/content_887.htm, accessed March 2, 2010; Zhong Lu Wang [China Law Network], *Anjian Zhenzha Zhongjie Hou Dou Yao Yusong Qisu Ma* [Are All Cases Necessarily Prosecuted after Investigation?], available at http://www.148com.com/html/4018/460593. htm, accessed March 2, 2010; and Falu Jiaoyu Wang [Legal Education Network], *Zhencha Jieduan Faxian Shishi Buqing huo Zhengju Buzu Ying Yisong Shencha bu Qisu* [Cases That Have Been Transferred to the Court Should Not Be Prosecuted if the Evidence Is Unclear or Insufficient], available at chinalawedu.com/new/21601_21714_/2009_12_14_ ji61313151311421900224888.shtm, accessed March 2, 2010. I wish to thank Hsieh Peishieu (Edward) for his efforts in tracking down the distinction between these two terms.

16. The court aggregates economic crime differently from the procuratorate and includes a wider range of offenses.

17. In most cases, suspended deaths sentences are commuted to life after the two-year suspension if the accused shows appropriate remorse, cooperates with authorities in recovering illicit money, and is a model prisoner.

18. *Zhongguo Falu Nianjian* [China Legal Yearbook] (Beijing: Zhongguo Falu Nianjian Chubanshe, various years).

19. Amnesty International, "Peoples Republic of China: The Death Penalty Log," various years, available at http://www.amnesty.org/library, accessed February 24, 2010.

20. *Zhongguo Jiancha Nianjian,* various years. Although data on the total number of senior official investigated are available for all years, the breakdown of cases by level is not available for 1990, 1997, and 2007.

21. *Zhongguo Falu Nianjian,* various years.

22. In the case of the Chen Xitong case, informants said that officials in Beijing spent months on edge fearing that the next knock on their office door could be party investigators or prosecutors. More recently, informants have recounted officials' dread of being detained under the party's "double regulation."

23. Forty percent of officials convicted on felony charges of public corruption in the United States received prison sentences.

24. Sampling is an obvious issue. The report from the Public Integrity Section only contains information on one in ten cases pursued in 2005. As such, the data culled from it are necessarily only a small subset of the total. But like my database on Chinese corruption cases, we can assume it contains the most visible, more egregious cases. As such, I would contend that the samples are comparable, at least in broad terms. In making these comparisons, I fully understand and appreciate that there are not only differences in the two countries' legal definition of corruption but also that the qualitative nature of the offenses is obviously quite different. Public Integrity Section, Criminal Division, United States Department of Justice, "Report to Congress on the Activities of the Public Integrity Section for 2005" (Washington: U.S. Department of Justice, 2006). In some instances, sentencing data were obtained from later editions of this annual report.

25. For purposes of comparison, I have not included those executed in my calculation of the total number of those sent to prison, and I have assumed that all those give a suspended death sentence had their sentences commuted to life after two years (I am not aware of cases in which the death sentence was later imposed, although is it possible that it is in some instances).

26. Staffan Andersson and Paul M. Heywood, "The Politics of Perception: Use and Abuse of Transparency International's Approach to Measuring Corruption," *Political Studies* 57 (2009): 746–67.

27. I treat the game as an iterated lottery because corrupt officials not only face punishment when they commit a crime but also remain criminally liable forever afterward (or until some statute of limitations has been reached). This is true of officials who engage in single-shot corruption (e.g., accepting a single bribe) and those who engage in repeated acts of serial corruption.

28. For a more complete explanation of this method and detailed examples of use of the chained probabilities and comparative static modeling, see Andrew Wedeman, "Win, Lose, or Draw? China's War on Corruption," *Crime, Law and Social Change* 49:1 (2008).

29. If the odds of getting caught are set at one in ten, then in the first round 10 percent of corrupt officials will get caught. If the odds of getting caught are discounted by half for each pervious round (that is, if there is a 10 percent probability of capture in the present round, the odds of getting caught for crimes committed in the previous round would be 5 percent, in the round before that 2.5 percent, etc.), then the odds of getting caught for

crimes committed in either the current round or in previous rounds climb to 14.5 percent in the second round, 16.6 percent in the third round, and so on.

30. I choose to use two years as my metric of quick capture rather than one year because the nature of corruption is such that we should assume that an official will evade capture for some period before investigators get wind of his or her illegal activities.

31. This section on the Chen Xitong cases summarizes materials in Andrew Wedeman, "Corruption and Politics," in Maurice Brosseau, Suzanne Pepper, and Tsang Shu-ki, eds., *China Review 1996* (Hong Kong: Chinese University Press, 1996), 61–94.

32. David Dixon and David Newman, *Entering the Chinese Market: The Risks and Discounted Rewards* (Westport, Conn.: Quorum Books, 1998), 29–30.

33. Li Ka-shing, who had close ties to Deng Xiaoping and other senior party figures, was never officially implicated and denied any wrongdoing. See Richard Baum, *Burying Mao: Chinese Politics in the Age of Deng Xiaoping* (Princeton, N.J.: Princeton University Press, 1994): 469.

34. All figures in *renminbi* converted to dollars using the exchange rate in the appropriate year.

35. *New York Times*, August 1 and July 31, 1998. Chen was granted a medical parole in 2006 and released from prison after serving only eight years. China Vita, "Chen Xitong," available at http:www.chinavita.com/biography/Chen_Xitong%7C2864, accessed July 16, 2011.

36. Chen's mistress seems to have been the only person to escape. She reportedly fled to Hong Kong as soon as the scandal broke, taking with her a substantial part of what Chen had stashed away.

37. Associated Press, November 7, 2006; and *South China Morning Post*, October 20 and September 26, 2006.

38. *New York Times*, April 12, 2008; and *The Times* (London), April 12, 2008.

39. Cheng Li, "Was the Shanghai Gang Shanghaied? The Fall of Chen Liangyu and the Survival of Jiang Zemin's Faction," *China Leadership Monitor* 20 (2007): 1–17.

40. Xinhua, April 4, 2008.

41. Ibid.

42. *Wen Wei Po*, August 8, 2007; *Yomiuri Shimbun*, July 27, 2007; and *China Daily*, August 5, 2008.

43. Xinhua, April 11, 2008.

44. Li, "Was the Shanghai Gang Shanghaied?"

45. Shawn Shieh, "The Rise of Collective Corruption in China: The Xiamen Smuggling Case," *Journal of Contemporary China* 14:42 (2005), 71–72.

46. James Mulvenon, "To Get Rich Is Unprofessional: Chinese Military Corruption during the Jiang Era," *China Leadership Monitor* 6 (2003): 21–35.

47. Shieh, "The Rise of Collective Corruption in China," 72.

48. For an entertaining account of the lurid goings-on in the Red Mansion, as well as a detailed description of the totality of Lai's operation, see Oliver August, *Inside the Red Mansion: On the Trail of China's Most Wanted Man* (Boston: Houghton Mifflin, 2007).

49. Ji was particularly instrumental because he provided registration papers that enabled Lai and his confederate to make the cars they smuggled in legal and thus sell them on the open market. Dali L. Yang, *Remaking the Chinese Leviathan: Market Transition and the Politics of Governance in China* (Stanford, Calif.: Stanford University Press, 2004), 114.

50. Mulvenon, "To Get Rich Is Unprofessional," 24.

51. Like the Chen Xitong case, the Zhanjiang and hence the Yuanhua cases were allegedly exposed by an "accident." In September 1998, a customs patrol boat intercepted a boat carrying smuggled cigarettes. The smugglers assaulted and beat the crew of the patrol boat, which allegedly triggered alarm bells in Beijing. In reality, the central

government had initiated a major antismuggling campaign some months earlier, and it is likely that investigators were already aware of both operations. Benjamin C. Ostrov, "The Anti-Smuggling Investigation Bureau's War on Smuggling in China," *Police Practice and Research* 3:1 (2002): 41–54; Benjamin C. Ostrov, "The Fight Against Smuggling," *China Business Review*, July-August 2000, 44–47; and Chong Zhubian, *Zhonggong Haiguan Heimu* [The Inside Story of Communist China's Customs] (Hong Kong: Xia Fei Er Guoji Chuban Gongsi, 2001), 78–109.

52. According to Gong, the total value of goods smuggled through Zhanjiang was ¥60 billion (US$8.6 billion), including ¥10 billion (US$1.4 billion) worth of petroleum, which would mean it was a larger operation than Yuanhua. Ting Gong, "Dangerous Collusion: Corruption as a Collective Venture in Contemporary China," *Communist and Post-Communist Studies* 35:1 (2002): 94. Yang, however, puts the total value of goods smuggled through Zhanjiang at ¥30 billion. Yang, *Remaking the Chinese Leviathan*, 111.

53. Shieh, "The Rise of Collective Corruption in China," 83–84.

54. Yang, *Remaking the Chinese Leviathan;* Ostrov, "The Anti-Smuggling Investigation Bureau's War on Smuggling in China"; and Ostrov, "The Fight Against Smuggling."

55. Joseph Fewsmith, "Bo Xilai Takes on Organized Crime," *China Leadership Monitor* 32 (2010): 2.

56. *The Sunday Telegraph*, October 18, 2009.

57. Fewsmith, "Bo Xilai," 5. Because of his age (he will be 63 when the 18th Party Congress meets) and strong evidence that a decision has already been made that Xi Jinping will succeed Hu Jintao when Hu retires in 2012, Bo is not considered a contender for general secretary. Emerging convention suggests the retirement age for the general secretary is 70 and that an individual can serve only two five-year terms as general secretary. Bo will, therefore, be too old to become general secretary if Xi serves two full terms. It is also assumed that Li Keqiang has been selected to succeed Wen Jiabao as premier. Alice Miller thus speculates that Bo and Wang are possibly in contention for the chairmanship of the National People's Congress, which she considers the number two position within China's political hierarchy. Alice Miller, "The 18th Central Committee Politburo: A Quixotic, Foolhardy, Rashly Speculative, but Nevertheless Ruthlessly Reasoned Projection," *China Leadership Monitor* 33 (2010): 6–7.

58. According to rumors, gangsters in Liaoning put a ¥5 million (US$725,000) price tag on Wang's head and, after he started attacking crime in Chongqing, the local gangsters were said to have offered pay ¥12 million (US$1.7 million) to anybody who could kill him. *South China Morning Post*, August 22, 2009.

59. Deng Hai, "Chongqing War on Gangs Claims Ex-Top Cop," *Caijing*, August 11, 2009.

60. Xinhua, October 26, 2009.

61. *China Daily*, November 5, 2009.

62. *South China Morning Post*, August 14 and 15, 2009; *New York Times*, November 4, 2009; Xinhua, October 26, 2009; and *China Daily*, August 18, 2009.

63. *Straits Times*, July 11, 2010; and *South China Morning Post*, October 21, 2009.

64. Agence France Presse (AFP), April 14, 2010; and *The Times* (London), November 4, 2009.

65. *China Daily*, April 24, 2010.

66. *China Daily*, September 2, 2009.

67. *South China Morning Post*, August 22, 2009.

68. Associated Press, July 29, 2010.

69. *China Daily*, August 21, 2009; and *South China Morning Post*, December 31, 2009.

70. *China Daily*, December 26, 2011.

71. *China Daily*, December 25, 2009.

72. *China Daily,* December 17, 2009.

73. *South China Morning Post,* December 2, 2009.

74. *China Daily,* October 10, 2009.

75. *South China Morning Post,* August 22, 2009.

76. Xinhua, January 31, 2011.

77. AFP, January 26, 2011.

78. AFP, August 11, 2010.

79. Xinhua, December 22, 2009.

80. *South China Morning* Post, September 26, 2009.

81. *China Daily,* February 6, 2010.

82. Xinhua, June 22, 2010.

83. Xinhua, December 20, 2010.

84. *China Daily,* November 2, 2009.

85. *China Daily,* December 15, 2009.

86. *China Daily,* January 12, 2011; and *South China Morning Post,* December 4, 2009.

87. Li Ling, "Performing Bribery in China: Guanxi-practice, Corruption with a Human Face," *Journal of Contemporary China* 20:68 (2011): 1–20.

88. Xinhua, August 3, 2008.

89. If the odds of getting caught are 10 percent as suggested previously, after ten years the mathematical probability of successfully evading detection would be about 35 percent. In other words, even at this putatively low risk, there is still 65 percent chance of eventual capture.

90. Jeffrey Becker, "Tackling Corruption at Its Source: The National Corruption Prevention Bureau," *Journal of Chinese Political Science* 13:3 (2008): 292; and Guo Yong, "People's Republic of China," in Transparency International, "Global Corruption Report 2009," 253–57, available at http://www.transparency.org/publications/gcr/gcr_2009, accessed March 2, 2010.

91. Guo Yong and Liao Ran, "China," in Transparency International, "Global Corruption Report 2006," 142–45, available at http://www.transparency.org/publications/gcr/gcr_2006, accessed March 2, 2010.

92. Auditors, for example, reportedly played the key role in breaking the case of Liu Zhijun, the minister of railways and chief architect of China's high-speed rail initiative. According to *Caijing,* a routine audit of a state-owned construction company revealed that it had made a ¥100 million (US$15 million) payment to Ding Shumiao, a woman who had made a substantial fortune first in the coal-shipping business and later as a mediator between Liu and firms bidding for lucrative rail contracts. Company executives told the auditor that such payments were routine and that companies winning contracts generally paid 3 percent commissions to various intermediaries. According to investigators, over the previous several years, Ding had collected close to ¥800 million (US$119 million) from various companies, half of which she retained on Liu's behalf and invested following his instructions. Working with Ding and Luo Jinbao, the head of China Railway Tielong Container Logistics, Liu also allegedly steered subcontracts to relatives and friends, rigging bids so that only those firms designated by Liu won contracts. Several years earlier, Liu's younger brother Liu Zhixiang, who was the deputy director of the Wuhan Railway Bureau, was convicted on charges of embezzlement, bribery, and unexplained assets after he allegedly hired a train conductor to murder a businessman with whom he had tangled several years earlier while serving as director of the Hankou Railway station (*Caijing,* March 2, 2011). If the 3 percent figure was applied to the total spending on new high-speed rail lines, it would imply illicit payments of ¥60 billion (US$8.9 billion) since the advent of the program.

93. In key respects, the establishment of such centers harkens back to the American Progressive Era and the establishment of public administration departments to train civil

servants and to devise new "scientific" methods of government. In fact, some of the leaders of the new public administration centers in China hold doctorates in public administrative from U.S. universities and explicitly acknowledge the link between their efforts and the Progressive Era.

94. For an enlightening discussion of the political use of anticorruption in kleptocracies and specifically how the rulers of such political systems use strategies that combine the carrot of opportunities for corrupt income and the stick of harsh punishment for those who come to be seen as disloyal, see Daron Acemoglu, James A. Robinson, and Thierry Verdier, "Kleptocracy and Divide-and-Rule: A Model of Personal Rule," *Journal of the European Economic Association* 2:2/3 (2004): 162–92.

CHAPTER 7

1. For the most part, structural corruption in Japan, South Korea, and Taiwan flourished in the days before indices such as those now published by Transparency International existed.

2. Caution must be exercised in comparing scores from the mid-1990s to more recent scores because TI's sample changed significantly in the later 1990s as more counties were added. Many of these countries, particularly those in the former Soviet Union, Eastern Bloc, and Sub-Saharan Africa were scored as fairly corrupt. Thus, as TI's sample increased from 54 in 1995 to 133 in 2003, the average jumped from 4.63 to 5.77. We might say the mean was rising toward China's score at the same time that China's score was decreasing.

3. Among the top quarter of economies measured by average growth in GDP 1978 to 2008, the average TI score was 6.02.

4. According to the PRS Group, its estimates of corruption measure the probability that corruption could trigger popular unrest, cause the government to fall, and either result in significant restructuring of a country's political system or internal disorder. See PRS, "International Country Risk Guide Methodology," available at http://www.prsgroup .com/ICRG_Methdodology.aspx#EconRiskRating, accessed July 22, 2011.

5. Huang Yasheng, *Capitalism with Chinese Characteristics: Entrepreneurship and the State* (New York: Cambridge University Press, 2008).

6. Quoted in William L. Riordon, *Honest Graft: The World of George Washington Plunkitt* (St. James, N.Y.: Brandywine Press, 1997), 53.

7. Yan Sun, "Reform, State, and Corruption: Is Corruption Less Destructive in China than in Russia?" *Comparative Politics* 32:1 (1999): 10–11.

8. In the run up to the 1872 presidential election, for example, President Ulysses S. Grant's campaign operatives in the Midwest conspired with whiskey makers to generate political monies. Distillers would falsify the production and sales figures they submitted to the U.S. Treasury and then hand over part of their profits from evading the federal excise tax to party operatives, who used the money to finance Grant's reelection campaign. After the election was over, the Whiskey Ring continued to operate and by 1873 was skimming off an estimated $1.5 million a year. When the secretary of the U.S. Treasury attempted to break up the main ring in St. Louis, and similar rings elsewhere, by shuffling local tax collectors, he was initially thwarted by political opposition. He persisted in his efforts and obtained sufficient evidence for federal agents to arrest 300 alleged members of the ring. In the investigation that followed, evidence surfaced that appeared to implicate President Grant's private secretary Orville Babcock, who had allegedly tipped off members of the ring about the Treasury investigation in the spring of 1874. Babcock was, however, acquitted. Timothy Rives, "Grant, Babcock, and the Whiskey Ring," The U.S. National Archives & Records Administration, *Prologue* 32:3 (2000), available at http://www.archives.gov/publiations/prologue, accessed April 18, 2008. In a second scandal, the so-called Star Route

case, a U.S. senator (Stephan Dorsey) and an assistant postmaster general (Thomas Brady) were among those indicted on charges involving the rigging of bids for postal routes in the western United States; neither was convicted. J. Martin Klotsche, "The Star Route Cases," *Mississippi Valley Historical Review* 22:3 (1935): 407–18.

9. Mark W. Summers, *The Era of Good Stealings* (New York: Oxford University Press, 1993).

10. See, inter alia., Matthew Josephson, *The Robber Barons: The Great American Capitalists, 1861–1901* (New York: Harcourt, Brace and Company, 1934); Matthew Josephson, *The Politicos, 1865–1896* (New York: Harcourt, Brace & World, 1938); Lincoln Steffens, The *Shame of the Cities* (New York: Hill and Wang, 1904); Ida M. Tarbell, *The History of the Standard Oil Company* (Gloucester, Mass.: P. Smith, 1963); David Loth, *Public Plunder: A History of Graft in America* (New York: Carick and Evans, 1938); Gustavus Myers, *History of the Great American Fortunes* (New York: Modern Library, 1936); and Gustavus Myers, *The History of Tammany Hall* (New York: Boni & Liveright, 1917). For a more scholarly analysis of the period, see Mark W. Summers, *The Plundering Generation: Corruption and the Crisis of the Union, 1849–1861* (New York: Oxford University Press, 1987); and Mark Wahlgren Summers, *Party Games: Getting, Keeping, and Using Power in Gilded Age Politics* (Chapel Hill: University of North Carolina Press, 2004).

11. At the state level, machine-like organizations emerged as a means of controlling not only the state legislature but also the selection of U.S. senators, who were elected by state legislatures until the passage of the 17th Amendment in 1912. Control over Senate seats was considered particularly valuable because senators had de facto control of all federal appointments within their state, including postmasters, a key position not only because postal workers accounted for 60 to 70 percent of federal employment in the nineteenth century but also because the postal service penetrated into virtually every locality, thus allowing those who controlled their appointment to create networks of local political allies. In the original construct, senators were to represents state legislatures in Washington. The power relationship between the state legislatures and their supposed senatorial agents was, however, inverted in the 1830s with the advent of public canvassing (i.e., campaigning). Whereas in the early years of the republic, would-be senators would await the election of the state legislature and conduct their campaign within the state house, it became increasingly common for candidates to "stump the state" in support of legislative candidates, with the result that the candidate would arrive in the state capital backed by a corps of legislators he had helped elect. As incumbency increased, the endorsement of sitting senators became increasingly important for would-be legislators, with the result the original servant-master relationship linking senators to state legislatures gave way to a relationship in which the senator exercised considerable influence over the makeup of the body that would, in turn, elect (or re-elect) him to his seat. Powerful senators often controlled the machines that dominated their state's politics. State bosses included Roscoe Conkling and Thomas C. Platt in New York; John A. Login in Illinois; Oliver H.P.T Morton in Indiana; James McMillan in Michigan; John Coit Spooner in Wisconsin; Nelson W. Aldrich in Rhode Island; Marcus Alonzo Hanna in Ohio; John S. Barbour, Jr., in Virginia; William J. Sewell in New Jersey; Arthur P. Gorman in Maryland; and Simon and James Donald Cameron and Matthew Stanley Quay in Pennsylvania. See William Alan Blair, "A Practical Politician: The Boss Tactics of Matthew Stanley Quay," *Pennsylvania History* 56:2 (1989): 77–92; Donald Barr Chidsey, *The Gentleman from New York: A Life of Roscoe Conkling* (New Haven: Yale University Press, 1935); Peter McCaffery, "Style, Structure, and Institutionalization of Machine Politics: Philadelphia, 1867–1933," *Journal of Interdisciplinary History* 22:3 (1992): 435–52; James A. Kehl, *Boss Rule in the Gilded Age: Matt Quay of Pennsylvania* (Pittsburgh, Penn.: University of Pittsburgh Press, 1981); Brooks M. Kelley, "Fossilism, Old Fogeyism, and Red Tape," *Pennsylvania Magazine of History and Biography*

90:1 (1966): 93–114; William H. Riker, "The Senate and American Federalism," *American Political Science Review* 49:2 (1955): 452–69; Peter Swenson, "The Influence of Recruitment on the Structure of Power in the U.S. House, 1870–1940," *Legislative Quarterly* 7:1 (1982): 7–36; John D. Stewart, "The Great Winnebago Chieftain: Simon Cameron's Rise to Power 1860–1867," *Pennsylvania History* 39:1 (1972): 20–39; Harold Foote Gosnell, *Boss Platt and his New York Machine: A Study of the Political Leadership of Thomas C. Platt, Theodore Roosevelt and Others* (Chicago: University of Chicago Press, 1924); Harold F. Gosnell, "Thomas C. Platt—Political Manager," *Political Science Quarterly* 38 (1923): 443–69; Francis Russell, "The Easy Boss: Thomas Collier Platt," in Francis Russell, ed., *The President Makers: From Mark Hanna to Joseph P. Kennedy* (Boston: Little, Brown, 1976), 46–58; John R. Lambert, *Arthur Pue Gorman* (Baton Rouge: Louisiana State University Press, 1953); Walter S. Sanderlin, "Arthur P. Gorman and the Chesapeake and Ohio Canal: An Episode in the Rise of a Political Boss," *Journal of Southern History* 13 (1947): 323–37; Francis Russell, "The Red Boss of Cleveland: Marcus Alonzo Hanna," in Russell, ed., *The President Makers,* 1–42; Hebert D. Croly, *Marcus Alonzo Hanna: His Life and Work* (New York: Macmillan, 1912); and Clarence A. Stern, *Resurgent Republicanism: The Handiwork of Hanna* (Ann Arbor, Mich.: Edwards Bros., 1968).

12. The forms of vote fraud were legion, ranging from tampering with voter registration lists to ballot-box stuffing, use of "repeaters" (men hired to vote who would be marched from precinct to precinct to vote under different names), and vote counting irregularities. Vote buying quickly developed into an art, with buyers using a variety of mechanisms to ensure that the bought stayed bought. Many of the irregularities were possible because at the time there were no regular ballots and the parties frequently printed their own. Peter H. Argersinger, "New Perspectives on Election Fraud in the Gilded Age," *Political Science Quarterly* 100:4 (1985–6): 669–87; Horace Bell, "Getting Out the Vote," excerpt in Horace Bell, *Reminiscences of a Ranger* (Los Angeles, 1881), 92–95, reproduced in John and LaRee Caughey, eds., *Los Angeles: Biography of a City* (Berkeley: University of California Press, 1977), 145–47; Richard Bensel, "The American Ballot Box: Law, Identity, and the Polling Place in the Mid-Nineteenth Century," *Studies in American Political Development* 17:1 (2003): 1–27; Ray Boomhower, "'To Secure Honest Elections': Jacob Piatt Dunn, Jr., and the Reform of Indiana's Ballot," *Indiana Magazine of History* 90 (1994): 311–45; Fabrice Lehoucq, "Electoral Fraud: Causes, Types, and Consequences," *Annual Review of Political Science* 6 (2003): 233–56; Genevieve B. Gist, "Progressive Reform in a Rural Community: The Adams County Vote-Fraud Case," *Mississippi Valley Historical Review* 28:1 (1961): 60–78; John Reynolds, "'The Silent Dollar': Vote Buying in New Jersey," *New Jersey History* 48 (1980): 191–211; John F. Reynolds, "A Symbiotic Relationship: Vote Fraud and Electoral Reform in the Gilded Age," *Social Science History* 17:2 (1993): 227–51; and Mark Wahlgren Summers, "Party Games: The Art of Stealing Elections in the Late-Nineteenth-Century United States," *Journal of American History* 88:2 (2001): 424–35.

13. From colonial times onward, public-sector jobs were allocated on the basis of connections and political loyalty. According to Fish, the prevailing belief was that "public office constituted a fund, from which the most deserving party workers were to be paid for their service." As a result, public employment largely operated on the basis of the spoils system wherein in politics, as in war, "to the victor go the spoils." It was not until the election of Andrew Jackson in 1828 and the end of two decades of Democratic Republican control over the federal government, however, that the first sweeping political purge was conducted. Thus, even though Jackson is popularly viewed as having initiated the spoils system, he was in fact simply following established precedent. See John Denton Carter, "Abraham Lincoln and the California Patronage," *American Historical Review* 48:3 (1943): 495–506; Carl Joachim Friedrich, "The Rise and Demise of the Spoils Tradition," *Annals of the American Academy of Political and Social Science* 189 (1937): 10–16; Carl Russell Fish,

The Civil Service and the Patronage (New York: Longmans, Green and Company, 1905); Carl Russell Fish, "Lincoln and the Patronage," *American Historical Review* 8 (1902): 53–69; and Erik McKinley Eriksson, "The Federal Civil Service Under President Jackson," *Mississippi Valley Historical Review* 13:4 (1927): 517–40.

14. Public employees were expected to volunteer during elections and kick back a percentage of their salaries in what was commonly known as "the assessment"—generally somewhere between 5 and 10 percent depending on the size of the employee's salary. According to those involved, because they owed their job to the elected boss, employees should kick back a portion of their earnings to make sure the boss remained in office and they kept their jobs. The link between assessments and jobs was never absolute and, particularly in later years, public employees might find ways of avoiding payment. The link was, nevertheless, implicit and widely understood. During the 1880 presidential election, for instance, one would-be federal judge in New York sent his $500 assessment along with a note asking when the Republican Party would approve his nomination for office. Thomas C. Reeves, "Chester A. Arthur and Campaign Assessments in the Election of 1880," *Historian* 31 (1969): 573–82.

15. Criminal gangs were, in fact, often integral to the power base of many machines because they were responsible for organizing repeat voting operations, intimidating opposition candidates, and preventing opposition supporters from voting on election day. Saloon operators also played a key role in many cities by acting as local political organizers in return for the police allowing them to remain open on Sundays when blue laws legally banned the sale of beer and alcohol, as well as protecting illegal gambling and prostitution rings operating out of their establishments. See Philip A. Bean, "The Irish, the Italians, and Machine Politics: A Case Study: Utica, New York (1870–1960)," *Journal of Urban History* 20:2 (1994): 205–39; Daniel Czitrom, "Underworlds and Underdogs: Big Tim Sullivan and Metropolitan Politics in New York, 1889–1913," *Journal of American History* 78:2 (1991): 536–58; John Kyle Davis, "The Gray Wolf: Tom Dennison of Omaha," *Nebraska History* 58 (1977): 25–52; V. O. Key, "Police Graft," *American Journal of Sociology* 40:5 (1935): 624–36; Lawrence H. Larson and Nancy J. Hulston, "Criminal Aspects of the Pendergast Machine," *Missouri Historical Review* 91 (1997): 168–80; and Thomas J. Noel, *The City and the Saloon: Denver, 1858–1916* (Lincoln: University of Nebraska Press, 1982).

16. See Lyle W. Dorsett, "Kansas City Politics: A Study of Boss Pendergast's Machine," *Arizona and the West* (1966): 107–18; Lyle W. Dorsett, *The Pendergast Machine* (New York: Oxford University Press, 1968); Richard McCormick, "The Discovery that Business Corrupts Politics: A Reappraisal of the Origins of Progressivism," *American Historical Review* 86:2 (1981): 247–74; Orville Menard, *Political Bossism in Mid-America: Tom Dennison's Omaha, 1900–1933* (Lanham, Md.: University Press of America, 1989); J. Paul Mitchell, "Boss Speer and the City Functional: Boosters and Businessmen versus Commission Government in Denver," *Pacific Northwest Quarterly* 63:4 (1972): 153–64; Harvey Molotch, "The City as a Growth Machine: Toward a Political Economy of Place," *American Journal of Sociology* 82:2 (1976): 309–32; John R. Logan and Harvey J. Molotch, "The City as a Growth Machine," in John R. Logan and Harvey J. Molotch, eds., *Urban Fortunes: The Political Economy of Place* (Berkeley: University of California Press, 1987); and William Elliott West, "Dirty Tricks in Denver," *Colorado Magazine* 52 (1975): 225–43.

17. Riordon, *Honest Graft*, 53.

18. In defending honest graft, Plunkitt used the example of a municipal project that would drain a swamp and replace it with parkland. Why should not he, as an insider, buy the land before word got out about the project from its owners rather than allowing developers and speculators to buy it for resale to the city? Why, in other words, should people who had nothing to do with bringing the project to fruition be allowed to cash in? Plunkitt did not seem to consider that perhaps the city should have cut the middlemen

out altogether and that the original owners alone ought to profit or that the city ought to have simply paid the owners the fair market value of their land. Ibid., 54–56.

19. In a biting and overtly anti-Irish satire, Shapley portrays the boss as an uneducated, drunken lout obsessed with plundering his social betters and emptying the city's coffers. Rufus E. Shapley, *Solid for Mulhooly: A Political Satire* (Philadelphia: Gebbie and Company, 1889).

20. Andrei Schleifer and Robert W. Vishny, "Corruption," *Quarterly Journal of Economics* 108:3 (1993): 599–617.

21. Mancur Olson, "Dictatorship, Democracy, and Development," *American Political Science Review* 87:3 (1993): 567–76.

22. Monte A. Calvert, "The Manifest Functions of the Machine," in Bruce M. Stave, ed., *Urban Bosses, Machines, and Progressive Reformers* (Lexington, Mass.: D. C. Heath, 1972), 45–55. Also see Amy Bridges, *A City in the Republic: Antebellum New York and the Origins of Machine Politics* (New York: Cambridge University Press, 1984); Amy Bridges, "Rethinking the Origins of Machine Politics," in John Mollenkopf, ed., *Power, Culture, and Place: Essays on New York City* (New York: Russell Sage, 1988); Amy Bridges, "Another Look at Plutocracy and Politics in Antebellum New York City," *Political Science Quarterly* 97:1 (1982): 57–81; and Leonard Chalmers, "Fernando Wood and Tammany Hall: The First Phase," *New York Historical Society Quarterly* 52 (1968): 6–37.

23. Douglas Bowers, "From Logrolling to Corruption: The Development of Lobbying in Pennsylvania, 1815–1861," *Journal of the Early Republic* 3:4 (1983): 439–74.

24. The most widely known example of these forms of support comes from the federal programs that helped support the construction of the transcontinental railroad.

25. Bowers, "From Logrolling to Corruption," 439–74.

26. Although stories of suppliers selling the federal forces shoddy goods and inoperable weapons abound, to date I am not aware of a detailed study of the extent of corruption in military procurement during the Civil War.

27. Richard Franklin Bensel, *Yankee Leviathan: The Origins of Central State Authority in America, 1859–1877* (New York: Cambridge University Press, 1990); and Richard Franklin Bensel, *The Political Economy of American Industrialization, 1877–1900* (New York: Cambridge University Press, 2000).

28. The extent of true corruption is, however, uncertain. There were certainly notorious cases such as the Tweed Ring, which allegedly plundered scores of millions of dollars from the New York City treasury during 1870–71, and it was commonly assumed that politicians left office much richer as a result of their service. In some cases, politicians undoubtedly lined their pockets. Sometimes they accepted cash bribes and kickbacks. In other cases, they received corporate shares or bonds that could be held or quickly resold if the stock suddenly rose in value after the enactment of a particular piece of legislation. In many cases, however, it appears they made more of their money by providing legitimate business services to powerful interests, often in the form of legal services since there were few restrictions on lawyer-politicians continuing to provide legal advice and representation to private clients. See Oliver E. Allen, *The Tiger: The Rise and Fall of Tammany Hall* (Reading, Mass.: Addison-Wesley, 1993); Alexander Callow, *The Tweed Ring* (New York: Oxford University Press, 1966); Leo Hershkowitz, *Tweed's New York: Another Look* (Garden City, N.Y.: Anchor, 1977); Fletcher M. Green, "Origins of the Credit Mobilier of America," *Mississippi Valley Historical Review* 46:2 (1959): 238–51; Mark D. Hirsch, "More Light on Boss Tweed," *Political Science Quarterly* 60 (1945): 267–78; Denis T. Lynch, *"Boss" Tweed: The Story of a Grim Generation* (New York: Boni and Liveright, 1927); Seymour Mandelbaum, *Boss Tweed's New York* (New York: Wiley, 1965); General John McDonald, *Secrets of the Great Whiskey Ring* (Chicago: Belford, Clarke & Company, 1880); Rives, "Grant, Babcock, and the Whiskey Ring"; Jerome L. Sternstein, "Corruption in the Gilded

Age Senate: Nelson W. Aldrich and the Sugar Trust," *Capital Studies* 6 (1978): 13–37; and Samuel J. Tilden, *The New York City "Ring," Its Origins, Maturity and Fall* (New York: J. Polhemus, 1873).

29. See James Gimpel, "Reform-Resistant and Reform-Adopting Machines: The Electoral Foundations of Urban Politics, 1910–1930," *Political Research Quarterly* 46:2 (1993): 371–82; Harold F. Gosnell, "The Political Party versus the Political Machine," *Annals of the American Academy of Political and Social Science* 169 (1933): 21–28; Fred I. Greenstein, "The Changing Pattern of Urban Party Politics," *Annals of the Academy of Political and Social Science* 353 (1964): 1–13; and Michael P. McCarthy, "On Bosses, Reformers, and Urban Growth: Some Suggestions for a Political Typology of American Cities," *Journal of Urban History* 4 (1977): 28–38.

30. Hilton Root, "Corruption in China: Has It Become Systematic?" *Asian Survey* 36:8 (1996): 741–57.

31. Huang, *Capitalism with Chinese Characteristics:* 109–12.

32. David C. Kang, *Crony Capitalism: Corruption and Development in South Korea and the Philippines* (New York: Cambridge University Press, 2002): 116–20.

33. On the concept of political business, see Edmund Terence Gomez, "Introduction: Political Business in East Asia," in Edmund Terence Gomez, ed., *Political Business in East Asia* (New York Routledge, 2001), 1–33.

34. See Naomi R. Lamoreaux, *The Great Merger Movement in American Business, 1895–1904* (New York: Cambridge University Press, 1984).

35. Theodore H. Davis, Jr., "Corporate Privileges for the Public Benefit: The Progressive Federal Incorporation Movement," *Virginia Law Review* 77:3 (1991): 603–30; Samuel Dickson, "The Development in Pennsylvania of Constitutional Restraints upon the Power and Procedure of the Legislature," *American Law Register and Review* 44:8 (1896): 477–508; John W. Eilert, "Illinois Business Incorporations, 1816–1869," *Business History Review* 37:3 (1963): 169–81; L. Ray Gunn, "The New York State Legislature: A Developmental Perspective: 1777–1846," *Social Science History* 4:3 (1980): 267–94; Stanley E. Howard, "The Limited Partnership in New Jersey," *Journal of Business of the University of Chicago* 7:4 (1934): 296–317; Edward Q. Keasbey, "New Jersey and the Great Corporations," *Harvard Law Review* 13:3 (1899): 198–212; Edward Q. Keasbey, "New Jersey and the Great Corporations, II," *Harvard Law Review* 13:4 (1899): 264–78; William C. Kessler, "Incorporation in New England: A Statistical Study, 1800–1875," *Journal of Economic History* 8:1 (1948): 43–62; W. C. Kessler, "A Statistical Study of the New York General Incorporation Act of 1811," *Journal of Political Economy* 48:6 (1940): 877–82; and Melvin I. Urofsky, "Proposed Federal Incorporation in the Progressive Era," *American Journal of Legal History* 26:2 (1982): 160–83.

36. See Dorothy Ganfield Fowler, "Precursors of the Hatch Act," *Mississippi Historical Review* 47:2 (1960): 247–62; Harlan Hahn, "President Taft and the Discipline of Patronage," *Journal of Politics* 28 (1966): 368–90; Ari Hoogenboom, "Thomas A. Jenckes and Civil Service Reform," *Mississippi Valley Historical Review* 47:4 (1961): 636–58; Ari Hoogenboom, "The Pendleton Act and the Civil Service," *American Historical Review* 64:2 (1959): 301–18; Ari Hoogenboom, *Outlawing the Spoils: A History of the Civil Service Reform Movement, 1865–1883* (Urbana: University of Illinois Press, 1961); Ronald N. Johnson and Gary D. Libecap, "Patronage to Merit and Control of the Federal Government Labor Force," *Explorations in Economic History* 31:1 (1994): 91–119; H. Eliot Kaplan, "Accomplishments of the Civil Service Reform Movement," *Annals of the American Academy of Political Science* 189 (1937): 142–47; Samuel Kernell and Michael P. McDonald, "Congress and America's Political Development: The Transformation of the Post Office from Patronage to Service," *American Journal of Political Science* 43:3 (1999): 792–811; Martin J. Schiesl, *The Politics of Efficiency: Municipal Administration and Reform,*

1880–1920 (Berkeley: University of California Press, 1977); Sean M. Theriault, "Patronage, the Pendleton Act, and the Power of the People," *Journal of Politics* 65:1 (2003): 50–68; and Leonard D. White, "Politics and Civil Service," *Annals of the American Academy of Political and Social Science* 169 (1933): 86–90.

37. In 1996, the Procuratoratial Work Report received a 59.6 percent approval rate. The following year, it passed with only 55.3 percent of the delegates voting to approve. By contrast, the Government Work Report submitted by Premier Li Peng received a 97 percent positive vote. The Supreme People's Court Work Report was also subject to a higher than normal negative vote in these years. Since 1998, the approval rate for the Supreme Procuratorate's Work Report had averaged 73 percent.

38. The World Bank's Worldwide Governance Indicators, on the other hand, shows a degree of deterioration during this time, with China's score worsening from –0.08 in 1996 to –0.67 in 2005 on a scale that ranged from 2.5 (least corrupt) to –2.5 (most corrupt). In the past several years, the score improved, rising to –0.44 in 2008. The authors of the Worldwide Governance Indicators caution, however, against placing too much weight on small changes and emphasize the importance of statistical variance. Recast in those terms, movement of China's score suggests minor fluctuation rather than clear-cut movement. Moreover, China remains relatively close to the mean. See Daniel Kaufmann, Aart Kraay, and Massimo Mastruzzi, "Governance Matters VII: Aggregate and Individual Governance Indicators, 1996–2007," World Bank, Policy Research Working Paper no. 4654, June 2008, available at http://ssrn.com/abstract=1148386, accessed June 24, 2008.

39. Guo Yong, "Corruption in Transitional China: An Empirical Analysis," *China Quarterly* 194 (2008): 349–64; Andrew Wedeman, "Guilt and Punishment in China's War on Corruption," in Jean C. Oi, Scott Rozelle, and Xueguang Zhou, eds., *Growing Pains: Tension and Opportunity in Contemporary China* (Stanford, Calif.: Walter H. Shorenstein Asia-Pacific Research Center, 2010), 117–42; and Andrew Wedeman, "Win, Lose, or Draw? China's War on Corruption," *Crime, Law and Social Change* 49:1 (2008).

40. Melanie Manion, "Issues in Corruption Control in Post-Mao China," *Issues and Studies* 34:9 (1998): 1–21.

41. Gordon G. Chang, *The Coming Collapse of China* (New York: Random House, 2001); and Minxin Pei, *China's Trapped Transition: The Limits of Developmental Autocracy* (Cambridge, Mass.: Harvard University Press, 2006).

42. Justin Yifu Lin, Fang Cai, and Zhou Li, *The China Miracle: Development Strategy and Economic Reform* (Hong Kong: Chinese University Press, 2003).

43. Huang, *Capitalism with Chinese Characteristics*. In 1999, Pei in fact argued that China could experience the same sort of economic collapse and political crisis that brought down the Suharto regime in the wake of the 1997 Asian Economic Crisis. Minxin Pei, "Will China Become Another Indonesia?" *Foreign Policy* 116 (1999): 94–109.

44. Thomas Bernstein and Lu Xiaobo, *Taxation without Representation in Contemporary China* (New York: Cambridge University Press, 2003), 109–14.

Index